The Old Songs are Always New

Indigenous Music, Language and Performing Arts

Associate Professor Myfany Turpin, Series Editor

The many forms of Australia's Indigenous music and temporal arts have ancient roots, huge diversity and global reach. The Indigenous Music, Language and Performing Arts series aims to stimulate discussion and development of the fields of Aboriginal and Torres Strait Islander music, language and performing arts, in both subject matter and approach, as well as looking beyond Australia to First Nations cultures around the world. Proposals are welcomed for studies of traditional and contemporary performing arts (including dance), popular music, art music, experimental and new media, and the importance of First Nations languages for culture and empowerment, as well as theoretical, analytical, interdisciplinary and practice-based research. Where relevant, print and ebook publications may be supplemented by online or audiovisual media.

Archival Returns: Central Australia and Beyond
Edited by Linda Barwick, Jennifer Green and Petronella Vaarzon-Morel

For the Sake of a Song: Wangga Songmen and Their Repertories
Allan Marett, Linda Barwick and Lysbeth Ford

Music, Dance and the Archive
Edited by Amanda Harris, Linda Barwick and Jakelin Troy

Recording Kastom: Alfred Haddon's Journals from the Torres Strait and New Guinea, 1888 and 1898
Edited by Anita Herle and Jude Philp

Reflections and Voices: Exploring the Music of Yothu Yindi with Mandawuy Yunupingu
Aaron Corn

Singing Bones: Ancestral Creativity and Collaboration
Samuel Curkpatrick

Songs from the Stations: Wajarra as Sung by Ronnie Wavehill Wirrpnga, Topsy Dodd Ngarnjal and Dandy Danbayarri at Kalkaringi
Myfany Turpin and Felicity Meakins

The Old Songs are Always New: Singing Traditions of the Tiwi Islands
Genevieve Campbell with Tiwi Elders and knowledge holders

Wurrurrumi Kun-Borrk: Songs from Western Arnhem Land
Kevin Djimar

The Old Songs are Always New

Singing Traditions of the Tiwi Islands

Genevieve Campbell
with Tiwi Elders and knowledge holders

SYDNEY UNIVERSITY PRESS

This book contains the traditional knowledge of Tiwi people and has been presented and published with the consent of Tiwi knowledge custodians. Repurposing any part of this Tiwi material herein without consent may breach Indigenous Cultural and Intellectual Property rights.

First published by Sydney University Press 2023

© Genevieve Campbell and Tiwi Elders and knowledge holders 2023
© Sydney University Press 2023

Reproduction and Communication for other purposes
Except as permitted under the Australian *Copyright Act 1968*, no part of this edition may be reproduced, stored in a retrieval system, or communicated in any form or by any means without prior written permission. All requests for reproduction or communication should be made to Sydney University Press at the address below:

Sydney University Press
Fisher Library F03
Gadigal Country
University of Sydney NSW 2006
AUSTRALIA
sup.info@sydney.edu.au
sydneyuniversitypress.com.au

 A catalogue record for this book is available from the National Library of Australia.

ISBN 9781743328750 paperback
ISBN 9781743328767 epub
ISBN 9781743328842 pdf

Cover image: Jikipayinga (crocodile) fabric design by Agnes Portaminni; tawutawunga (clapping sticks) made by Leroy Portaminni, courtesy of Leonie Tipiloura. Photo: Roger Press.
Cover design: Miguel Yamin

We acknowledge the traditional owners of the lands on which Sydney University Press is located, the Gadigal people of the Eora Nation, and we pay our respects to the knowledge embedded forever within the Aboriginal Custodianship of Country.

Aboriginal and Torres Strait Islander readers are advised this publication contains names and images of people who have died. The inclusion of any names, voices and/or images of deceased people is done with the permission of their family.

Acknowledgements

I must firstly thank the people of the Tiwi Islands who have been very generous to me personally. I am grateful for the welcome to Tiwi land shown by the Tiwi Land Council committee members and their ongoing support for this project. This book is in large part the result of study undertaken for my doctoral thesis, guidance for which I am so glad to have received through Charles Darwin University and the University of Sydney.

I am honoured to have spent time with the senior song and culture men who have shown patience, grace and sincerity in methodically explaining and documenting their skills and knowledge. I acknowledge my great respect, esteem and love for the Strong Women's Group who have been beacons of pride, drive and energy in the sharing, creating and animating of Tiwi song culture with the view to ensuring its continuing central place in Tiwi culture.

They are the Elders, the singers, the poets, the ceremony leaders, the artists, the teachers and the custodians, and it is really only with their expertise and support that any of this has happened.

Nginja nguwuri mantawi, kapi ngininuwila kuruwala.

Payinga

Thank you, friends, for your stories and songs.

Genevieve

Contents

Acknowledgements	v
List of figures	xi
List of music transcriptions and notes	xiii
Explanations of markings used	xv
List of song texts	xvii
List of audio examples	xix
List of other recorded material in the AIATSIS archive	xxiii
List of plates	xxv
Preface	xxxi
Notes on orthography	xxxv
Orthography for Tiwi language used	xxxv
Variations to pronunciation	xxxvi
List of Tiwi Elders, singers, culture and knowledge holders, and research consultants	xxxvii
Names used to refer to singers in the Palingarri recordings	xli
Glossary of terms	xliii
Prologue	1
Murntankala, the ancestral woman who created the Islands	1
Chapter 1: An introduction to the Islands	3
Early visitors	5
The ephemeral nature of Tiwi songs	9
An archive of old, new songs	15

Chapter 2: The archived recordings … 23
   Gaining access to the recordings … 23
   Taking voices away … 26
   Song as artefact … 27
   Ongoing engagements with collections … 31
   Repatriation, reclaiming, returning family to Country … 33
   Embedding the songs back in the continuum of tradition … 43

Chapter 3: Singing identity … 53
   Kinship … 55
   Singing mother, singing father … 64
   Pukumani … 68
   The role of the Yoi songs … 73

Chapter 4: Kulama … 89
   The role of Kulama in education … 92
   The role of Kulama in social politics … 96
   The role of Kulama songs in social history … 98
   The role of Kulama in maintaining an artistic space … 100

Chapter 5: The Tiwi Language(s) … 107
   The spoken language … 107
   The effects of language change on the song tradition … 114
   Song language … 119
   Vocalisations … 137
   Indicators of time … 139
   Kulama stage markers … 142
   Interpretation of song subjects … 147
   Continuing versification and cantillation techniques in modern song forms … 155
   What happens when the Old language is lost … 157

Plates … 160

Chapter 6: The classical Tiwi music … 177
   Performance context and variability … 181
   Melody … 183
   Pitch … 184
   Structure … 186
   Tempo … 191
   Rhythm … 193
   Text … 193
   1. Jipuwakirimi … 203
   2. Jalingini (sugarbag) and Timilani (mosquito) call … 208
   3. Arimarrikuwamuwu (tree-climbing) … 210

4. Ampirimarrikimili (women's songs)	212
5. Amparruwu (widow songs)	214
6. Mamanunkuni (sorrow songs)	215
7. Arikuruwala (Kulama songs)	219
8. Ampirikuruwala (Kulama songs)	222
9. Ariwangilinjiya (lullaby)	225
10. Apajirupwaya (love songs)	228
11. Ariwayakulaliyi (individuals' songs)	230
12. Modern Kuruwala (the Strong Women's Group songs)	233
Chapter 7: Emerging musical genres	**235**
Daniel Paujimi's melody	237
Singing current events into a 21st-century oral tradition	244
Imparting cultural knowledge in new musical ways	248
Continuing traditions despite (and because of) cultural change	253
Murrakupuni melodies in a new musical genre: the aural landscape changes	259
Darwin Entertainment Centre 2021	269
On stage cultural negotiations	273
Returning to the archives: The old songs are new songs	280
Epilogue	**283**
References	**291**
Index	**303**

List of figures

Figure 1: Ethnographic Tiwi song material housed at AIATSIS.	24
Figure 2: Joe Puruntatameri's song about Long Stephen Tipuamantimeri.	39
Figure 3: Spencer recordings, 1912: song subjects and cylinder numbering.	49
Figure 4: Pukumani and Kulama song subjects recorded in the archive.	55
Figure 5a: The Tiwi Skin groups and associated clans.	58
Figure 5b: The Tiwi Skin groups and marriage connections.	59
Figure 6: Tiwi Dreaming groups.	62
Figure 7: Mortuary rituals sequence.	71
Figure 8: The bereavement symbols of kinship status.	76
Figure 9: The framework of the Yiloti Pukumani ceremony.	79
Figure 10: Functional classification of Kulama songs and their use in ceremonial context.	95
Figure 11: Selection of Ayipa song subjects that were current news the year they were sung.	100
Figure 12: Language shift from the 1960s to 2020s.	112
Figure 13: Text breakdown of Arikuruwala song by Barney Tipuamantimeri.	133
Figure 14: Ritual stage and time-of-day markers used in song texts.	143
Figure 15: Morning time marker in a healing song by Clementine Puruntatameri, 2011.	146
Figure 16: Two iterations of the same song, at different times of the day (Eustace Tipiloura, 2012).	147

Figure 17: Train song showing text change between 1912 and 2011.   149

Figure 18: Four possible interpretations of one line of Murli la, 2011.   156

Figure 19: Overview of the Tiwi song-types.   179

Figure 20: Pitch of Sugarbag and Mosquito calls.   185

Figure 21: Structural analysis of song-types.   189

Figure 22: An indication of the tempi (beats per minute) of recorded Kulama and Yoi song-types.   192

Figure 23: Transliteration of Crocodile song texts sung at a Yiloti (Final Ceremony) in 1977.   195

Figure 24: Performance context of Tiwi songs, early 20th century.   200

Figure 25: Functional correlation of traditional song-types and Modern Kuruwala songs.   255

Figure 26: Comparing song subjects in the archive with Modern Kuruwala song subjects.   258

Figure 27: Functional correlation of traditional song-types and Modern Kuruwala songs and how they were incorporated into a public performance in 2021.   273

Figure 28: Tiwi song performance contexts today.   279

List of music transcriptions and notes

Music Transcription 1: Example of altering the metre in sung form. Christopher Foxy Tipungwuti (Audio 38).	132
Music Transcription 2: Melody in relation to text. Barney Tipuamantimeri.	133
Music Transcription 3: Love song melody showing relationship between text and melody. Unidentified female singer 1954 (Audio 23).	135
Music Transcription 4: Six musical treatments of Kurukangawakawayi (Audio Examples 16, 27, 38, 46, 48, 51).	138
Music Transcription 5: Outline of melodic contour for each of the Tiwi song-types.	201
Music Transcription 6: Two examples of rhythmic interest within the constant pulse of the Jipuwakirimi/Yoi song-type (Audio 7, 55).	206
Music Transcription 7: 1912 Yoi performance showing alteration of rhythmic pattern between first and second sections. Yirrikapayi, Tungutalum (Audio 6).	207
Music Transcription 8: 1976 Yoi performance showing alteration of rhythmic pattern between single-beat and double-beat percussive accompaniment (Audio 7).	208
Music Transcription 9: Arimarrikuwamuwu tree-climbing song. Wampayawityimirri Bartholomew Kerinaiua, 1955 (Audio 17).	211
Music Transcription 10: Two Ampirimarrikimili melodies.	213
Music Transcription 11: Two examples of the Amparruwu melody.	215

Music Transcription 12: Full performance transcription of Mamanunkuni song. Long Stephen, 1975 (Audio 26). 217

Music Transcription 13: Mamanunkuni melodic contour. Unidentified woman, 1954 (Audio 15). 218

Music Transcription 14: Five examples of Arikuruwala incipits showing individuals' variation. 220

Music Transcription 15: Two examples of the Arikuruwala melody. Foxy Tipungwuti (Audio 37) and Tractor Joe (Audio 29). 221

Music Transcription 16: Arikuruwala with Ampirikuruwala response. Tractor Joe and unidentified woman. 1975 (Audio 29). 223

Music Transcription 17: Showing relationship between Arikuruwala and Ampirikuruwala vocal lines. Foxy and Dorothy Tipungwuti, 1975 (Audio 37). 224

Music Transcription 18: Ariwangilinjiya (lullaby), 1954 (Audio 22). 226

Music Transcription 19: Apajirupwaya (love song) melody. Unidentified woman, 1954 (Audio 75). 229

Music Transcription 20: Ariwayakulaliyi melody, Long Stephen 1975 (Audio 47). 231

Music Transcription 21: Ariwayakulaliyi melody, Eustace Tipiloura (Audio 48). 231

Music Transcription 22: Ariwayakulaliyi/Nyingawi melody. Enrail Munkara, 1954 (Audio 56). 232

Music Transcription 23: Three Ariwayakulaliyi melodic contours, composers unknown. 234

Music Transcription 24: Six variations of Daniel Paujimi's Ariwayakulaliyi melody (Audio 41, 42, 43, 44, 45, 46). 239

Music Transcription 25: Three treatments of the word rrakwiyangili (dugong) in the Modern Kuruwala Kupunyi song. 2008. (Audio 46). 241

Music Transcription 26: Football song examples of line extension. 246

Music Transcription 27: Line 1, Wurrumiyanga Wellbeing Centre song. 2009 (Audio 51). 248

Music Transcription 28: Example of rehearsed Ampirikuruwala singing. Strong Women, 2010. 252

Music Transcription 29: Kulama introduction to Murrntawarrapijimi. Clementine Puruntatameri, 2008 (Audio 54). 265

Music Transcription 30: The chorus of the Modern Kuruwala version of Murrntawarrapijimi 2008 (Audio 54). 265

Music Transcription 31: Text/Melody relationship comparison between "Happy to be on an Island in the Sun" and "Tikilaru Song" (Audio 73). 266

Music Transcription 32: Four classical Ariwayakulaliyi melodic contours used across multiple songs. 271

Music Transcription 33: Going to Canberra, Yikliya Eustace Tipiloura. Full performance transcription. 287

Explanations of markings used

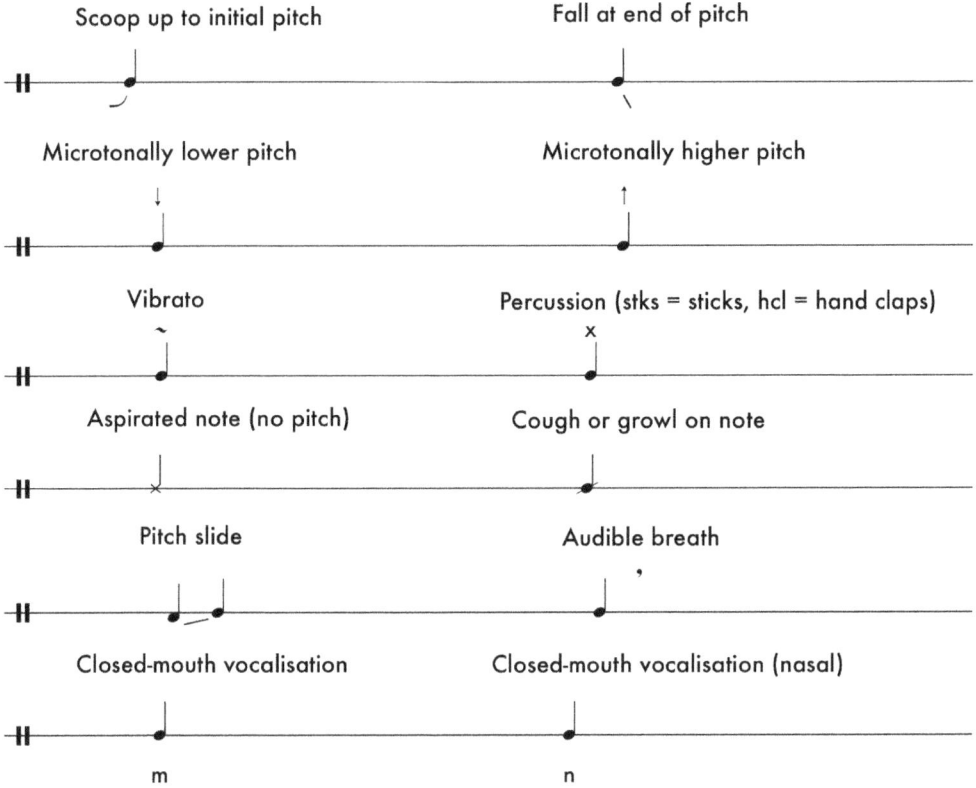

Where space requires that I use "ML1" to indicate "Musical Line 1" and so on, "L1" etc., refers to lines of text. Notated rests are used where the break between notes is in time with the syllabic pulse. This does not imply that the singer is singing in a time signature. Where there is a non-timed break between notes or text phrases I use visual spacing to indicate its length; i.e. a blank space on the stave indicates a period of silence between notes. I do not use bar lines unless the music has a time signature (such as in the case of more recent songs in non-traditional music style). Partial/dotted barlines are added where appropriate to clarify an example and open-ended staves indicate a continuation of phrase or unit. As much as possible, complete melodic phrases are presented on one stave, hence a variation of size in the transcriptions. Similarly, I have not attempted to transcribe exact rhythm, but rather to give an educated representation using musical notation (crotchet, quaver, etc.) as close to the performance as possible while retaining clarity.

All examples are transcribed at the pitch of the recording, unless otherwise stated. In some examples, for instance, I have transposed to a common key for ease of comparison (and this is indicated on the relevant music transcription). In the case of semitone pitch change I use an accidental at the first change, and then a natural to indicate a change. As an example, below (part of Music Transcription 15), the reader should infer that from the quaver on the syllable *tyi* until the semiquaver on *ta* all the notes are B♭. I have re-indicated B♭ (on *na* and *mwa*) when that pitch returns, and then similarly, subsequent notes are also B♭.

I have used stemmed and unstemmed notes in my examples for the sake of clarity, where the pitch and/or melodic shape is the only element I wish to focus on.

Because of unreliable recording speed in old recording technologies, I have not included tempo markings in many of my music transcriptions.

I have indicated rhythmic treatments as closely as possible in order to give a clear documentation of the performance being presented and so that it can be read by a reader familiar with western musical notation if the audio example is not available. I do, however, presume and hope that my written descriptions are read in tandem with the audio files. It is only when accompanied by the recordings of the songs themselves that my explanations will be fully useful.

List of song texts

Song text 1: Warlakurrayuwuwa Paddy Sawmill. Murrukuliki (Macassar Man), 1975. — 6

Song text 2: Jimalipuwa. Recorded by Hart in 1928. — 7

Song text 3: Jipapijingimirri, recorded by Spencer in 1912. — 8

Song text 4: Tungutalum. Gramophone, 1928; Warabutiwayi Allie Miller. Rijya (Radio), 1954. — 45

Song text 5: Wampayawijimirri Black Joe. Pitapituwi (Spirit children), 1954. — 56

Song text 6: Karla (Tractor Joe). Yipunjinga mayingi (Calling spirit), 1975. — 57

Song text 7: Warlakurrayuwuwa Paddy Sawmill. Mayimampi (Goose), 1975. — 66

Song text 8: Tungutalum. Yirrikapayi (Crocodile), 1912. — 75

Song text 9: Jipwarlamparripa Stanley Munkara. A song for his father at Yilaniya (Smoking), 1969. — 77

Song text 10: Warlakurrayuwuwa Paddy Sawmill. Yirranikara Pajimuna (Burning leg), 1975. — 80

Song text 11: Jipwarlamparripa Stanley Munkara. Mangulumpwarni (Tide), 1975. — 80

Song text 12: Clementine Puruntatameri. Mingatalini Mamanunkuni (Sorrow), 2011. — 82

Song text 13: Yirripungiwayamirri George Norm. Kujupurruwatuwu (Turtle), 1975. — 84

Song text 14: Jipwarlamparripa Stanley Munkara. Pajipajuwu (Turtle eggs), 1975. — 84

Song text 15: Kilupwarlapiwiyi Romuel Puruntatameri. Wantangini (Firewood), 1975. ... 85

Song text 16: Justin Puruntatameri song for Kulama 1970. ... 95

Song text 17: Eunice Orsto. Jinarringa (Black-headed python), 2011. ... 125

Song text 18: Unidentified singer. Tatuwali (Shark), 1948. ... 127

Song text 19: Calista Kantilla, Jacinta Tipungwuti and Leonie Tipiloura. Wutawa kuwayi (They call out), 2010. ... 131

Song text 20: Calista Kantilla. Awungarra Jiliyarti (Here in Darwin), 2011. ... 134

Song text 21: Spoken, metrical and sung forms of love song, 1954. ... 136

Song text 22: Unidentified man. Ngiya mampini (I am a canoe), 1912; Timarralatingimirri Daisy. Ngiya kulumurrunga (I am the crocodile), 1966; Warlakurrayuwuwa Paddy Sawmill. Ngiya jipilonti (I am the goose), 1975; Kitiminawulimguwi Declan Apuatjimi. Ngiya purrungi (I am the feather ball), 1975. ... 140

Song text 23: Jimalipuwa. Use of *-ingilimpange-* as temporal marker in Tamunga (Cotton Tree), 1928. ... 144

Song text 24: Warabutiwayi. Allie Miller, Sorrow for his father, 1954. ... 152

Song text 25: Unknown singer. Ariwangilinjiya (lullaby), 1954. ... 226

Song text 26: Strong Women's Group. Kupunyi (Canoe), 2008. ... 242

Song text 27: Kilupwarlapiwiyi Romuel Puruntatameri. Rrakwiyangili (Dugong), 1975. ... 243

Song text 28: Strong Women's Group. Yiloga (Football), 2010. ... 246

Song text 29: Strong Women's Group. Wurangku Murrakupuni (Wurangku Country), 2022. ... 250

Song text 30: Strong Women's Group. Tikilaru Murrakupuni (Tikilaru Country), c. 1995, and John Louis Munkara, 1993. ... 267

Song text 31: Yikliya Eustace Tipiloura. Kapi Canberra (Going to Canberra), 2012. ... 284

List of audio examples

This is a list of the audio examples referred to in this book which can be found at https://open.sydneyuniversitypress.com.au/old-songs.html. I include the AIATSIS catalogue number and, when the audio example is edited out of a larger sound file, I give a timestamp to indicate the position of the song item in the complete sound file. For example: Audio 42 is a recording of Foxy Tipungwuti's song about a pearling boat that can be found at 41:03 into AIATSIS catalogue number C04-003855 among the Osborne collection. The Hart and Mountford examples are numbered according to their numbering in the original collection. Among the recorded archive are numerous Tiwi singers who were not credited by name by the recordist. Those individuals whom I have not been able to confidently name are listed as 'unidentified', while some, while not named in the archive, have been identified by Tiwi Elders so I have included their name.

Audio example	Singer	Year of recording	Song subject	Song-type	Recorded by	Catalogue	Timestamp
1	Allie Mungatopi	1954	Prince of Wales	Arikuruwala	Mountford	C01-002916-37	0:29:42
2	Unidentified man	1948	Turtle	Jipuwakirimi	Simpson	Island of Yoi	0:25:44
3	Clementine Puruntatameri	2008	Murrntawarrapijimi	Arikuruwala	Ngarukuruwala CD	NG2008-1	
4	Calista Kantilla	2011	Being in Darwin	Arikuruwala	Campbell	111019GC3	
5	Calista Kantilla & Leonie Tipiloura	2011	Ngariwanajirri	Arikuruwala	Davies	SKS2011-3	
6	Orsto	1912	Yirrikapayi	Jipuwakirimi	Spencer	C01-00701A	0:13:29
7	Aloysious Puantiloura	1976	Yirrikapayi	Jipuwakirimi	Moyle	18425	0:05:43

The Old Songs are Always New

Audio example	Singer	Year of recording	Song subject	Song-type	Recorded by	Catalogue	Timestamp
8	Romuel Puruntatameri	1975	Dugong	Jipuwakirimi	Osborne	C04-003851A-41	0:30:46
9	Unidentified man	1928	Tirupi Country	Arikuruwala	Hart	C01_004240B-D30	0:02:40
10	Justin Puruntatameri	1975	Genie	Ayipa	Osborne	C04-003854-155	0:40:44
11	Barney Tipuamantimeri	1975	Argument with Maninkuwila	Arikuruwala	Osborne	C04-3855A-157	0:02:11
12	Stephen-Paul Kantilla	2012	Sorrow for father	Mamanunkuni	Campbell	120225GC1	
13	Allie Miller Mungatopi	1954	Cards	Arikuruwala	Mountford	CO1-0020917	0:22:40
14	Dorothy Tipungwuti	1975	Sorrow	Amparruwu	Osborne	C04–003855B-205	0:42:19
15	Unidentified woman	1954	Why Did you leave me?	Mamanunkuni	Mountford	A02917	0:05:09
16	Eunice Orsto	2010	Coiled like a snake	Amparruwu	Campbell	100420GC1	
17	Black Joe	1955	Goose	Arimarrikuwamuwu	ABC	ABC_36-004069-4	0:05:37
18	Male Group	1948	Jalingini and Timilani Calls	Calls	Simpson	Island of Yoi	0:26:10
19	Unidentified man	1981	Sorrow	Mamanunkuni / Amparruwu	Grau	A01-009278-4	0:03:49
20	Unidentified woman	1981	Kinship	Ampirimarrikimili	Grau	A01-009277	0:44:31
21	Unidentified women	1948	Yirrikapayi	Ampirimarrikimili	Simpson	Island of Yoi	0:16:25
22	Unidentified man and woman	1954	Lizard, flea	Lullaby	Mountford	CO1-002916-19, CO1-002916-20	0:17:00
23	Unidentified woman	1954	Light	Love song	Mountford	CO1-002916-16	0:24:24
24	Tractor Joe	1967	Tatuwali	Arikuruwala	Doolan	J02-000628A-1	0:00:33
25	Long Stephen	1975	Father	Arikuruwala	Osborne	C04–003852B-81	0:03:31
26	Long Stephen	1975	Drinking together	Mamanunkuni	Osborne	C04-003855B-198	0:30:55
27	Long Stephen	1975	Waking up	Mamanunkuni	Osborne	C04-003855B-199	0:32:15
28	Eustace Tipiloura	2012	Sorrow for wife	Arikuruwala	Campbell	120320GC1	
29	Tractor Joe and wife	1975	Sister	Arikuruwala	Osborne	C04–003852b-88	0:28:51
30	Tungutalum	1912	Train	Arikuruwala	Spencer	C01-00701A	0:16:59
31	Stephen-Paul Kantilla	2012	Sorrow for wife	Mamanunkuni	Campbell	1200225GC3	
32	Tungutalum	1928	Boat	Mamanunkuni	Hart	04240BD38	0:12:55

List of audio examples

Audio example	Singer	Year of recording	Song subject	Song-type	Recorded by	Catalogue	Timestamp
33	Unidentified man	1954	Sorrow for wife	Arikuruwala	Mountford	C01-002918	0:09:02
34	Mrs. Duke?	1928	Mopaditi	Mamanunkuni	Hart	04240AD8	0:08:02
35	Mariano?	1928	Sorrow for father	Mamanunkuni	Hart	04240AD11	0:12:55
36	Unidentified woman	1948	For son	Mamanunkuni	Simpson	Island of Yoi	0:08:11
37	Foxy Tipungwuti / Dorothy Tipungwuti	1975	Pangityiarri man	Arikuruwala	Osborne	C0-0003855B-193	0:06:38
38	Foxy Tipungwuti	1975	Honey	Mamanunkuni	Osborne	C04-003855B-208	0:47:55
39	Foxy Tipungwuti	1975	Rainbow Serpent	Amparruwu	Osborne	C04-003855B-207	0:45:59
40	Unidentified woman	1928	Tractor	Ampirimarrikimili	Hart	4240A-D13	0:15:23
41	Daniel Paujimi	1972	God in the Bush	Ariwayakulaliyi	Sims	M03-002480-2	0:06:15
42	Foxy Tipungwuti	1975	Pearling Boat	Ariwayakulaliyi	Osborne	C04-003855-204	0:41:03
43	Schoolboys	1962	Army Tent	Ariwayakulaliyi	Moyle	Songs of the NT-7a	
44	Schoolchildren	1965	Yinjula, Dugong	Ariwayakulaliyi	Wurm	508A	0:19:32
45	Leonie Tipiloura	2011	Yinjula	Arikuruwala	Campbell	111018GC7	
46	Women's group	2008	Kupunyi	Modern Kuruwala	Ngarukuruwala	NG2008-2	
47	Long Stephen	1975	Yamparriparri	Ariwayakulaliyi	Osborne	C04-003854-132	0:28:04
48	Eustace Tipiloura	2012	Brolga	Ariwayakulaliyi	Campbell	120319GC1	
49	Women's group	2010	Wrangku	Modern Kuruwala	Campbell	100412GC7	
50	Women's group	2010	Football	Modern Kuruwala	Campbell	100311GC7	
51	Women's group	2009	Wellbeing Centre	Modern Kuruwala	Campbell	091014GC2	0:39:49
52	Women's group	2008	Murli la	Modern Kuruwala	Ngarukuruwala	NG2008-11	0:02:11
53	Francis Orsto and group	2011	Murli la	Modern Kuruwala	Ngarukuruwala	SKS2011-6	
54	Women's group	2008	Murrntawarrapijimi	Modern Kuruwala	Ngarukuruwala	2008NG-1	
55	Eustace Tipiloura	2011	Country calls/Parakajiyali	Jipuwakirimi	Ngarukuruwala	SKS2011-1	
56	Enrail Munkara	1954	Nyingawi	Nyingawi	Mountford	C01-002916-1	0:04:25
57	Casmira Munkara and women's group	2008	Nyingawi	Nyingawi	Ngarukuruwala	NG2008-5a	
58	Ngarukuruwala	2011	Ngariwanajirri	Modern Kuruwala	Ngarukuruwala	SKS2011-2	
59	Allie Miller	1954	Mary Elizabeth	Arikuruwala	Mountford	C01-002916-9	0:11:39
60	Unidentified man	1980	Name giving	Arikuruwala	Grau	A009275-1	0:03:05
61	Unidentified man and woman	1967	Sorrow	Arikuruwala	Doolan	J02-000628A	5:35:00

The Old Songs are Always New

Audio example	Singer	Year of recording	Song subject	Song-type	Recorded by	Catalogue	Timestamp
62	Mariano	1928	Sorrow	Mamanunkuni	Hart	C01_004240B-D48	0:21:07
63	Foxy Tipungwuti	1975	Sorrow	Mamanunkuni	Osborne	C04-003855B-202	0:36:33
64	Mary Curry	1975	Jealous women	Amparruwu	Osborne	C04-003855-197	0:27:24
65	Francis Orsto	2009	Yirrikapayi	Jipuwakirimi	Campbell	090309GC2	
66	John Louis Munkara	2021	Jikilaru	Ngarukuruwala	Campbell	210319GC1	
67	Women's group	2008	Yirrikapayi	Modern Kuruwala	Davies	NG2008-8	1:25:00
68	Women/band	2008	Yirrikapayi	Improvisation (Instrumental)	McMillan	NG2008-7	
69	Long Stephen	1975	Silent land	Mamanunkuni	Osborne	C04-003855-201	0:34:38
70	Jimalipuwa	1928	Cotton Tree	Arikuruwala	Hart	C01-004240B-D29i	0:00:12
71	Unidentified group	1948	Tatuwali (Shark)	Vocable	Simpson	Island of Yoi	0:13:32
72	Tungutalum	1928	Gramophone	Arikuruwala	Hart	C01-004240B-D33	0:04:52
73	Women's Group	2007	Tikilaru	Modern Kuruwala	Campbell	070221GC6	
74	Unidentified group	1981	Yoi, Jingalini, end cues	Jipuwakirimi, Calls	Grau	A01-009270	0:00:27
75	Unidentified woman	1954	Waiting All Night	Love Song	Mountford	C01-002916-9	0:26:52
76	Ngarukuruwala	2011	Ngariwanajirri Dance Mix	Hip-Hop	Campbell	SKS2011-9	
77	Clementine Puruntatameri	2008	Purrukapali	Arikuruwala	Davies	NG2008-10	
78	Eustace Tipiloura	2012	Going to Canberra	Arikuruwala	Campbell	120319GC6	

List of other recorded material in the AIATSIS archive

To facilitate locating these recordings within the AIATSIS collection, I include the catalogue number and the song item position within the larger recording. The song item numbering follows either the accompanying written documentation of the collection, the numbering spoken on the audio, or, in the absence of either, the start of each new song item as determined by my Tiwi consultants. For example, the song noted as "ship" by Paujimi/Lopez in 1912 will be found in the collection of recording made by Spencer, catalogue number C01-00701, at song item position 3. I list the performers according to the names used in the accompanying documentation.

Footnote	Singer (Tiwi/English name)	Year of recording	Song subject	Song-type	Recorded by	Catalogue code-item number.
CH1, 5	Paujimi/Lopez	1912	Ship	Jipuwakirimi	Spencer	C01-00701-3
5	Jimalipuwa/Danny Bubu	1928	Man o' War	Arikuruwala	Hart	C01-004240B-D29ii
5	Allie Miller/Warruputuwayi	1966	Ship	Jipiuwakirimi	Holmes	S02_000181A-2
5	Long Slim	1967	Old time boat	Arikuruwala	Doolan	J02 000628B-4
6	Unidentified man	1948	Bombing of Darwin	Arikuruwala	Simpson	LA4730-7
6	Wampayawityimirri/Black Joe	1954	Enemy plane	Arikuruwala	Mountford	C01-002917-63
6	School boys	1962	Bombing of Darwin	Ariwayakulaliyi	Moyle	Songs NT-7b
6	Harry Carpenter	1966	Aeroplane bombs	Amparruwu	Holmes	S02-000182B-30
6	Karla/Tractor Joe	1967	Japanese	Arikuruwala	Doolan	J02-000628A-3

The Old Songs are Always New

Footnote	Singer (Tiwi/English name)	Year of recording	Song subject	Song-type	Recorded by	Catalogue code-item number.
6	Deaf Tommy	1975	Fighter plane	Arikuruwala	Osborne	C04-003851A-48
6	Pujuta/Long Stephen	1975	Fighter plane	Arikuruwala	Osborne	C04-003854B-135
6	Awunjingijimirri/ Christopher (Foxy) Tipungwuti	1975	Pearling boat Japanese lover	Ariwayakulaliyi	Osborne	C04-003855B-204
6	Leo Tungutalum	1975	Aeroplane	Arikuruwala	Songs of the Tiwi	ST2.2
6	Jipuwankini/Aloysious Puantiloura	1976	Bombing of Darwin	Jipuwakirimi	Moyle	018425-1
CH2, 31	Karla/Tractor Joe	1967	Tatuwali (Shark) Japanese Hauling in a rope	Arukuruwala	Doolan	J02-000628A-1-6
CH4, 9	Big Jack	1967	Trouble over fight Getting fined Magistrate's Court Trial	Arikuruwala	Doolan	J02-000628A-9-12
12	Mirrirawayuwu/ Dorothy Tipungwuti	1954	Thoughts from afar	Amparruwu	Osborne	C04-003855B-206
CH5, 19	Tyurruptimirri/Tony Charlie	1975	Cargo ship Marella	Arikuruwala	Osborne	C04-003854B-137
21	Jipulimatu/Dorrie Tipakelipa	1975	Faithful wives	Amparruwu	Osborne	C04-003855B-213
CH6, 19	Unidentified woman and man	1981	Sorrow	Arikuruwala Mamanunkuni Amparruwu	Grau	A01-009278
22	Unidentified group	1981	Yilaniya ritual, Yoi	Jipuwakirimi	Grau	A01-002970-1-35
CH7, 3	Awunjingijimirri/ Christopher (Foxy) Tipungwuti	1975	Japanese lover	Ariwayakulaliyi	Osborne	C04-003855B-204
15	Jipapijingimirri/ Capstan	1912	Building houses	Jipuwakirimi	Spencer	C01-00701-2
15	Tungutalum	1912	Shipwreck	Jipuwakirimi	Spencer	C01-00701-11
15	Munkara	1928	Nyingawi	Ariwayakulaliyi	Hart	C01-004240B-D49
15	Tuki	1954	Storm	Arikuruwala	Mountford	C01-002917-53
15	Pujuta/Long Stephen	1975 (composed 1970)	Man on the moon	Arikuruwala	Osborne	C04-003854B-129
15	Barney Tipuamantimirri	1975	Cyclone Tracy	Arikuruwala	Osborne	C04-003855A-160

List of plates

Plate 1: The Tiwi Islands, looking north along the Arruwulupini Kirluwagamini (the Big Creek), Apsley Strait. Photo: Genevieve Campbell. 160

Plate 2: Marralyaangimpi waterhole, Bathurst Island. Photo: Genevieve Campbell. 160

Plate 3: Delegation to Canberra, November 2009. L-R: (standing) Regina Kantilla, Francis Orsto, Agnes Kerinaiua, Wally Kerinaiua, Stephen-Paul Kantilla, Eustace Tipiloura; (seated) Genevieve Campbell, Mary Elizabeth Moreen, Teresita Puruntatameri, Jacinta Tipungwuti, Leonie Tipiloura, Mel Sheba Fernando. Photo: Terrilee Amatto. 161

Plate 4: Performing Kupunyi (Canoe) at NFSA, November 2009. L-R: Wally Kerinaiua, Teresita Puruntatameri, Stephen-Paul Kantilla, Eustace Tipiloura, Mary Elizabeth Moreen. Photo: Genevieve Campbell. 161

Plate 5: Unidentified man dancing Yirrikapayi (Crocodile), Bathurst Island. Still taken from footage by Baldwin Spencer, 1912. Photo: AIATSIS. 162

Plate 6: Performing with the 1912 archive footage. L-R: Gemma Munkara, Regina Kantilla, Frances Therese Portaminni, Katrina Mungatopi. NFSA, May 2021. "Eyes and Ears" presented by Canberra International Music Festival. Photo: William Hall. 162

Plate 7: Francis Orsto performing at NFSA, Alex Boneham in background, November 2009. Photo: Genevieve Campbell. 163

Plate 8: Collecting pandanus, Tikilaru Country, June 2014. Photo: Genevieve Campbell. 163

Plate 9: Eustace Tipiloura and Roger Tipungwuti in Wrangku Country, June 2014. Photo: Genevieve Campbell. 163

Plate 10: Marcella Fernando, Emerentiana Tipiloura and Tallulah viewing the 1912 footage. Wurrumiyanga, Bathurst Island, February 2010. Photo: Genevieve Campbell. 164

Plate 11: Jacinta Tipungwuti and Francis Orsto composing for an upcoming funeral. Wurrumiyanga, Bathurst Island, June 2012. Photo: Genevieve Campbell. 164

Plate 12: Performing at PULiiMA Indigenous Language and Technology Conference in Darwin, August 2019. L-R: Frances Therese Portaminni, Mary Elizabeth Moreen, Nola Tipungwuti, Regina Kantilla, Gregoriana Parker, Calista Kantilla, Concepta Orsto. Photo: Genevieve Campbell. 165

Plate 13: Jules Palipuaminni singing Kuruwala songs at a funeral for the first time, guided by Francis Orsto. At the funeral for Teresita Puruntatameri, January 2020. Photo: Genevieve Campbell. 165

Plate 14: John Louis Munkara performing his Jikilaru song. Darwin Entertainment Centre, March 2021. Photo: Libby Collins. 165

Plate 15: Performing Nyingawi at the Magic Mirrors Spiegeltent. L-R: Regina Kantilla, Mary Elizabeth Moreen, Jacinta Tipungwuti, Francis Orsto, Karen Tipiloura. Sydney Festival, January 2016. Photo: Prudence Upton. 166

Plate 16: Rehearsing the opening of Ngarukuruwala Yoi! Darwin Entertainment Centre, March 2021. Photo: Roger Press. 166

Plate 17: Mary Elizabeth Moreen and Eustace Tipiloura performing Yirrikapayi (Crocodile) at the Magic Mirrors Spiegeltent. Sydney Festival, January 2016. Photo: Prudence Upton. 167

Plate 18: Turtuni placed at the Milimika in preparation for Yiloti Ceremony. Wurrumiyanga, October 2012. Photo: Genevieve Campbell. 167

Plate 19: Calista Kantilla painting up for Yiloti. Wurrumiyanga, October 2012. Photo: Genevieve Campbell. 167

Plate 20: Transcription session. L-R: Marie-Carmel Kantilla, Regina Kantilla and Augusta Punguatji (behind). Wurrumiyanga, July 2017. Photo: Genevieve Campbell. 168

Plate 21: Ratifying the Tiwi display, part of the *Ambassadors* exhibition at Chau Chak Wing Museum, University of Sydney, 2021. L-R: Calista Kantilla (seated), John Louis Munkara, Regina Kantilla,

Augusta Punguatji, Frances Therese Portaminni, Katrina Mungatopi. Photo: Genevieve Campbell. 168

Plate 22: Performing the Bombing of Darwin dance. L-R: Bobby Fernando, Ivan Fernando, Harold Munkara, Paul Tipungwuti. Bathurst Island, 1982. Photo: Patakijiyali Museum, Bathurst Island. 169

Plate 23: Justin Puruntatameri dancing at Kulama. Pirlingimpi, 1981. Photo: Andrée Grau. 169

Plate 24: Cornelia Tipuamantimeri dancing Winga (Sea) towards her husband, Long Stephen. Pirlingimpi, 1981. Photo: Andrée Grau. 169

Plate 25: Yilaniya (Smoking) ritual. Pirlingimpi, 1981. Photo: Andrée Grau. 170

Plate 26: Calista Kantilla leading singing at the funeral for Augusta Punguatji. Wurrumiyanga, September 2022. Photo: Genevieve Campbell. 170

Plate 27: Nina Black and Calista Kantilla, Bonnie Bush, Gabriel Wommatakimmi and Marcellus Mungatopi, Yanna Fourcroy, Doriana Bush, Nelson Mungatopi. Milikapiti, March 2010. Eunice Orsto, 2010. Casmira Munkara and Regina Kantilla, February 2008. Photos: Genevieve Campbell. 171

Plate 28: Eustace Tipiloura, Calista Kantilla, Teresita and Barry Puruntatameri, Stephanie Tipuamantimeri. Wurrumiyanga, February 2010. Photos: Genevieve Campbell. 172

Plate 29: Juliette Puruntatameri and Clementine Puruntatameri. Wurrumiyanga, March 2010. Photo: Genevieve Campbell. 173

Plate 30: Calista, Clementine, Genevieve and Eustace. Women's Centre, Wurrumiyanga, 2010. Photo: Katherine Wood. 173

Plate 31: Justin Puruntatameri explaining language and Kulama to Francis Orsto, listening to the old recordings. Munupi Arts, Pirlingimpi, Melville Island, 2012. Photo: Genevieve Campbell. 174

Plate 32: Recording in the Old Church, Wurrumiyanga. L-R: Teresita Puruntatameri, Francis Orsto, Regina Kantilla, Genevieve Campbell, Karen Tipiloura. Photo: Simon Bartlett. 174

Plate 33: Shirley Puruntatameri and Regina Kantilla watching archive materials with Pularumpi Primary School children. Pirlingimpi, April 2016. Photo: Genevieve Campbell. 175

Plate 34: Singing "traditional way" songs at the Nguiu Social Club, 2010. L-R: Brian Ullungura, Eustace Tipiloura, Stephen Paul Kantilla, Walter Kerinaiua Sr, Leonard Tungutalum, Regina Kantilla, Calista Kantilla and Bede Tungutalum. 175

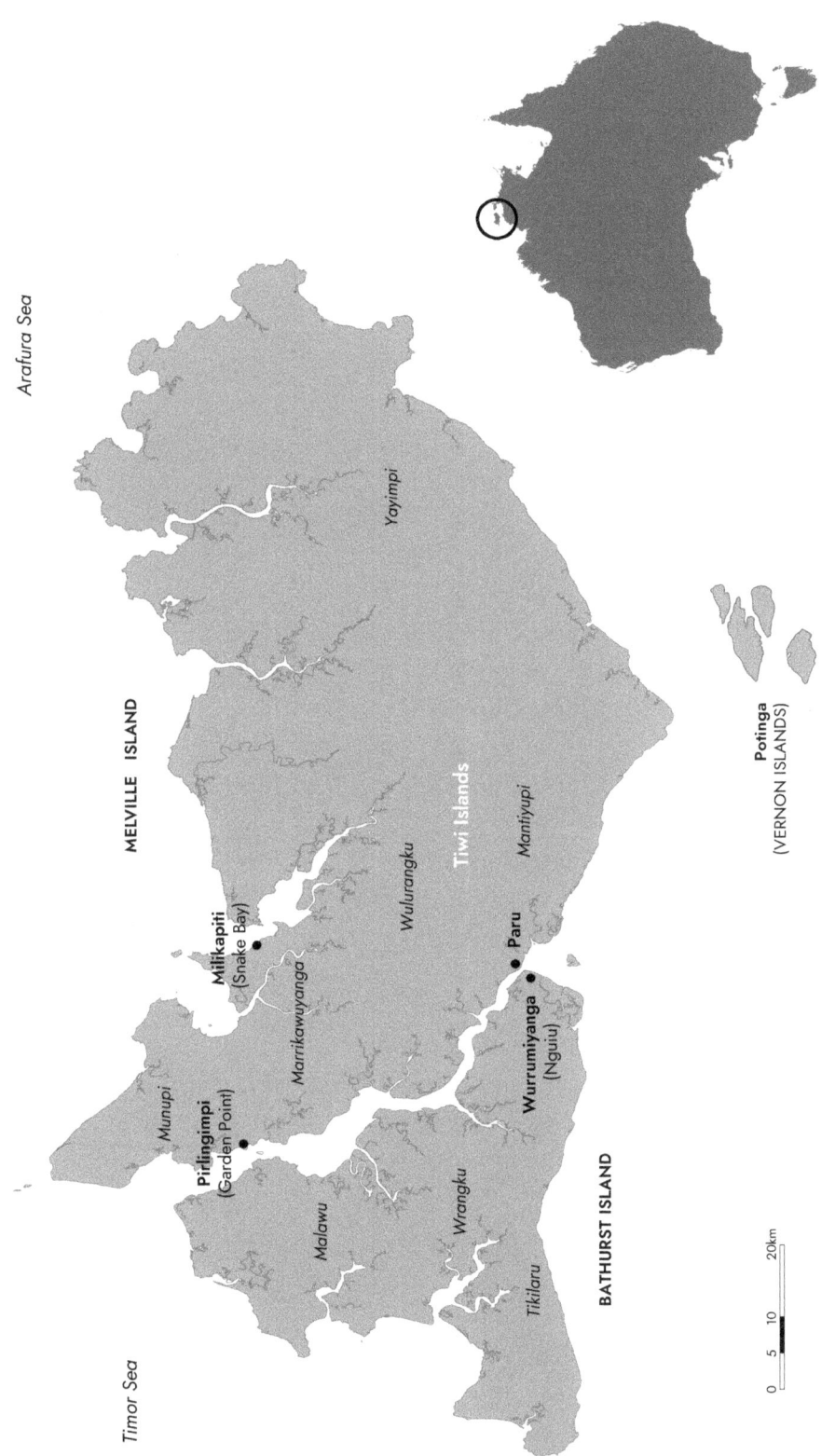

Map 1: The Tiwi Islands. (Map: Nathan Grice)

Preface

This book is about the song practice of Yirrara Ratuwati (Two Islands), known in English as the Tiwi Islands, northern Australia. It aims to provide as complete as possible a resource and documentation of the traditions of Tiwi song composition and performance, the musical and linguistic elements of the core song-types, and an explanation of the place of song in ritual. It does not set out to provide the definitive or final word on Tiwi song, however – that would be impossible and inappropriate. As a fundamentally oral, embodied art form and vehicle for accumulating knowledge, culture and identity, Tiwi song cannot be confined to the written word and this book is merely a drop in the ocean of the deep and ongoing accumulation of sung history.

My first experience of Tiwi song was in Sydney in 2006 when I heard a recording made on a family friend's mobile phone of the Tiwi Strong Women's Group singing at a local Tiwi community event on Bathurst Island. I knew nothing about what I was hearing but I loved how it sounded and I devised a plan to get myself up north. When I arrived in February 2007 at Nguiu, now called Wurrumiyanga, on the southern coast of Bathurst Island, I met the women and we very quickly became friends, our relationship firmly planted in those old ladies'[1] songs, me wanting to hear them and them wanting to share them. Teresita Puruntatameri, Regina Kantilla, Jacinta Tipungwuti and their sisters made me feel welcome and useful as we chatted and they sang. Right from the start there was no plan or agenda aside from allowing the women, and the songs, to take the lead. With the support of Arts NT and the Darwin Festival,

---

[1] The term "old lady" is used widely in the Tiwi community as one of respect and love for the Elder women.

our initial project came to life as a week-long get-together between the Strong Women's Group and a group of Sydney instrumental musicians. Our first performance, at the Darwin Festival in August that year, was semi-rehearsed, largely improvised and not at all predictable. Being in Darwin we had a sold-out local crowd, and the women were immediate stars, taking to the stage with the confidence and integrity of people whose identity, as individuals and as a group, was defined by the songs they knew. Not the songs they performed or rehearsed but the songs they just got up (or sat under a tree) and sang.

The women and I had to find a name for the collaborative group (the Tiwi women and the band) when we first performed publicly. After some discussion, Teresita called me to say that they had decided on Ngarukuruwala (We sing). This, she said, is "who we are … what we the ladies do, that's why we are a group of strong women", a collective noun encompassing how and why they come together and the power they have as that group through the knowledge and the words they hold in their songs. In the 16 years since then, with a dozen performances, three published recorded albums, a song book, numerous conferences and event appearances, and all of our study together, their identity as women who sing their culture remains the heart of what they do.

My initial role in Ngarukuruwala was as a musical colleague and co-performer (French horn), planner, secretary, budget wrangler, tour manager and bus driver. However, over the years as we talked more about the ownership of songs, derivations of words, and the origins of stories, melodies and dances, I found myself adding student, researcher and academic collaborator[2] to our relationship as we focused on the preservation of Tiwi songs in both traditional and contemporary composition and performance contexts. Respecting the forms, richness, complexity and intellect of Indigenous systems of philosophy, learning and communication, and giving them the value that we'd give any lived cultural heritage is the only way I can see truly successful research happening.

In 2009, as a result of our mutual interest in what the women called the "old songs"[3] and our discovery of the Tiwi collection held in the Australian Institute of Aboriginal and Torres Strait Islander Studies (AIATSIS) and the National Film and Sound Archive (NFSA), a group of Tiwi Elders and I went to Canberra to reclaim the audio and visual recordings made by researchers and visitors to the Islands between 1912 and 1981 (these are listed in Figure 1). Among these

---

2   Much of the musical analysis herein is based on work carried out by myself and senior Tiwi singers during the period of my PhD candidature from 2011 to 2014.
3   As I will explain in this book, what constitutes "old" and "new" songs, stories and language is not straightforward. In this instance, I refer to those songs that comprise the old language and what I refer to as "classical" musical forms.

recordings are hundreds of unique songs, composed specifically for particular events, both ceremonial and secular. Together they form a rich historical and cultural archive and a meaningful social and personal record of ancestors, place and family. More than that, though, they hold the voices of past knowledge holders. In the context of a traditionally oral knowledge system that relies upon the passing on of language, lore and culture through song, these recordings have become a document – a proof – of Tiwi educational, artistic, spiritual and social systems and of poetic, musical and danced creativity. Their repatriation[4] proved a pivotal point in our work together as the returned recordings became the focus of our musical collaboration, as well as the starting point of our documentation of the classical songs.

The Old Songs are Always New is fundamentally a document of and reference to Tiwi song practice, but Tiwi songs are and always have been part of a living oral culture. My aim is for this book to be a conduit through which the skills and knowledge of Tiwi song practitioners and custodians past and present can pass into writing, to create a resource for future Tiwi singers, and also place Tiwi song in the scholarly literature.

I was encouraged to compile this book by senior songman and Elder Yikliya Eustace Tipiloura (now deceased). He and I had many conversations about the conflict between the difficulty of preserving in writing the intricacies of Tiwi song – inherently extemporised and unique to each singer and each performance – and the power and value that a written volume holds. Many further discussions were had with Elders and young singers about the degree to which song holds knowledge and enables connections between Tiwi people and their place and each other. It was decided that the complexity of Tiwi song poetry and the detail and idiosyncrasy of melodic, rhythmic and vocal techniques, accumulated across generations of experts, made it important to document it in writing. Put most simply, Tiwi song practice is a rich part of our heritage – local and global – and it deserves to be marvelled at and its science is worth preserving. I use the word "science" here on purpose. Tiwi song practice is a complex and systematically organised body of knowledge and its musical, linguistic, artistic and spiritual elements are worth attempting to understand. My Tiwi collaborators and I hope many non-Tiwi people will read this book and add Tiwi song practice to their knowledge of world music. We also hope that Tiwi people will find it a valuable resource of the song words, phrases and melodies that can be used to continue this culturally significant practice.

---

4   In Chapter 2 I explain my part in the process of repatriating Tiwi song material to the Tiwi community.

Notes on orthography

Orthography for Tiwi language used

This orthography applies to Modern Tiwi, which is the basis for information and song texts given to me by my consultants, with advice from Nguiu Nginingawila Literacy Production Centre and referring to Lee (1993).

a as in "a cow"; before **y** it sounds like **e** as in "met"

i when in the middle of a word as in "bit"; at the end of a word as in "beet".

j preceding **i** or **u**, as in "cheese"; preceding **a** or **o**, it is a soft **d** as in "indigo".

k as in "ken"

l as in "like"

ly as in "million"

m as in "man"

n as in "now"

ng as in "sing"

ny as in "menu"

o between the **o** in "gong" and that in "port"

p as in "pat"

r as in "cheery" but with tongue tip curled back

rl digraph: like **l** but with tongue tip curled back

rr as in Scottish "sporran" with rolled **r**

rn like **n** but with tongue tip curled back

rt digraph: like **t** but with tongue tip curled back

t as in "tea"

u as in "put"

w as in "wand"

y when at the start of a word it is short as in "igloo"; when within a word it is like the y in "yes"

Variations to pronunciation

i becomes neutralised to schwa **ə** when it is preceded or followed by **p**, **w**, **m**, **ng** or **k**.

i and **u** sound like **a** as in "about" when in a non-stressed syllable.

Consonants differences between Osborne's and Lee's orthography:

tye is now spelled **ji**

agha is now spelled **aya**

e is no longer used (replaced by **i**, with no distinction between the two in current spelling)

The following abbreviations are used in text translations when Osborne's translation is presented for ease of cross reference:

eve: evening word form

caus: causative

dur: durative

em: emphatic

f: feminine

ic: incompletive

lk: linking syllable

morn: morning time prefix

np: non-past

nz: nominaliser

p: past

vol: volitional

List of Tiwi Elders, singers, culture and knowledge holders, and research consultants

The following is a list of Tiwi singers, knowledge holders, cultural leaders and Elders who have contributed their expertise and experience to the research and analysis undertaken in the course of compiling this book. Those who have since died are noted with † and their names are included with the permission of family, who are proud to have them included here to honour their role in the continuation of Tiwi cultural traditions.

Clementine Majitiwaya Kantilla Puruntatameri†

Concepta Milika Palipuaminni Orsto†

Emerentiana Tipungampurrimau Palipuaminni Tipiloura†

Eugenie Tipirrapulawu Kerinaiua Tipungwuti†

Eustace Yikliya Tipiloura†

Hyacinth Tungutalum†

Augusta Purruwurrika Portaminni Punguatji†

Barberita Tipamaetua Tampilaningimau Tipungwuti†

Barry Puruntatameri†

Casmira Milangimpanimauru Palipuaminni Munkara†

Consolata Kuraringawayu Portaminni Kelantumama†

Cynthia Timaepatua Portaminni†

Eunice Mirrukuku Palipuaminni Orsto†

The Old Songs are Always New

Genevieve Portaminni†

Justin Wamunkinimirri Puruntatameri†

Leah Kerinaiua†

Madeline Puantilura†

Marina Pirijipijawayu Portaminni Tipungwuti†

Patrick Puruntatameri†

Philippa Ngangurrumawu Kantilla†

Roger Tipungwuti†

Stephanie Tipilipatu Tipungwuti Tipuamantimeri†

Stephen-Paul Jamingi Tankarriyamari Kantilla†

Teresita Kilapayu Timaepatua Puruntatameri†

Theodore Pirrakiningimiri Tipiloura†

Walter Pirranuwamiya Kerinaiua†

Yanna Fourcroy†

Aileen Wurandabalu Ilortaminni

Ainsley Kerinaiua

Alice Munkara

Amy Joy Moreen

Ancilla Kurrupuwu Puruntatameri

Anita Moreen

Anna-Maria Polijiyapila Tipiloura Babui

Anne Marie Ampilipiyanu Puruntatameri

Annunciata Pirrnupantatila

Anthea Kerinaiua

Bernadette Tipuluwaningalayuwu

Bernard Tipiloura Mandilimiyu

Bertram Tipungwuti

Bonaventure Timaepatua

Bonnie Bush

List of Tiwi Elders, singers, culture and knowledge holders, and research consultants

Calista Jukura Tipuamantimeri Kantilla

Carol Puruntatameri

Charlotte Portaminni

Clancy Puruntatameri

Crystal Love Portaminni

Cypanthea-Rose Puluwamijayu Puruntatameri

Deborah Ampurrayumawu Kerinaiua

Della Kerinaiua

Doreen Kimarringilayu Orsto Tipiloura

Doriana Bush

Dulcie Pungantiluwayu Kelantumama

Edwina Portaminni

Elaine Tiparui

Elizabeth Tipungwuti

Ella Lamaturrujimawu Puruntatameri

Fiona Kerinaiua

Frances Therese Portaminni

Francilia Kutuwapijimawu Puruntatameri

Francis Jules Manginjirrimi Orsto

Gabriel Wommatakimmi

Gabriella Tumurayilawayu Alimankinni

Gemma Raparrulla Puruntatameri Munkara

Georgina Porkilari Portaminni

Gerarda Puliwitjimawu Tipiloura

Gibson Farmer Illortaminni

Glen Farmer Tipomurrayl Illortaminni

Greg Orsto

Gregoriana Porkilari Parker

Katrina Mungatopi

The Old Songs are Always New

Jacinta Tipulumuntayu Portaminni Tipungwuti
Jeman Tipiloura
John Louis Puwanikiyawayi Munkara
Judith Wiyalupuwayu Puruntatameri Fernando
Karen Kujarrapijila Tipiloura
Kay Piripanirila Brown
Leonie Tipiloura Pukutungumi Tipuamantimeri
Leslie James Tungutalum Enrail
Makarila Tipungwuti
Marcella Pulakatu Fernando
Marcellus Mungatopi
Marguerita Kerinaiua
Marie-Carmel Tipurupilimau Kantilla
Marie-Simplicia Tipuamantimeri
Mary Elizabeth Mungatopi Moreen
Mary Pungantiluwayu
Mel Sheba Pampiyamo Portaminni Fernando
Melinda Lakurrapiyanayi Kerinaiua
Michaeline Makarila Tipungwuti Puruntatameri
Nelsina Portaminni Mungatopi
Nina Kerinaiua Black
Pamela Brook
Paulina Jedda Puruntatameri
Pedro Wonaemirri
Regina Ampurulumi Portaminni Kantilla
Richard Tungutalum
Robert Tipungwuti
Rosemary Pupantuwu Portaminni Tipungwuti
Stanley Jipwarlamparripa Munkara

List of Tiwi Elders, singers, culture and knowledge holders, and research consultants

Tony Pilakui

Virginia Pirringitapijimawu Pangiraminni Garlaga

Walter Jr Kerinaiua

Wesley Kerinaiua

Names used to refer to singers in the Palingarri recordings

Nicknames given to some of the Tiwi men and women from the 1930s through to the 1950s are used in much of the literature and on the recordings, and this has made correct identification difficult. English names and nicknames were given to men by members of the Australian Defence Force stationed on the islands during the Second World War, and also by priests and nuns during the mission period because as Leonie Tipiloura told me "they couldn't pronounce our hard Tiwi names". Paddy Sawmill, Tractor Joe and Allie Miller were named (by non-Tiwi people) for the labouring jobs they had at the time. Others such as Long Stephen and Slim were, Tiwi people now presume, physically descriptive. Although some of these were initially nicknames for the fathers, the children have now inherited them as some have become surnames. The name Brown, for instance, was given to Jipuwampi, who then became known as Danny Brown. He was the father of a woman called Kaye with whom I worked. She was therefore christened Kaye Brown. Another of my consultants, Nina Black, knows her father was Bartholomew Kerinaiua Wampayawityimirri (having been given a Christian name at the mission as well as the Tiwi names he was given by family). He was called Black Joe by missionaries and so is referred to by that name by Charles Mountford, both in his written account (Mountford 1958) and on the recordings he made.[1] His son, Paul, inherited Black as a surname and this has been further established as a surname through his children. Other descendants took one of his Tiwi names, Kerinaiua, and it has also become a surname. Paddy Bush is another senior songman whose Tiwi name was passed over for the sake of simplicity.

The Brown, Black and Bush families have expressed concern that these names, given to their forbears in a derogatory context (albeit a paternalistic and perhaps well-meaning one) have become entrenched in Tiwi society at the expense of the Tiwi family names that should have been respected. The fact is, however, that these names are used so widely in the literature and in the recordings that I include them for the sake of cross-referencing. I have, wherever possible, included singers' Tiwi names in the complete list of recorded material. Since

---

1   C01-002917.

the practice of baptising children into the mission began, most Tiwi people now have a Christian name as well as Tiwi names. Calista Kantilla explained it this way:

> I have one Christian name that Bishop Gsell gave me when I was a baby. That is Calista. Then big mob other names from my mother and Jukura that my father gave me when I was five years old at Kulama. That is what everyone calls me and myself. It is in my heart.

Glossary of terms

Ayipa: *Free-form verb.* to perform the final songs of or to finish *Kulama* ceremony. The songs performed at the end of Kulama that tell of news and current affairs.

Country: an area of land that holds cultural and ancestral significance for a particular group who identify as traditional owners through paternal inheritance. I capitalise "Country" because this term is used as a proper noun to indicate the area of land with which each Tiwi person identifies as a spiritual and ancestral home.

Dreaming: a widely used Aboriginal English term for one's totemic/spiritual identity. (See *Yoi* definition 2.)

Kulama: *Variant:* kurlama. *Noun, Feminine.* round "cheeky" yam; the annual ceremony and (obsolete) lead up ceremonies of initiation towards *Kulama*.

Kuruwala: *Verb.* to sing, songs in the "singing" or "lyrical", "individualistic" style.

Mamanunkuni: *Variant:* Mamanukuni. *Noun, Masculine.* sad song or dance following death; dirge.

Milimika: *Variant:* Milimuka. *Noun, Feminine.* circle, cleared space, for dancing, sleeping, etc.

Mopaditi: *Variant:* Mapititi; Mapurtiti; Moputiti. *Noun, Masculine.* **1.** evil spirit, spirit of dead person, ghost, devil, Satan, sin, magic things.

ngirramini: *Variant:* ngarramini. *Noun, Masculine.* story, talk, message, words, news; law.

Nguiu/Wurrumiyanga: Until mid-2010 the largest town on the islands was called Nguiu (Bathurst Island). It is now officially called Wurrumiyanga but is still widely known as Nguiu by many locals. In order to respect this and to aid cross-referencing I will refer to the community by the name Wurrumiyanga for contemporary statements but will use Nguiu when within historical references or quotes from Tiwi people or other sources when referring to the town before the name change.

Pitapituwi: *Noun, plural.* Spirit children. *Feminine:* Pitipitinga. *Masculine:* Pitiputini.

Pukumani: a term that refers to mourning restrictions, items and rites connected with mortuary rituals.

song/song item: For the purposes of this study a "song" or a "song item" refers to one composition. Depending on the song-type and performance context, a song might be one line of sung text, of about 10 seconds duration, and that song might be repeated a number of times, before another song is presented. The change of singer and/or of subject matter will delineate separate song items within a larger recorded event.

Strong Women: The term "Strong Woman" is a designation given to Elder women who hold a particular degree of cultural knowledge.

tiwi: *Noun, plural.* people. specifically Tiwi (capitalised) people but often extended to all people, particularly in Modern Tiwi. *Masculine:* tini. *Feminine:* tinga.

traditional: The word "traditional" is problematic in this context due to the fact that the "tradition" of Tiwi song practice is itself based on innovation and variation. Tiwi singers refer to the "traditional" or "old" songs, however, and so I include it here where appropriate.

traditional owners: This is a term widely used in Australia to indicate the Indigenous owners and/or custodians of Aboriginal land and extends to cultural knowledge and heritage.

Yilaniya: *Variant:* Yilaninga; Yilaniga. *Noun, Masculine.* non-final funeral dance.

Yiloti: **1**. *Adverb.* forever; final. **2**. *Noun.* final mortuary ritual.

Yiminga: *Variant:* Yimunga; Yimunga. **1**. *Noun Feminine.* spirit, life, breath, pulse. *Syn:* pukwiyi. **2**. Matrilineally inherited Skin group identity

Glossary of terms

Yiminga + verb with root: -angirri to breathe. *Syn:* wunijaka + verb with root Þ -angirri. *See:* jiringa Yiminga + verb with root Þ -angirri; pumpuni Yiminga + verb with root Þ -angirri. *Category:* Body functions.

Yiminga [number] + verb with root: -muwu time of day, o'clock. Karri yimunga punginingita ampiri-ki-muwu. when it is five o'clock/at 5 o'clock. *Syn:* Yiminga.

Yoi: *Variant:* Yoyi. **1**. *Noun, Masculine.* dance, ceremony **2**. *Noun, Masculine.* Patrilineally inherited dance of a particular totemic identity (see *Dreaming*) **3**. *Free-form verb.* to dance

Prologue

Murntankala, the ancestral woman who created the Islands

Parlingarri karri karrukuwapi purumuwu murrakupuni, api yartijanga yipingima nginingaji ngatawa murrualupuni apingimi. Karrikamini yirringarni, karlawu jupunyi, yirritji. Karlawu yanamurluwi, tokwampuwi, miputuwi, jarrakalani amintiya yirrikapayi.

Long ago there were no people on the earth and darkness covered the land. There were no hills or valleys or waterholes or creeks. No animals or birds, no fish or turtles or crocodiles.

Kuriyuwu kapi yuwunka purumuwu awuta yamparriparri. Yilaruwu murrakupuni jiyimuwu yinjula yintanga Murntankala, kapi nyirra mwaruwi. Natinga wumunga niyrra papi jinirimi kapi awinyirra mupuka. Nyirra kularga jiyimi yinkiti amintiya kularlaga jiyama kapi yartipuranji ngini kapi pimantamajirripi nyirra mwaruwi. Karluwu wupunga, karluwu kukini.

Above the sky were the Yamparriparri spirits and underneath the earth lived an old woman called Murntankala and her three children. One day she dug upwards through the earth and arrived on the land. She looked around for food for her children and for soft ground where she could lay them down, but there was no grass, no bushland, nothing.

Murntankala jipamukurigi nyirra-mwaruwi yilaruwu kapi tunga kapi jukwartanga kapi pirrartimarti ngini marruwapa awuta kakarijuwi. Api nyirra jimarnuwa awungarruwu murrakupuni. Karri jimanuwa api jiyikirimi yangamini kapi murruakupuni awinyirra mirripaka kalikali yinipajimangimi kapani nyirra jukwartanga.

Murntankala put her children in a basket and carried them on her back as she was afraid of the Yamparriparri because they might want to eat her children. Then she began to crawl around the earth and as she crawled along, she made tracks in the ground and the sea rushed in behind her.

Waya piyaki kiyi awinyirra papi jiyimi kapi nyiraa pakinya jipilikirimi, amintiya nyirra awungarra naki yirrara ratuwati.

She crawled all around and back to where she started, and she had created these two islands.

  Story and translation given by Calista Kantilla and Jacinta Tipungwuti

Chapter 1
An introduction to the Islands

Yikiyikini, wayayi, kipiwura, awurnanka amintiya alawuntawini yirrima kapi yungunkwa. Kirawirratingama, kirilima, tarnikuwi, jipwarringa, wuninga wuta apulipamiya murrakupuni wuta arrayi, muputi, kuluwarringa, jarrakalarni, kirimpika, yiriwirli, marntuwunyini, yirrikapayi wuta tatuwali kapi mirrimpaka.

Cockatoos, bush stone-curlews, pelicans, magpie geese and masked owls fly across the sky. Snakes, junglefowl, fruit bats, wallabies and possums hide in the bush and oysters, fish, mud mussels, turtle, crab, mangrove worm, dugong, crocodile and sharks are found in the surrounding coastal waters.

Concepta Orsto

The Tiwi Islands are located 80 kilometres north of Darwin at the confluence of the Timor and Arafura seas (see Map 1). They are known today by their English names, Bathurst Island and Melville Island, and are separated by the Apsley Strait. With a combined area of 8,320 square kilometres they comprise mallee scrub bush, eucalypt forest, pandanus, spring-fed waterholes, estuarine creeks, mangroves, and a coastline of rocky outcrops and wide sand beaches. Also part of the Tiwi traditional lands are numerous smaller uninhabited islands including Yirripurlingayi (Buchanan), Purrumunupi (Harris), Pirripitiriyi (Seagull), Purrapinarli (Karslake), Yipinuwurra (Clift), Turiturina, Matingalia, Nodlaw and Muma (East Vernon), Warabatj (North West Vernon) and Kulangana (South West Vernon) – known collectively as Potinga (Vernon Islands), dotted around the coast to the north and south.

The word Tiwi means "people" – the plural of tini (man) and tinga (woman). Living on islands since palingarri (for ever, long ago, from the beginning), the people had no need for a "national" label. Ethnographer C.W.M. Hart first used the term "Tiwi" to refer to all inhabitants of the Islands (Hart 1930, 169). While Jane Goodale reported that in 1971 the term was not used by the locals (Goodale 1974, 14), since then it has come to be used commonly among Islanders to refer to themselves as a group when talking about the entire community or when introducing themselves to non-Tiwi people in order to distinguish themselves from other Australians. Within their community, however, people most often identify with the Murrakupuni (Country) to which all Tiwi people belong. At the local level, the Murrakupuni groups and the land management and custodianship of the Country areas are extremely important.

The Australian Bureau of Statistics (ABS) census figures show the official total population of the Tiwi Islands to be 2,453 in 2020.[1] There are approximately 1,700 inhabitants on Bathurst Island, living in Wurrumiyanga, and about 30 at the small outstation Wurangku. Melville Island has about 900 people spread across (in descending order of population) Milikapiti (Snake Bay), Pirlingimpi (Garden Point), and the outstations at Paru and Pickertaramoor.

Since the beginnings of the Catholic mission on Bathurst Island in 1912, the Government Ration depot in 1939 (which later became a mission at Garden Point (Pirlingimpi)) and the Government Settlement at Snake Bay (Milikapiti) in 1941, Tiwi people have lived in and around these organised settlements rather than in their own Murrakupuni. There is nonetheless a very strong sense among everyone of affiliation with and ownership of Country. This is best explained by the Tiwi Land Council:

> Land plays an important role in kinship and relationship networks, with each person belonging to a landowning group and having particular connections to spatially defined areas. Similarly, there are aspects of managing and allocating land and natural resources that are inseparable from kinship and relationship ties. While landowning rights are inherited from the father, the responsibility for the care of important sites comes through the mother's line. (Tiwi Land Council 2020)

Whenever the opportunity arises, people will go out bush and spend time on their own land. The realities of modern life mean that they live, for the majority of the year, in the towns. The Country groups determine the ownership of the

---

1 Australian Bureau of Statistics (2020). Census QuickStats: Tiwi Islands. Canberra: ABS. Retrieved 23 July 2020.

land, with its use and that of any resources remaining under the control of the traditional owners.

To avoid a Eurocentric version of the last 200 or so years of Tiwi Islands "history" I have included only those events that have been recorded in Tiwi song. It must be said that the sung record (preserved in the form of audio recordings made of Kulama and Yoi song in 1912, 1928, 1948, 1954, 1966, 1972, 1981)[2] contains a wealth of social and local history, and the songs quoted here form only a small sample.

Early visitors

The song shown at Song text 1[3] was performed by Warlakurrayuwuwa Paddy Sawmill in 1975 (and recorded by linguistic anthropologist Charles Osborne). He recounts an old story from sometime in the late nineteenth century about the lone survivor of a shipwreck off the western coast of Bathurst Island who lived, left alone and not troubled by locals, near the shoreline of the south-west coast. He was known as Murrukuliki (Macassar Man) and the story goes that, after living in a rock cave near Tangiyawu on the south-western tip of Bathurst Island for some years, he made himself a raft and disappeared out to sea. People presume he found his way home. The fact that the song mentions he ate zamia palm nuts suggests that he was from one of the islands to the north of the Tiwi Islands and so he knew that he had to soak the nuts before he ate them to make them ingestible. Tiwi recounting the story say if he had been a murrintani (white man), he would have made himself sick and died, not knowing they are poisonous unless one leaches them of toxins first. The Murrukuliki song and story belong to and are still retold by people of the Tipungwuti patriline, after Tipungwuti, the then senior man of the area and leader of the group who spotted the castaway.

---

2   Kulama and Yoi constitute the two main song performance contexts and are described in Chapters 3 and 4.
3   Ayipa is a section of the Kulama ceremony when songs telling of current events and newsworthy stories are performed. The musical form of the Ayipa song-type is described in Chapter 6.

Song text 1: Warlakurrayuwuwa Paddy Sawmill. Murrukuliki (Macassar Man), 1975.

> **An Ayipa song for the third evening of Kulama, telling the story of the Macassar Man**
>
> Ngila Juwarlarrapi Murrukuliki ngintuwarinjirrikipurramukuriyi
> *I am the Macassar Man camped at Juwarlarrapi [on the south-west coast of Bathurst Island]*
>
> Jipiliwula kwampi putiminginjirrikipurrarumunayi
> *Jipiliwula big men found me there at my camp*
>
> Wiyapurali ngirrajinipingimarri kipantingimuwu
> *I sat at Wiyapurali beach cracking zamia nuts*
>
> Ngintwijirrikipi ngimakepantingimayaji ngirrawira
> *I dropped the nuts and ran away*
>
> 'Puwankupwanayi!' nimpujingipingimapi kiripwiyamami
> *I hold up my hand to say 'peace!'*
>
> Pungikiliyiwula Jakupwayinga nginta ripiya kilimayaoungarliyi
> *I pushed my canoe out and escaped*
>
> Ngampi maningintuwu winga Jiminijingipingimajirramawinamani
> *The sea carried me far away*
>
> Ngampi ngili yeti Mankaja timani ngirriwunjingipimaya majinarlayi
> *I got there ashore in my Macassar Country*

From the seventeenth century, annual expeditions were made to the trepang[4] beds along the northern coast of western Arnhem Land[5] by Macassans, Malays and other fishermen from the islands of the Indonesian archipelago (McIntyre 1977; McMillan 2007; Toner 2000). A theory that the music of northern Australia might have connections with long-past influences from these visitors has been suggested and more research into this area may well discover deeper cultural links than previously supposed (Marett 2005, 208; Toner 2000). Although there is no direct evidence of musical influence of this kind on Tiwi culture there are songs that mention visitors and visiting boats from the north.[6] The sea route from the Indonesian archipelago to Arnhem Land would have

---

4 Trepang is a common name for the marine invertebrate *Holothuria scabra* (also known as the sea cucumber).
5 The Cobourg Peninsula, north-western Arnhem Land, is approximately 30 kilometres from the east coast of Melville Island across the Dundas Strait.
6 Doolan J02 000628B-4; Hart C01-004240B-D29ii; Holmes S02_000181A-2; Spencer C01-00701-3.

taken fishing boats close to the north-eastern coast of Melville Island, although the trepang beds there were not rich, so contact was probably not as intensive. There is one mention of Tiwi Islands in relation to the Portuguese and I quote from Pilling (1960), who quotes George Windsor Earl (1853, 210), who wrote:

> According to … the older inhabitants of Timor, Melville Island was only less a source of slavery than New Guinea, in proportion to its smaller extent of surface, at the period in which the slave-trade was encouraged or connived at by the European authorities.

Although otherwise not well documented in the literature, Tiwi oral history recounts that at least a generation prior to the five-year British settlement at Fort Dundas on Melville Island from 1824, the Portuguese had already been taking Tiwi men from Melville Island as slaves. Such oral history as this is of course impossible to prove, and also impossible to discredit with any real certainty. There are intriguing elements to this, with some loan words in the old songs in the archive such as pirrawa (from "prau", an Indonesian sailing boat) and manuwa (man o'war) indicating there was some degree of relatively close contact, either between Tiwi and Portuguese or Tiwi and Macassans, who themselves had incorporated some Portuguese into their language. The song at Song text 2 was sung by Jimalipuwa at a recording session by Hart in 1928. It is considered by current senior singers to be a historical song as Jimalipuwa would have inherited the story from his grandfather, describing a large, masted "man o'war" sailing ship of the type seen off the coast around the early nineteenth century. While it doesn't directly suggest shipwreck, oral history recounts a number of shipwrecks in the time before 20th-century ships or sustained contact with non-Tiwi. We can hear the two old words for the ship/boat: pirrawa and manuwa.

Song text 2: Jimalipuwa. Recorded by Hart in 1928.

An Arikuruwala song for the first evening of Kulama

Ngiyapirringi limpangi**pirra** waningimawu
The ship/boat is coming

Ngiyapirima Jingi**pirrawa**nuwa
I am the tide I am pushing the ship

Ngiyapirripi majingi**pirra wamanuwa**
I am a strong wind and I am pushing you [the boat] onto the shore

Pantirriwini atumwutirru puntingayinti
The flag is standing up [on a mast]

Japanese pearlers had been visiting the islands seasonally from the 1880s, when they first had a temporary base on the southern coast of Melville Island. For some years there existed a seemingly mutually agreed-upon trade of goods for the sexual use of Tiwi women (Osborne 1989; Pye 1977). In 1930 the Australian government attempted to stop this arrangement by transporting all of the Tiwi people in the area (the Yeimpi) to Darwin, and by patrolling the waters around the coast. A government rations depot was set up at Garden Point (Pirlingimpi) in 1939, and more Tiwi women were removed to Darwin in a further attempt to stop the contact (Hart and Pilling 1988). In 1940 a Catholic mission was established to care for the so-called half-caste[7] offspring of these contacts, the mothers having been taken to Darwin. This has resulted in a group of Tiwi people who identify themselves as part of the Stolen Generations. At the outbreak of the Second World War, Australian government intervention stopped the Japanese from pearl fishing in waters off the islands. There are many references to Japanese fishermen (and the unconnected Japanese air raid on Darwin in 1942) among the recorded songs.

Robert (Joe) Cooper (an Anglo-Australian) first visited Melville Island in 1895, for a short buffalo shooting trip, bringing with him a group of Iwaidja people from the mainland. In 1896, when the shooting was paused to let the buffalo population renew, Cooper left for the Cobourg Peninsula (on the Australian mainland) taking with him 11 Tiwi people, including babies (Hart and Pilling 1988). In 1905, Cooper returned with another group of Iwaidja people and the Tiwi who had been taken 10 years earlier (apart from one man, who died at Oenpelli) and set up a permanent base at Paru on Melville Island, where they remained until 1916. Five of the Tiwi women had married Iwaidja or Gagudju men. A number of Tiwi families today have close links with Iwaidja people and a number of Iwaidja loan words have entered the language (Lee 2011).

Song text 3: Jipapijingimirri, recorded by Spencer in 1912.

> A Jipuwakirimi song.
>
> Watimanuwampjirri kiliyarumi jipilimuwinkuwa
> *The white men have lined up their houses in their camp*

---

[7] This derogatory term was used for many years to label Aboriginal children with mixed-race parents or grandparents, as part of a systematic segregation and suppression of Indigenous people in Australia by governments and missions. It was only in 2008 that a formal apology to the Stolen Generations was given by the Australian government. I include the term here to remind the (non-Tiwi) reader of the offence it has caused and with the knowledge and permission of Tiwi consultants.

Songs including that at Song text 3 documented the increasing presence of visitors from the mainland.

The permanent interruption of Tiwi sovereignty of their islands came in 1912[8] when a Catholic mission was established on the shore of Bathurst Island by Father (later Bishop) Francis Xavier Gsell, a French priest of the Missionaries of the Sacred Heart. The then-government-appointed "Protector of Aborigines" Baldwin Spencer[9] declared Bathurst Island an "Aboriginal Reserve"[10] and granted 10,000 acres (approximately 40 square kilometres) to the Catholic Church. Gsell is most famously known for his 150 "wives": the female children he removed from their families between 1921 and 1938 to stop the traditional Tiwi family system, which did not adhere to the values of Catholicism (Gsell 1955). I discuss the disruption of Tiwi family systems and its impact on culture and language further in Chapters 4 and 5.

The ephemeral nature of Tiwi songs

Song is the primary framework for Tiwi ceremony and ritual as well as for the transmission of cultural knowledge, the documentation of current affairs and a vehicle for maintaining language. The body of knowledge of the Tiwi people – the spiritual, historical, geographical and customary record – has been passed on orally, most of it through song. Perhaps the most defining feature of Tiwi song is the importance placed on the creative innovation of the individual singer/composer. Tiwi songs are fundamentally new, unique and occasion-specific, and yet sit within a continuum of an oral artistic tradition. Performed in ceremony, at public events, for art and for fun, songs form the core of the Tiwi knowledge system and historical archive. Held by song custodians and taught through sung and danced ritual, generations of embodied practice are still being created and accumulated as people continue to sing.

Tiwi song practice is primarily one of extemporisation, with songs created contemporaneously with and specific to the performance event.[11] Rather than

---

8   Having arrived on the island in 1911, Gsell began taking young Tiwi girls into dormitory housing in 1912 and the first nuns arrived at the mission in 1914.
9   Spencer espoused the paternalistic value judgements of many anthropologists at the time with the idea that Indigenous peoples were "primitive", and were worth observing and documenting as examples of a dying race. It is only due to the legacy of his recordings that he is mentioned in this book.
10 Melville Island was declared an Aboriginal Reserve in 1933.
11 Each song in this book is noted in terms of the purpose and context of its performance. Most were not given a title by their composer/singer. The captions for songs in transcriptions, in text and in the lists of audio examples and AIATSIS material are for the purposes of cross-referencing with existing literature, the archive catalogues and/or identification by Tiwi singers.

comprising a corpus of songs that is passed down through generations, it is the skill of composing within a framework of prerequisite metrical, melodic and poetic knowledge that is passed down through a long process of heuristic learning. Individuality and creativity are highly regarded and there is therefore much variation to be found across the more than 1,300 song items preserved in ethnographic field recordings made on the Tiwi Islands over the past century. In the face of language loss and a shrinking traditional song culture, the repatriated recordings from the Canberra visit (see Chapter 2) may be seen as an important educational tool, but there is also concern among Elders that the recordings might cause a move away from improvisatory song composition to the creation of a canon of learned songs.

Being the central oral art form in an ancient and (traditionally) non-written culture, Tiwi song is also a living document of ancestral, seasonal, spiritual, social, political and genealogical history, making it vital to the Tiwi community and to Australian heritage.

As the central focus of this book, both in terms of content and inspiration, the songs will as much as possible be the vehicle through which the reader learns about the practice. Rather than writing about the songs, I will include the songs themselves. Song is the vehicle for oral instruction, the holder of embodied knowledge, culture and spirituality, so it is through the texts that have been sung by Tiwi ancestors that we will most successfully learn something. The Tiwi words and their English equivalents are presented here as the result of close, careful and respectful consideration by senior song custodians and knowledge holders in order to encapsulate as much of the complexity and richness of a continuing sung culture as can be captured in written and recorded form.

Among the archive recordings are hundreds of unique songs, composed specifically for particular events, both ceremonial and secular. Together they form a rich historical and cultural archive and a meaningful social and personal record of ancestors, place and family. More than that though, they hold the voices of past knowledge holders. In the context of a traditionally oral knowledge system that relies upon the passing on of language, lore and culture through song, these recordings have become a document – a proof – of Tiwi educational, artistic, spiritual and social systems and of poetic, musical and danced creativity.

The Tiwi singers with whom I spend time refer to their songs as their history books. The songs are their almanac, their genealogy, weather chart, calendar, constitution, spirituality – all actively known through intergenerational transmission and performative, heuristic learning. I am re-presenting Tiwi sung knowledge and by writing songs down I'm transcribing unique, sung moments in time into finite symbols and words. While this removes them from their enacted place and potentially alters their essence as lived, performed, embodied actions, my Tiwi colleagues want the song forms, words and melodies documented, for preservation and for acknowledgement and so we try to find sensitive ways of enabling the oral and embodied transmission of that knowledge while recording finite examples of it.

It is important from the outset to appreciate the role of the individual in Tiwi song culture. The passing down through generations of epithetic phrases, ancestral names and places, and poetic devices means that some repeating of parts of songs occurs, but fundamentally it is the innovation of one's own words that is characteristic of Tiwi song practice. Just as a jazz musician or a writer of poetry might incorporate existing harmonic or rhythmic structures, metrical patterns or metaphorical imagery to fashion their own unique and new compositions, so too does the Tiwi singer compose a song unique to them, which may draw on the imagery of composers before them and that is based around a recognised melody. Among many hours of song items there are no two exactly the same, and fewer than a dozen share a full phrase with another song. Considering that for all of the songs captured in the recorded archive there are thousands more that have been sung over the ceremonies, days, months, years outside of those recorded periods and for the millennia before the 20th century, the 1,300 or so songs in the recorded archive are a drop in the ocean of the Tiwi song corpus.

A core element of an oral and embodied knowledge and essential to its continued teaching is the time that its teachers and learners share together. The flexibility of time spent listening, existing. The openness to metaphysical aspects of intuition and cultural practice (which also encompasses the physical, spiritual, environmental and intuitive) and the depth of inherited confidence and grounding. Through a decade of listening and learning from the Tiwi songwomen, I have re-learned some of my ways of approaching notions of inherited knowledge, practised skill, cleverness, ownership and responsibility.

Senior Tiwi singers know that the knowledge they hold is best passed on and most successfully documented through their voices, their songs, their language, their art and with Tiwi-specific cultural understandings. Working out how to do that within the framework of an imposed colonial socio-political environment is our task and challenge as researchers, and theirs as knowledge holders. Whatever our systems are they are all rich and complex and we are so very fortunate to be in a place of being able to appreciate them. The core of our method as researchers – and as people – has to be to listen and, I think, not just to listen, but to hear.

Taking into consideration the improvisatory nature of Tiwi singing, one must always be aware that a song recording is the record of *one* performer on *one* particular day. Although the song will feature textual, melodic and rhythmic patterns characteristic of its particular song-type, it is still essentially unique and must be accepted as only indicative of the song and/or song-type. Microtonal fluctuation, ornament, vocal timbre, vibrato and rubato are performance-specific and impossible to represent exactly via music transcription using western notation. A transcription can also never represent fully the embedded meaning, emotional response or technical skills of the performer nor (and this is equally important) the response of the listener (Knopoff 2003; Marett 2005). It is, however, an essential tool that I have used to represent the music in a way that makes it accessible to non-Tiwi readers and to facilitate detailed analysis that will place Tiwi music in the literature.

Although there has been observation and research into Tiwi culture (Brandl 1971; Goodale 1974; Grau 1983a; Hart and Pilling 1988; Mountford 1958; Spencer 1914; Venbrux 1995), as far as I am aware there is thus far little specifically relating to Tiwi song. Charles Osborne's assertion that the musical forms of Kulama and Yoi songs are "merely monotoning" and "entirely inexpressive" (Osborne 1989, 155) comes from the point of view of someone uneducated in Tiwi music.[12] Any music will only be fully appreciated for its technicalities and quality when the listener has some level of knowledge of the subtleties of harmony, melody, timbre and performance qualities that are unique to those musical traditions. Far from being monotonic, Tiwi song is melodically and performatively expressive, interactive and vocally complex. Steven Knopoff suggests there is a cultural basis for musical understanding, stating: "It is precisely because our musical ears are so culturally biased that we need analysis for a very practical purpose, as a sort of game or exercise to help us hear music in different ways" (Knopoff 2003, 45). I therefore use musical notation with as much visual clarity as possible, and intend the reader to make use of the accompanying audio examples to facilitate an appreciation of the pertinent features I refer to in each. I have used symbols for rests, sparingly, between sung phrases when the break is in "time" in relation to the notes around it. Otherwise, I have indicated breaths and/or breaks between phrases with spacing. Similarly, percussive beats often do not exactly align with a particular note and so are indicated as such. I have transposed transcriptions within some examples to a common "tonic" in order to facilitate comparison and have indicated as such. Unless otherwise

---

12 As I will describe in Chapter 6, even those melodic forms that centre on a repeating pitch incorporate accentuation of rhythmic patterns, dynamics, vocal timbres and microtonal fluctuation that make them highly expressive.

stated, all musical examples are transcribed at performance pitch. With no drone or accompanying pitched instrument,[13] there is no implied harmony or tonal centre, although each melodic shape does centre on, lead to or otherwise create the sense of a primary pitch. In the case of Tiwi music this is rarely the final note. I refer to this primary pitch as the "tonic". (Please refer to the List of music transcriptions and notes for an explanation of the markings used in the music transcriptions.)

The centrality of text to Indigenous Australian song is well established in the literature. In all studies of song, from communities around the Arnhem and Kimberley regions in particular, the recurring finding is that text is fundamental to song and informs the structuring of the rhythmic elements and the durational features of melodic elements, often called "melodic sections" (after Ellis 1984, 90; see also Marett 2000, Barwick 2003, Treloyn 2003, Garde 2006). The interconnectedness of language and song in terms of meaning, subject matter and function therefore result in multiple levels of understanding for different audiences (Feld and Fox 1994; Garde 2006; List 1963; Roach 1982; Tiparui 1993; Turpin and Stebbins 2010; Walsh 2007). I do not pretend to have a thorough knowledge of the Tiwi language, nor to present in this study a detailed analysis of the language itself. Although my connection with the Tiwi Strong Women,[14] the Elder men and the community is primarily based on study of song, it has become clear that the change Tiwi language has undergone since the arrival of the mission is relevant to my work because of its effect on song practice. Tiwi has undergone rapid change in the last 100 years, rendering the language that was spoken by Elders in 1960 incomprehensible to all but a very few old people in the community today. Linguist Jennifer Lee's discussion of the changes that have occurred in the language over the last 50 years (Lee 1987, 1988, 1993, 2011) have been a valuable aid in navigating the complexity of the language situation in the community, as I explain further in Chapter 5. (See also Notes on orthography.)

Linguistic anthropologist Charles Osborne's detailed analysis of Old Tiwi (Osborne 1974) provides background for work on song texts, because they are in the "Old" language,[15] and my Tiwi listeners have deferred to Osborne in the cases where their own knowledge of the language is insufficient. Allowing for development through the generational transmission of improvised, individually

---

13   This relates to the classical Tiwi song-types. The guitar-accompanied song-types do have a pitch centre and harmonic progressions.
14   "Strong Women" is a term used by Tiwi people to acknowledge the women as collective cultural knowledge holders and their role as matriarchal Elders.
15   "Old Tiwi" is the now archaic language in which traditional song is composed. The shift in Tiwi language is the subject of Chapter 5.

created contemporary practice, there is still a wealth of information to be generated from Osborne's transcription of the sung texts. Most of Osborne's song texts (Osborne 1989) are, however, in metrical form (the midway step in the process of song composition, which I explain in Chapter 5), not as they were actually sung. Tiwi song texts have three stages:

1. The text in prose (in spoken form).
2. The text structured into the standard Tiwi songs metrical form: any number of units of five syllables, followed by one unit of four syllables.
3. The text as iterated at the moment of performance (often the same as the metrical form, but not always, and in some song-types, most often *not* the same as the metrical form).

The various additions and deletions made by the singer at the metrical and then the performance stage make transcribing the sung form quite difficult. With no living regular speakers of the Old language, we rely on auditory recognition of each sung syllable. I have found that those older Tiwi people who do have a good knowledge of the Old language, and of the poetic devices used in extemporised song, ignore the additions and/or deletions and hear just the words. Speakers who still use some (and remember) Old Tiwi have native speaker intuitions about which syllables fulfil a communicative function and which fulfil a purely metrical function, as they leave the latter out when speaking the song text. The additions/deletions are a feature of the metrical form and/or the sung form (not the spoken form). When reiterating a song text so that I can transcribe it, what Elders offer as the song text is not what I am hearing but is, instead, the underlying spoken form. Indeed, I have found that singers find it very difficult (and often impossible) to speak the text of a song (rather than singing it). As soon as they speak it, they automatically revert to the spoken form. Added to this, most do not have a good enough knowledge of the Old language to recognise which added (or missing) syllables and changes of pronunciation belong solely to the sung form and which belong to the spoken form. The fact that Osborne has transcribed the metrical form of many song texts, without the irregularities and variations of individual performances, means that the metrical forms of the words have been documented, providing a resource for those interested in learning the correct way to create their own new songs with the texts as source material for their own compositions.

Being on relatively remote islands, the Tiwi people have not had the degree of contact and exchange of song genres that has happened across the mainland. Further research is required to investigate the extent to which a sharing of songs might have happened, although I have found only a few instances of non-Tiwi song genres among the recordings, either as a result of mix-ups in the materials' archiving or recording performances by non-Tiwi visitors. Many studies have shown the degree to which songs have moved across language groups in northern mainland Australia, with Ronald and Catherine Berndt first raising the possibility of contact and cultural trade among Indigenous people around the Cobourg Peninsula and western Arnhem Land (Berndt and Berndt 1947, 1964). Sharing and exchange of songs between the Wadeye (Port Keats) area and the Kimberley and western and central deserts as well as into the Daly and Arnhem Land regions occurred via overland trade and stock routes. The renegotiation and variegation of song genres also occurred as people from different language groups were brought together into mission settlements during the 1950s and 1960s. Neither of these phenomena occurred on the Tiwi Islands. As far as I am aware, the Tiwi do not sing genres from other areas of Australia. Unlike Junba, Lirrga, Wangga, Nurlu and Manikay that have moved across wide areas and have been shared across language groups, there are very few examples of non-Tiwi genres being performed at Tiwi events, and these have been by visitors. There is evidence of Iwaidja songs being performed by Iwaidja singers on Melville Island (recorded in 1912)[16] and the Tiwi and Iwaidja people share the Buffalo Dance (although the associated songs are different).[17] There is also a long association between Tiwi people and Wadeye (formerly Port Keats) through the Catholic Sacred Heart mission (established on Bathurst Island in 1912 and in Wadeye in 1935). The Anglican mission at Belyuen (then Delissaville) established in 1946 and the Methodist mission at Minjilang (on Croker Island) also created a context for ongoing contact between those communities. While these three proximate-community links are long and ongoing there is no evidence of sharing or mixing of song genres. Tiwi people sing Tiwi songs when they visit Wadeye, Belyuen or Minjilang for ceremonial gatherings and Murriny Patha and Iwaidja people sing their own songs when they visit the Tiwi Islands.

An archive of old, new songs

As this is intended as a reference book it focuses mostly on what I will call "classical" Tiwi music, in an attempt to differentiate it from the "modern" Tiwi music that has evolved across the 20th century. Without suggesting that "modern" Tiwi

---

16 The Djanba song recorded by Spencer in 1912 is not Tiwi, but was performed by Iwaidja people who were on Melville Island temporarily. This pre-dates what was previously thought to be the earliest recording of Iwaidja song, made by Mountford in 1948 (Barwick, Birch and Evans 2007).
17 The Buffalo dance, now firmly established as a dance performed by Tiwi people with Jarrangini (Buffalo) Dreaming, most likely travelled with the people who moved between Melville Island and the Cobourg Peninsula at the turn of the 20th century. It is now considered Tiwi, with Tiwi people leading Buffalo dancing when they attend events involving both communities.

music is not an integral part of Tiwi song traditions, it has to be acknowledged that the permanent arrival of Europeans in the form of the Catholic mission in 1912 was a turning point in Tiwi cultural autonomy. I do though need a way to differentiate between the ways in which Tiwi singers composed and performed before Europeans changed things, the ways in which Tiwi singers composed and performed after that, and the changes across the subsequent century. I am wary of using the terms "pre/post-invasion" or "pre/post-colonisation" as they are potentially divisive in the Tiwi community itself, and I don't intend to criticise or cause offence to those (Tiwi and non-Tiwi) now older people for whom the mission time holds happy memories. The modern Kuruwala song-type created by the Strong Women's Group in the 1980s is a combination of the church choral guitar-accompanied style and elements of traditional Tiwi linguistic and metrical techniques. It relates to music syncretism that has occurred in other communities as a result of similar history of mission influence and the introduction of non-Indigenous music to the culture (Corn 2002; Lawrence 2004; Magowan 2007; Wild 1992). The embedding of traditional song practice, language and cultural knowledge into new musical forms is being achieved in other parts of Australia and the world, with the senior custodians of endangered traditions embracing new ways of continuing the transmission of songs. This "grafting" (Wild 1992) of popular western culture into Indigenous traditions is a feature of other Australian song genres today. The deeply rooted connections with traditional song language, subject matter and musical elements place senior songmen and songwomen in positions of high esteem and, with increasing engagement with recordings, both as educational tools and as the starting point for new music, as protagonists in the future of their song traditions (Corn 2007; Corn, Marett and Garawirrtja 2011).

Consider too that Tiwi songs are/were intrinsically contemporary. Composers were always innovative. The melody, rhythm and tempo were adapted for performance context and the language was altered from prose through poetic and musical ornamentations in performance. Restrictions on the use of certain words, phrases and names following deaths and associated protocols of closure, and the movement of people and their songs around the islands, resulted in lexical change over the course of time. Taking into consideration the fact that Tiwi song practice celebrates novelty and innovation and that one should sing one's own song (they are not passed down word for word by any means), this then also makes the distinctions "old" and "new" problematic. Tiwi people today refer to "old" songs and "new" songs. The musical and linguistic form of an entirely new and contemporary song might be what I would describe as "old" (pre-colonial), while a song containing choral harmonies and a rhythm and blues backbeat on guitar will be considered "old" because the linguistic and cultural content are old. The word "traditional" doesn't quite work either. Traditions are what cultures, communities and families follow, have "always done" and one could say that the traditional Tiwi song practice is defined by change and innovation. To describe the songs composed for ceremony in 1928 as "traditional" makes sense, as long as only those "old fashioned" song-types are called "traditional", whether composed in 1912 or in 2021. The traditional way of composing song text continues within non-Tiwi musical contexts and so the women's songs are now called "old" songs – even with their guitar-accompanied style and borrowed American pop song melodies. I will therefore call the Tiwi songs that do not include non-Tiwi influence "classical", regardless of when they are sung.

Translations presented here are the result of work with a group of women and men with cultural authority to speak about songs. As they each bring to the task their own accumulated knowledge and experience of song and ceremony, there is some variation in their explanations of what song texts mean. As well as actual text words, the translations I have been given include associated information, potentially inferred in different ways by the people who are listening to the song. Again, this is due in large part to differing levels of knowledge of the Old language and of song-specific idioms, with allusive references often only recognised by the older listeners, and younger listeners understanding a more literal meaning. Following advice from song custodians I have provided glossing and/or poetic free translations that are included below the transcriptions. The presentation of all song texts is the result of close consultation with Elders.

When approaching the text of recorded songs, younger Tiwi people tend to hear what I hear because they do not expect to understand the text. I have found, too, that people often think they hear the syllables in a word that they know – they incorporate their accumulated knowledge and experience into their physical (aural) and intellectual response, adding or omitting syllables to make the word fit what they know is correct rather than reporting what is actually in the recording. This has resulted in some contradictions between transcriptions and translations. Some recordings have poor sound quality and not all text has been clear enough for people to hear in its entirety. Consonants can be particularly unclear, and a different consonant can change the meaning of an entire word, and therefore an entire text phrase. Some songs include Old Tiwi words that are not used today and so Elders are uncertain (or have conflicting opinions) as to their meaning. In most cases we have however been able to produce a transliteration in English that they are happy with in terms of documenting the song in a meaningful way and as a valuable tool and resource for the community. In examples that focus on musical elements I give a free translation that indicates the general (rather than deeper) meaning of the text.

The spelling of Tiwi words is not standardised, and over the years there have been several different spelling systems based on (sometimes flawed) phonetic assumptions on the part of the non-Tiwi speakers transcribing them. Especially across the early literature and in museum collections (Spencer in 1912, Hart in 1928 and Mountford in 1954, for example) there are wide discrepancies in how consonants and vowel sounds are notated and this has, at times, rendered names and other words undecipherable when comparing them to current understandings. Although there was some defining of Tiwi written language in the form of school materials in the 1970s, most written Tiwi follows phonetics and so can change across writers. The spelling I use for Tiwi words in this book is therefore flexible. When quoting from existing literature I use the spelling used therein. When presenting old song texts transcribed and translated by Osborne (Osborne 1989), however, I have used Osborne's spelling and linguistic gloss only where the text is in an old form of the language that today's Elders wish to have documented here. This includes some words that are no longer spoken, whose meaning has either been forgotten or, through lexical change, whose translation into New Tiwi (the current form of the spoken Tiwi language; see Chapter 5) does not correspond, but which are being passed on as "song only" words. These songs, words or phrases now carry inherent inferred meaning and connection to ancestors and they have been deemed important enough to be remembered in their original form. It is hoped that students will learn them as they are.[18] All other song texts are presented using current spelling and, after consultation with senior singers, indicating the sung (performance) form of the text, with word breaks indicated in the clearest possible way to enable Tiwi students of song to learn, whether by rote (if that is their choice) or to pick up words that they can use in their own new songs. There are also some variations in the spelling of vowel morphemes as the process of transcribing song texts directly from audio recordings has resulted in differing opinions among senior singers as to the sounds created for artistic effect by the recorded singers. It is important to keep in mind that the written versions of the songs are an indication only, and that in sung form the words are quite different to how they would appear in prose.

For the texts of the women's current songs I use their preferred spelling, and for all other Tiwi words I refer to the dictionary compiled by Jennifer Lee (1993)

---

18   As I will explain further in Chapter 5, there is the potential for a shift from the classical practice of newly composed songs, extemporised using heuristically learned poetic devices, to the creation of a repertoire of song texts that can be taught in their complete (already composed) form.

(now online (Lee 2011)). For consistency, equity and correctness of record I spell the unique names of Tiwi people quoted in the literature as they appear in that publication and current knowledge holders' names as they prefer. Current surnames which appear in the literature with different spellings have been updated to align with current spellings.

Every personal Tiwi name is unique and, over a lifetime, one can be bestowed numerous names.[19] When a person dies their name becomes closed for Pukumani (a mourning restriction or taboo).[20] The restriction on the use of names of deceased people (as well as their songs and images) does not continue indefinitely but is lifted after the Yiloti (Final Ceremony) which is held about one year after death, or at a time deemed appropriate by immediate family. Although the deceased can then be referred to by name, that name would not normally be used again to name a new child.[21] During the early mission days Tiwi children were renamed by the nuns and babies were baptised with Christian names. While they were still also being bestowed Tiwi names, these were often not documented in written records. Some Tiwi people have found that their Christian name became Pukumani and so now use another European name. If two Tiwi people share a Christian name (which has occurred as babies were baptised with names that were already the names of older people in the community), when one dies the other has to change their name. In 2008 an older Tiwi woman whose Christian name was Genevieve passed away. This meant that my name became Pukumani, and so I was given a Tiwi name by the women who had welcomed me into the community. Those particular women dance Crocodile as their Yoi (Dreaming) and so I was given the name Payinga, from Jikapayinga the female crocodile. Since then I have rarely been called Genevieve by my Tiwi colleagues, and only to non-Tiwi audiences (performances or conference presentations, for example). Many young Tiwi people, who never heard me called Genevieve, only know me by my Tiwi name. I have since been given three other Tiwi names, each bestowed by a senior woman: they are Mungurruwamirrila, Janjilawayuwu and Portamininga. Also, with people from the mainland joining the community, there is increased likelihood of two people having the same Christian name, although it is still uncommon and would most likely be due to the presence of a non-Tiwi staff member or visitor. In the era of colonial structures and the Eurocentric suppression of culture came the simplification of adults' names to suit white bosses and so we find names such

---

19   These are given for special occasions or as marks of life events.
20   Pukumani is discussed further in Chapter 3.
21   In the last few years there has been some relaxing of this tradition, such as a little girl named Teresita in honour of her great grandmother, the revered songwoman and community leader mentioned a number of times in this book.

as the aforementioned Black Joe, Jacky Navy, Long Stephen, Paddy Sawmill and Tractor Joe in the literature. These men are now remembered as leading songmen, having been recorded in the archive. As much as their English names might now cause unease for many readers, they are widely accepted, used (especially by older Tiwi people) and recognised in relation to songs. So I refer in this book to these men by both their Tiwi and their non-Tiwi names in order to facilitate cross-referencing with the archives. The names of all Tiwi people herein are presented as accurately as possible, following the guidance of current Tiwi cultural authorities, and using the name by which a person is known best.

The inclusion of any names, voices and/or images of deceased people is done with the permission of their family. It is inevitable that at some stage in the future a person whose voice, image or name is included here will pass away and I therefore ask that any reader be sensitive to this fact when using any part of the text, sound files or images.

I'm not Tiwi and I don't intend to speak on behalf of Tiwi people in any way other than to present their knowledge. I intend to create a narrative that most faithfully and intelligently presents the data as well as the opinions and voices of my Tiwi colleagues and the very relevant and important issues surrounding the study, preservation and use of Indigenous knowledge from the point of view of the non-Indigenous researcher and the subject of the study itself. Writing down an embodied, sung knowledge system (even in the cause of preservation) is of course problematic. Taking into consideration the improvised nature of Tiwi songs and the fact that it is the skill of song composition at the point of performance that is so important and highly respected, capturing one performance on tape, designating it as the definitive example of a particular song style, or indeed of a particular singer's technique, is misleading. It does not allow for either an appreciation of the improvisatory skill that was employed, of the occasion and audience, or of the performance's place on the trajectory of a developing, changing and fluid art form.

> What does it mean to take knowledge developed in a complex oral tradition where it was evolving in a dynamic process and freeze it in a database, outside of the community from which it derived its meaning? (Nakata 2003)

The integrity of the current song practice and the respect commanded by the senior holders of song knowledge can be at risk of being undermined by the return of recorded material (and with it the return of voices, skills and knowledge of preceding practitioners) with the responsibility of continuing the traditions being felt deeply by some. The perceived favouring of some singers, families, ancestors or kinship groups over others, having been recorded, and so constituting the "heritage" – the describing of Pukumani songs composed for a particular person, for instance, or the memorialisation of individuals because songs about them were recorded at the Kulama that happened to be documented – is another issue to be negotiated by Tiwi custodians. Certain singers have been recorded by a number of researchers, and we also see family lines of singers building long-term recorded repertoires. Whether this was by coincidence, by the logistics of where researchers spent their time or by the accumulation of respect that befell those singers, having been chosen to represent the song practice, or whether they were already designated leading singers is unclear. What has transpired though is that particular names have become revered as song and culture men and women and those who connect to them through family lineages are today either senior singers themselves or actively involved in matters of cultural maintenance and engagement with the archive. The content in returned recordings also has the potential to raise conflicting understandings of what was fundamentally an oral and dynamic social and cultural system. Seen in hindsight and plucked out of the context of slowly evolving modifications, changes to inter-clan kinship obligations and land ownership can cause a questioning of the status quo for current cultural authorities. The process of returning these previously unheard recordings to the islands has therefore been one treated with sensitivity. The repatriation of recordings to Indigenous stakeholders has, quite rightly, become a central consideration of ethnomusicological research in the Australian region (and indeed all over the world), with the return of recordings itself becoming an object of research (Anderson 2005, Kahunde 2012, Lancefield 1998, Niles 2012).

While there is little doubt or argument that the artistic and moral rights of the songs belong to Tiwi traditional owners, ownership of the recordings themselves is a complex issue. The complications and implications of the repatriation of Indigenous materials highlight the need for the re-evaluation of some of the practices of past approaches to First Nations cultures generally. Although perhaps well meaning, the attitudes of paternalism and voyeurism underlying some of the collection of material for the study and preservation of Indigenous cultures can be seen in hindsight as culturally insensitive at best and destructive at worst. The discussion of how best to ameliorate power imbalances, theft or appropriation of artistic material or intellectual property and, in the circumstances of legitimate collection of cultural materials (tangible and intangible), now that we know more, must continue to be open and frank, and must be a two-way discussion between institutions, researchers, artists, and Indigenous owners and stakeholders. The issue of ownership is ongoing. The wait for permission to be granted (and sometimes rejected) to use song recordings that, by any ethical reasoning, belong to the Tiwi people and contain voices of their direct ancestors – and sometimes even their own voices – is often uncomfortable, with unresolved questions and discussion circling around the group of Tiwi song custodians with whom I have been working over the years. At all stages I have followed the direct advice of and responded to the wishes of Tiwi custodians. As the holders of the moral rights and cultural authority, they were (in some paperwork, literally) signatories, both as the party requesting release of material and as the party granting permission for its release – a circular process we grappled with through 2008, some of which I describe in Chapter 2. Their experience with the repatriation process has motivated Tiwi community leaders to ensure that these recordings and the voices and knowledge within them are reclaimed in an artistic and cultural sense, as well as by having them physically returned. All of this is to say that it is a complex process that requires patience, trust and communication as we all navigate the ever-changing ramifications of the collection and storage of people's intellectual, artistic, spiritual and personal (tangible and intangible) property.

Chapter 2
The archived recordings

Kuwa [yes]. It was good to go down there, you know. Get those recordings out from that place. Maybe we don't know why they ended up there. My grandfather was a big man for singing. My dad too. Now me, I'm a community leader so I have to make decisions about culture. What's best for our young people. Teaching them our language, you know. Those old songs. They have all our stories in them. Bringing those old fellas' songs back so we can listen. Yeah it's important. We keep going.

Wally Kerinaiua

In this chapter I will give an account of the process undertaken by a group of Tiwi people to reclaim[1] a large collection of ethnographic recorded song material, including the emotional, socio-political, legal and ethical issues that my Tiwi colleagues and I encountered, as well as the effect that the material is now having on Tiwi song tradition itself. Documenting the experience of the group, as the Indigenous owners of the material, is essential to give an understanding of how their journey to Canberra informed the reception given to the recordings and how they've been regarded by their Tiwi custodians since.

Gaining access to the recordings

The desire (the women's and my own) to find the old Tiwi recordings came about largely through the process of workshopping the Ngarukuruwala music

---

1   I use the word "reclaim" here because that is how the Tiwi people regarded the purpose of the journey to AIATSIS.

project,[2] especially when we made the first of our new musical arrangements of Tiwi songs with (non-Tiwi) instrumental accompaniment. Questions asked by the band about the meanings, melodies and functions of Strong Women's Group songs sparked conversations about the lineage and associations each song had, as well as notions of how "old" the songs were. Then when we recorded some of those "new" versions of "old" songs, it was essential to register them correctly and fairly for artists' creative and moral rights, decisions around future reproduction, live performance and potential royalties. A can of worms of ownership, copyright and intellectual property was opened, which necessitated a deeper enquiry into the songs than simply their subject matter and melodic structure. I became aware of a large amount of Tiwi song material housed at the Australian Institute of Aboriginal and Torres Strait Islander Studies (AIATSIS) and, after discussions with the Tiwi women and members of the Tiwi Land Council, I requested the material listed in Figure 1.

Figure 1: Ethnographic Tiwi song material housed at AIATSIS.

Collector	Year
Baldwin Spencer	1912
Charles Percy Hart	1928
Colin Simpson	1948
Charles Mountford	1954
ABC Radio (collection of Alice Moyle)	1955
Helen Wurm[3]	1965
Sandra Holmes	1966
Jack Doolan[4]	1967
Michael Sims[5]	1972
Alice Moyle	1976
Charles Osborne	1975
Andrée Grau	1981

---

2   While Ngarukuruwala was initially, and still is, in the main voiced by the Strong Women's Group, we do enjoy the support of senior and emerging songmen as guest performers and on matters of authority related to song custodianship.
3   In the AIATSIS collection inventory, the recordist is named Helen Wurm (her married name). In the academic literature she is referred to as Helen Groger-Wurm. To facilitate cross-referencing with the recordings catalogue, I will refer to the recordings as the Wurm collection.
4   Jack Doolan was superintendent with the then Department of Aboriginal Affairs and living at Milikapiti when he made these recordings.
5   Father Michael Sims was a priest at Nguiu at the time he made these recordings.

2 The archived recordings

These recordings housed at AIATSIS became the focus of my activities with the Tiwi women throughout 2008 and 2009. While it is not the aim of institutions to make access difficult for Indigenous stakeholders, there is evidence that it is by no means a smooth and easy process, and the experience I had reclaiming recordings on behalf of my Tiwi colleagues is not an isolated one, with recent reports indicating that this is not unique to Australia (Kahunde 2012; Niles 2012). It was immediately clear that the process of requesting copies of the Tiwi recorded material – either for the purposes of study (at that point only in the context of our studying the old songs for interest and artistic inspiration) or for any public sharing in the Tiwi community – was going to be complex and lengthy. My initial enquiries were (quite rightly) met with questions as to my authority to be asking on behalf of Tiwi owners, and followed by complex paperwork requirements that seemed to be more about protecting the ownership rights of the anthropologists and the institutions than about offering the material to the Tiwi community. It was from this point on that the idea of "reclaiming" the recordings began to generate talk around the Tiwi community about ownership, stakeholders' rights, why they had been "taken away" in the first place, and that Elders felt a sense of duty to arrange for their return, with a repeating theme of discussions around how these recordings came to be in the collection without them (the Elders and/or the Land Council) having been officially informed already.

I was advised by AIATSIS in April 2009 that the only way to have the material digitised and processed for release was to have Tiwi Elders listen to it in order to assess potential cultural restrictions. Although Tiwi songs are not affected by secrecy or gender restrictions, none of the metadata accompanying the material specifically noted this and so AIATSIS, following correct procedure, was unwilling to release the material without Tiwi approval. There had been no previous request and no impetus for repatriation on the part of AIATSIS, so the material was not in line for digitisation, but instead was in storage. Our request (mine for "research" and my Tiwi colleagues' for "personal use") was not logistically possible because it had not had cultural restriction appraisal (which could only happen if the Elders listened to it). This posed a catch-22 problem: the Elders could not listen to it unless it was digitised and sent to the islands (in effect, released) which could not happen until the Elders had listened to it. With time stretching on, and potentially running out for older Tiwi people with direct interest in and knowledge of this material, it became imperative to the Tiwi Elders that they take affirmative action.

Taking voices away

Senior culture woman Clementine Puruntatameri spoke up at a meeting in Nguiu in mid-2008, as I reported the latest on our attempts to navigate the bureaucratic hurdles of repatriation and grappling with the idea that, although traditional owners' intellectual property was acknowledged for the songs, it was the (white) person who pressed the record button who owned the actual recordings. She compared the voices in the recordings with the bones of Indigenous people taken to museums in England in the nineteenth century, pointing out that these voices are part of the person, they are the person, they are not tape recordings. The distinction between tangible and intangible cultural heritage becomes more blurred when we consider this. Both the musical composition and the poetry held within a song are without question that person's artistic property, just as much as the painted carved designs of a spear, but, as Clementine made clear, the voice of a person is their own as well. As we would find over the years to come, the very tangible presence of these voices made the recordings far more than the cassette tapes or computer files they were held in, and certainly not something that Tiwi people could fathom should be owned by anyone other than family. Accompanying our discussions about the archives is a continuing consternation as to why this very significant material was in Canberra in the first place, owned by collectors and not available in the Tiwi community.

We struck an impasse, with no conceivable way to have the recordings put into a format that would enable Tiwi authorities to listen to them and give approval, to then allow for the process of repatriation. We were advised that the only way was for the Tiwi authorities to go to Canberra. To fund the journey, and because we were now interested in knowing what Tiwi artefacts might be in other collections in Canberra, I was able to secure co-funding[6] for a week-long trip to visit the collections at AIATSIS, the National Museum of Australia (NMA), the National Film and Sound Archive of Australia (NFSA) and the University of Sydney's Macleay Museum,[7] with a view to consultation between Tiwi delegates and curators on the Tiwi collections at each institution. In November 2009, I accompanied a group of Tiwi people to Canberra; it was made up of four men and seven women representative of different Countries and Skin groups to show as broad a spread of cultural authority and knowledge as possible.[8] The primary aim was to spend two days at AIATSIS auditioning the audio material so that Elders could give authorised permission for its release.

---

6   The visit was supported by NMA, NFSA, AIATSIS, the Mantiyupwi Family Trust and the federal government (Office of the Minister for Arts and Environment).
7   The Macleay Museum is now part of the University's Chau Chak Wing Museum.
8   The group appears in Plate 3.

I include here a brief account of the visits to the other collections because, although not focused on song, they had a direct impact on the attitudes the group had during their time at AIATSIS and brought into sharp focus the interrelatedness of material and performative Tiwi culture.

Song as artefact

A symposium on the expedition to Arnhem Land by C.P. Mountford in 1948 was, coincidentally, being held at the NMA that same week as the Elders' visit. The recordings made by Colin Simpson (who was on the Arnhem Land expedition) on Melville Island in 1948 and Mountford's recordings there in 1954 were among those we would be auditioning at AIATSIS and so there was a sense of the Tiwi group "connecting the dots" between the written history; the collected painted, carved and woven pieces; recorded song; and filmed and photographed dance and ceremony. Indeed, all week we continued to find connections between the audio recordings (at AIATSIS), the material artefacts (at the NMA and the Macleay Museum) and the film material (at the NFSA). The audio recordings and filmed footage by Spencer in 1912, and the recordings and artefacts collected by Hart in 1928, provided rich and visceral meaning and context to both collections. At the NMA we saw bark paintings by Black Joe, Tractor Joe and Kardo Kerinaiua, collected in the 1950s and 1960s by Mountford and Groger-Wurm, whose songs, recorded by those collectors, we then heard at AIATSIS. Also viewed were a number of items that were collected by Torrance McLaren for use in the film *Coorab in the Island of Ghosts*, made on Melville Island in 1928 and then acquired by the National Museum in 1969, having been purchased from the owner (the daughter of the collector). Although this selection comprised items for ceremonial use (pandanus and feather armbands, seed pendants, spears, stone axes and bark baskets), the group considered them free of any spiritual sensitivity. Once objects such as these have been used for a ceremony they are generally discarded, so it made sense that they might have been sold or bartered to the film maker after the event.[9]

This strong correlation between the collection of song/performance recordings and the collection of material pieces served to strengthen the feeling among the Tiwi group that their predecessors had given a lot to the visitors, and it was time for them to be offered something in return.

---

9   This film was in the collection at the NFSA, but it was not available to view because it was marked in the collection metadata as being restricted as it includes "confirmed culturally restricted material which may not be viewed by the public". It was not possible to have the film made available in the time we had. AIATSIS had an open-access edited version of this film, but they were also unable to make it available while the group was in Canberra.

At the NMA the group was shown a large collection of Tiwi artefacts, including ceremonial spears, woven pandanus armbands and headbands, message sticks, sculptures and paintings on bark, some on public display and others kept in an NMA storage building. To the surprise and dismay of the group, apart from a collection of carved poles on public display, none of the items was marked with the name of the Tiwi person who made it; instead each was labelled with the European collector's name. The painted designs, specific to particular Skin groups and Country groups, helped identify the artist in a number of cases (knowing the year in which they were made and who would have been the senior artist then) and this information was added to the NMA's metadata.

The group was shown photographs of four Turtuni poles (commonly referred to as Pukumani poles) collected by Herbert Basedow in 1911. Basedow's notes say these poles were from a Pukumani Yiloti (Final Ceremony) held for a baby some years beforehand; at Basedow's direction the baby's body was exhumed for collection, but was deemed to be in too poor a condition (Basedow 1913, 291–323). Basedow had the poles repainted, by Tiwi men, and then removed from the site and shipped to Adelaide, where they were eventually housed at the South Australian Museum in 1934.[10] This caused great sadness and some anger among the group, with much discussion as to how the Tiwi locals must have been coerced in some way – either through payment in cigarettes or other goods, or through the position of power held by the stranger/white man – because no-one would normally ever move Turtuni poles, or even suggest it. The Turtuni poles serve in a similar manner to gravestones, marking the place of the burial, but more so to mark the place of the soul or spirit of the deceased.[11] Teresita said:

> I can't believe they pulled them out of the ground. That is bad for the spirit of the child. It breaks the spirit of the place. They should never be moved.

They agreed the Tiwi men must have had little understanding of the reality of these poles leaving the island and being displayed elsewhere. Wally, Eustace, Stephen-Paul and Francis resolved that on their return home they would perform ceremony to attempt to heal the situation.

---

10   Later that week we visited the collection of Tiwi Turtuni poles on display in the Art Gallery of New South Wales in Sydney. These Turtuni were, in 1958, the gallery's first Indigenous Australian objects to be commissioned as works of art rather than acquired as artefact. Since then, so-called Pukumani poles are painted as artworks to be sold and, like the gallery's collection, they are not associated with an actual ceremony.

11   The relocation of most people off Country and into towns, as well as government regulations, mean that most people are now buried in the town cemetery. Some families still place the person's Turtuni pole/s in their Country, which is where their spirit resides (regardless of where their body is buried).

2 The archived recordings

The equivalency of songs with paintings and artefact as items of cultural and artistic heritage and as physical "ownable" objects became clear to my Tiwi colleagues over the course of the week, and I am certain that this has had an ongoing effect on the way the Palingarri recordings[12] are regarded among the Tiwi community.

It was within the context of these discussions about the collection and ownership of Indigenous cultural property and heritage, as well as a heightened sense of pride and purpose, that the group arrived at AIATSIS ready to reclaim their song material. The older members of the group found it particularly powerful to hear familiar voices among the recordings. They expressed their concern at the songs (and the singers' voices) being trapped in recordings and removed from the community in the same way that some of the objects had been, and their sense of duty to return them to the islands was strong. Some of the younger members of the group had the opinion that they were also the rightful owners of the recordings themselves and that there should be no impediment to their being given compact discs to return home. These discs became objects emblematic of the artefact in the other institutions and, as Sheba Fernando said at the time, "holding on to them" became just as important as listening to them.

There was an expectation among the group – as well as from the Tiwi community and the Tiwi Land Council (which had also given significant financial support) – that they would return with some song material.[13] Although most of the requested material had been cleared by the copyright holders, and was digitised and ready to be auditioned, only the Hart material was on a CD ready for repatriation (pending the Elders' approval). The Mountford, Sims and Osborne material was in stasis because the copyright holders could not be traced. With the copyright issue the only impediment, the Elders signed the required request forms and cultural authority forms[14] and so it was hoped that the process of release would, from this point on, be relatively smooth. We learned that Holmes had not given permission for the release of her recordings. In 1966, Mary Elizabeth Mungatopi Moreen was the twelve-year-old daughter of Polly and Allie Miller, Holmes' primary consultants. Holmes' recordings were very moving for Mary as they contained the voice of her father (as lead singer) and of her mother and Mary's sister

---

12   Palingarri translates as the deep past continuing traditions, "like we always have", forever or long ago. The repatriated recordings have come to be called the Palingarri recordings.
13   Considering it had been 18 months since I first requested Tiwi song material, and for four months AIATSIS knew of our planned visit (partially funded by AIATSIS itself).
14   Some of these had already been signed and posted in 2008.

Eleanor as informants. It was with understandable confusion and sadness that Mary learned that Holmes would not release the recordings.

Unfortunately, at the end of our week in Canberra, only one disc (the 1928 Hart material[15]) was ready for the group to take home and there was clear frustration among the group that they were not being given what they deemed rightfully theirs. After some discussion, and perhaps as a result of our noticeable disappointment, the acting director gave discretionary permission for release of the Osborne and Sims material, and these were posted to the group eight months later. These were not, however, allowed to be copied or played publicly in the community, nor was the Sims recording released for "research purposes". While the diligence with which permissions and digitisation of the rest of the material were eventually organised is impressive, it took a physical visit from the group to Canberra – with accompanying time, money and effort – to obtain a result after many months of inaction. The release of material under different usage permissions caused great confusion and very quickly all of the recordings were being copied (by me) and shared around the Tiwi community regardless. I understood at the time that this was in potential breach of the release conditions but, under the circumstances, family members wanting to hear their own antecedents, old people wanting to hear themselves, and the sense of the songs as cultural property overrode any moral concerns I had. CDs break or get scratched very easily, and the logistics of travel between the towns on the islands meant there was no practical way those 11 copies, which constituted the repatriated material, were going to last long. Indeed, three of the women had left their copies with me in Sydney because they didn't have the means to play them. Frustrations aside, the overall experience was invigorating and powerful as each member of the group discovered something deeply personal among the recordings, and all of them felt that going to Canberra in person had been the right thing to do.

In late 2011 I was advised by AIATSIS that the Holmes material had been released, at the discretion of the director, to the 11 Tiwi individuals for personal use only, but I was not authorised to use it for research. It therefore did not appear in my PhD dissertation. I have listened to it many times with Tiwi colleagues, partly due to logistics as my laptop was their only means of playing it. With Eustace Tipiloura, the designated senior custodian of the content, I also made some cursory transcriptions and annotations of the songs, primarily

---

15 The Hart material is out of copyright and so was a simpler process. The quality of this recording is very poor and much of it is inaudible.

significant to a particular clan group on Melville Island.[16] Among the recordings Holmes made are the voices of women singing widow songs. Widow songs are sung in a ritualised, performative manner in certain stages of the mortuary-related rituals. They are, however, also sung in moments of solitary mourning. The vocalisation of intense personal grief in these instances on the recordings caused great upset among my Tiwi colleagues, who were of the opinion that the women may not have known they were being recorded, and that it was an invasion of their privacy at a deeply personal time. Discussions about the Holmes recordings have informed the descriptive content of widow songs in this book but I don't include any specific material relating to those sections of the recordings.

Ongoing engagements with collections

In May 2021 a group of Tiwi custodians travelled again with me to Canberra, this time as performers in the Canberra International Music Festival and as artists-in-residence at the Australian National University's School of Music. One of the events we were involved in was a speaking and performance presentation at the NFSA. The idea was for the group to respond to the Tiwi archival film material in any way they chose – anecdote, song, dance – and the material was made available to us prior to the public presentation so that we could prepare. Only one of the group had seen the footage back in 2009, so the experience was a discovery process again, and brought up many of the emotions that I had witnessed 11 years earlier. The footage provides visceral reminders of the social and environmental history of the Tiwi Islands in the mission era – from a 1938 Cinesound Review showing the Bathurst Island mission through to home movies taken by tourists in the 1960s. The oldest in the group, 84-year-old senior woman Calista Kantilla, had personal memories of the years featured in the footage and all present (all in their sixties and seventies) remembered the mission days and had emotions of nostalgia and sentimentality, as well as some strongly negative memories, seeing the era of their childhoods. Throughout the viewings was the uncomfortable reality of the power imbalance, cultural misunderstandings and prejudice that pervaded much of the material. While of historical and sentimental value, some of the footage is now (and indeed always was) offensive and patronising, and it causes new levels of discomfort for Tiwi and non-Tiwi viewers to acknowledge how recently these attitudes

---

16   The material was closed for a period on Eustace's death in 2018 and, although no longer restricted, there has been a sense that he was the authority to speak about it, so comprehensive documentation has not been done at time of writing.

existed.[17] The group at the NFSA in 2021 presented a spoken, danced and sung performance in tandem with a screening of the film material.[18] During the viewing and discussion prior to the event, the group decided that some of the footage was particularly demeaning and disrespectful and would not be shown publicly. The footage that was shown, they chose to share and to comment on from their own point of view with the aim of reclaiming some of that power imbalance. One small unedited section of the footage was shown to the audience without the Tiwi group present, but only after Calista gave an introductory speech explaining why the footage was offensive to Tiwi people. It was therefore a powerful reclamation of "voice" as the films were then shown (with the group on stage) with the sound removed so that the group could speak and sing over them, creating their own narrative and their own soundtrack to these films that nevertheless contain such rich historical, cultural and sentimental Tiwi heritage.

There had been another revisiting of the archives in 2019 when a small group of Tiwi singers[19] was in Sydney to perform with Ngarukuruwala.[20] We took the opportunity to make another visit to the Macleay Museum collection, with three of the group returning after ten years. This time they made the first of four consultations with the museum's curators, helping to correct, add to and give cultural approval of design and layout for the display of Tiwi items (for the first time) in the University of Sydney's newly opened Chau Chak Wing Museum. A number of correlations were again made between the song items and the tangible objects and photographs in the Hart collection in terms of ceremonial context, likely artists and singers, reference to kinship and Country identities, and ancestral totems. A decade later, we knew a lot more about the links between the material. However, Hart's photographs, taken in 1928 of ceremony being performed, were new to the group. To the delight of the curators, Jacinta Tipungwuti was able to put the dozen or so photographs in order, creating a sequence that shows the progression of the actions and dances of a particular part of Pukumani rituals. Jacinta's first-hand knowledge had made performative sense of an until then apparently random collection of images. Showing particular dance gestures that matched song items among the

---

17   With titles such as *Civilisation Comes to Primitive Children* alongside footage of bare-chested teenaged Tiwi girls sitting at desks learning needlepoint, musical soundtracks and scene-setting following the tropes of exoticism and the "noble savage", the community is portrayed as having been "tamed" and "saved" by the arrival of the mission.
18   The group comprised Calista Kantilla, Elizabeth Tipiloura, Katrina Mungatopi, Frances Therese Portaminni, Gemma and John Louis Munkara, Regina Kantilla and Augusta Punguatji.
19   Augusta Punguatji, Jacinta Tipungwuti, Regina Kantilla, Gregoriana Parker, Anthea Kerinaiua, Frances Therese Portaminni and Francis Orsto.
20   The performance was in the Sound Lounge, a theatre venue on the University of Sydney campus, and produced by the Sydney Environment Institute.

recordings and confirming the performative context of the kinds of spears held in the collection, Hart's photographs created a circle of collection, reclamation and re-animation that traditional owners' knowledge and experience can give to otherwise static collections. In May 2021 we were back again, as eight Tiwi singers[21] performed in the new Chau Chak Wing Museum and viewed the newly installed Tiwi display for the first time. They decided to officially give their "blessing" by performing a small Yoi. As the singers approached the glass display case, Calista Kantilla, in her role as the most senior songwoman, called out the Tiwi ancestral countries and kinship groups, acknowledging the group's presence as visitors to others' ancestral lands and as representatives of their own ancestors as current Elders. Just as they would in ceremony (and just as we had seen in the filmed and photographed archives) they carried painted ceremonial spears. Two of these spears are of the same kind as those in the display[22] and one is a double-barbed Arawanikiri, made by Bede Tungutalum, a current senior culture man and artist and a direct male descendant of Tungutalum who was photographed and recorded by Spencer in 1912 and Hart in 1928.

Repatriation, reclaiming, returning family to Country

The material repatriated from AIATSIS has an aura of specialness about it and people approach the auditioning of it with a heightened level of interest and concentration. The material that pre-dates living singers and involves song texts in "hard" language[23] is listened to with reverence for the culturally significant heirloom that it has become. Older people who recall having researchers around in the 1950s, 1960s and 1970s did not know there were resultant recordings kept in Canberra.[24] Even Elders' engagement with the material is therefore not as peers, nor as students, but as descendants discovering an old relic such as an old family photo album or piece of estate jewellery.

The fact that the AIATSIS recordings' return was a result of proactive engagement on the part of the Tiwi people themselves has informed the way they have been received. Rather than being lodged (by a non-Tiwi visitor) in a library or school or council office, the CDs went directly into people's homes. The physical CDs

---

21 This was part of the visit to Canberra for International Music Festival.
22 The two spears have no confirmed artist or age. They are "very old" according to Calista. They bear a close similarity to those in the collection.
23 The language used in songs is referred to as "hard" language because it is a form that is no longer spoken or understood by anyone but a few Elders. More on this in Chapter 5.
24 Recordings were made in 1975, by Osborne, of senior songman Justin Puruntatameri. I played these to Justin in 2012. He was by then aged 87 years and had never heard them before. To hear his own voice, strong and much younger, was (he told me) a marvellous but also upsetting experience.

were, at first, the property of the people to whom they were posted (directly to each of the 11, in the mail), who then decided which family or individual should be given particular material – a renegotiation of the ownership of the recordings and of the songs on them. Certain people, for example, were given CDs (that contained the voice of their direct ancestor) even though they had no way of playing them, but because it was decided among the group that they should be the "custodian" of that particular material. A Tiwi song is owned by its composer, and then to whomever they have taught it (if it has been passed down). The vast majority are, however, unique to the point at which they were first performed and so today's listeners delegate ownership to their direct family. Usually people felt that the (long deceased) singer owned the song, but that their family now owns the recording. Among several hours of material are numerous singers with different Country and kinship affiliations, so sections of the recordings belong to different people. I have been asked to create "playlists" of sections of different collections that relate to a particular family or hold particular interest for an individual.

Discs are played at informal gatherings and, especially when children are present, the material becomes the subject of talk ranging from family to language to hunting to geography. They are played in vehicles' CD machines and in people's houses. At the towns' social clubs, where the music is usually firmly in the realm of rock and roll hits from the 1970s and 1980s, a few times I have been present when someone has put on a palingarri CD.

The women's group has used the material as a starting point for new song projects, incorporating old recordings into arrangements by playing them through the sound system either as introductions to songs or with live performance accompanying the recording. Although it has proved difficult and time-consuming to organise permission to play the recordings at public performances, it is a matter of principle to the group that they be able to use their own cultural material. The fact that they have had to ask permission from AIATSIS to use segments of the reclaimed recordings in our performances and new recordings has been perplexing for my Tiwi colleagues. From the point of view of the Indigenous stakeholders the songs belong to them as items of cultural heritage, but from the point of view of an archive (such as AIATSIS) it is more complicated than that. There are many other considerations for a library charged with the protection of intellectual property of the collector, of usage (commercial or otherwise) and of protecting the Indigenous community in terms of respect for the voices, images and names of the deceased, all of

2 The archived recordings

which make this an area of very recent debate.[25] One outcome of this is that, in applying for permission to use a section of an old recording for a music project aimed at engaging Tiwi children with their Dreaming songs in 2011, the same Tiwi Elder signed both the request form and the authorisation form for AIATSIS. This adds an extra element to the story of the recordings, with issues of ownership, legalities and cultural property never far from people's minds.

Niles and others[26] reported motivations for repatriation (relevant to my engagement with the Tiwi recordings) that include:

- a response to direct request from (Indigenous) people with direct ownership claims
- the facilitation of analysis and collection of essential accompanying metadata
- as source material proving ownership in land rights cases of Country and kinship affiliations[27]
- the enhancement of cultural maintenance activities within the stakeholders' community
- because it is the right thing to do (Seeger 1987; Treloyn 2013).

The power of repatriated recordings to reinvigorate interest in song practice is only one of the benefits. Old recordings hold great social and historical significance as well as holding ancestral and cultural knowledge of land management, sustenance and protection, of ritual procedure, and of the Country and kinship relationships that are fundamental to Tiwi societal organisation. One of the key themes to emerge is the emotional response of Indigenous owners to the material.

There have been three important and distinct areas of response to the Tiwi recordings that I can report on directly.

1. Emotional, personal responses

Hearing the voices of ancestors, of deceased loved ones or of their younger selves had a powerful effect on some Tiwi people, with strong (positive and negative) sentimental reactions to songs. Older people heard the voice of their deceased parent, sibling or spouse, bringing up personal memories, and with those, associated emotions of happiness, reminiscing for their youth and past achievements. Also of course are the painful memories that regularly come up,

---

25 Brown et al. 1998; Anderson 2005; Barwick and Thieberger 2006; Thomas 2007a; Kahunde 2012; Niles 2012.
26 Stubington 1989; Lancefield 1998; Barwick and Marett 2003; Toner 2003; Thieberger and Musgrave 2007; Niles 2012; Treloyn 2012.
27 Among the recordings made by Groger-Wurm in 1965 is a segment in which a Tiwi woman lists family names and the Country groups they belong to. It has been used by members of the community in discussions with the Tiwi Land Council.

especially as much of the material is associated with mortuary rituals. This has had a marked effect on the process and timeframe of auditioning the collections, with many occasions requiring breaks, or not listening to sections at all. Some of the songs record interpersonal and interclan disputes or information about land ownership, creating tension for some and vindication for others. Many of the songs inspire laughter as they poke fun, employ clever word play and tell comical stories. Then quiet reflection and gathering of women to listen to the lullabies and love songs of their female antecedents. With mostly very scant accompanying metadata we were often listening with a degree of anxious anticipation: Who will we hear next? Whose memory will be evoked in the next song or ritual, and so who in the room now listening will experience a rush of grief or be thrust into the mourning ceremony for their own long-dead mother or hear her as a younger woman, singing for her father (the current listener's grandfather)? In some ways it was like looking through the pages of a large family album, the contents of which none of us could anticipate. With each song item we turned the page, not knowing what we'd come across: the face of a smiling loved one, a death notice of a husband, an announcement of marriage or the birth of a grandmother.

Younger listeners with a more distant attachment to the people in the recordings tended to listen with more of a sense of its historical value. Hearing the voices of great-grandparents (and earlier) and a language they could decipher very little of, their reactions were more of family and cultural pride. Through Elders' descriptions of the song content, younger listeners experienced snapshots of a way of life unlike their own, as well as points of connection to places and people they know or had heard about through the songs and stories they've been taught, now verified in a recorded document. They reported feelings of pride and fascination in discovering their own social history, told by their own family. Turning the aural "pages" sparked curiosity, reverence, laughter, tears, anger and joy. The first listening sessions of the collection were an emotional rollercoaster.

2. Questions of ownership

Differing understandings and opinions emerged regarding the cultural, physical and intellectual ownership of Tiwi song material. In the case of the old recordings there are multiple layers of "ownership"; the moral and legal rights of Indigenous traditional owners, including (but not restricted to) the family of the (deceased) composer; the kinship groups with claims to the cultural content held in a song, such as ancestral stories, inherited songlines, items of cultural significance; non-Tiwi copyright holders such as the person who made the recording, or in the case they are deceased, the family or estate of the person who made the recording; and finally the archive holding the collection and the organisational structures around the collection and its acquisition. The relationship between all of these, the researcher and current Indigenous stakeholders with regard to access and usage is an issue that is an ongoing underlying concern for myself and my Tiwi colleagues.

Questions of ownership were raised among Tiwi people in relation to individual and/or family associations with particular (recorded) songs, ceremonies or singers and therefore the use of those recordings and the documentation, transcription and translation of the songs. Especially as Tiwi songs are in the main individually composed and not repeated after an event (except by the composer), the containment of particular songs and particular singers in the collection raised some conflicting concerns. Why were some songs "preserved" while the vast majority went undocumented by way of being one-offs and never recorded? Were certain singers or Country groups favoured over others by virtue of their being chosen as subjects by researchers (and so their songs preserved for posterity)?[28] What are the financial ramifications of embedding old songs, melodies and/or actual recordings within new musical arrangements? Fundamentally it is the content of the songs – the knowledge of Country places, ancestral stories and genealogies passed down through the songs – that is what is "owned". This makes the singer the current custodian of that content (not its owner) and so people speak not so much of who *owns* a song as who is the *holder* of it. Having then to register "composer" for songs for royalties and copyright purposes is a complex issue and one that we negotiate by listing senior singers as "composer" or by listing Skin group, Country or family groups as "arrangers" as each song and each recording requires.

3. Recordings as archive and as a teaching resource

Tiwi song culture is primarily based on occasion-specific improvisatory composition. There has been significant (sometimes negative) impact, from an artistic point of view, of hearing old recordings that demonstrate higher quality linguistic and performance values and therefore confirm perceptions of cultural loss. This is a very sensitive issue, especially among senior men in the community. In the face of language loss and dwindling numbers of singers with knowledge of composition, the old recordings are becoming a resource of

---

28   Charles Hart, for instance, suggested that the Tiwi people living away from the mission area were more valuable as subjects of his anthropological observations and collections because they were less affected by cultural intrusion. The suggestion that people living in and around the mission on Bathurst Island, and similarly those affected by the Garden Point mission, were less culturally "authentic" through the last century, and have lost more cultural authority as a result, is an unfortunate undercurrent to our work even now.

song text to be learned by rote. This has the potential to create, with a library of recorded material, a canon of songs that might eventually take the place of the Tiwi tradition of improvisation.

The recordings are important as an archive for preservation, as a focus for active engagement in the continuation of song traditions and as a primary resource for learning language, song poetry and vocal technique. As well as from a musical point of view, the recorded songs represent an important piece of cultural heritage. Individual creativity is highly regarded in Tiwi song culture and so ideally (in the opinion of older singers) it is not so much a matter of learning from these recordings by rote but to learn words, phrases and the required poetic devices to be able to create one's own song. A result of the current, topical and context-specific nature of most Tiwi song, we find among the old recordings a wealth of social, ancestral and ritual information embedded in song texts. As well as this they are an invaluable resource for a new method of teaching song composition skills.

From the mid-1970s the marked changes to the spoken Tiwi language, and the shrinking of attendance at (and involvement in) Kulama (an annual ceremony centred on the attainment of cultural knowledge, language and song composition skills), fewer singers were able to compose. This saw people beginning to use cassette recorders to capture the songs of a highly regarded singer, not with long-term preservation in mind, but as a means of entertainment. Venbrux (1995, 122) notes "relatively few people were able to 'copy' (re-enact) these [songs] themselves". Grau noted (speaking of the changes in instruction in Kulama singing):

> … from what I saw it seems that modern technology in the form of cassette recorders has helped a great deal … Every Kulama is taped by a number of people and these tapes are played over and over during the following weeks … Few people state [learning] as the reason for listening to the tapes, and usually say they just enjoy listening to them. (Grau 1983a)

Listening to Kulama songs on tape was also a modern means of dispersing the messages within the songs themselves as it became more difficult for people to attend ceremonies. The songs composed for the first day of the Kulama ceremony that celebrate deceased kin, for example, remain important as a way of remembering and respecting their lost loved ones. Listening to recorded performances of these has become a soothing, healing and almost spiritual experience for some, replacing the actual ceremony. The thought of archiving these recordings was, for the Tiwi people, however, not on the agenda. One wouldn't want to hear the voice of a departed loved one. Venbrux (1995) mentions a cassette tape being destroyed after the death of the man leading the singing, rendering his voice Pukumani. Venbrux and Grau also report men in the 1970s and 1980s learning songs via cassette tapes and many of the older men with whom I've spoken (who are the leading singers today) say they mostly learned this way too. This might have been the beginning of a shift away from what was traditionally an oral and heuristic learning process. Coupled with the almost complete loss of a spoken command of the language in which these songs were composed, there has been a demonstrable change from unique, performance-specific composition, to rote learning from stock phrases. This has led to the atrophying of the text resource material, because men are learning from recordings, from finite performances, rather than learning the skills to create their own word patterns.

I present at Figure 2 the translation of part of a song composed by Joe Puruntatameri in February 1981 in honour of Long Stephen Tipuamantimeri, a well-respected singer, culture man and leader of ceremony. I don't have a recording or the Tiwi text of this song, but the English summary, noted down by Grau, is interesting and sufficient for the purpose of making this point.

Figure 2: Joe Puruntatameri's song about Long Stephen Tipuamantimeri.

They all say "That man from Irumakulumi he is a good singer"

People from Nguiu send tapes to him saying, "Sing for us so we can hear your voice and your words and know what is right"

They all make tapes of him singing

He has got to sing in this tape Imerikungwamili, Imerikiyanuwa and Ayipa [first, second and third night of Kulama]

We will have every word in the tape and everybody will listen

People will listen the meaning of the right words

They all say, "He had Yilantjini [special necklace worn by the initiates, thus he went through all the initiation grades] it is why he is a good singer, we know about him"

All the government, really old men and ladies come to listen to his songs.

The song text says something of how conscious people were of the role of recordings as a teaching tool and as a means of preserving knowledge held in song. The fact that this was a song, not simply a discussion, provides an example of the community business of the day continuing to be put on the oral (sung) record, and confirmed tacit approval of this new way of learning by the current singers at the time. It also suggests that there was a sense of what was being lost, even 40 years ago. Just as in 1981, today there is a sense of reverence towards those few left who can sing and a desire to learn from them, using recording as a means of preserving their knowledge. The senior men, on whom the responsibility of performing at funerals falls, have described to me their anxiety at the thought of not being able to sing the required Country, ancestral or Dreaming songs[29] at funerals. Some songmen are turning to the archival recordings as source material for their own compositions. As of 2022, discussions continue between Elders, the Tiwi Land Council and myself as to how (and where) best to house the recordings to enable access and engagement by the local community.

At this stage there is no evidence that recordings are replacing live performance in ceremony. Apart from the handful of songs (no more than about a dozen) that can be successfully repeated because of their direct function as Dreaming Yoi songs the vast majority of songs are of the moment, and not ever intended to be repeated. There are a number of dances through which a member of a certain Dreaming will embody the animal or entity (Turtle, Shark, Crocodile, Rainbow for example) that is that Dreaming. As one dances Crocodile (for example) one becomes the ancestral crocodile and sings/speaks as that totemic being. Perhaps due to the individual and one-off nature of Tiwi song, the idea of learning a particular song from the recordings by rote for repetition is beyond the current thinking. The current, topical nature of their text and the overriding culture of the individualism of composition and artistic ownership make most Tiwi songs unsuitable for long-term repetition.

In the face of dwindling numbers of singers who can compose these songs (as would traditionally have been the case) there is talk of "setting" a list of the required songs that would be taught to young people, enabling the ceremonies to continue to be held in the proper way.[30] It is in this context that the repatriated recordings have the potential to change the entire basis of Tiwi song practice, from one that was primarily about extemporisation to one that is based on the rote learning of a finite set of songs. Deciding which songs these will be is something that has already begun to cause some concerns among Elders. The "privileging" and reification of certain songs over others due to their inclusion in recordings is a problem that people are starting to think about (Kirschenblatt-Gimblett 2006; Treloyn 2012). Preserving an orally transmitted tradition by making it finite brings with it complications of ownership of the songs themselves and of the associated connection through esoteric knowledge that is passed on through oral transmission.

---

29   Some Tiwi songs include reference to all three of these within one text, but many songs are specifically about Country, tell ancestral stories or refer to Dreaming totems.
30   I was present at a meeting at the Literacy Centre in late 2012, and again in 2020, where this was discussed.

2 The archived recordings

Respect for singers of the past

In the process of studying and documenting archived Tiwi song recording, my Tiwi colleagues and I are constantly negotiating the balance between individualism and community.

Tiwi notions of where the music came from and why it was created were very different to my understanding of what music and art were. As we have performed, studied, travelled and created together over the past fifteen years we have had many conversations about what music is, why it is created and what 'our' music means.

Certain singers (within the recorded archive and in current practice) are known for and often have been identified by their vocal embellishments, melodic motifs and poetic artifice. It is frustrating for Tiwi listeners to confront the anonymisation of the archive documentation, as composers, singers and the context of many performances go unacknowledged and – if named at all – Tiwi people are referred to only by the names given by white colonisers.

Among the recordings repatriated from AIATSIS are performances showing a high level of vocal talent. The strength of tone, length of phrasing, and quality of diction and pitch of some recorded performances can objectively be regarded as being at a technically higher quality than found today. Over the years, through the process of oral transmission, songmen have made their own variations to vocal techniques and rhythmic and melodic ornamentation. It is only by hearing the "old men" again after 60 years or more[31] that these incremental changes become apparent. The singer who had attained the skills of composition through Kulama was a highly respected person in the community; there is a sense of performance as a means of impressing those around them. In a recording made by Jack Doolan of a Kulama ceremony in 1967[32] we hear the singer, Karla's,[33] performance inspiring enthusiastic response from the "audience". While not a performance in the sense of him being on the stage, Karla's singing was of a particularly impressive quality both in terms of words and in the vocal strength, tone and length of phrases. I have played this file to a number of Tiwi colleagues and they have often given the same spontaneous response (like "bravo") at the end of Karla's songs. In this case, the recording itself has become a performance by Karla, because, although he is not physically present, his recorded voice

---

31 The 1912, 1948, 1954 and 1955 recordings have had the biggest impact in this regard.
32 Karla sings six songs in succession, heard at items 1–6 on DOOLAN_J02-000628A with the appreciative response heard at 05:32.
33 Karla (aka Tractor Joe) was also known as Prijina Lokemup. He is remembered as a particularly talented singer and the older men listen to his recorded performances with the aim of emulating him.

manifests his presence and (Tiwi) listeners respond to that presence as a tangible experience of the man himself. Well-respected senior singers are anecdotally remembered for particular performances and for the ceremonies they have led. Hearing them in recordings confirms this collective memory and, for younger listeners, adds their voices to the lineage of singers.

Elders recall being present as children at ceremony when these men sang. During the course of our work together, song leaders at Wurrumiyanga[34] have been very interested to hear the stylistic differences between their way of performing particular parts of ceremony and that of the men on the old recordings. While novelty and change are inherent in Tiwi song practice, it was a difficult experience for the men to hear so clearly the degree of quantifiable loss that has occurred. The numbers of people singing, the "strength"[35] of people's voices, the length of phrases, the linguistic complexity and the number of songs in each event are all elements that Elders had to admit to themselves have lessened in the last 50 years. This is a difficult thing to accept, especially for those Elders who feel the responsibility of sustaining the traditions.[36]

Rediscovering song traditions

The reverse can also occur as rediscovering an element of song practice can be exhilarating and empowering for the song leaders. One such instance occurred during our visit in 2009 to the NFSA in Canberra when the group was shown a collection of film footage with Tiwi content. Among this was film of a Tepuwaturinga (Wallaby) Yoi dance (filmed by Spencer in 1912) that has not been performed for many years. Wallaby had been "forgotten", having fallen out of practice because the men who would have danced Wallaby had stopped leading ceremony. Wallaby is not among Spencer's audio recordings, but the visual had a great impact regardless. Basedow (1913) describes the Kangaroo[37] dance, but there is no further mention of it in the literature until Grau, who writes that she never witnessed it and was told that:

---

34 Stephen-Paul Kantilla, Eustace Tipiloura, Roger Tipungwuti, Robert Biscuit Tipungwuti and Walter Kerinaiua Sr. These men are now deceased, and I have permission to include their names here.

35 The strength and volume of the lead voices is a feature of the old recordings that a number of singers have remarked upon, comparing their "short wind" when singing today.

36 My role in analysing the songs has necessitated sensitivity in this area and respect for senior singers. I therefore note only those examples of loss of quality that were discussed openly.

37 Among the native fauna of the Tiwi Islands are wallabies (not kangaroos). It seems to have been a matter of using the generalised term that has meant that at times in the Tiwi literature we read about kangaroos (Basedow 1913; Hart and Pilling 1988).

... at Pularumpi only one old man, Mickey Geranium Warlapini, knew the dance but that he was too old to perform it, the series of jumps requiring a lot of stamina. (Grau 1983a)

We know from the recording made by Alice Moyle in 1976 at the South Pacific Festival of Arts at Rotorua, New Zealand, that Aloysious Puantilura, Leo Tungutalum and Max Kerinaiua performed Wallaby, but without video it is difficult to make a comparison with 1912.

The group in 2009 was invited to give a performance in the outdoor courtyard at the NFSA. This was a free lunchtime concert and was very well attended, with about 100 people in the audience. The men and women performed Kulama songs and Yoi songs and dances, and Wally Kerinaiua[38] spontaneously performed Wallaby. It was a marvellous moment, one that the audience would not have been aware of, but one in which the other Tiwi performers suddenly found themselves also among the audience. Wally had brought this Yoi to life again. The 1912 footage has been viewed around the Tiwi community since then, with Wally's performance in Canberra now part of its accompanying story.

Embedding the songs back in the continuum of tradition

While the vast majority of recorded Tiwi songs is unique, there is a strong degree of continuity of text elements and melody, especially along hereditary lines (of singers) and this has had an important effect on the people directly connected with the songs. It seems likely that each few generations have a horizon of living memory of knowledge: one's father learned from his father, who learned from his father, with that being about as far back as it goes. By the time the current grandfather is passing on his knowledge he has defined and perhaps refined the knowledge he was taught and now owns it in order to pass it down. So we find in Tiwi songs passed along kinship lines a clear correlation, and some exact stability of text and melody, but with a large degree of individual imprint and expression and a moving away from the old to create the new. This moving is so imperceptible that the Elders themselves only realised it when they heard the old recordings. The Nyingawi song gives us one such example of the transmission of a song text through nearly 70 years. In March 2010 old lady Stephanie Tipuamantimeri listened to the Nyingawi recordings made in 1928, 1954 and 1975 (shown wearing headphones in Plate 28). She then spontaneously sang her Nyingawi song, saying that she remembered the words from the old days.[39] Stephanie sang

---

38 Walter Kerinaiua Jr, more widely known as Wally.
39 This was an informal meeting on 5 March 2010, and I did not record Stephanie. She died a few months later.

three lines that compare very closely to the old recordings, and one that she created. Although she sang only four lines (whereas the old recordings had up to seven lines), she told me she was singing it "the old way".

When Casmira Munkara recorded her Nyingawi for our CD in 2008 (see Plate 27) she also told me she was singing it in "the old way". Although it contains some text that is identical to the old recorded songs, Casmira's performance is noticeably different, rhythmically, from the "old way". People's perception, however, not having heard the recordings, is that she sings it how it always has been sung, continuing the transmission of this song through her family line. It also became a point of pride for Casmira that she sang it at exactly the same pitch as her predecessors even though she had not heard the old recordings when she made her recording. This connection, through a recording, directly to the voices of her ancestors is another powerful and tangible outcome of the return of the recordings.

The effect of recording on performance

A recurring point of discussion during listening sessions has been whether the singers were aware they were being recorded and how that might have had an effect on performance style and song choice. When basing analysis on recorded examples one must take into consideration the fact that a performance will most likely be affected by the context, the intended audience, and relationship between the singer and the researcher. The reason for the performance, especially in elicited recordings, is necessarily altered, as are the social, functional and performative contexts. The venue (indoors or outdoors) has a marked effect on both the quality of the sound and the way the singer will relate physically to the microphone. Sitting in a room across the table from the microphone will result in a very different performance from one recorded sitting outside on the ground with birds, dogs, children, cars and passers-by distracting the singer and adding to the sound that is captured.

The audience aspect is perhaps the element that most affects the performance. I have had occasions, during a recording session, when a palpable sense of respect and import is felt by the group, witnessing an older woman recording her song, or a group of three senior singers correct each other's performances as they sing. The desire to be correct, preserving the song (and the performance) for posterity that the singer might (or might not) have been experiencing can be heard among the repatriated recordings. Among Osborne's recordings, for example, we hear some singers correct themselves as they sing, reiterating a line of text with the syllabic count corrected. This is how it would be done in a "real" performance context and suggests that the singer is approaching their task of recording a song in much the same way as they would a performance in ceremony. My experience is somewhat different. Perhaps it is the result of hearing their antecedents make mistakes that has meant some singers ask me to delete a recording if they make a mistake, or they ask me not to record until they have practised a few times. There might well have been similar re-takes during recording sessions in the past, but it is certainly a feature of my recording sessions that singers are aiming at a correct performance to be recorded for posterity. Perhaps this is due to a heightened sense of creating an archive in the light of the repatriation of the Palingarri recordings.

Tungutalum sang an Ayipa (news-telling) song into Hart's recorder in 1928. He had already experienced Spencer's recording machine (in 1912) and so was, quite likely, singing as a teller of knowledge, as a man of experience. Whether he was singing about Hart's recording machine[40] or noting his previous experience with a sound machine, Tungutalum was clearly aware of the fact that voices were recorded in it, as he recorded himself remarking on the very action he was engaging in. Among songs recorded by Mountford as part of a Kulama ceremony held on Melville Island in May 1954 is a similar example of the self-awareness of the research subject and the fact that the singer uses the performance to comment, in song, on the process he is going through at the time. It is most likely Ray Giles, the ABC radio recordist who worked with Mountford, to whom the singer Allie Miller is referring. The text is at Song text 4 (translation given by Eustace Tipiloura).

Song text 4: Tungutalum. Gramophone, 1928; Warabutiwayi Allie Miller. Rijya (Radio), 1954.

Gramophone: Tungutalum 1928.

Jontayampinga ngapujingipi yaninkilirri pujingayawu kalawiyi
Come and see the talking machine

Ngipingipiyaminkirati minkimawula
I turn the handle

Radio: Warabutiwayi Allie Miller 1954.

Ngilaghama karirijiya waliji miningu merreke wanga pinguwangamini
I am the radio talking

Ngiyawungarri karra apuji yintawayalangimi
I am putting it in the radio

Kalipulijimani rijiya yinuwalumurri
He is talking on the radio

---

40 Translated as a gramophone by Osborne, the word jonta ("hard item", such as a shell or iron) in the text means "engine" or "machine". In 1928 Hart's machine would more correctly be referred to as a phonograph.

Listening to the recordings, Eustace Tipiloura told me:

> … he's telling people about something new. That's the main part of the ceremony, around about 3 pm. He must be talking about the white bloke being there with his recorder I think.

While Tiwi people filmed and/or recorded by Spencer and Hart may well have had very little understanding of the long-term implications of their participation, the fact remains that they were being asked to sing for a visitor and this must have had some effect on their motivations and resulting performance. If singing into a machine that could play sound back immediately, the singer would have been aware that their voice was being reproduced and stored in some way. The experience of hearing their own singing replayed would have changed the nature of performance as a one-off. As any musician will perform in a slightly heightened state in front of an audience or at a recording session, so too Tiwi people may have altered their performance when they were being recorded or filmed. In Spencer's 1912 footage, for example, we see the Tiwi men dance as a group towards the "audience" as if on stage, and individuals breaking out of the traditional circular formation of ceremony to perform solo straight to camera – in effect breaking the so-called fourth wall. The sense of presenting the culture in the best possible way for the cameras (or recorder) might arguably result in a performance that is not entirely natural. It is very difficult to decide whether this is a problem or not. If being recorded (or having a non-Tiwi audience) inspires a more elaborate version or a more enthusiastic dance or more rehearsal, then that is a valid part of the notion of performance.

Among my Tiwi colleagues there have been widely differing opinions as to the ethics of the collection of some of the recorded material, especially the recordings of mourning songs in the Pukumani (mortuary-associated) ceremony. Some (Tiwi) people listened with interest to the melodic and linguistic artistry of a performance, some recognised the voice of a deceased loved one with sentimental joy, and some heard personal grief and pain and thought it inappropriate for anyone other than close family to listen. I have witnessed a number of heated discussions about the difference between singing for family and singing for visitors/researchers (in the context of a mortuary ceremony), with many people concerned that singers might not always have been aware of the intrusion of the recorder, or of the long-term ramifications of being recorded. In the following quotation Holmes makes the distinction between a ceremony and performance. The Pukumani ceremony for Polly and Allie Miller's young son was held in May 1966, at the then Bagot Aboriginal Reserve in Darwin.[41] The segment below indicates the occasion was seen by the government welfare department as a

---

41   The ceremony was held in Darwin because the child had died in Darwin en route to hospital.

good opportunity to give (white) people a new cultural experience. The Tiwi people do not seem to have been given much of a choice in the matter. Allie is quoted as having been upset at the lack of understanding and respect for his son's ceremony: "Too many white people come … we never ask them to come, only Welfare man can say." (Holmes 1995, 22)

> The Welfare Branch had declared an Open Day for tourists and locals … Polly sang softly to the ghost of her dead son and signalled for me to record it … Crowds of white visitors jostled each other for photo opportunities, staring expectantly up the hill to where the Tiwi mourners were assembled in full ceremonial regalia. (Holmes 1995, 22)

By Holmes' accounts the ceremony was just as it would have been (in terms of structure and ritual) without any non-Tiwi onlookers. Clearly, though, they were being watched as spectacle. Holmes goes on to report:

> At this point a senior welfare officer stood up and made a speech to thank the public for attending the ceremony and the Tiwi people for the performance. By prior arrangement the sculptures and grave posts would be sold to various dealers and other outlets. (Holmes 1995, 29)

The distinction between "ceremony" and "performance" in the welfare officer's words (or in Holmes' reporting of his words) implies there was a difference in perception between the audience's and the mourners' experience of the event. It should really have been the other way around; the white audience was watching a performance (although with the extra exoticism of knowing it was a ceremony) while the mourners were attempting to have ceremony, knowing they were being watched and photographed. Yes, the mourners knew they were being recorded, but it is arguable whether they were aware of the legal and moral consequences of that recording's journey to Canberra and eventual return to the community four decades later.

This example brings us back to the notion of a performance, and a song (owned by its performer) becoming an item, trapped in a recording which then becomes an artefact (owned by its collector). In the moment it is recorded the song's ownership shifts and it is only the process of repatriation that enables that ownership to be shifted back. I have explained some of how the "discovery" of the recorded song material in the AIATSIS catalogue, the process of going to Canberra to reclaim it, and the ongoing associated negotiations regarding usage rights have created a story around the repatriated recordings. The fact that they have been "reclaimed" gives them a presence in the Tiwi community as highly valued and important cultural property that has been returned. The repatriated recordings have been the focus of close study, from the point of view of their historical, cultural, social and artistic significance, and their return has had substantial positive and empowering outcomes for Elders, as they share with young Tiwi people the knowledge in the songs. While some Elders feel that many of these recordings should perhaps not have been made in the first place, others believe that with the tenuous state of Tiwi song, language and ceremony the recordings are now of great value to the community for the preservation of culture as well as being a meaningful source for the continuation of existing and new forms of Tiwi music making. Whatever the differing opinions as to the ethics of such recordings being made and collected, it is evident that the process of their return, even with (and perhaps due to) the difficulties and lengthy bureaucratic processes, has imbued these old recordings with an extra significance. The repatriation process has also opened a new chapter of engagement between Indigenous knowledge holders and researchers in the recording and documentation of song.

Clarifying some misinterpretations of the 1912 recordings

The 1912 recordings are the earliest recordings of Tiwi songs. This makes them a very important collection for comparative analysis and as an item of Tiwi heritage. I include here a brief account of some findings that have come out of auditioning this collection.

These were originally recorded by Baldwin Spencer in 1912 on hand-cranked Edison wax cylinders. Spencer had visited Melville Island on two occasions previously (March 1911 and June 1912), but he did not have recording equipment with him. He notes in his diary that Cahill, a colleague, had brought a phonograph with him from Melbourne, arriving in Katherine on 26 October 1912, and that he had that machine with him when he travelled to Bathurst Island on 29 November (Spencer 1928), with the recordings made presumably in early December. He recorded on 20 cylinders in the Northern Territory from October to December 1912. Copies of the cylinders were sent to Cambridge University in England (sometime between 1912 and 1914) and were then acquired by the British Institute of Recorded Sound in 1959 where, in 1978, they were transferred to cassette and then deposited at AIATSIS (then called AIAS, the Australian Institute of Aboriginal Studies) in Canberra in 1979. Each cylinder is two minutes in length. They were digitised at my request in March 2008. The numbering on the cylinders in Spencer's written work and in the (renumbered) written documentation of the cassette tape catalogue do not correspond, and so it is impossible to say exactly how many cylinders of Tiwi songs there were. Osborne (1989) states that there were five cylinders stored at the National Museum of Victoria and four others that were not (he doesn't state where these were). As far as we are currently aware there are five surviving cylinders of Tiwi songs recorded by Spencer on Bathurst Island. Some of the written and spoken notes on the audition document accompanying the AIATSIS collection are incorrect, most likely due to the inconsistent numbering of cylinders and boxes and from attempts to decipher people's handwriting. The notes on cylinder 3, for example, state "Identification on this cylinder is number 3 … taken in Bathurst, Qld." The songs on cylinder 3 are Tiwi, made on Bathurst Island, but perhaps one of the cataloguers along the way misread a cursive script "Ild." (an abbreviation of Island).

Spencer's visit resulted in separate audio and video recordings, as he recorded sound on the wax cylinders and also took photographs and film footage, but almost certainly not at the same time. In the course of my work with Tiwi colleagues on this material I was often asked whether the songs correlate with the ceremony that was filmed. An Yirrikapayi (Crocodile) Yoi dance is recorded on film and a Yoi song on audio. The film is taken from a distance of about 15 metres. To get a good audio result the singer would have to be standing close to the wax cylinder machine and sing straight into the input. I therefore surmise that the audio was probably recorded at a separate event. Spencer mentions making recordings of songs associated with a Pukumani ritual he observed. Not all the song subjects he refers to are on the cylinders that have survived. Buffalo and Wallaby dances are in the footage, for instance, but we do not find those songs on the recordings. Figure 3 lists the surviving song recordings and those mentioned by Spencer. To aid any future researcher into this, I have included the song subject and the timestamp entered on the handwritten audition document that accompanies the collection at AIATSIS.

Figure 3: Spencer recordings, 1912: song subjects and cylinder numbering.

Timestamp on complete digitised file	Cylinder	Tiwi/English name of performer(s)	Subject	Song-type
0:14	1	Unidentified group	Calls of Country	Call
1:29	1	Jipapijingimirri/ Capstan	Building houses	Jipuwakirimi
3:39	3	Paujimi/Lopez	Ship	Jipuwakirimi
4:38	3	Unidentified man	Pushing a saw	Jipuwakirimi
5:26	3	Paujimi/Lopez	Flour	Jipuwakirimi
7:07	4	Iwaidja		

Timestamp on complete digitised file	Cylinder	Tiwi/English name of performer(s)	Subject	Song-type
10:31	16	Unidentified man	Boat and Tide	Arikuruwala
13:29	20	Purruntilayi/ Orsto	Crocodile hunts flying foxes	Jipuwakirimi
14:54	20	Purruntilayi/ Orsto	Ship's funnel	Jipuwakirimi
16:59	24	Tungutalum	Train	Jipuwakirimi
18:22	24	Tungutalum	Ship awaits tide	Jipuwakirimi
Filmed material[42]				
08:10		Men	Wallaby	Jipuwakirimi
10:20		Men	Buffalo	Jipuwakirimi
16:20		Men	Crocodile	Jipuwakirimi
05:20		Men	Ritual preparation, smoking	Call
07:25		Women and children	Non-specific	Jipuwakirimi

The vocalisations

A musicological study was carried out on Spencer's recordings in 1957 by Alice Moyle (A. Moyle 1959). Moyle noted that the songs on three of the cylinders are melodically different from the others on Spencer's Tiwi recordings but, presuming they were Tiwi, wrote:

> Spencer's recordings of the "conch" are important. Those from Bathurst Island (Cylinder Nos. 4 and 6) point to a wider distribution of this "aerophone" ... than is indicated by later recordings from Arnhem Land and the Kimberleys. And the sample from Katherine (Cylinder No. 24), in which several "conches" deliver high-pitched, unmusical sounds is unique among Australian records ... The Bathurst Island performances

---

42   Time-stamp indicates a clear example, bearing in mind there are several iterations and some cross-over of the dances among the performers and also some repetition of footage in the archive item. As there is no audio in the film, the song-types are based on rhythmic and gestural indicators of each dance and the songs they traditionally accompany.

> may have resulted from a recent importation of the trumpet from the mainland. It is possible that didjeridu players from Port Essington accompanied Cooper to Melville Island. Spencer, however, says nothing of a new importation. On the contrary, he seems to imply a widespread and already well-established use of the conch on Bathurst Island. (A. Moyle 1959, 13–14)

Tiwi listeners immediately recognised that the song on Cylinder 4 is not Tiwi but Iwaidja. We know there was a group of Iwaidja people (from Cobourg Peninsula, north-west Arnhem Land) working for Robert Joe Cooper, a (white) buffalo hunter who had a camp on Melville Island. It is surprising that Spencer would not have guessed that some of Cooper's party of Iwaidja people might have joined in the performance put on for his benefit.[43] My most current information suggests the performance is related to an open ceremony belonging to groups from north-west Arnhem Land and is perhaps the same ceremony as Ngurlmak also known at Oenpelli as Ubar.[44] It is also possible of course that the Iwaidja performance was not recorded on Bathurst Island at all, but that (as Osborne noted from his investigation of the material) some of the cylinders had been put back in the wrong boxes, causing confusion when they were transferred to cassette. All the literature, however, lists these as Tiwi and there are at least two publications that discuss the interesting departure from tradition by the Tiwi singers in this segment of the recording. Osborne transcribed and translated the Tiwi songs on the recordings in 1967 with assistance from Tyukuliyanginila (who also identified the singers). Osborne must have found the Iwaidja songs with the help of his Tiwi consultants. Written correspondence between Alice Moyle and Charles Osborne in 1967 confirms clarification of the discrepancy of these mis-credited songs.[45] Unfortunately, Osborne didn't publish this clarification, and indeed sixteen years later he criticised Moyle's "confusion" and "incorrect identification" of Spencer's recordings (Osborne 1989, 422).

There is no cylinder 6 listed in the AIATSIS collection and so I have to presume this is a misprint, and Moyle meant cylinder 16. The song on cylinder 16 is about a boat being marooned on the tide and is in the melodic style characteristic of Tiwi Kulama Ayipa songs.

---

43 Similarly, a photograph taken by Axel Poingant on Melville Island in 1948 depicts a Tiwi ceremonial event, with a man seated playing didgeridoo. Current Tiwi Elders believe that this is another example of an Iwaidja performer joining the Tiwi group, either spontaneously or at the invitation of the non-Indigenous viewer. Photograph: National Library of Australia nla.obj-151240574.
44 Discussions with colleagues in the field are ongoing.
45 AIATSIS online collection of Alice Moyle's correspondence. Retrieved 17 June 2010.

Cylinder 24 was another, quite different misinterpretation. It is identified (probably again from being in the wrong box) as having been recorded at Katherine River, Northern Territory. From Spencer's diary we know that he was in Katherine, recording in the Victoria River Country, with Waduman and Mudburra people (Spencer's terms; Spencer 1928) between getting the phonograph on 26 October and the end of November (just prior to his going to Bathurst Island). Moyle describes "high-pitched conch 'blasts' in the 'Tjadpa' corroboree (cylinder 24)" and her experiments with tubes of various lengths until she found a 3 foot (1 metre) length with which she could produce a note "approximately 82 cycles or the first 'E' below the bass stave. In contrast to this the pitch of the recorded 'blasts' is approximately E5 (660 cycles)" (A. Moyle, 1959, 14). Although her attempt produced a note three octaves too low[46] she did not entertain the possibility that the notes might be vocalisations and theorised that they "may have been produced from a short tube; the method may have differed; or the blowers may have been learners" (A. Moyle 1959, 14). The fact is that these "blasts" are vocalisations; imitating the whistle of a train in the train song composed by Tungutalum (Audio 30). It is not clear why the train song on cylinder 24 is identified as a Tjadpa corroboree. This word, or anything similar, is not Tiwi. One presumes it is simply that the box in which cylinder 24 was incorrectly stowed was inscribed with "Tjadpa corroboree from Katherine River natives, the Marungga Tribe, Oct 28, 1912."[47] I have not been able to establish where the actual recording from Katherine is, or if it exists. At some stage the cylinders were transferred to reels and at that point the incorrect inscriptions must have also been transferred to the reels.

---

46 Moyle's note corresponds to E2 which is 82.4069HZ and is two below middle C, whereas that sung by the Tiwi men in the recording is 659.255HZ, the second E above middle C.
47 AIATSIS. Audition notes accompanying archive tape 701a.

Chapter 3
Singing identity

If all the old songs are lost then we don't remember who we are. When I pass away there is no-one to sing my song, so I sing now to my grandchildren so they will know too. From palingarri, way back, all them papirrimaruwi [ancestors], they are there. Out bush you know, in my Country. They still sing too, you know. Singing to us about all our people.

Leonie Tipiloura

The Pukumani and Kulama ceremonies are the focus and manifestation of as well as the reason for song composition and performance. The changing relevance, form and size (the numbers of participants and the length of the ceremony itself) of both Pukumani and Kulama can be tracked alongside changes to song practice. It is important therefore to have an understanding of the foundational principles of the two ceremonies and the role of songs in each.

Of over 1,300[1] song items among the recorded archive material, fewer than 30 songs are unrelated to Pukumani or Kulama.[2] Most Tiwi songs pertain in some way to either or both of those ceremonies and the poetry found in their texts relates very closely to them. As I will explain in Chapter 6, certain

---

1   Especially when listening to recordings of Pukumani in which songs are often presented in a continuation of theme, by one singer at a time, it is impossible to exactly define the end of one song and beginning of the next. Some listeners will hear (for example) seven Tatuwali (Shark) Yoi phrases performed in turn by the one singer and describe seven separate song items, whereas others will hear the entire segment as one Shark song, with seven phrases.
2   While the secular song-types (the love songs and the lullabies) may well have been sung just as often, they have not been recorded to the same extent, perhaps because, not being ritual-related, they were not of sufficient interest to anthropologists and/or because they were sung by women.

melodic forms belong to each part of Pukumani and Kulama, and Tiwi listeners recognise the function (and therefore create an inferred understanding and emotional response) of songs recorded out of performance context often solely by hearing the melody. While there are melodies that relate specifically to (and are always sung at) particular rituals or ritual stages, it is not the melody alone that determines a song's function. One must also take into consideration the subject matter and the song's place within a ceremony to determine its function. When songs are heard (in person or in recordings) within a ritual, the function can be determined by where in the proceedings it comes (for instance, songs marking the relationship of mourners to the deceased are presented in Pukumani following a defined order, and songs with particular motivations and functions are presented on the first, second and third day of Kulama) so Tiwi composers are always aware of when, where and why they are singing and, as I'll explain later, the language used refers to these in various ways. It is perhaps surprising to think that highly poetic and oblique song texts, which very rarely refer to an event explicitly, can be quite succinctly pinned down to time, place and performer. Especially among the oldest archived recordings that do not name performers or describe the context of the recording, it is the melodic and linguistic conventions and the poetic imagery and allusion that help contextualise a song within the ritual stage, function, to whom it refers and often even the part of the day it was sung.

Individual artistic idiosyncrasies notwithstanding, there are general conventions of language, musical form and vocal style that place songs into specific ritual functions. Figure 4 gives an idea of the focus of each ceremony by tallying the numbers of songs of each function performed at Pukumani and Kulama ceremonies that were recorded in the archive. Although this is only an indication of what was being practised, it does provide a macro-overview of the shape the ceremonies followed.[3] We can see from the song subjects that the songs that make up the Pukumani-associated mortuary ceremonies are primarily to do with the process of the rituals, the bereavement status of participants (their relationship to the deceased) and affirmation of their kinship, Dreaming and Country identity. There are multiple understandings of the function of the Kulama ceremony, which can be regarded as an annual thanksgiving, remembrance and renewal. Its numerous stages focused on artistic achievement, memorialising the deceased, and the communication of matters of importance such as announcing and naming new babies and bestowing names on children as

---

3   It is important to note that there is a degree of overlap with imagery of the Dreamings, bereavement, kinship and ritual context often alluded to within the one song. It is an indication therefore of the songs' primary subject matter/function.

they progress through initiation stages and on adults to mark special occasions. The fact that there have been fewer Kulama ceremonies (and songs) recorded is not surprising, considering the likely reticence of locals to include outsiders in activities focused on initiation, ritual thanksgiving and the airing of personal matters, and then the dwindling of the practice of Kulama across the 20th century. Kulama ceremonies tend to be longer and spread out across three days, with periods of rest and changes of venue (without singing) and so there are fewer complete Kulama ceremonies recorded. In elicited recordings there are Pukumani and Kulama songs, sung out of context and in no particular order. I have not included those in the tally below.

Figure 4: Pukumani and Kulama song subjects recorded in the archive.

Songs presented within 16 recorded Pukumani ceremony events		Songs presented within 9 recorded Kulama ceremony events	
Ritual activity	128	News, ancestral stories, bestowing names	81
Dreaming, Country	122	Sorrow, remembrance	69
Bereavement kinship status	120	Ritual activity	38
Kinship/Ancestors	38	Local social politics	27

Kinship

As rituals held around the death of a person, Pukumani ceremonies are fundamentally centred around kinship: how people are related to each other. Kulama has a broader social role but also includes songs directly related to the reaffirmation of kinship. The Skin group, Dreaming and Country of every Tiwi person are central to their identity, and the vast majority of all Tiwi songs pertain to at least one of these. In order to appreciate the importance of Tiwi people's connection through Skin groups, Dreaming and Country to songs and dances, it is important to first understand how Tiwi people identify their kinship through all three of these.

For the Tiwi there are three states of existence (unborn, living and now deceased), all existing concurrently and through which all people pass once. The Pitapituwi (the as yet unborn) live on the same Country and within the same kinship affiliations as do the living and when they are "found", "sung" or "dreamed" by their father they are born. This symbolic finding of the unborn child by the father is why people have their father's Dreaming and inherit obligations of care and custodianship of the Country of their paternal ancestors.

In his song about Pitapituwi (Song text 5), Wampayawijimirri (Black Joe) sees his (unborn) children running on the beach. Their big shoes symbolise the fact that they are still too small to be wearing shoes at all, but he places them in their own future.

Song text 5: Wampayawijimirri Black Joe. Pitapituwi (Spirit children), 1954.

> **Arikuruwala, Kulama, recorded in Milikapiti by Mountford 1954**
>
> Wutamaluwi wilimpungarri wunitimingi limpangi nikirimi
> *They are walking around*
>
> Mulintamini arrukulani wungitimini rramingati
> *They are all wearing big shoes*

After living, a person becomes Mopaditi and joins the world of the dead, returning to the place of their birth and living on the same land in the same way as living people do. In that world all of the kinship systems, interactions and activities that happened in the world of the living continue. The relationship people have with the Mopaditi is one of care and love – as the Mopaditi are after all their deceased loved ones – having respect for them as they move into the realm of the ancestors. Yet there is also a degree of wariness, with the need to protect oneself from being taken by Mopaditi informing much of the ritual processes of the mortuary-related rituals and Pukumani protocols. Death is not regarded as the end, but as a removal to another state of being within the same time and place. The imagery in song texts related to mourning therefore includes aloneness, silence, going away, being separated from the group or being unheard in some way. Even with the addition of the Catholic faith to many Tiwi people's spiritual beliefs, the return of a person's spirit to their Country place is the overriding truth and whenever (living) people travel through Country, they call out in greeting to the ancestors who reside there. All exist simultaneously, so the voice of a departed ancestor can still be heard in the bush, and the unborn are there too, waiting patiently to be dreamed and sung.

Add to that the tangible and spiritual connection to the land that people who are living in the place of their deep-past ancestors have. Walking the same paths, following the songlines, maintaining oral transmission of stories and knowledge, one can imagine a real sense of communication between the three states and multiple layers and overlappings of time, physicality of actions, place and existence. This metaphysical connection with all of one's successors and predecessors, within one place and at one time, has a profound effect on the way Tiwi people view time, "history" and embodied knowledge.

In Song text 6 Karla (Tractor Joe) sings in the voice of his father's Mopaditi spirit as he calls out in the bush and people respond. The spirit calls out as he follows the path through the bush that he did in his life, and which his (living) Country people also do. The Mopaditi are sometimes described as the tiny dots on the horizon far out to sea and they are said to be able to walk across the water with no trouble.

Song text 6: Karla (Tractor Joe). Yipunjinga mayingi (Calling spirit), 1975.

> **Karla. Ayipa, Kulama. Recorded by Osborne, Pirlingimpi 1975.**
>
> Ngiya urrungwarra pripiyapi marrarla yipunjinga mayingi
> *I am a spirit that keeps calling*
>
> Muninjirrikipingi marrarlatiyarra Niyinginta kuwani?
> *They ask "Who are you?"*
>
> Murawatinga wakari Ngiwinjirrikipingi marrarla yipunjinga yiriyi
> *I call out to them in the distance*
>
> Ngangilawa jarrumwaka Ngipijingipingi marrarla yipunjinga yampunya
> *I call out as I walk along my path*
>
> Ngampi mangimirntata tinguwa Ngipijingipingimangirraringinamami
> *I am a tiny dot as I walk on the calm sea*
>
> Pungjingipingimangirranyuwurrumami
> *To my Country over there*

Each Tiwi person identifies themselves on three levels: Yiminga (Skin group), Murrakupuni (Country) and Yoi (Dreaming dance). A system of matrilineal and patrilineal moieties gives each person a particular relationship to their father, father's brother, father's sister, father's mother, etc. These affect behavioural practice and also determine the songs and dances children are taught in ceremonial contexts (Goodale 1974; Grau 1994; Ward 1990). I will discuss each of these in turn.

Yiminga (Skin group)

The system of Yiminga or Pukwiyi (Skin groups) determines social and family protocols, loyalties and responsibilities. In the Tiwi–English dictionary the entry for Yiminga is "sun, hour, time, breath, pulse, maternal totem group, gall bladder" – an indication of how fundamental it is to one's existence. The Skin groups are fundamentally important to social etiquettes: whom one can partner with, whom one can and cannot embrace or sit near.[4]

The term Yiminga has been translated variously as "totemic groups" (Spencer 1914, 200), "matrilineal totemic clans" (Berndt and Berndt 1964, 67), "matrilineal sibling sets" (Goodale 1974, 71). Grau describes Yiminga/Pukwiyi as "the principle of, or essence of life" (Grau 1983a, 201). The term today refers to the four Skin groups: Warntarringuwi (Sun), Miyartuwi (Pandanus), Lorrila/Marntimapila (Rock) and Takaringuwi (Mullet), with numerous sub-groupings (called "clans" in English) related to particular areas across the islands. A person's Yiminga, inherited from their mother, is the primary kinship group to which they belong.

Figure 5a shows each Skin group's associated clan sub-groups and we can see how they are emblematically connected with the group to which they belong. The clans associated with the Sun group, for example, are all red-hued, and those associated with Mullet all relate to the estuarine areas and the flora and fauna that are found there. The connection to Country is so strong that people call particular places by relationship names. Wulinjuwu (a small island off the coast of Melville Island), for example, would be called ngintinganinga (aunty) by people of the Wulinjuwula (Mosquito) clan (within the Takaringuwi Skin group) because this is the Country belonging to their father. He would call the place yipunga (sister). Similar to the concept of the soul, found in other religions, at death it is the Yiminga that leaves the body and joins the spirit world. Figure 5b shows the four major Skin groups and the marriage connections between them. The arrows indicate allowed associations; so, for example a person from Lorrila/Marntimapila can marry someone from the Warntarringuwi or Takaringuwi group but not a member of Miyartuwi.

Figure 5a: The Tiwi Skin groups and associated clans.

Yiminga Skin group	Internal associated clans
Miyartuwi PANDANUS	White Cockatoo, Flying Fox, Fresh Water
Lorrila/Marntimapila ROCK	Oyster, Fish, March Fly, (small sea) Bird
Warntarringuwi SUN	Mud Crab, Red Ochre, Fire, Stingray, Woollybutt Flower, Red-flowered Swamp Grass
Takaringuwi MULLET	Brolga, Ironwood, Crocodile, Mosquito

---

4   The "wrong-way" love that is talked quietly about is a sensitive issue that everybody is aware of even in a thoroughly 21st-century community, and with varying degrees of cultural orthodoxy. It is also touched upon in a number of songs in the recorded archive and so is mentioned here to add context for those potentially using those texts in the future.

3 Singing identity

Figure 5b: The Tiwi Skin groups and marriage connections.

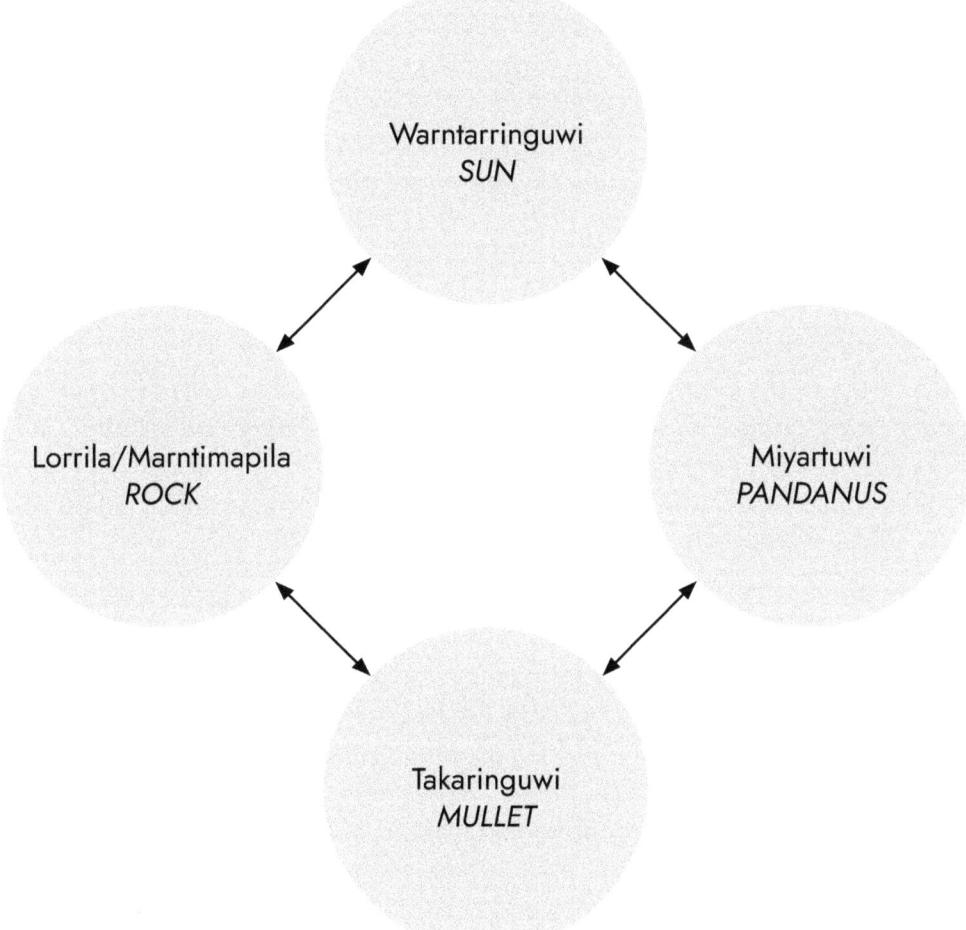

Murrakupuni (Country)

As well as identifying with a Skin group, every Tiwi inherits a Murrakupuni (Country place) affiliation from their father at birth depending upon where they were "found" or "dreamed" by him. Today there are eight Murrakupuni on the Tiwi Islands. They are Munupi, Marrikawuyanga, Yimpinari, Wulurangkuwu on Melville Island, and Tikilaru, Wurangkuwu and Malawu on Bathurst Island. Mantiyupi Country straddles the channel between the two islands.[5]

The exact boundaries of these Countries, and indeed the number of Countries, have changed quite a bit over the period in which they have been documented in

---

5 www.tiwilandcouncil.com. The differences in spellings of Country names are the result of differing opinions as to correctness.

writing.⁶ Although most people now live in one of the three main towns rather than in their Country, the spiritual connection with the land is still paramount to one's place in the community, where one's paternal ancestors are buried and/or have ceremony held and which songs one owns and performs. After the *Aboriginal Land Rights (Northern Territory) Act 1976* (Cwlth), the Tiwi Land Council was formed, made up of representatives of each Country group. The emergence of land rights as an indicator of the Indigenous cultural voice led, at least in part, to what is regarded by many Tiwi people as an unbalanced shift of power towards patrilineal ownership rights and male-dominated decision making. The Land Council has remained as the structure for the system of decision-making and power on the islands. Goodale notes that:

> … the patrilineal *aminiyiati* land-based units, which Hart noted in 1929, composed of the descendants of an important and powerful father's father *(amini)* are reappearing as important units in Tiwi society in the 1980s under a dual influence of the Mission and of the Land Rights Act. (Goodale 1988, 143, 144)

This meant too that from the late 1970s the names of the important men of the past (the leaders of those patrilineal Country clans) came to be taken as family surnames. Notwithstanding these changes, there is firmly in place today: a balance of affiliation between the Skin group (with ancestral Country connection) of one's mother and the Dreaming and Country group of one's father. The relatively recent, non-Tiwi system of women taking the surname of their husband in marriage does not disrupt the patrilineal or matrilineal system. Children take their father's surname, their father's dance and their father's Country, while they have their mother's Skin group.

Yoi (Dreaming dance)

As well as identifying with a Country group, a Skin group and a clan, every Tiwi person has a Yoi (Dreaming dance) that they perform at all ceremonial and many social occasions. The Yoi dance and song are referred to, in English, by Tiwi people as their Dreaming dance (and song), a widely used Aboriginal-English term that implies connection with the deep-past ancestors (there is no direct Tiwi translation of the term Dreaming). The Yoi dances are taught from a very early age, with children being encouraged from when they begin to learn to walk to also begin dancing their Dreaming Yoi whenever the opportunity

---

6   Maps of the islands showing the Countries vary. This is a potentially contentious issue as areas of land are increasingly becoming important as they draw land ownership royalties, administered through the Tiwi Land Council. It is evidenced by different versions of the Murrakupuni maps that land ownership areas have shifted.

arises. By school age, dancing one's Yoi is natural and uncontrived, so much so that the moves of someone's dance often spill over into conversation as a gesture or spontaneous few steps.

The Dreaming Yoi dances have been created over the years by songmen in ceremony. The Dreamings relate to animals or other features of the different Country areas and so groups of families with Country affiliation will also tend to share a Dreaming. New Dreamings – and so new Yoi dances – are said to have emerged as people moved around the islands and formed family groups, and the current Yoi are evidence of the continuation of this in the last century or so and reflect the changes on the islands. As well as Indigenous flora and fauna such as Sugarbag,[7] Rainbow, Turtle, Junglefowl and Shark, we find people who dance Horse and Cart, Ship, and Buffalo. When they perform their Yoi they "manifest as representations of these things. When they dance Shark or Crocodile or whatever, they are not therefore mimicking the animals … they are showing another facet of their personalities" (Grau 2005, 147). There have been variations and changes to the Yoi Dreamings recorded over the past century and we can safely assume for generations before. As clans and family groups combined and new groups emerged, new Dreamings, entities from their land, were taken on as totems. With the 20th-century arrangement of family lines under surnames (most of which were the "first" name of descendants) and the introduction of married names, the delineation of family groups into Dreamings became overlapping and one's surname doesn't necessarily define one's Dreaming. While this may seem complicated to non-Tiwi readers, Tiwi people know exactly how they fit into the Yoi (and the Yiminga) system. The Dreaming Yoi groups are listed in Figure 6 (sourced from Ward (1990) and confirmed, with some changes, by Elders at time of writing this book).

The word Yoi

I am inclined to title this paragraph "read this first!" as it is fundamental to being able to follow much of what is to come. The Tiwi word Yoi is complex and multi-layered. Andrée Grau, who wrote extensively and sensitively about Tiwi danced culture, summed up the potential confusion but also beautiful logic of what Yoi is. Tiwi people explain this the best, of course, but from the point of view of someone who knows what it means and feels it's obvious! For the rest of us, Grau puts it as well as I could attempt so I'll quote her here:

---

7   A general term for the honey of native bees.

> Yoi is not only defined by the Tiwi as "the dance" and "to dance", and "the event including dance" but also as "the song used for dance", "the rhythm of these songs" and "to sing for a dance". Thus Yoi denotes the phenomenon, the act of dancing, the music associated with dance, and the performance of that music. (Grau 1983a, 49)

Added to the above is the meaning closest to the English speaker's understanding of Aboriginal Dreaming. A Tiwi person's Yoi is their Dreaming. Dreaming is a widely used English word to refer generally to Aboriginal stories of deep-past ancestry and identity. While the words Dreaming or Dreamtime have various connotations in the context of Aboriginal cultures – from creation stories and the deep-past time of ancestral spirits, to states of existence and metaphysical connections with the land – in the Tiwi context it specifically applies to a person's Yoi dance through which one's totemic ancestor manifests when dancing. I will use the word Dreaming when referring to Yoi because that is how Tiwi people explain the patrilineal identity that each person has, relating to an ancestral "first" embodiment of the animal with which they identify. More about the Tiwi Dreamings later.

The most important thing to grasp here is that Yoi does mean Dreaming. Regina Kantilla says, "My Yoi is Crocodile, which I inherited from my father. It is who I am, because I dance Crocodile." So Regina's Yoi (Dreaming) is Crocodile and her Yoi (dance) is Crocodile.

It's also a verb – older women call out encouragingly, "Yoi, mana!" ("Come on, dance!") to young people stepping into adult ceremonial roles or to toddlers as they learn their first steps of Crocodile or Dingo or Shark or Rainbow. Then, as Grau explains, Yoi is the section of a larger ceremonial event (or indeed these days in a concert performance) when people dance *and* it is the song that accompanies those dances. In fact, Yoi (dance) and Yoi (song) are so intrinsically intertwined and codependent that it makes perfect sense that they share the same word.

Figure 6: Tiwi Dreaming groups.

Dreaming	English name
Alijarraka amintiya Pakitiringa	*Frog and Rain*
Ampiji	*Rainbow Serpent*
Jarrangini	*Buffalo*
Jipankuna	*Boat*

3 Singing identity

Dreaming	English name
Kapala	*Battleship*
Karlapurti	*Black Whip Snake*
Kirilima	*Junglefowl*
Mantupwawi	*Sugarbag Fly*
Maratinga	*Ship*
Nyarringari	*Goose*
Nyingawi	*Mangrove spirit people*
Pika	*Horse*
Purutjikini	*Owl*
Rawaturrunga	*Pig*
Tarangini	*Snake*
Tarikulani	*Turtle*
Tatuwali	*Shark*
Tayamini	*Dingo*
Timilani	*Mosquito*
Tuwiyika	*Whirlwind*
Wunijaka	*Wind*
Yingwati	*Sugarbag*
Yirrikapayi	*Crocodile*

Teresita Puruntatameri explained Tiwi identity and the inextricable connections between person, family and Country this way:

> So I dance Tatuwali [Shark] because my father was Timaepatua, but my children dance Junglefowl for their father [a Puruntatameri man]. I sometimes dance Junglefowl too because I am Mrs Puruntatameri and I have to teach my children.

> Yiminga. Also, for when we breathe that's Yiminga, pulse, culture … and also the Skin group. Yiminga is the life … also a life, life, from the four Skin groups. So when we sing, we also make song for our Country

> Yiminga, like Skin group. The Yiminga the four Skin groups, Yiminga comes from the mother. So I'm Takarringa, my mother was Takarringa, my grandmother, her mother before her, always Takarringa. And the dance that we do comes from our father's side. So my dance, Shark, comes from my father and his father and so on. It's always been like that. I teach my grandchildren about the four Skin groups. I teach them that we are related to Miyartuwi, but not the Rock and the Sun. So that's the first thing grandmothers do, they teach the young ones the Skin group system, so they know that they can't marry Miyartuwi. They can marry Warntarringuwi or Lorrila.

It is significant that Teresita called the Yiminga the "Country Yiminga". Both the Murrakupuni (Country) group affiliation (determined patrilineally) and the Yiminga sub-groups (matrilineally) are connected to Country places. An unborn child has the Yiminga of their mother and therefore ancestral connection to her Country. They are the breath, the pulse, the life of the Country. A part of the natural world. They are in existence in the same way as seeds that are yet to grow then fall to the ground to germinate exist or as rain that is still in the state of moisture evaporating upwards to the clouds is still rain, though not yet falling as rain. Having been "dreamed" or sung by their father they are then born. Old men tell of hearing their unborn child's voice in their mind as they walked out bush one day, or how the child's name came into their mind as a song. Having been "found" by the father in his Country, they are then born with their Yoi (Dreaming) with connection to the Country of their father. We can say, therefore, that all three levels of Tiwi identity – Yiminga, Murrakupuni and Yoi – relate back to Country.

Singing mother, singing father

This brings me to another fundamental aspect of Tiwi culture, which is the closeness and fluidity of gender roles in knowledge holding, teaching and in cultural practice. While men traditionally lead the song in Kulama and in Pukumani, there are no songs or parts of ceremony that women are forbidden to participate in. In fact, in 2020 a group of young women held Kulama entirely without male participation and they were congratulated for doing so. As I will touch on again, in today's context of a fragile song practice, Elder men and women are coming together to support younger singers, and are equally involved in the teaching of dance and ritual. This co-participation goes back to pre-invasion culture in the gender equality of kinship marking in dance. Right back through the archives and today, the ritual/sung/danced role of "mother" is often performed by a man, when that man is (for example) the maternal uncle of the deceased. They will dance and sing Yoi symbolic of breast, womb and breast milk with no suggestion of awkwardness or disrespect. Senior women are able to sing in the role of paternal responsibility too, singing mourning songs in the role that their husband should/would have sung if they were still alive.

Warlakurrayuwuwa (Paddy) Sawmill sang Song text 7 at Kulama in 1975. Singing in place of his father (who had already died), he takes the parental kinship role, and because the deceased is his father's sister's daughter, he sings not as "father" but the role of mother. Knowing the type of song Paddy was singing, the ritual context (here, the second day of Kulama, when the deceased are remembered) and his family affiliations, knowledgeable Tiwi listeners understand that he means to mark this woman's Country. In this case it is Yangarti, north-eastern Melville Island, the Country area of a deceased woman whose Dreaming Paddy marked in his Kulama song, through reference to her father's ancestral Country, the Country associated with Goose Dreaming, where, now deceased, she has returned. We hear Paddy first speak in the voice of the woman's (long deceased) father who, as senior man, would be clearing the dance ground. He now speaks (through Paddy) in the voice of the Goose ancestor. Listeners hear the voice then of the daughter herself, now returning to her Country, and as a goose and as the spirit of the deceased the image of her flying off and away, to join her ancestors in her Country where she now stays. The swampy water adds an extra layer of significance here. In this context, a song performed in mourning, to mark the journey of this woman, the singer's classificatory daughter (whom we might call "niece"), the water becomes the earth's lifeblood and nourishment – the mother's milk. It isn't by coincidence that the deceased is depicted *in* the water, surrounded by, embraced by, nourished by her Country. Paddy's poetic reference to mother's milk is another clue to listeners that he sings in this context as "mother". Again we find continuity of meaning through performance that withstands written alteration. One can imagine how, without the connection of actual speakers and singers, words get lost in the translation of a superimposed external system of recording knowledge. At the time he sang, Paddy knew there was no need to directly name the place – and indeed perhaps at the time he thought it inappropriate to do so as it may still have been closed due to Pukumani. We rely absolutely on the continuing transmission of these songs to keep the sounds of the written words alive.

Song text 7: Warlakurrayuwuwa Paddy Sawmill. Mayimampi (Goose), 1975.

> Ngiya jipilontimajiyawatiwuwa
> *I am the goose clearing the ground*
>
> Wayangirikangintuwinjirriki lontiyipunji ngangarlayi
> *I sit with a flock of other geese all honking/talking*
>
> Waya manguluwumpamenjirrikilumangiliyajumanguwu
> *Now I am here in the swampy water*

Pre-mission-era Tiwi girls and boys proceeded equally through the Kulama initiation stages towards adulthood, and only in the later stages when the marriage system necessitated a split path did they learn different skills of engagement with the land. Girls and boys/women and men dance in gendered groups, but they dance the same kinship and Yoi dances. As previously mentioned it is only over the past half century (perhaps with the influence of Western gender inequality?) that a socio-political gender imbalance has developed. Increasingly the community is calling for the women to be heard, to be included on the Land Council and in community decisions, and that their knowledge and opinions be considered, mirroring similar conversations in the wider world, which seems ironic when palingarri (old way) Tiwi society had less imbalance than the one they inherited from Europeans.

This gender fluidity in ritualised dance and associated song comes to some degree from the dual identity Tiwi people have: their maternal Yiminga and their paternal Yoi: both equally important to the ego, to self-esteem and to an individual's position in society.

The Tiwi community has a small, proud and well-loved group of transgender people known collectively as sistagirls. While they have experienced sadness, loss and a struggle to be accepted in the past, and they continue to speak out on LGBTQI+ issues, they are, at time of writing, very much a part of the community. A number of sistagirls[8] play a very important role in cultural maintenance and – in the context of pre-20th-century cultural, sung and danced gender roles – it is essential they are included. Sistagirls are free to dance (and, if they can, sing) with the men or with the women as they choose and feel most comfortable. Some dress overtly as women and always dance as a woman while others sometimes dance with men in classical Tiwi performance contexts and also dance in drag in non-Tiwi arenas. As in any culture, there are as many

---

8 The sistagirls formulated this small section with the author and gave permission for it to be included in this book.

variations to personal opinion, belief, need and identity as there are people. The Catholic mission implanted traditional European gendered stereotyping on the upbringing of Tiwi children. Girls lived full-time in dormitories, whereas boys attended by day, and children were taught the gendered skills of the time. The girls learned to sew, to cook and serve meals, and clean and wait on the Brothers, while boys worked on the mission farm and did outside tasks. The systemic and conscious disruption of the Tiwi "marriage" system and the switch to the Catholic one for an entire generation of children meant there was an abrupt alteration to the social and cultural system through which Tiwi youngsters were schooled and in which they learned their values and identity, as well as gender roles in terms of leadership, decision-making and – in this context, perhaps most importantly – cultural and artistic practice. It was the disruption to the Tiwi marriage system that had a marked knock-on effect on Tiwi song culture by removing much of the relevance of Kulama.

Built into the traditional Tiwi practice of young women (and girls) being "promised" to older men was a system of multi-generational support. Older people were learned from and revered, cared for and embedded into the fabric of why people needed to learn the songs, the rituals and the language, with senior men holding responsibility for the care and structure of family organisations also being the teachers of intellectual, spiritual and artistic practices. When a woman was widowed, responsibility for her care passed to the next senior man in the family group, so women were always "married" and therefore supported for their entire lives within the family circle, enabling long-term intergenerational connection and teaching. Although the Catholic missionaries thought it to be unseemly (as they saw it as child and/or forced marriage), in reality the system ensured that older men were given direct responsibility for the young women of other families, which helped ensure a social and relatively peaceful community. This ongoing cycle nurtured boys and taught young men so that they would in turn become senior and learned enough to become heads of families, with a duty of care for the older women in their family units, and created an ongoing respect and need for older men as they took on the care of young girls (who were in turn in the presence of knowledge holders as a matter of course). With the introduction of Catholic marriage and there no longer being the need for attaining adulthood/initiation through language and song in order to be married, the need for Kulama dwindled quickly; more on that later. Here it is worth noting that children are born with equally strong spiritual ties to identity through their mother and their father. Both men and women dance, sing and compose. While there are song-types that men or women traditionally sing there is a crossover through the communal song context at which all of the community sings and/or witnesses the songs. Today especially, as Elders with song knowledge are few, women and men share the singing, often within the one song, taking over mid-phrase if the singer tires or loses the words.

Pukumani

The word Pukumani has a number of meanings, all related to the death of a person and the associated rituals. Pukumani is used as an adjective to describe the state of a person's name, a place or a song that is closed or "taboo" because of a death. It also refers to the overall state of a person affected by the death of a close relation. For example, the deceased's name is Pukumani (not to be uttered), the Country to which they belong is Pukumani (not to be visited), a song they composed is Pukumani (not to be sung) and the deceased's closest kin are said to be Pukumani (following the restrictions associated with mourning).

I will not embark on a detailed description of the Pukumani ceremonies because they are already the subject of anthropological description (Hart and Pilling 1988; C.W.M. Hart 1930; Levy 1975; Mountford 1958; and Spencer 1914). One pertinent point to make here is that any reader of those works must be aware of the third-party, observational and non-Tiwi lens through which those descriptions were made. I certainly don't presume to think that I can describe the multi-layered spiritual, social and philosophical meaning of Tiwi rituals, and so will only describe the elements of song as I'm qualified and authorised to and document the knowledge of those who actually enact the rituals themselves. Aside from the language barrier (especially in the early 20th century) and cultural differences around the social etiquettes and protocols of passing on information, there are questions to be considered as to the level of inclusion any outside observer would (and should) have been given to deeply personal matters of death, grieving and religious observance. Reading through the early anthropologies with Tiwi people uncovers numerous examples of a non-Tiwi observer's descriptions in writing (or recorded on field tapes) that either present only part of the picture or misinterpret the occasion entirely.

One such example is Hart's surprising assertion in material first published in 1960 that the dances performed at Pukumani rituals "had no relation whatever to the death or the deceased" (Hart and Pilling 1988, 101). A footnote added to the 1988 edition reads: "Goodale, who probably has seen more Tiwi mourning dances than Hart, pointed out in 1986 that the individually owned and performed dances, in fact, do bear some relation to the deceased" (Hart and Pilling 1988, 101). Subsequent observation and study of the ceremony and its dances (and, by association, songs) show without doubt the centrality of the deceased and their relationship to all present in all songs and dances performed for Pukumani (Goodale 1974; Grau 1983a; Holmes 1995; Mountford 1958; Osborne 1989). One can only guess that Hart was watching ceremony without any attempt to understand either the metaphysical role or the deeply allusive meaning of the songs themselves. This is a recurring problem in the conversation about song and language loss in Indigenous cultures, when most of the "study" and "documentation" is done through the colonialist, positivist point of view.

In the face of significant social and religious change, Tiwi people have embedded aspects of the Palingarri (old way) ceremony into modern practice. It is a matter of record that there was strong opposition to and active dissuasion of ceremony by the missionaries on Bathurst Island. The Pukumani-associated rituals were banned in the community around the mission on Bathurst Island in the 1950s and 1960s (Goodale 1974; Mountford 1958; and contemporary Tiwi accounts), and children at the mission school were not allowed to attend those ceremonies held away from the township area. This upset the system of holding ceremony at the place of the burial (which should be in the Country to which the person belongs). Goodale reports on a burial in 1954 of a newborn child (on Melville Island, away from the mission) on the day the infant had died. She describes a burial largely unaltered from Tiwi traditions, but with the "innovation" (Goodale 1974, 245) of a wooden coffin lined with flowers for the burial of a newborn infant. Her reports from that time suggest that there was the beginning of an overlap between Tiwi traditions being followed by the older generation (and those with less contact with the mission) and the introduced Anglo/European traditions. This and the fact that most people now lived in the town rather than on Country perhaps saw the beginning of the changing connection between the burial and the Pukumani ceremony.

As a result of persistent disapproval of Tiwi ceremony by the mission and the gradual establishment of Catholic ceremonies in their place, Holmes notes that, by 1985, the funeral she witnessed comprised a Catholic Mass said by the priest, followed by Yoi songs and dances (Holmes 1995). Grau however reported that during her 18-month period of fieldwork from 1980 to 1982 she witnessed 27 Yilaniya and 19 Yiloti ceremonies, indicating that there was a continuing desire to follow Tiwi traditions of mortuary ritual (Grau 1983a). Goodale observed a change between her time on the islands in 1954 and in 1986 in "the [lesser] length and elaborateness of these most important rituals" but that "the basic structure and obligatory roles of kin and spouse remained as they always have been" (Goodale 1988, 141).

It cannot be ignored that the Catholic mission influence since 1912 has had a massive impact on when and how the mortuary rituals are held. A number of researchers have commented on the situation of ceremonial practice in relation to the mission (Brandl 1971; Goodale 1988; Grau 1983a; Grau 2001a; Mountford 1958; Osborne 1989) and this general consensus confirms the lived experience of senior Tiwi community leaders – that while there has been significant loss in terms of the extra richness of ceremonial practice and paraphernalia, such as painting up,[9] making of head-dresses and ceremonial spears, the size and number of Turtuni poles and the duration of and participation in song-based ritual, the essential elements of the Pukumani practice – in particular the Yoi songs – are still performed and, comparing my observations in 2010 with those in 2022, there is a noticeably stronger push among community leaders for the revival of traditional ritual as well as (and increasingly in the place of) elements of Catholic ritual.

The ritual songs associated with Pukumani

Pukumani is the overall state of mourning and associated ritual observance, but within that are ritual stages, each having their own distinct purpose and protagonists. In the past, the burial was just one of these, and the Pukumani process comprised several weeks or months worth of rituals involving dance, painting, weaving, smoking, and inter-clan communications, arrangements and preparations. The five main stages that are followed at time of writing are shown in Figure 7. Stages one and two occur soon after death, while stages three, four and five occur at least one year later. At all Pukumani (mortuary-related) rituals, song provides the framework and lays out the structure that mourners follow. Some of these stages are omitted, or performed in varying degrees depending on the wishes of the immediate family, obligations of work, financial situation and schedules of the community as well as increasingly unpredictable weather patterns.

---

9   Painting up is a term used by Tiwi people to describe painting one's face and/or body with ochre designs, in preparation for a ceremonial or performance event.

3 Singing identity

Figure 7: Mortuary rituals sequence.

1. Burial: Digging of grave, interment of deceased. Today often also includes (Catholic) rites. (Seldom practised is the moving and preparation of the body).

2. First Yilaniya (Smoking): Smoking of the deceased's possessions, house and places frequented by them throughout town.

3. Preliminary rituals: a) Nitipaurini taka: cutting the poles, b) Nitaumi taka: burning/singeing the poles, c) Jilimarra: painting the poles.

4. Main Yilaniya (Smoking): Healing/smoking ritual, preliminary to the Final Ceremony.

5. Yiloti (Final) Ceremony: Includes some or all of Yoi event, Pamati (mock spousal fight), Makatinarri (ritual washing).

---

1. <u>Burial</u>

The important point to make about the changes that have occurred to the Pukumani-associated ceremonies is that until about the 1950s, the burial was a relatively small occasion held a day or so immediately after death, and attended by only a small group, and it was the series of rituals leading up to and comprising the Yiloti (Final) Ceremony, held about one year after death, that were the most important and involved large numbers of mourners. Grau notes increasingly larger attendances at the burial in the 1980s (Grau 2001a), and it is the case today that what is now referred to as the Funeral is the main (and sometimes only) mourning event. The Funeral today usually combines elements of a Catholic service with elements of the Pukumani-associated rituals.

2. <u>First Yilaniya (Smoking)</u>

This is a ritual held as soon as possible after the death, usually within a week or so. Today a small group of singers moves through buildings or areas the deceased had frequented such as the shop, the school or the club and their house. Songs particular to Yilaniya are performed and smoke (from burning green leaves in a tin bucket) is wafted around the area in order to cleanse the place of the deceased's spirit and to discourage the Mopaditi (spirits of the deceased) from staying around and perhaps stealing someone else away. Yilaniya is also now often held the evening before a funeral, with a combination of Catholic prayer and songs (in Tiwi and/or English language) and classical Tiwi Yilaniya songs. At this event, now commonly called "Healing" in English, family and close friends walk through the smoke to cleanse and to disguise themselves from the Mopaditi.

3. <u>Preliminary rituals</u>

The sourcing and cutting of wood for the Turtuni and their carving and painting have ritual-specific songs that are now seldom performed by those doing the work (usually because they are younger men who do not have the singing skills) but are sometimes sung by old men if they are around. These activities happen at mutually convenient times in the lead-up to a Yiloti (if one is being planned). Other small rituals occur – such as travelling through Country to the ceremonial ground (asking permission to enter from ancestors as they go), preparing the Milimika (the dance ground), painting up and small smoking rituals – as they traditionally would, to suit the logistics of the environment and location of family and depend on the motivations of individuals involved.

4. <u>Main Yilaniya (Smoking)</u>

The Yilaniya is the last preliminary ritual before the Final Ceremony. A series of Yoi songs (with their dances) is performed by those with corresponding Dreaming and kinship status. As they dance, each person moves through the smoke made by burning green leaves. This action has a symbolic healing effect and also helps to mask the living person's identity to avoid their being taken away by the Mopaditi.

5. <u>Yiloti (Final) Ceremony</u>

Traditionally held over a few days, this was the culmination of the numerous smaller lead-up rituals comprising songs of appropriate function. While many of the lead-up rituals have fallen away, and the Ceremony itself is completed in one day, the Yiloti remains the largest of the rituals, attended by the entire community, and at which the main Yoi dance and song event occurs. It is followed by payment of ritual workers and symbolic cleansing and washing. Today this is often simply called "Yoi" or "Ceremony" and so in this description, I refer to it as Ceremony (as a proper noun). It is this Final Ceremony that releases the spirit of the deceased and signals the end of the period of Pukumani and the lifting of the mourning restrictions.[10]

The Yiloti (Final) Ceremony is ideally held one year after the death so, as Elders explain, all the seasons go around while the close family stays in mourning. There are slightly differing reports of the timing of Yiloti in the anthropological literature, but I cite here the opinion of the current community and Elders at time of writing. The responsibility falls on the closest relation to the deceased

---

10   It can become unclear to refer to Ceremony as Yiloti (Final Ceremony) because within that event there is a smaller ritual also called Yiloti (final, the end), which serves as the end and closing of the rituals in their entirety.

(so the spouse, parent or child) and people often feel the burden of planning their loved one's Ceremony for months or even years. People cite problems with finding the money required for paying the workers (the dancers, the singers, those who clear the area and those who make the poles) as being the main reason people put off holding one. This creates some tension and anxiety because the spirit of the deceased remains around town, restless and in limbo, and until it is held, their name remains Pukumani (closed/taboo) and people are waiting for the cathartic event to be able to move on and let the person go.

There are differences of opinion over the degree of Yiloti to be included in the funeral, with some people suggesting that the Yilaniya and Yoi stages should be included in order to expedite the spirit's release, fearing that it will likely be quite some time before Ceremony is held, if indeed at all. Others believe the traditional way should be adhered to even if that means waiting a long time for Ceremony to happen.

While most Tiwi are baptised Catholics, there is (as in any religion) a range of adherence to religious practice and orthodoxy. The eschatological importance of Tiwi ceremonies pertaining to death has endured notwithstanding the addition of Catholic ritual, as is noted in the following statement, from the voice-over narration on the soundtrack of the documentary film *Mourning for Mangatopi*:

> … for many Tiwi, Christian funerals have failed to ensure the ritual journey of the dead to the spirit world and have also failed to provide the emotional release of the Pukumani ceremony. (Levy 1975)

While the (Catholic) funeral Mass and burial provide a framework that satisfies the 21st-century Australian process after a Tiwi death, it is primarily the surrounding Tiwi rituals that ensure the successful release of the deceased from the life they have just finished, the enabling of mourners to fulfil their spiritual and emotional grieving, and the confirmation of communal identity and cohesion.

The role of the Yoi songs

Looking at the list of Yoi song items among the old recordings by subject, one might infer that the vast majority of Tiwi songs recorded across the 20th century are about apparently everyday topics such as tractors, ships, electric lights or bulldozers, and that therefore the songs composed in the millennia prior to that had equally mundane and ubiquitous subjects such as rocks, trees, fires or turtles. A feature of Tiwi songs recorded post-invasion is that new subject matter has been added into the traditional practice, with those non-Tiwi subjects imbued with the same degree of rich symbolism and spiritual meaning as those of the natural world. With song texts centred on features and animals of the natural world, there is always also a level of meaning deeper than (simply) rocks or turtles as those rocks are the ancestors in Country, or mark the place where a kin group belongs and the turtle plays various metaphorical roles in songs about nesting, mothers or journeying across the sea.

Ayipa[11] Kulama songs (about a ship seen on the horizon or electricity being installed, for example) do concern prosaic subjects for their value as news, and so Ayipa songs can be regarded as more overt and explicit. However, most often a song (even those of the Ayipa function) will carry a meaning deeper than the words at the literal level. The subject matter for each song is determined by the stage of ceremony at which it is being performed. When there were numerous singers able to compose, there would have been many newly created (Jipuwakirimi) Yoi songs performed at regular song/dance events across the islands, created by senior men and women in each kinship group and so containing imagery, names and stories related to those groups and their Murrakupuni (Country) areas. This resulted in a wealth of poetry that is intrinsic to specific people, times and places.

Symbolism is perhaps the most important feature of Tiwi song poetry in terms of obfuscated meaning and in the context of current attempts to translate old song texts. Before detailing the various forms of symbolism it is worth giving an overview. There are three general types of symbolism in Tiwi song texts: mourning/bereavement; ritual; and Yoi (in this case, Dreaming totem). The role of Yoi songs can be broadly summarised with these subsections.

Kinship and bereavement status songs

The kinship status songs are the most important songs in the Pukumani context. Kinship is the central means of connecting people to each other, and the entire Yoi event can be regarded at one level as a means of reaffirming the kinship status of everybody present. Grau says similar of the dances, stating that "the kinship dance system is not merely a reflection of Tiwi kinship" but "it is the Tiwi kinship" (Grau 1983a, 333). Perhaps the most important thing to understand is that Yoi is central to one's identity and, through that, to the earth. It is the ancestral totemic animal from whom one is descended and, through connection to the land that animal lived (and lives) in, it firmly situates a person as a current manifestation of that ancestor and all of its descendants, placing the person therefore as both a continuation of the unbroken link to and a current

---

11   Ayipa is the section of the Kulama rituals in which songs about current affairs and social politics are composed. I discuss these further in Chapter 4.

custodian of that land. In Song text 8, Tungutalum sings as a Crocodile man in ceremony, wearing the traditional ritual goose-feather ball neckpiece.

Song text 8: Tungutalum. Yirrikapayi (Crocodile), 1912.

> Ngiya perimrringurrumwiyankerlatayuwu
> *I am the crocodile that watches and waits*
>
> Ngiya perimrringurrumwiyankerluwankerlipi liwayini
> *I am the watching crocodile with goose-feather balls*

As Yoi means "dance" as well as "Dreaming" and "Dreaming dance" it also means *who you are when you dance*. At any celebration a person with Crocodile Yoi/Dreaming will dance Crocodile. At a funeral they will dance Crocodile and they will also dance the Yoi of their kinship status to the deceased.

The overall structure of Pukumani rituals (shown at Figure 9) is consistent across the recorded archive and current practice. The Yilaniya (Smoking) rituals are performed a number of times: prior to and on the day of the Final Ceremony, as well as prior to and/or on the day of Funeral and burial. The order of the bereavement status Yoi songs and dances (at point 3) also forms the structure for the ritual (also called Yoi) that is held alongside funerals (and would therefore be repeated within the later Pukumani ceremony). The performance of the dance appropriate to one's relationship with the deceased is essential to the wellbeing of both the living person and the spirit of the dead person. In much the same way that other religions include "paying respects" to the deceased, which are shaped by family relationship protocols, following this structure enables the physical expression of each person's relationship to the deceased as well as providing comfort and support through participation within one's kinship group. For example, as well as next-of-kin sisters (Putaka), all those women who call the deceased "sister" will dance Mijuni together, each supporting the other (through dance and singing) as they come forward to pay respects and grieve. The bereaved spouse is protected from isolation through this system too, as all those who call him or her sister or brother (whether actual or classificatory) will dance as widow with them.

Songs composed for mortuary-related Yoi events refer to the parts of the body that symbolise each kinship status. Following palingarri conventions the imagery in these song subjects note the person's bereavement as some sort of injury, symbolising the emotional hurt and grief that must be made overt and shared by embodiment through dance, bringing it out, carrying it to the deceased and stamping it into the ground so it leaves the living and goes with the dead.

Figure 8 lists (in the order in which they are performed in Ceremony) the kinship symbols and how they are represented in the grieving/bereavement context of Yoi. Injury to, pain in or weakness of a leg (sung by siblings of the deceased) or to breasts, breast milk or the womb (sung by mothers) are some examples. These symbols can be referenced overtly in song: *I limp on one leg* (sung by a bereaved sibling) or *my milk doesn't flow* (a bereaved mother) or more obliquely *my shoes are torn* (sibling) or *I have run out of water* (mother). A grieving cousin-sister might sing *the harsh wind makes my face bleed* or *I am hit in the jaw.*

This convention of injury in kinship bereavement songs is inherent across the recorded archive and continues in songs created today with modern/non-Tiwi references. A song referring to a brother being bitten on the foot by a snake or one in which he is cut by stepping on a piece of broken glass fulfils the same ritual purpose.

Figure 8: The bereavement symbols of kinship status.

Kinship status	Symbolised in dance and song by:	Symbolised in bereavement as:
Performed as Yoi whether within Yiloti (Final Ceremony) or as part of Funeral.		
Patrilineal Ngunantani – Father	Penis, groin	Injury to or pain
Mijuni – cousin-sister or –brother (half siblings)	Face/cheek	Hurt face, bleeding face
Matrilineal Ngunantani – Mother	Breast Womb	Lack of milk Pain, emptiness
Putani – brother Putaka – sister	Leg	Injury to leg, limping, weakness
Amparru – widow	Shoulder	Jealousy, fighting
Performed at Yilaniya (Smoking)		
Mamirampi – children of fathers	Spear	Killing of father

To further veil the meaning and to include reference to the deceased's (and/or his own) ancestral Country, a man might sing of stepping on sharp rocks at Wurangkuwu – placing himself as a man from Wurangkuwu who mourns his brother. A grieving mother might sing in the voice of a heron who can't find water to drink. This imagery places her as the wife of a Crocodile Dreaming man, with a number of song texts in the recorded and remembered archive either mentioning herons or women singing in the voice of the Heron ancestor

Revenge songs

Singing one's grief and anger is an important part of mourning. Songs symbolic of revenge and hatred for the perpetrator of a death (real or imagined) give the singer and their audience a ritualised context for grief. At Song text 9, for example, are three poetic images of revenge created by Jipwarlamparripa (Stanley Munkara) as he sang at the ritual smoking of his (then recently deceased) father's house. He sings of his anger (the fire noting both the ritual stage and his rage), then places himself in the family lineage of men who have to take on the burden of responsibility for avenging a death (symbolically, not literally). Symbolically unloading the blame of a death onto a third party helps people move on and to not internalise suffering.

Song text 9: Jipwarlamparripa Stanley Munkara. A song for his father at Yilaniya (Smoking), 1969.

> Jurrumumiyirrura nguwati wingawirri kuwirraniyamiiningaji
> *My stomach burns with fire*
>
> Nginginaji Ngiyawaminawungani Ngimawatuwinjirri nguwalimimi
> *I might kill in revenge like my grandfather did*
>
> Ngilarawunikiri Ngintimawatuwunjingimji
> *I take my spears and go*

Among the recordings are songs about knives and murderers, or that point the blame on the doctor or the hospital, that are not literal but fulfil this revenge function. Tiwi beliefs do not include magical or divine reasons for death, and so every death must have a cause (and something to blame) as part of the rationalisation and acceptance of a death. This blame is often exacted through the symbolism of songs performed at mortuary rituals and at Kulama. Elders recorded up to the early 1970s (those who held the old form of the language composed a generation before them) include bad water, angry Mopaditi or totemic animal beings or malevolent natural phenomena to blame for deaths (even in the absence of those as the reason for death). Topics such as a hospital stay gone wrong, a disliked nurse or an unknown killer, a visiting stranger or a mysterious poison are found in more recent songs. Unnamed murderers are very often blamed in songs presented by men singing in classificatory son roles. The responsibility for a man's death is traditionally put on his son's shoulders, whether he had anything to do with it or not. The duty of organising and leading singing at the funeral and related events falls on the son. The symbolism of the spear for the sons of deceased fathers is more than phallic. It implies responsibility for the father's death when a son takes on the social position of his father on his death. The Amparruwu songs, sung by the grieving widow or her classificatory sisters, take the imagery of revenge and make it one of jealousy – for the man who has left her in order to start his next life, and so also of the imagined new wife he has. In Audio 64, Mary Curry sings, "Winikunjurru punjingami [They are calling me]. Yimuluwila ruwunjiyi [Yimulu women]." She is telling the audience that the (Mopaditi) women now have the deceased man and are daring her to come and fight for him.

Dreaming songs

The most widely performed Yoi songs today are those belonging to the Dreamings that are associated with the Dreaming dances. They are performed at most funerals, at Yiloti (Final) Ceremonies, at weddings and many other community events. We have found evidence of continuity between old recordings of Dreaming Yoi and those same Yoi today. The text is partly epithetic, in that certain phrases and names known to signify ancestors or Skin groups through flora, fauna or geography would be used within an extemporised text setting. The Dreaming Yoi, therefore, while showing some variation, is more stable, with each Country group singing their own version. Across the recordings are Yoi events lasting several hours, each containing numerous individual song items relating to one particular Dreaming. In the Yoi event recorded by Holmes in June 1966 at Milikapiti,[12] for example, there are 15 distinct versions of Moonfish song performed by a number of singers. These were newly created for that day and related to specific creeks in the Country of the deceased (as well as his Moonfish Dreaming) so as to identify exactly with the occasion.

Most if not all Yoi specifically sung for the purpose of announcing each kin relationship are now old songs that are sung (with perhaps some small text variation) at each ceremony, and there have been very few occasions of new songs being composed for the Yoi section of a Funeral or a Final Ceremony. The kinship songs are less easily generalised in the way that the Dreaming songs in the last decade or so are, due to the multiple cross-generational and Yiminga Skin group ways in which individuals are related to each other as compared with the larger groupings of Dreamings and Countries. At Figure 9 the stages of the Yiloti Pukumani ceremony are shown with an indication of the subject of the songs presented in each. It must always be acknowledged that these are general stages of a longer ritual process and not all ceremonies follow this exactly.

---

12 This was part of the Yilaniya in a Final Ceremony held for Mamburringamirri (Charlie Fourcroy Pilakui).

3 Singing identity

Figure 9: The framework of the Yiloti Pukumani ceremony.

1. Yilaniya (Smoking). Walking through smoke to protect and cleanse the mourners.
   Songs of Dreaming Yoi, calling out to ancestors and Country, songs about blame and revenge.

2. Encouraging the spirit of the deceased to move on. Displays of sorrow and grief.
   Songs about spears, killers, injury and anger.

3. Bereavement status songs.
   Songs marking the relationship of each participant to the deceased.

4. Acknowledgement of those who helped provide the ceremony.
   'Payday' songs and songs to enact the presentation of money or goods.

5. Singing around the Turtuni pole(s).
   Songs about spears, jealousy, departure.

6. Final sorrow: sometimes people will move to the grave (as the Yoi is usually held away from the cemetery) and sometimes they will stay at the poles at the Milimika.

7. Washing off (body paint) ochres.
   Songs about water, rain, washing.

Allusion to ritual

Among the recordings of Pukumani-associated ceremonies there are songs that describe the action that the singer is performing at the time. Ritual actions are often the subject of a song almost as though the singer has sung in a stream-of-consciousness manner what they are doing at the time. For example:

> I am ... clearing the dance ground; lighting the fire; painting my face; painting the poles; calling the next dancer ...

are all loose translations of song texts that have been heard among the recordings. There are also Payijayi (payday) songs that are sung towards the end of the Final Ceremony when the workers (those who prepared the dance ground, those who painted the poles and the singers, for instance) receive their payment. Other songs refer to stages of ritual. Songs sung at the Yilaniya (Smoking) rituals allude to fire, sometimes literally, but more often via a ship's engine or boiler room, a generator or a blowtorch. At the Jilamara stage of ritual, when the participants apply painted body and face designs are songs that refer to painting up (repainting a boat or a house) and in later stages of ceremony we hear songs alluding to ritual washing (the sea or water). Two examples of allusion to ritual stages in songs are at Song texts 10 and 11 (translations by Justin Puruntatameri).

Song text 10: Warlakurrayuwuwa Paddy Sawmill. Yirranikara Pajimuna (Burning leg), 1975.

> **Sung at Yilaniya (Smoking) stage of ritual and kinship status Warlakurrayuwuwa Paddy Sawmill. Yoi, Pirlingimpi 1975**
>
> Ngipintirrikirrayanikurikipajiumuma
> *I am scorching my leg in the fire*

Song text 11: Jipwarlamparripa Stanley Munkara. Mangulumpwarni (Tide), 1975.

> **Sung at ritual washing performed at the end of a Yiloti (Final) Ceremony. Stanley Munkara, Yoi, Pirlingimpi, 1975**
>
> Ngimangrrupawuntimirri
> *I am a man of the rising tide*
>
> Wiyapurali munjingirampirramangima
> *At Wiyapurali backwater the sea flows in*

In Song text 10 Paddy Sawmill refers simultaneously to the fire/smoking stage of the ceremony and to his relationship with the deceased (brother, symbolised by the leg) as well as his bereavement (the injury). Song text 11 was sung at the final stage of the ritual when people wash off their ochre paint in a ritual and emotional cleansing. It refers to this indirectly, via the sea, and also places the deceased in his Country (which is Wiyapurali, on the south-western coast of Bathurst Island).

Many song texts include names of either the singer or the kin of the deceased. As well as adding import to the song through the inclusion of the actual names, this serves to evoke a sense of ancestry and mark connections between the singer, the audience and the song subject, whether an individual, a place or a narrative. The recorded bereavement songs (sung at Yoi and Kulama) are now a source of important family knowledge. Calling the names of ancestors brought them to the place while also making clear to listeners the credentials of the singer, in the context of his ancestry and Country affiliations. Elements of ritual song functions have been maintained in the non-traditional music forms of Tiwi song (described in Chapter 7). In a song composed by Clementine Puruntatameri in 2011, for example, only one of the eleven lines of text expresses literal meaning. Each of the other ten lines has a specific symbolic function. Clementine composed this song (translated as Her Father Sorrow song) to be sung at her own funeral.

Song text 12 is a translation of the text. It tells the story of Clementine's ancestors (whose names I have marked in bold font) leading a large and elaborate ceremony on Melville Island for a relative with Crocodile Dreaming and is a piece of oral history that only the eldest people hold. In fact, in 2011 when the song was composed, none of the women younger than about 50 recognised the significance of the names in the text, and the process of discussing the connections through symbolism to Country and allusions to historical events lasted across a number of days and has inspired a thread of talk and song in the years since then.

The text includes allusion to the ancestral story and Dreamings that Clementine wanted to document and, through this song, pass on to her children. Line 6 is sung in the voice of the performer of the song (in this case, members of the women's group), telling the story of the brothers who (in the story) were singing at ceremony. Line 7 is sung in the voice of Clementine's father who says, in first person present tense, that Alungurumirri, the ancestral dog, is teaching the song (in the historical ceremony) to another female ancestor. This continues traditional practice, bringing the ancestor into the body of the performer and the story into the present. Line 8 returns to the voice of the (current) performer of the song, telling us how the ancestors are singing sorrow for the deceased (understood by most to be Clementine, and also, by the eldest listeners, to be the deceased for which the historical ceremony was performed).

The fact that it is Clementine who has passed on this knowledge through the song is embedded in the text with the inclusion of her Dreaming Piki Piki (Pig) (Line 9) as well as the bloodline of her brother (Line 6). There is reference to Crocodile in order to mark the Dreaming of her classificatory brother, a much older relation of her father's generation who was a leading songman. In Line 5 the reference to a female crocodile building a nest is taken to be a manifestation of Clementine, connecting her to a female ancestor with Crocodile Dreaming.

Song text 12: Clementine Puruntatameri. Mingatalini Mamanunkuni (Sorrow), 2011.

L1. Mantirijipi rijipi agayi, yatipili-wati winkirinjimi aga
The sound of the bird singing in the morning, lets us know that it's morning.

L2. **Mingatalini, Pilajimarri** Mamanunkuni pirratuwujingi-waya-mukuriyi
[Ancestors' names] sorrow they are singing.

L3. Ngini kamini nginjirriki-majiliya-punguni-ngiyatiyi naninga-nani ngawurayi
What has happened to my daughter? I lost her.

L4. Ngiya yimajulujinginta **Pirrawuyati Ngumanampi Juwunjirrati Ngurrumayi**
I am [Crocodile names]

L5. **Arntilimingila**, ampatilaya murrungumani jiwatipaki Juntuwingurrumumanyayi
She builds her nest she built it strong like a basket to protect it from the tide.

L6. **Tampurruwayi, Pilakirrawujimi** wuta pirratuwujingi-wangimiji, ngirringaniya
[Two brothers' names] they continued on with the songline calling out to their father

L7. Ngiya **Alungurumirri** pili ngiya-minijingikuwaluwamamni wangi **Marrakitijimawu** wangini
[Father speaking] I am Alungurumirri [name of the dog] so the dog says, "I am teaching you the song."

L8. **Purruntawulimi** ampatimingu-jurruwilingi-rrangiraga
[Ancestors' names] he is singing Mamanunkuni

L9. Jiwatiyingujingiwanga ngiya **Pikipikinga**
She calls herself I am (female) pig [Clementine speaking]

L10. Yirrikapayi kuruta-nguluwu kangi kulinjini
Crocodile is in that swampy area, in the water and long grass

L11. Mawunga awungaji ngimpitu-wu-ji-ngi-ma-jili-ki-rimani
Where she built that mound digging in the swamp

The words rijipi rijipi in Line 1 are an onomatopoeic reference to early morning birdcall and can be translated as "the sound of a bird that calls in the morning". Wati winkirinjimi is a linguistic marker for morning. Wati is the sung marker for morning. Kirinjimi or wunkirinjimi (which becomes win … when sung) means the sun rising or coming up.

I was told this line was especially clever and followed the old way because funerals are always held in the morning, so Clementine composed the song using the correct grammar; that is, the time-of-day words/affixes appropriate to the time at which she knew it would be sung. Clementine's skill at song poetry is evident in this text and the depth of associated meaning and use of old word forms[13] were often commented upon as the women learned the song in preparation for the funeral at which they would perform. It is regarded as probably the last song in the modern Kuruwala style to use "hard" words. The fact that Clementine composed this song for her own funeral added extra significance when the women sang it at her funeral in August that year and it is something which is still spoken about.

At Line 11, mawunga was translated as mound (the nest built by the crocodile). It is listed in the current Tiwi dictionary, however, as "native bee". Opinions differ: the mound looks like a beehive in its construction, perhaps, or native bees are sometimes found in discarded crocodile nests.

Tiwi singers find intellectual and artistic reward in composing songs that combine symbolism and therefore embed layered meaning within seemingly prosaic phrases. By combining the symbolism of kinship, Dreaming and the relevant ritual stage, the Country and/or family lineage of the deceased, and perhaps adding reference to the way somebody died or the anger the bereaved feel as well as using veiled or oblique symbolic references, many Tiwi songs become richly poetic and hold far more meaning to Tiwi listeners than to anyone attempting translation at face value.

The connection through song to the earth is pervasive. Mentions of water, for instance – in myriad forms (creeks, swamps, waterholes, waves, rain, tides) – give extra meaning to the actions, the placement of those actions, and the originating essence of identity through Yoi and through Yiminga. Country, Dreaming and kinship overlap in many song texts and again I can give only a few examples from the hundreds. Song texts 13 and 14 are sung by and for Turtle people.

---

13 There are some words that the women could not translate.

Song text 13: Yirripungiwayamirri George Norm. Kujupurruwatuwu (Turtle), 1975.

> Yitatayupu ngarawirtapu rrawurrijurru punjingami
> *At the coral at Tayupu the turtles are calling out [singing]*
>
> Purrunjerrawu rrinturrupunji ngapaluwu
> *The turtles sing in the deep water*
>
> Nitawarrawu nuwatipawu rriturrupunji ngayaputi
> *The tide coming up at Warrawu brings the turtles*
>
> Purratuwunji rrawurriturru punjingayama jikutuwa
> *The Turtle [Dreaming] people are there*

Song text 14: Jipwarlamparripa Stanley Munkara. Pajipajuwu (Turtle eggs), 1975.

> Nginingajipa jipajuwari ngintuwujirriki ningiyamaru rimijarra
> *Like the turtle's eggs are my many daughters*
>
> Pipiliyaku larritiyimur nupitimana menjirrikilimu ngarlingiyi
> *Pipiliyakularritiyi [in] Murnupi [Country] is worried for me.*

In Song text 13 (sung at Yilaniya) the turtles are the people who are dancing their Yoi. They are singing/calling out as they manifest and embody their Turtle Dreaming. Tayupu and Warrawu are coastal areas in the Country of the deceased and so the singers/dancers are also, through this song, in their Country. Yirripungiwayamirri (George Norm) sang at Yilaniya (Smoking) for his classificatory father. As "son" he was responsible for the holding of ceremony and for the composition of most of the songs. At this smoking stage he is setting the scene by describing the participants and their actions. The turtles singing are the people at the ceremony who share that Dreaming. The tide brings them in just as the dance brings them into the Milimika and the ritual itself brings them all together. Tayupu and Warrawu are in Munupi Country on the north-western coast of Melville Island, and turtles can be heard and seen in the waters and bays around there. The Munkara daughters mentioned in Song text 14 are hatchling turtles and the Country worries for the deceased. In both songs, the words were sung to focus on placing the deceased in Country and on the enactment of the ritual, which itself is enacting his journey to the land of his next existence.

Singing as classificatory mother (maternal uncle of the deceased), Romuel Puruntatameri presented the following (Song text 15) at Yilaniya (Smoking) at the start of Yiloti (Final Ceremony) at the Yoi for Pilampijimirri in Milikapiti in 1975.

3 Singing identity

Song text 15: Kilupwarlapiwiyi Romuel Puruntatameri. Wantangini (Firewood), 1975.

> Nginingajiwanjaputipurramaripiya kitimunga
> I put firewood in the boiler

Stoking the fire refers to the Yilaniya (Smoking) stage at which the song was presented. The boiler in this case serves as the ship's womb, and so the singer conveys his maternal uncle status and the performance context in one line. The fire inside the boiler is also understood by Tiwi listeners to convey the singer's pain and anger (hot or hurt inside) at his son's death.

As we have seen, across the song texts are a number of conventions of imagery that are widely used to imply particular meanings. A Tiwi listener will recognise the barbed spear as referring to senior men and the tunga basket to senior women. The tail of a crocodile is also very often referred to as the barbed spear (and this therefore can refer to male ancestors of Crocodile Dreaming). A song that describes flags strung up on a ship as being like flying foxes hanging off a branch; a revered man is a shooting star; a helicopter is a puffer fish; a man singing as he sweeps the sand dance-ground is a grader clearing a path. With most songs comprising some form of metaphor and/or symbolism it is safe to say that Tiwi songs are rarely (if ever) literal. One can presume that the songs composed across the millennia before the nineteenth century (the period from which songs in the archive first refer to non-Tiwi objects) comprised metaphorical references to the natural world, just as many songs in the archive do, and indeed as do songs being composed today. "I am the crocodile hiding in the mangroves. I (the brolga) sit high up watching over my Country." A songman sings, "Junglefowl clears his mound of sticks", and the audience hears the voice of a man of Junglefowl Dreaming as he clears the dance-ground for ceremony. Connecting ego to Country through song texts that draw the flora and fauna of a place with the actions of the people living in it, people through their Yoi are the embodiment of their ancestors – human and non-human – and of the Country from which all sprang. Everybody says, "He's *singing* Crocodile", not "He's singing *about* Crocodile." Note that the Aboriginal English verb "to sing" takes a direct object: in this case, Crocodile Dreaming.

In the songs recorded across the 20th century there are, not surprisingly (considering the contemporary nature of Tiwi composition), many songs with this same metaphorical poetry but with non-Tiwi objects where natural objects would likely have been. The Junglefowl clearing the dance-ground becomes the bulldozer or the grader. The Moonfish turning on the tide becomes the ship being caught on low tide. The fire glowing in the heart of the forest becomes the fire being stoked inside a ship's boiler. The composition of song as a vehicle for connecting kin – to each other and to ancestors – as a means of progressing through ritual stages and as a record of news and society has not changed in its structure or form, the devices of poetry and the oblique, veiled and multi-layered ritual connotations have not lessened with the introduction of non-Tiwi subject matter.

As I have said, this book is not the place to describe the Pukumani ceremonies themselves. There are descriptions of Pukumani in the literature which are the result of observations as far back as the early 20th century. I won't add anything to these except to suggest the reader keeps an open mind when reading them, especially the early ones, and that with the relationship between visiting anthropologists and Tiwi locals (with very little language in common), vast differences in cultural and religious points of view, and the power imbalance between white Australians and Indigenous Australians, it is likely that misunderstandings were recorded in print. I won't pretend to have a deeper understanding than researchers before me but I have, in the process of working with Tiwi custodians through audio recordings of Pukumani events that coincide with some of those written descriptions, discovered a number of misinterpretations or generalisations. It is important to recognise too that there is no "best" way to hold Pukumani, and perhaps there never was. The overarching structure of songs, rituals and dances is followed to enable those in attendance to move through the process of mourning, to pay respects in ritualised ways and allow for the cathartic release and lifting of emotional (both personal and social) sadness and restrictions. Just as the songs within Pukumani are occasion-specific, so too the ceremony itself is tailored to the people for and by whom it is held.

In the 21st-century Tiwi community, elements of the "ideal" or "traditional" practice of Pukumani-related procedures are being incorporated to different degrees in funerals and at Yiloti (Final Ceremony). The preliminary rituals (such as those at which a person's effects and regularly visited venues are smoked so that the spirit of the deceased is chased away or helped to move on, for instance, and the songs that would be sung with them) that are held immediately after the person's death are now sometimes performed on the return of the coffin to the family's home and/or either the evening before or the morning of the funeral. Many funerals also begin with a Catholic Mass, led by the (non-Tiwi) priest and include hymns and healing songs in English and in Tiwi. There is a varying amount of Yoi performed at a funeral (and sometimes none at all), depending on the wishes of the direct family members who make the arrangements.

3 Singing identity

Regardless of the relative amounts of Catholic and/or Tiwi ritual, it is essential that the Dreaming and kinship Yoi are performed. These bereavement kinship status songs (denoting the relationship of each person in attendance to the deceased), the Dreaming songs and the ritual activity songs (describing what is happening at various points of the proceedings) are performed at various stages throughout. The Yoi event (whether part of the longer Yiloti ceremony or the shorter funeral) is fundamentally about the group dynamic. The attendance of all people connected through kinship is essential and every person will dance the Yoi appropriate to their relationship with the deceased. Everyone knows their Dreaming dance. From a very young age, children are taught and encouraged to do so. By adulthood it is instinctive.

While the Pukumani rituals have changed, the role of the songs to support the main Yoi dance processes has not. As I will further explain in subsequent chapters, increasingly the role of the Strong Women's Group in creating a musical bridge between the traditions of Pukumani and the conventions of Catholicism is becoming relied upon. Their healing songs are being sung at Yilaniya and at Funeral alongside – and sometimes in the place of – the classical mortuary ritual songs. Their Kuruwala songs (explained in Chapter 7) also fulfil a function of passing on stories and recording important events, a continuation of much of the function of Kulama songs, the subject of the next chapter.

Chapter 4

Kulama

It comes from the Kulama, when they sing. Us old ladies, we understand what they're saying, what they're singing about. It's the old way of doing that. Old people used to do that in the past. They've been there, all the time. They were out in the bush – they did that – they had that knowledge, how they were, together, out in the bush. They had lots of words come in their mind and they sing about that. Old people used to tell us about that ... Today we have that knowledge passing down to our young people. Telling them about it. We try to bring them back. There's always culture there. In them, in us.

Jacinta Tipungwuti

This chapter is about the Kulama ceremony. Once the central activity of song composition performance and instruction for Tiwi people, its almost complete loss can be correlated to the loss of the old Tiwi language, with both having a large impact on the continuation of certain song-types in particular and song composition, song transmission and the skills of singing in general. While there have been various opinions as to the purpose of Kulama it is beyond doubt that it was central to the functioning of the Tiwi culture, with the primary goals and focus being the transmission of cultural knowledge and instruction in linguistic, artistic and musical skills. The importance of song to Tiwi society is made clear when one understands that a Tiwi man was fully initiated only when he composed his own song at Kulama. The Kulama-associated rituals and the main ceremony itself were structured by the performance of songs specifically composed for each stage, and instruction in the language, how to compose and how to sing were firmly embedded in the entire process. The regularity of song-focused activity (as all young Tiwi people moved through the initiation process) would have resulted in a community in which song composition was a far more widely practised skill than it is today.

Today, rather than Kulama being the vehicle for attaining knowledge, prestige and standing in the community, it has become the focus of that prestige, with knowledge of the actual ceremony and how to perform it becoming what people learn. Kulama is now spoken of with reverence, a remnant of the past that only a few older people feel strongly enough about to persevere with. The intricacies of song composition, so reliant upon a thorough knowledge of the language and on regular and repeated instruction and practice, are becoming beyond the reach of singers these days. Elders who know how to perform at Kulama are revered as holders of knowledge of a bygone era, rather than as active participants in an ongoing artistic tradition. The shift of Kulama from an all-inclusive schooling system to the preserve of a few culture-holders has rendered Kulama songs items of cultural heritage rather than a means of communication.

Before the arrival of the mission, the main Kulama ceremony, held annually over the course of three full days and nights at the start of the dry season, comprised numerous rituals: body painting, and singing and dancing, as well as the cooking, washing and eating of otherwise poisonous native yams according to specified methods. Fully initiated men and women composed and performed song and dance in order to ensure good health, community wellbeing and, most importantly, to ceremonially elevate young men and women through a series of initiation grades. Regular ceremonies meant that Tiwi singers lived within a sustained rich cultural atmosphere that was passed from one generation to the next with heuristic learning of extemporised composition through immersion at ceremony. Goodale notes:

> The aesthetic achievements are mentioned in connection with initiation, particularly one's ability to compose the songs. The presentation of one's first song was said to be the high point of the sequence of initiation. (Goodale 1970, 359)

A man was not considered adult and eligible for marriage until he had passed through all the stages of Kulama. It was only older men – who had gained respect and knowledge through initiation – who were in a position to partake in the reciprocity of wife bestowal among senior men.

Ideally one would ask Tiwi cultural leaders to explain Kulama, but as so much of its rituals has faded from all but the oldest memories, to a degree we do have to rely on anthropologists' observations and opinions of Kulama practitioners of the past. There are numerous descriptions in the literature of the Kulama ceremony, with differing opinions among researchers as to the exact reason for holding it (Brandl 1970; Goodale 1970; Grau 1983a; Hart and Pilling 1988; Osborne 1989; Spencer 1914). It is clear that Kulama was important for spiritual, intellectual and personal growth into adulthood (Goodale 1970; Grau 1983a; Lee 1987; Mountford 1958; Spencer 1914). It is, however, now impossible to say exactly what each stage signified. There is some difference of opinion as to the primary motivation behind the Kulama ceremony, and Elders today describe numerous spiritual, emotional, artistic and physical benefits of equal, interwoven value. Spencer was of the opinion that it was a ritual held in order to ensure good food supply (Spencer 1928). Mountford, Goodale, Grau and Lee have expressed different opinions, questioning the likelihood of a food-increase ritual in a place with such abundance of fauna, seafood and bush food as well as a relatively temperate climate. By all accounts, the preparation of the otherwise poisonous yam is symbolic. With so many other edible foods (including other types of yam) it is very unlikely that this yam would become relied upon as a food source. One theory of the yam's significance in the ceremony, postulated by Goodale (1970), is that it may have taken on the symbolic embodiment of the harmful magic that had been brought to the islands by the Iwaidja in about 1913.[1] She suggests that as Kulama's role in long-term initiation receded, the cleaning and preparation of the yam became the focus of a relatively new need for ritual cleansing (against the magic). As the years have gone by, the shift of emphasis from young initiates to the yam has made it more abstract and now, in a modern world, less meaningful to the everyday lives of the people.

If we are to fully understand the effect the almost complete loss of the Kulama ceremony has had on the art of Tiwi song composition, we must attempt to understand the course of and reasons for its dwindling over the past century. The main thing to make clear is that, pre-mission, the Kulama ceremony consisted of not only one annual event (called the Kulama ceremony) but also of two associated rituals held months apart, and a number of intermediate periods of instruction given by Elders to young initiates.

There are a number of descriptions of the annual Kulama ceremony in the literature (Brandl 1970; Goodale 1970, 1974; Grau 1983a; Hart 1930; Mountford 1958; Osborne 1989; Spencer 1914). Maria Brandl made recordings of 190 Kulama songs and an unknown number of mortuary songs.

---

1   Goodale also cites a discussion among the men at Kulama held from 30 April to 3 May 1954: "the people of the island are small in numbers, because the white people brought other tribesmen into this land who sang magic songs of poison that caused the tribe to dwindle" (Goodale 1974, 224). My eldest consultants also tell stories they heard in their childhood of poison and sickness that came with the Iwaidja and wondered if that "magic" might have been disease brought from the mainland.

Unfortunately, all of these were lost in Cyclone Tracy in 1974. Mountford suggests that in 1954 the pattern of the annual Kulama ceremony itself had hardly changed from that which Spencer described in 1912. He does, however, also state that the related, but separately performed, rituals associated with Kulama initiation had ceased entirely (Mountford 1958).

Although Grau witnessed a number of the main Kulama ceremonies during her fieldwork in 1981, she wrote that:

> Since the fifties all the information we have about the [associated] initiation is second hand, what informants told the anthropologists should happen rather than what the anthropologists witnessed themselves. (Grau 1983a, 155)

While we therefore cannot make assumptions about the exact nature of these associated rituals, we can form a picture of a society in which ritual activity was regularly occurring.

The following overview of Kulama is based on what would have been the complete set of rituals, keeping in mind that all but the three-day annual Kulama yam ceremony had gone out of practice by 1954. I do not intend to describe the rituals as this has been done in previous research (see above) but I will explain Kulama's place in Tiwi society in terms of it being the focal point of education in linguistic, cultural and artistic matters and how, when it was performed in full, it provided an ongoing source of newly composed songs.

The role of Kulama in education

The path to full initiation for Tiwi youth comprised, along with instruction in kinship systems and basic skills for life, a comprehensive bestowal of the linguistic, musical and intellectual skills needed to compose the songs required for regular ceremonies that were central to Tiwi social and spiritual life.

There were six grades of initiation to progress through, with the initiate moving up a grade at each annual Kulama ceremony. Other ritual events were held throughout the year. One, for instance, occurred a few weeks after the annual Kulama, to introduce a new round of initiates. Another marked the progression from grade two to grade three, and another involved the collecting of the Kulama yams that were used in the main ceremony. When the full initiation process was in action there would have been some form of Kulama ritual going on every few months, and at any one time there would have been young men and women at various stages of initiation, so some were leading up to the annual Kulama while others were following up after it. Based on his fieldwork in 1928–29, Hart gives a brief explanation of the stages of the associated rituals. He calls Kulama "periodic collective ceremonies when the youth was ritually advanced from one stage of initiation to the next" (Hart and Pilling 1988, 103).

With the initiation process beginning at about age ten (involving girls as well as boys (Spencer 1914, 94)) and with approximately six years' instruction, Kulama can be regarded as having been a form of schooling. That this was a long, ongoing and continuous part of a youth's life is also evident in the literature (Gsell 1955; Ritchie 1934) and the memories of Elders. Hart reports the practice of removal of young men for initiation between about 14 and 24 years of age at various periods during the year for individual secluded instruction, in a relationship with their Elder instructors not unlike that of monk and novice, learning "all the things – chiefly ritual matters – that grown men should know" (Hart and Pilling 1988, 103). He also makes the point that the long periods of instruction in isolation, elaborate body painting (that must remain intact for months so was constantly renewed) and periodic ritual restrictions on food handling meant that for much of the year a large proportion of the young male population was not available for hunting or provision of food to the family group. He contrasts this with mainland communities and suggests this is an indication of the wealth and security the Tiwi people enjoyed, leaving more time for artistic and intellectual pursuits. All aspects of the Kulama rituals involved singing, and so a large part of instruction focused on attaining the skills required for song composition. The poetic intricacies, knowledge of Country and ancestral lore, as well as metrical rules needed to compose were imparted by senior men over the course of these years of instruction.

Grau, Goodale and Brandl in particular have made interesting observations on the changes that have occurred in the practice, goals and relevance of Kulama over the mid-20th century (Brandl 1970; Goodale 1970; Grau 1983a). One of the most important changes was to the motivation for initiation. With the changes to the Tiwi marriage system brought about by the arrival of the Catholic mission in 1912 – the most profound of which was the cessation of a polygamous system (see Goodale 1974; Gsell 1955) – the need for a long initiation period through Kulama was no longer apparent. Father (later Bishop) Gsell, a French priest of the Missionaries of the Sacred Heart, is famously known for his "150 wives" (Gsell 1955): the female children he removed from their families between 1921 and 1938 in order to stop the traditional Tiwi system of family structures that did not adhere to the values of Catholicism. In the past the reciprocal bestowal of wives occurred between senior initiated men. Whereas in the past a man was eligible to marry only once he was fully initiated, the end of the Tiwi marriage system over the course of a generation meant men could marry at a much younger age, and without the former prerequisite initiated status.

A contributing factor was that most Bathurst Island children, and many from Melville Island, were at the mission school (the girls boarding full-time) and so were not able to spend time with their Elders, with attendance at Kulama either discouraged or banned. It was only after they had left school that Tiwi people took part in Kulama (if they were interested in reconnecting with their culture). By 1954 the age at which initiation began had moved to at least 30 years, with those seen as ready for initiation being "a mature man, usually married and with children" (Mountford 1958, 128). It can be safely assumed that at least part of the reason for the demise of Kulama was mission opposition to local ritual practice.[2] "There is no doubt that this decline in the initiation procedures over the years is largely due to the influence of the Catholic Mission" (Grau 1983a, 156). The initiation function of Kulama was no longer regarded as essential to the path towards adulthood. Rather, the focus began to shift to learning the ritual procedures and singing skills required to perform the Kulama ceremony itself, and so become a respected cultural Elder. Venbrux states:

> Pragmatically, the initiation procedures were shortened and limited to the performances of the yam ritual … Tiwi call this initiation "short cut" and it must be seen as very different from the pre-mission period when all men were kept from marrying until they had completed initiation. (Venbrux 1995, 29)

Kulama did not cease entirely though, and in February and March 1981 Andrée Grau witnessed four Kulama ceremonies. She sums up the changes that had occurred:

> Initiates were still "captured" and they had to perform certain rites during preliminary mortuary rituals … but they did not have to go through all the grades until it was time for them to take part in the Kulama as full participants composing and singing songs for all the stages of the ceremony. (Grau 1983a, 156)

Grau mentions Mickey Geranium Warlapini as one of the last remaining men who had been through all the initiation stages. He was born in 1905 and so he would have been close to the final stage of initiation at the age of about 23, when C.W.M. Hart was on the islands in 1928. In 1975 he sang for Osborne's recorder and by 1981 he was a highly respected Elder and culture man. Grau also mentions Justin Puruntatameri among the few initiated men who were able

---

2   Priests' opposition to Kulama and to Tiwi burial rituals is reported by Elders who themselves witnessed it, and in Goodale (1974), Hart and Pilling (1988), and Morris (2003).

to perform Kulama in 1981. Mr Puruntatameri learned to sing from Mickey Warlapini. At Justin's request, I worked with him and his daughters in 2010–12, transcribing his own songs, recorded by Charles Osborne in 1975, so that Justin could use them to teach young people how to compose.[3] He lived in Pirlingimpi, and mourned the loss of Kulama there since, as he told me, "everybody's gone and I'm too old to hold one on my own". In this song, composed by Justin in 1970, he is (his Dreaming) Kirilima (Junglefowl) preparing the Milimika (dance-ground) on the afternoon of the second day of Kulama.

Song text 16: Justin Puruntatameri song for Kulama 1970.

> Ngiajipilontiya jimaturrawukarirrapijimirri
>
> Maka ningani kirirrawukuwayi Ngiwanjirrikilontiyipunjingamani
>
> *I am the Junglefowl calling out as I do my work clearing and scratching in the ground.*

Kulama songs told of ancestral lineage, personal achievements and important contemporary events, using a poetic artistic medium to entertain and inform, forming an oral living public record. The Tiwi had no need for a printed register of births, deaths and marriages, honour roll, a dictionary, a bible or an almanac. All such knowledge and information were put into songs. Everybody aspired to sing at Kulama and everyone was expected, when they were ready, to create their own new musical work. This inclusiveness meant that Tiwi people lived in a richly artistic atmosphere. At the main annual Kulama ceremony, songs were performed in order to satisfy various social, spiritual and community needs. Songs of all or some of the six functions listed in Figure 10 were observed by Mountford and Goodale in 1954 (Goodale 1970; Mountford 1958), Brandl in 1969 (Brandl 1970) and Osborne in 1975 (Osborne 1989).

Figure 10: Functional classification of Kulama songs and their use in ceremonial context.

- Mourning songs: Remembering deceased loved ones.
- Grievance songs: Airing issues of concern.
- Songs about fathers or patrilineal Dreamings: Similar in function to mourning songs.
- Free-subject songs for entertainment: Serving as the community noticeboard.

---

3   There had been plans to bring young men to Pirlingimpi to spend time with Justin in informal teaching sessions on Kulama and song in general, but Mr Puruntatameri died in August 2012, aged 87 years.

- Songs to summon spirits of putiputuwi (unborn children) and to bestow names on babies and young children.
- Ritual activity songs, descriptive of each of the stages of the ritual.

Within this framework the songs of the Kulama ceremony were a vehicle for teaching, healing, reverence, social discourse, familial connection and artistic outlet. As it involved all ages and was based on innovation, the recorded song texts display a richly poetic overlapping of contemporary society with tradition. On the second day of Kulama, for example, the Milimika (the central performance area) was cleared in preparation for subsequent activities. Songs composed for this stage allude to clearing in some way: birds scratching at the dirt or a bulldozer clearing an area in town. Songs sung at the ritual washing stage (the evening of the second day, when the participants are ritually cleansed of their ochre paint and "reborn" higher up in the initiation process) tell of water, rain, and canoe or boat journeys. By extension of the theme of newness are songs about children and visitors (strangers). Through context-specific subject matter, songs alluded to ritual and added to the oral transmission of cultural knowledge. Among the recordings made by Mountford in 1954 is a song "for placement of yams in centre of Milimika".[4] The text was translated by Tiwi listeners as: "You have money in your pocket and you grabbed two packets of cards." The cards are symbolic of the yams and so fulfil both a ritual function and allow the performer to air a grievance at the same time. Another song recorded by Mountford tells the singer's audience that he has dreamed his unborn children. He sings with the aspirations of a proud parent that they will wear shoes and go to school. Again we find current subject matter being used in a traditional ritual context.

Fundamentally important to society were the songs "put up"[5] at Kulama in which fathers told of having found their unborn child, allowing them to progress to being born, and the naming of children.

The role of Kulama in social politics

As well as having great significance in terms of initiation, Kulama had a very important function in that it provided a public forum, a neutral place where anyone could, in the context of song, air a grievance, bring up a topic for discussion or get out in the open something that had been bothering them. "Singing it into Kulama" (as older people put it) placed the issue above reproach and gave the

---

4   At Audio 13, Mountford's voice is heard on the field tape.
5   A term used by senior songmen to refer to presenting a new song at a Yoi or Kulama.

singer the opportunity to make it known to people, in what functioned as a sort of "ceremonial truce" (Goodale 1974, 188). While using ambiguity and no direct names, everybody would know what the singer was referring to. Social responsibilities, obligations and hierarchies of respect were all embedded in the songs of Kulama. The loss of Kulama has been cited by many older Tiwi people as being part of the reason for much of the social dysfunction and disconnection of youth around the community. Without these three days of song and dance as the end-goal of initiation, there is also now no vehicle for the instructional connection between Elders and youth that used to occur.

Venbrux notes a number of occasions outside the ceremonial context when a song is performed seemingly on the spur of the moment in direct response to a need to clear the air, defend one's reputation or put forward one's point of view in a public setting (Venbrux 1995). Among the repatriated recordings there are songs pertaining to disputes over money owed, family obligations, and agreements (or disagreements) between men over "promised" women or proclamations of their intentions towards specific women. I have not heard of this happening today, although one Tiwi woman told me that about 15 years ago (when she had been recently widowed) a man sang his intentions towards her at Kulama. She told me that she sang back that she wasn't interested. While listening through cassette tapes of Kulama ceremonies at the Literature Production Centre at Nguiu in 2010, Marguerita Kerinaiua came across a Yoi that caused her to chuckle. She told me, "He's complaining he wasn't paid enough for the Pukumani pole he painted."

In today's circumstances, where Kulama is not often held nor well attended, these grievance songs can be sung at any stage. Stephen-Paul Kantilla described an occasion when he felt he had been treated disrespectfully by a younger man. Rather than risk a physical altercation or create ongoing or escalating bad feeling, he chose to "put up" a song at Kulama in which he asserted his position as a respected Elder by singing his names and Country affiliations. By presenting through song his ancestry and affiliations, he pointed out the wrong the younger man had committed against him and made clear his high standing in the community. He then used that song again at the club to resolve the matter once and for all:

> So when I go into the club and I say to that man – sing a song, you know. That man, the young boy like that he said, "Oh you're nothing" so I sang that Kulama for a long time. That's my pagan name: Jamingi. My uncle calls me that. That man, he was listening to me that I sing to him at the club like [whispering] we drink and argue. "Old man, you're nothing" and I sing a Kulama song. That one I got from old people. "That old man,

my uncle called me name" I said to him, and he believed me. It's in the Kulama song so he has to believe me. Now he won't talk to [bother] me again … We have to follow those rules.

Grievance songs are not sung so much these days, more because of the shrinking occurrence of Kulama and the very small numbers of people involved. Justin Puruntatameri told me, "If we do Kulama now, we want to be happy and make peace. We feel proud and don't fight, you know? We just sing together to make things good. No fighting anymore at Kulama, too important." From his words I got the sense that, with only the old men holding Kulama these days, it is more a restorative, spiritually important ritual, whereas in the past when everyone was involved, the grievance-songs stage of Kulama was more utilitarian and so these songs were prevalent.

The role of Kulama songs in social history

The annual Kulama ceremony is held to ensure spiritual and personal health and wellbeing. Deceased loved ones are mourned and celebrated, babies are named, young people are taught about culture and ceremony. During the third day of Kulama, the Ayipa songs are presented to negotiate community affairs and to put current events and important news on record. Among the recorded archive are Ayipa songs announcing marriages, outside intruders, shipwrecks, shark attacks, the first electric light, a meteor shower, cyclone damage and the moon landing. Among the 1928 recordings is an Ayipa song about singing into a white man's gramophone recorder (see Song text 4 and Audio 72).

The songs in Kulama are not connected into "song cycles" or "sets" that have a connecting narrative or theme. The songs presented by each individual do not therefore have any meaning in association with each other but stand alone. "Each singer's songs are an independent contribution to the ritual, composed and performed without any reference to any of the songs of any of the other singers" (Osborne 1989, 600). Each stage of the ritual does, however, comprise a collection of songs with similar function. The sorrow songs form the main part of the first evening of Kulama, for example, the free-subject news-telling songs are the focus of the third day, and the other songs related to community business and the activities of the ritual are scattered throughout the second day and evening.

The songs sung at Ayipa, on the third day of Kulama, in effect create an aural public noticeboard. Ayipa is the part of the Kulama ceremony where the newest composition is done. It is the singer's opportunity to impress their audience and Ayipa songs are anticipated with interest. Even today, with Kulama infrequently held, songmen talk about what they might sing at Ayipa. These are topical songs (also known as purakutukuntinga or "talk about" songs)[6] because their subject matter covers current events and items of novelty. Although Ayipa is a functional classification, rather than a musical one, Ayipa is also referred to as a style, indicating the composition and performance techniques involved in creating an Ayipa song. As well as being performed on the last day of Kulama they are also sung at the end of Yiloti ceremony, or these days at non-ceremonial occasions.

The oral record contained in the reclaimed recordings of Kulama songs has provided a rich historical record for the Tiwi community. Figure 11 gives a snapshot of the subjects covered in Ayipa songs among the recorded material to show the currency of subject matter for each year. Most songs recorded at Kulama are not repeated because the subject matter was contemporary to the time of performance. A particularly clear example of this is among the recordings made by Doolan in 1967.[7] Four songs, sung concurrently, tell of a current item of news: the singer getting in trouble over drinking and fighting; his attending the magistrate's court; the trial; and the reporting of the trial in the local (Darwin) newspaper. At Audio 10 is a performance by Justin Puruntatameri of an Ayipa song he composed in Kulama in 1970 noting a film he had recently seen on television about a genie.

It is interesting to note too that we can see the emergence of some song subjects as "favourites" being performed for various researchers. A song telling of the Japanese air raid on Darwin in 1942, for example, was first recorded by Simpson in 1948. Elders say that it would definitely have first been "put up" at Kulama in 1942. Bathurst Island was strafed during the raid and, with Kulama being held only a matter of weeks afterwards, it would have been a significant recent topic. Variations of the text have been sung at subsequent performance events, being filmed in a public performance at the Royal Botanic Gardens, Darwin, in 1948[8] recorded by Mountford in 1954, by Moyle in 1976 (at the Pacific Festival in Rotorua in New Zealand) as well as by Holmes in that same year. It has become a popular song often performed at public events by the Ngarukuruwala group in both the "traditional" and the "modern Kuruwala" style. Among the archival recordings there are also recurrences of songs about Fort Dundas (the British settlement on Melville Island in the years 1824–28), sailing ships and steamships, Japanese pearlers, army bases (American and Australian army personnel were

---

6   In the context of her study of dance, Andrée Grau called these "just a dance" Yoi (Grau 1983).
7   See List of audio examples: Doolan J02-000628A 00:29:35.
8   NT Archives, *Darwin – Doorway to Australia* (1949), C809, 1139364, Northern Territory Archives, Darwin.

stationed on the islands during the Second World War) and cyclones, as they would have had a significant impact on the social history of the islands. These songs, rediscovered as a result of the repatriation of the recordings, now provide a rich social history that is a source of great local interest.

Figure 11: Selection of Ayipa song subjects that were current news the year they were sung.

1912 (Spencer)	1928 (Hart)	1948 (Simpson)	1954 (Mountford)	1967 (Doolan)	1975 (Osborne)
- Steamship - Joe Cooper - Building houses - Train - Flour and tobacco - Using a saw - Sailing boat stuck in low tide	- Tractor - Boat - Man o'war ship - Gramophone - Man from the mainland - Announcement of impending tribal fight	- Visiting dentist - Bombing of Darwin - Japanese lover - A boy being taken by a shark	- Telephone - Going to Brisbane for the Queen's visit - Mission farm garden - Clearing trees for the airstrip - Policeman - Meteor - Wet season storm - Tractor	- Japanese pearlers - New local aeroplane - Magistrate's court trial - Being mentioned in the newspaper	- Cyclone Tracy - 1969 moon landing - Cowboy movie - Genie (from a movie) - Helicopter - Bulldozer - A visiting military band - Television

The role of Kulama in maintaining an artistic space

When Kulama was strong the Tiwi contemporary music scene was vibrant and busy. With numerous ceremonies (associated with Kulama and with Pukumani) held each year and with numerous singers composing especially for them, there would have been hundreds of new and topical songs on the oral playlist. The degree of novelty that was in Tiwi song composition cannot be overstated. Osborne lists 128 song subjects among the recordings he studied (Osborne 1989, 1275–79) and states that the Tiwi "are entirely without any body of traditional song" (Osborne 1989, 114), and that all songs are new to each ceremony or performance event.

One's creative talent was a matter of pride. In a community where everybody sang, there was a wealth of invention and a satisfaction in performing for each other and respecting the achievement of clever, beautiful or witty song texts. Goodale reports a consultant telling her that one's songs "must be newly composed or 'everyone would laugh at them if they sang an old song'" (Goodale 1974, 354). What Grau calls "just a song" dances were also created in this context of artistic innovation. Just as songs were created by individuals, so too were numerous dances that were performed by individuals. As well as the Dreaming dances that have been passed down patrilineally (and so have a continuity and conformity of actions and performance style), there is record of numerous unique/one-time dances. They were created by individuals either for entertainment or within Kulama or Pukumani ceremonies. The scope of action/gesture and movement is as broad in this category as there are composers. Generally these can be described as narrative dances,[9] telling a story acted out in mime and danced actions, the story being told by the composer as they sing. Some of these happened only once and we know about them either through their description in the written literature (Goodale 1974; Grau 1983; Mountford 1958; Simpson 1951) or in people's memories and retellings. Goodale describes a dance performed by Allie Miller Mungatopi at the point of Pukumani when the workers were to be paid[10] that told a fictional story of him stealing money and being locked up by the police, before creating a shop window through which workers are paid. He enlisted the help of family who danced the actions of pretending to be in handcuffs and then handing the money through the imaginary window and miming signing a receipt. This song/dance was just one imaginative treatment of this regular stage of Pukumani. Another is documented in the film *Good-bye Old Man, Or the Film of Tukuliyangenila (A Film About Mangatopi): A Tiwi Island Bereavement Ceremony* (MacDougall 1977) in which the singer dances as Crocodile with cash in his mouth. Another (which has been repeated and expanded into non-ceremonial contexts) is the Yinjula dance/song about the old blind lady that was danced/sung at Yiloti by men and women and which now has become a Kuruwala-style song performed by the Elder women out of ceremonial context. Some of the narrative or "just a song" dances enact stories symbolic to parts of the ritual while some are related to the news and storytelling segment of the Kulama ceremony. These are equally numerous and unrepeated, with subjects such as building houses with a saw, building canoes, cyclones and tribal fights. Some of these become favoured and repeated and enter the repertoire, perhaps aided by having been recorded and/or performed at non-ceremonial events, including those held for non-Tiwi researchers and audiences. It has been suggested by Elders that this is also how some seemingly incongruous non-Tiwi Dreamings have entered the culture. Some people dance "Ship", "Horse" or "Buffalo" as their Yoi, as ships on the horizon and introduced

---

9   Goodale coined this term (Goodale 1974, 304) and it fits well, although she also makes a distinction between dances that "are not traditional" and those that "have become traditional", which I will not. As I explained in Chapter 1, "traditional" is a term that sits uncomfortably in a description of a continuing cultural practice.
10 I explain this more elsewhere. Those who carve and paint the Pukumani poles and those who dance in particular roles are paid (palingarri payment would be in goods; today it is in cash).

horses and buffalo came to be associated with their traditional Country. These might initially have been narrative dances created at some stage in the past two centuries ("Ship" perhaps earlier), which were so well received they were repeated and became so popular among the family group of their creators that they became the mascots of those groups. These of course are relatively recent totems compared with the deep-past totems such as Crocodile, Junglefowl, and the other endemic animals and beings, but they have equally strong significance and association to Country for those people who dance them.

Grau notes that "there are many such dances and the repertoire keeps growing up, the Tiwi value innovation and creativity and they are prolific choreographers" (Grau 1983a, 246). When my consultants were shown photos of performers (taken by Grau), those older than about 50 years of age recognised the "just a song" dances recorded by Grau (Grau 1983a, 247–59). While they said they would have had accompanying songs, none of them (or the dances) is still performed, apart from the Yinjula Old Woman song (that I mention in Chapter 7) and the aeroplane dance (now performed as the Bombing of Darwin). Although I am not qualified to comment on the state of Tiwi dance, I am prepared to say that in my experience over the past 15 years I have not been made aware of any new dances. Further, in comparison to those recorded by Grau in the 1980s, there are fewer dances, mostly confined to the Dreaming dances connected with Yoi events. We can therefore surmise that there is a correlated shrinking of innovation in dance and in song, as Kulama, the main vehicle for song/dance performance, has dwindled.

In an understandable response to the perceived and actual reduction of knowledge of the traditional song and dance composition skills, it is easier to teach (and to learn) by rote a set of items than it is to teach the process of composition. Eustace Tipiloura explained:

> There used to be lots more dances … people made them for themselves, you know. Now we just dance the same ones all the time. Like the songs. Not many new ones anymore. Maybe we have to start singing the old ones instead because no-one is making new ones anymore.

As well as telling news in the Ayipa stage of Kulama, Tiwi singers used current topics to symbolically refer to ritual, bereavement and kinship, and simply for entertainment. Contemporary song subjects also appear in Yilaniya, the Pukumani-associated ceremony in the Jipuwakirimi/Yoi song-type and in Mamanunkuni (sorrow) songs. A sorrow song by Dorothy Tipungwuti (recorded by Osborne in 1975)[11] refers to the deceased being jealous, imagining he is seeing his wife on television with another man (the television being a very recent arrival at the time) and the television is, in this case, the vehicle for the placement of grief. As I discuss further in relation to song language in Chapter 5, Tiwi songs are richly metaphoric and have layered meanings, in the majority of cases using subject matter contemporary to the time.

Some songs did come to be repeated or reworked, and there are consequently a few songs that have been passed down through Kulama leaders, probably due to the significance of the historical event they describe, the important ancestor they name or the prestige the composer held. As I have mentioned in the context of Yoi, with fewer new songs being composed, these set pieces are becoming more valued and more often repeated.

As instruction in song through regular Kulama participation dwindled, the task of learning to compose became more difficult and a class of songman or woman emerged. While singing had always been a highly respected skill, it now became something just a few specialised in, having shown particular talents. Goodale mentions a particular man being singled out for initiation, having shown promise as a singer (Goodale 1970). Venbrux, who undertook fieldwork in 1988, mentions two men in their fifties who had tried but been unable to compose the "intricate and complex kulama songs … They hoped the seven grades of initiation would be restored so they and others would be able to learn in small steps and at a slower pace" (Venbrux 1995, 122).

Many of the songs performed in Kulama used contemporary subject matter while fulfilling traditional ritual function. The actual ritual is not usually mentioned, but the symbolism (that would have been apparent to initiated attendees) is strong. This is another facet of the process of repatriating the old songs, as most songs have topics which at surface level might seem secular, but which hold deep ritual symbolism – much of which is lost to Tiwi people listening to the songs today. One of the benefits of the return of old recordings is that many of the songs describe the process of the ritual itself and so provide a potential teaching resource. The reality is that the future of Kulama is very tenuous and all Elders agree that if it is to survive, it will be in a quite different form. It is no longer at the centre of linguistic, poetic and musical innovation, and social discourse but is now regarded as a culturally esoteric and ritualised art form, knowledge of which is held by only a few.

---

11   See List of other recorded material in the AIATSIS archive. Song 206 in Doolan, C04-003855B-206.

In Wurrumiyanga in 2012 there were three men (one aged 28, and two in their mid-thirties) who were regarded as "being initiated", which meant that they were learning the songs required for Yoi at funerals and ceremonies and that they would attend the Kulama held in 2012. One of them was doing this in the context of being a cultural leader and the other two because they were active singers of (non-Tiwi) contemporary music and had been targeted by the senior men and women to potentially take over from them.

Grau had already noted 40 years earlier:

> None of the writers looked at the problems for the men of learning, since they started to take a "short cut", as the Tiwi put it, not only the ritual procedures, but also the composition techniques and singing styles, learning which over the years had ceased to be acquired formally but which somehow the men had to make theirs in order to take part in the Kulama. (Grau 1983a, 156)

Old men and women I speak to now reminisce about when they were younger and they had what they now realise was a privileged opportunity to hear and learn from the last generation of men with any degree of initiation. The situation now is that as a result of changes to Kulama over the years its function as instruction in song composition has ceased entirely. The passing on of song composition techniques is no longer embedded in the formalised system of Kulama initiation but is reliant on individuals having the time and the inclination to learn, or to teach.

A small group of older men decided to have Kulama at the beginning of May 2010, after many years with no ceremony held. The decision by these men to have Kulama had come about after some heated discussions about the impending demise of Kulama and the senior men's responsibilities in terms of its survival in particular and of Tiwi culture in general. Eustace Tipiloura explained:

> Me, Walter, Stephen-Paul, Roger were there and Brian Wonaemura and Francis, Damon, the young fellas. We went Saturday night, Sunday, Monday, Tuesday morning. I taught the young ones. Very slowly, repeating the words so they could pick them up. They were a bit nervous but I said, "You'll be right, the second time will be easier and then the third time even better."

Speaking to me in 2010, Stephen-Paul Kantilla touched on the change that happened to Kulama. It is now something that is passed on, in the hands of custodians, to be preserved. There is the sense that it is only when the old men pass away that the younger ones will start singing in their place and that it has now become a case of preservation – saving intact what is left – rather than maintenance – passing on the skills of composition.

> I learned the Kulama from the old man ... [Bertram Kantilla] – I called him Uncle, like Dad. I went there when I was young boy to learn ... So he used to sing and I learned from him ... When my voice is good enough they say I'm ready. When I was probably about 60. When all those people passed away then I take over, that's why – so young people can come along and learn, the young ones, so when we pass away they have to take over ... So we have to sing that and the young ones have to learn now ... Hard to learn. Hard words, maybe later on.

At time of writing, Eustace, Walter, Roger and Stephen-Paul have all passed away. Two of those men who were learning in 2010 have emerged as senior singers in mortuary ceremonies and as cultural leaders for broader community matters. They still rely heavily on the few Elders, in their eighties, who overtly direct proceedings and correct or suggest text of songs put up for a funeral or Final Ceremony. The fact that they are learning "on the job" as they perform is an accepted necessity in the new reality of cultural maintenance. There is a clear correlation between fewer Kulama events and fewer trained singers/composers. It is a widely held view that singing incorrectly at Kulama is dangerous and disrespectful and so young people are loath to try to compose if they are unsure. As I will expand upon in Chapter 5, Old Tiwi is still considered essential for song composition, but it is all but lost. Kulama is now regarded as a piece of ritual to be preserved as an artistic and intellectual pursuit, for Elders (with the knowledge) and those younger people with incentive to learn "culture". It is now an esoteric rather than a pervasive and inclusive event and, because it has lost much of its social currency, it is no longer regarded as essential, but more of a relic of the past and of old, revered traditions. Elders have deep concerns for the spiritual balance of their society in which the positivist, renewing, discursive and instructional benefits of participation in Kulama are no longer experienced.

The art of creating extemporised song is less likely to survive than those songs that are required for the Yoi event in mortuary rituals. The deaths of senior culture men and women in the past ten years has had a devastating effect on the morale of Elders in the context of Kulama song culture. Although there is relatively detailed anthropological description of Kulama, there remains only a few men and one woman who can perform all of the required songs and the ritual processes, so the ceremony is at great risk of becoming at best an item of historical cultural heritage, reproduced for educational or tourist events rather than being a living practice. They feel a strong sense of obligation to help each other maintain and share the knowledge they have. They are aware of a looming vacuum of singers, and people are seeing a real need to create some form of teaching young Tiwi men and women that does not rely on oral transmission and immersive learning. At time of writing there is renewed interest in sustained development of engagement between young Tiwi adults and their Kulama traditions. Elements of Kulama have been held by a small group of men and women (but in the absence of younger learners or initiands) and at a few of those events, the local school took children to observe during school hours. Although the performance and observation of and participation in Kulama has become a "special event" and one certainly of heritage value rather than of normal life, its place in Tiwi culture is being increasingly valued again.

This leads me to the next topic essential to understand in the study of Tiwi song: the Tiwi language, how it has changed over the past two generations, and how that change has had an impact on engagement with and creation of song.

Chapter 5

The Tiwi Language(s)

You think about it and whisper it when you walking out bush or along the street, you think about it and the words come straight into your mind … some is what you want to put in, what you have to say, you know? Some is what just comes up, comes into your ears or maybe if you're asleep, in your dream. Then you sing at ceremony. The words have to fit. The sounds of them. That's what is important.

Eustace Tipiloura

The spoken language

Although spoken language is not the focus of this book, it is necessary to have some understanding of how the language has changed over the last century in order to appreciate the difficulties faced by Elders trying to maintain song culture, as well as the varying nature of engagement with the old song recordings. What Jane Goodale reported in the 1980s is relevant today:

> The composing of songs and performing of specific dance routines is still being transmitted to the younger generation, but not with as much emphasis or success as the elders wish. Part of the difficulty, they say, is the decline in language skills among those whose education is mainly, if not entirely, in English. (Goodale 1988, 142)

The fact that song relies on language may seem obvious. What needs to be explained here is that Tiwi song relies on a language that is no longer spoken. In this chapter I will therefore give a brief account of the Tiwi language situation in order to make clear just how tenuous the hold is on traditional song composition practice.

Charles Osborne's work *The Tiwi Language* (Osborne 1974) remains the major document on Old Tiwi language in terms of definitive analysis of word and grammatical structure.[1] When discussing songs that have been transcribed by Osborne, I present his transcriptions. In order that they are meaningful to contemporary Tiwi readers I have changed some spelling to conform to Lee's orthography.[2] Because much of my transcription of song texts from the repatriated recordings has been done phonetically, with the help of Tiwi singers who do not speak the language used in the songs, there have been differences of opinion as to how to spell various words. The variations between Old Tiwi, Modern Tiwi and New Tiwi create room for interpretation and choices of spelling.

Past researchers have each used their own orthography and so we find in the literature numerous spellings for many Tiwi words. For example, the Tiwi name of Allie Mungatopi is currently spelled Warabutiwayi. Simpson spells it Oruputuwae (1951) and Holmes spells it Wurraputiwai (1995). The town on Melville Island known in English as Garden Point is a good example of orthographic and phonemic inconsistency within one word. This site is currently spelled Pirlingimpi, with each /i/ pronounced slightly differently in the word itself and by individuals. The first three vowels sound like the schwa and the final like *ee* in "bee". The /ng/ is also variable, sometimes sounding closer to /mp/ and /r/, and so the town name is spelled across the written corpus Purlangimpi, Pilarumpi, Pulungimpi, Pulangimpe and (the current signage on the local primary school) Pularumpi.

A number of phonetic changes in the language (as a result of its transition from Old to Modern Tiwi) are described by Lee (1987, 33–48) and I have found that there are many phonetic differences between the singers in recordings taken in the 1960s and 1970s (within the corpus of songs in Old Tiwi). Some phonological changes might be a result of a word being removed from use because it is too close to the name of a deceased person and then having changed slightly by the time it returns. Some changes in consonants over the period 1930 to 1970 (in Old and Modern Tiwi) are documented by Mountford (1958) and Osborne (1974) and verified by Elders, who remember old people speaking in "the old way". These are manifest in the recordings of 1912, 1928 and 1954. Comparing the texts of songs recorded by Spencer with those recorded by Osborne, we can hear that there is

---

1   Aidan Wilson's recent study of Tiwi verb morphology is an important addition to this (see Wilson 2013).
2   Ngawurranungurumagi nginingawila ngapangiraga: Tiwi–English Dictionary (Lee 1993).

very little change in some of the words that appear in both, and that many words that had gone out of use for a period of time because of Pukumani had come back into use, with some changes to consonant pronunciation. There is great variation too in the pronunciation and writing of consonants. While it is impossible to determine how much of this can be attributed to front teeth (or lack thereof), Pilling mentions the effect of a lack of teeth on the /t/ sound among speakers in the 1960s (Pilling 1970). Osborne did use /t/ in his orthography (created in the 1970s) but it has disappeared from the spelling today. Lee noted a lack of contrast between voiced and voiceless stops and variation of voicing between speakers in the 1980s and there are certainly variations in the way individuals (both current speakers and performers on the archive recordings) pronounce /b/ and /p/ and in pre-nasalised or non-pre-nasalised stops; that is, pumpuni/pupuni (good).

Lee also notes that "[b]ecause there are so few contrastive vowels in Tiwi, the range of the allophonic variation for each vowel is much wider than for the corresponding vowel in English" (Lee 1987, 26).

The language has changed from what I will call (following current terms used by Tiwi speakers) Old Tiwi, through Modern Tiwi to New Tiwi.[3] All three languages are to some degree coexisting, while all are also in danger of disappearing. While there has probably always been some lexical replacement due to Pukumani protocols (Osborne 1974, 5; Pilling 1970, 268), Lee suggests that the major factor in the rapid shift from Old to New Tiwi is the grammatical change that has occurred as a result of exposure to English over the 20th century (Lee 1987, 2).

Old Tiwi

Old Tiwi is largely grammatically defined by noun incorporation, creating a language that has many morphemes joined together to form long words. Osborne describes Old Tiwi as "a polysynthetic mainly agglutinative language, predominantly prefixing, noun incorporating and of the type in which synthesis is in the verb" (Osborne 1974, 2). Lee defines 11 prefixes and three suffixes around the verb root in a grammatically correct Old Tiwi word (Lee 1993, 387), meaning that a word could comprise 15 syllables to include (as well as the verb) the noun, the time of day, the tense and the pronoun as well as indicators of mood, location of speaker, object and subject. Wilson (2013) adds to this to suggest Old Tiwi included 14 verb prefixes and four verb suffixes.

The embedding of the time of the day, in which an action takes place, is an important feature of Old Tiwi in the context of its use in song texts. The morphemes *watu* (morning) and *ki* (evening) in spoken Old Tiwi are, according

---

3   Lee (1987; 1993) refers to Old Tiwi as "Traditional Tiwi".

to Wilson "independent of tense; they locate the event with respect to the time of day rather than with respect to the time of utterance, so both morning and evening prefixes can occur in both past and non-past tense" (Wilson 2013, 98). Wilson suggests that in 2012 the use of *ki* had been lost from the Old language as his Tiwi consultant never used it, despite his attempts to elicit it. There are certainly many instances of *ki* being uttered in song performed currently by older singers. Going by what senior singers have told me, the use of these time-of-day markers has more to do (in singing anyway) with *when the words are said* than with what they tell.[4] It might also be that, similar to singers, speakers of the Old language created the sense of an event happening 'now' when telling a story with the aim of passing on cultural knowledge – which is timeless and ongoing. It is impossible to say definitely because the last speakers of Old Tiwi have passed away.

In Old Tiwi one might say, Ngirriwunimiwatijakurluwunyiyajirringinji, "I see you."

Broken down, this is:

ngi (I) rri (you) wuni (there) mi (singular) wati (in the morning) j (connective) akurluwunyi (to see) y (connective) ajirri (each other) nginji (you).

More than simply "I see you", it translates as "I see you, over there and you see me, and it is morning."

Modern Tiwi

All instruction at the mission school was almost entirely in English[5] until 1974, when a bilingual program (using Old Tiwi) was started at the request of Elders concerned at the children's loss of language (Lee 1988, 86). Lee reports that, because the children did not speak the (Old) language a simpler form was developed for use in the school. This is now called Modern Tiwi. It differs from Old Tiwi mainly in its simpler grammatical structure in which the long and complex multimorphemic verbs were replaced by separate words indicating noun, verb, tense and gender. Lexically, Old and Modern Tiwi have more in common than either does with New Tiwi.

In comparing the pronunciation of Old Tiwi with Modern Tiwi, Lee (Lee 1993) found that younger people were no longer using the retroflex sounds, or the velar approximant /g/ sound. Thus the suffix *-pagi* that we hear on old

---

4   Mr Wilson has since confirmed that he did not conduct any interviews in the evening, although he did attempt to elicit the *ki* morpheme by constructing examples of sentences in an evening context.
5   There is anecdotal evidence that the missionaries learned some of the language but Tiwi people who were at school in those years say that classes were always in English.

recordings with a velar approximant (the *g* is very soft at back of throat like the *ch* in German *Kuchen*), now sounds like the English word "pie". Similarly *-tiga* has become *-tiya*. The vowel glide *aa* occurs when the *g* in an Old Tiwi word such as kularlaga is removed to become kulalaa in Modern Tiwi. The *aa* is pronounced with a velar approximant glide between the two vowels. The *r* in the Old Tiwi word has also disappeared in Modern Tiwi. This has the effect of shortening and simplifying the pronunciation of the middle and final syllables.

In Modern Tiwi one could say, Ngi akuluwunyi nginji "I see you." Some older speakers might include *wati* to indicate the morning, but only if they wished to specify that it was morning (whereas in Old Tiwi one would include it if one was speaking in the morning).

New Tiwi

What Lee coined "New Tiwi" (Lee 1987; 1988) emerged from the 1960s as the language spoken by children and young adults. It has a further simplified structure with fewer Old Tiwi words and more English loan words. Many of the finer distinctions of tense, of time (of day), of person (such as inclusive or exclusive pronouns), and object and subject indicators have disappeared. A number of new sounds have been introduced to (spoken) New Tiwi via English loan words (Lee 1987, 19). The /sh/ sound in the word "fish", for example, is pronounced by young people as in English *fish* (in New Tiwi as pish) as opposed to the Tiwi version of the word, which, although still the same loan word, when spoken by older people sounds like pijipiji (another example of lenition).

By way of a very brief comparison, and to show how much the language has changed, I will repeat the three versions of "I see you".

Old Tiwi:
Ngirriwunimiwatijakurluwunyiyajirringinji
I-indirect object-morning action you see/look at-TVR[6] you

Modern Tiwi:
Ngi akuluwunyi nginji
I see/look at you

New Tiwi:
Lukim ngi ja
Look I you

---

6   Transitive verb root.

Some reasons for language shift

The Tiwi people were exposed to a number of factors with the potential to influence the Old language from the start of the 20th century,[7] but the biggest influence for the rapid and radical change in the language was the arrival of the mission on Bathurst Island (Goodale 1988; Lee 1987; Morris 2001; Mountford 1958; Osborne 1974; Pilling 1970). In the pre-mission family system, the complexities of the language were only fully acquired relatively late in life (Lee 1988, 88), as young girls and women learned from their older husbands or as they went through Kulama (like the young men). The removal of the majority of children[8] from their first language by separating them from their parents and Elders, and instead having full exposure to English, meant that, as Capell wrote in 1942, "the younger generation as a whole is losing the finer shades of usage in the language" (Capell 1942, 26). With the generational separation of speakers, in the mid-century, two forms of the language existed: Old Tiwi, spoken by adults away from the mission; and a language that Lee suggests was a type of pidginised Tiwi/English which has since become creolised (Lee 1988, 88). By the 1970s then, Modern Tiwi, a lexically similar but grammatically simplified version of Old Tiwi, was documented in written form in a conscious attempt to maintain the traditional language by teaching it in the school.

Figure 12: Language shift from the 1960s to 2020s.

	1960s	1980s	2020s
Old Tiwi Yungunki	- Understood by those over 30. - Spoken by those over 40. - Used for ceremony.	- Understood by those over 50. - Spoken by those over 60. - Used for ceremony.	- (Mostly) understood by those over 80 (four individuals). - Not spoken. - Dwindling use at ceremony.

---

7   The Iwaidja people who came with Joe Cooper, the missionaries (who spoke French and English), the Filipino workers they brought with them, the exposure of Tiwi men to Pidgin English during their time in the army in the Second World War, communicating with other patients at the East Arm leprosarium and Tiwi camps in Darwin, and the languages spoken by children from mainland Aboriginal communities taken to the Garden Point Institution, would all have had an impact on the Tiwi language.

8   Lee (1987; 1993) surmises that women's change from Tiwi to English has been more pronounced and at a younger age because they were educated in the dormitory system (which continued for girls until 1972).

	1960s	1980s	2020s
Modern Tiwi Yuwunki	- Understood by all. - Spoken by all.	- Spoken by those over 30 (with changes). - Used for songs.	- Understood by those over 60. - Spoken by those over 60 (with changes).
New Tiwi Langa/ Apiniapi	- n/a	- Emerging from changes made to Modern Tiwi. - Spoken by youth.	- Spoken by people under 60. - Understood by everyone. - Not used for ceremony. - Beginning to be used for secular songs.

Figure 12 indicates these changes, showing how in the 1960s both Yungunki (Old Tiwi) and Yuwunki (Modern Tiwi) were somewhat overlapping, while the language of ceremony and song was still firmly Old Tiwi. As the shift away from Old Tiwi continued and the spoken language changed even more, Modern Tiwi came to be regarded as the "proper" language compared with the even newer form, New Tiwi. Data from the 1980s (Lee 1987) suggest that only people over 30 or so spoke Modern Tiwi and the women's songs composed in Modern Tiwi were appearing in a newly defined "proper" language.

In the 1960s and 1970s there was some crossover among Old, Modern and New Tiwi as parents used varying amounts of the older language forms with their children and older people had varying exposure to English (Lee 1988). Among the recorded song material there is also incidental speech, and this has been of great interest to Tiwi listeners. For example, on sound file 508A recorded in 1962 by Helen Groger-Wurm, Tambu, then an older Tiwi man, is recorded telling the story of Purrukapali. He makes the comment "kalo kambakayiki" meaning "he's dead" or "he's not coming back". Elders were surprised to hear him use the loan word kambakayiki from English "come back". They were surprised that Tambu, an old man in 1962, therefore born and learning his own language in the first decade of the century, and who would have been singing and speaking Old Tiwi, would also have taken on a modern phrase in this way.

Today it is only those people (now in their late 60s and over) who have a working knowledge of Yuwunki (Modern Tiwi), since Langa or Apiniapi (New Tiwi) has emerged as the primary language of this generation.[9] The *Tiwi–English Interactive Dictionary* (Lee 2011) is intended to be a working dictionary based on Modern Tiwi, with a list of Old Tiwi words as a reference. Compiled in the late 1980s and first published in 1993, it retains most of the Modern Tiwi lexicon and grammatical forms and so includes many words that young Tiwi people do not recognise. There are differing opinions as to the relevance and usefulness of the dictionary, with New Tiwi now most often spoken. The online version of the dictionary contains New Tiwi updates, with the Modern Tiwi words documented in the dictionary regarded as the "proper" way of speaking. Hence, the dictionary is an important resource for the community, being used in the school and as a reference point for adults wanting to use correct spellings in printed material.[10]

The effects of language change on the song tradition

Language change is not in itself a problem, and it is only in the context of accessing archival recordings and in the capacity to compose ceremonial song that it has become an issue that Elders have raised. Lee observed in her time in the community that, although young people did attend Tiwi ceremonial events, they did not partake in composing songs due in part to a lack of interest and because they did not know the Old language well enough. She notes:

> It would seem, then, that this use of [Traditional Tiwi] is being lost and it is doubtful that [Modern Tiwi] will take over this function as MT is not regarded as being a fit medium for ceremonial songs. (Lee 1988, 331)

The issue of language change and its impact on capacity to conduct mortuary ritual is a sensitive one which the Tiwi community, led by Elders, is continuing to address. As with any cultural change (whether perceived as development or loss) there are differing opinions as to what the long-term effects on ritual observance and subsequent social wellbeing might be and what to do now. While most community leaders agree that singing "incorrectly" is not acceptable for ceremonial contexts, there is difference of opinion as to the way to resolve the problem. This is not a new conversation. Lee wrote in 1988:

> It is a very sensitive issue for many of the Tiwi people. The traditional language can only be acquired in all its intricacies through the regular and consistent use of it in the home and camp environments. However, this

---

9   During the course of a song translation project in 2021 it became clear that many phrases in the women's "Modern Kuruwala" songs, composed in Modern Tiwi during the 1980s and 1990s (see Chapter 7) are now beyond the comprehension of all but the women who sing them.

10 I have employed current spelling for words that are used at time of writing, so that it is meaningful to contemporary Tiwi readers. Only those song words that are no longer spoken are spelled using archaic forms where useful within an example.

5 The Tiwi Language(s)

> is an impossible situation as many of the parents of the children, being young adults themselves, do not speak the traditional language as their first language. (Lee 1988, 93)

It is clear in the context of traditional song composition skills that the ongoing and long-term heuristic process of acquiring knowledge of the language has already disappeared. Listening to the more recent recordings from the 1980s we are hearing text created by senior men, born in the 1920s and whose first language (and the language of their song initiation) was Old Tiwi. Although their spoken language would have changed, their use of Old Tiwi in songs continued. Thirty years on, knowledge of the Old Tiwi language has not disappeared entirely, although no-one speaks it today and there remain only three Elders who can compose in the old words. Eustace Tipiloura (1946–2018) remembered words ending in -*ti*, for example, and used this suffix when he sang.[11] While listening to the 1954 recordings in 2009 he commented, "These songs are in hard language. I know the hard language but kids today don't know it. When I was young I was there when the old men sang those songs." This is also having an impact on people's ability to engage with the repatriated recordings. The combination of an archaic language and complex poetic alteration renders much of the text of the old song recordings untranslatable for all but the eldest Tiwi listeners.

The lack of proficiency in the language is the main reason that fewer people can compose, but it is not just vocabulary that is the problem. The structure of the Old language (the long, agglutinative verb strings) is one factor that facilitates the metrical arrangement of song texts. It is the process of modifying the complex verb structures in Old Tiwi into metre and then into song that took lengthy learning, through trial and error relying on fluency in Old Tiwi as a spoken language. Without that, the comprehension of old songs and learning to compose songs using correct language is very difficult for people wanting to learn today.

The question of why the current Tiwi language does not fit with traditional improvisatory song techniques is problematic to report upon exactly. Senior singers consistently tell me that one cannot compose in the "proper/hard/old" way using New Tiwi and indeed, even Modern Tiwi is only partially successful. I have not been able to confirm that this is solely due to the grammatical changes. It is true that some critical vocabulary elements, such as place and time-of-day markers, have become obsolete in New Tiwi, but one could argue that words of any length can be combined, separated and altered to form units

---

11   *ti* exists as a verbal prefix in the old and current languages, but as far as I can ascertain, not as a suffix. It seems to be a vocable used in songs by Mr Tipiloura specifically (and I have not been able to clarify its linguistic provenance).

of five syllables (which, as I explain next, is the central metrical form for Tiwi song). Those words in New or Modern Tiwi that are made up of two, three or five syllables should be usable for song composition, but with the simplified verb structure, the continuous syllabic stream that facilitates classical Tiwi song metre is difficult to achieve.

As is evidenced by their Kuruwala songs, the Strong Women have been actively attempting to create a sustainable song tradition based on Modern Tiwi since the 1980s. In the opinion of senior songmen and songwomen, the numerous loan words and further simplified grammar in New Tiwi, as well as the absence of certain linguistic elements essential for song texts, make it all but impossible to compose classical song using New Tiwi. There is also a degree of cultural conservatism involved in this issue. There is anecdotal evidence that for at least a generation, older Tiwi people have regarded the changes in the language negatively and have been resistant to the normalisation of New Tiwi through its use in school, for instruction and/or in tutor books (Lee 1988). My own observations recently correlate, with Elders particularly mourning the loss of the "proper" language in the context of song, arguing that the current form of the language is not appropriate for ceremonial occasions, for reasons of respect to ancestors and to cultural traditions. It is not only in the transmission of cultural knowledge and lore that the linguistic disconnect between young and old is becoming a problem, but also in matters of social and familial obligations and mentorship, with the position of Elders as role models, teachers and figures of authority in danger of being undermined as communication at a deep spiritual and intellectual level becomes difficult with the language in the "half and half" state that it is in now. Elders have told me that there are some important elements of Tiwi identity that one simply can't say in English. As Teresita put it:[12]

> You can say more in your own language. Our children are stuck halfway between Tiwi and English. They need to know English of course, so they can move on into the world, but they still need to know their own language so they will always feel strong and proud about who they are and so they can learn about where they come from.

The general opinion of Elders is that the traditional Kulama and Yoi performance styles of singing might not survive in the extemporised form they are in now because the language has changed too much. I have been told a number of times that young people will have to "just keep singing the

---

12   Teresita Puruntatameri. From her speech at the launch of the *Strong Kids Song* CD. Parliament House, Darwin, Northern Territory, 29 June 2011. Mrs Puruntatameri died in 2019.

old songs" if they want to continue the tradition. These are in a language that fewer than a dozen people now can even partially translate. There is a real sense of sadness among those with whom I've worked that they are close to losing a large amount of their cultural history if the song texts are not documented to create a meaningful resource. During a listening session with the Strong Women's Group in Milikapiti in 2010 Nina Black said, "We should be studying our own language. It would be sad if we lost it. It is almost gone. I don't know that hard language. Only the old people know." She and others have realised, through listening to these recordings with older people, that the loss of the language is also putting at risk a wealth of social history. The texts of old (recorded) songs include place names, point to historical events, and document genealogies, ceremonial practices, and endemic fauna and flora. Also among the recordings are texts relating to kinship and Dreaming that are essential for mortuary rituals. In the face of the now very small numbers of singers with knowledge of composition, the old recordings are becoming a resource of song text to be learned by rote. This has the potential to create, with a library of recorded material, a canon of songs that might eventually take the place of the Tiwi tradition of improvisation. In 2023 Nina remains a core member of the Strong Women's Group, continuing to learn from the old recordings and encouraging her children and grandchildren to learn the songs she and the women continue to compose for their community.

The loss of traditional methods of song composition does not necessarily mean that innovation in song will cease. Just as there is evidence of lexical replacement in the Old language and the creation of new forms of words and phrases in traditional song (Osborne 1989; Pilling 1970), new ways of creating song texts that fulfil traditional functions are emerging. Since the 1950s, young Tiwi people have incorporated non-Tiwi music into their own, and just as the older women still sing "old" songs using guitar-accompanied music styles borrowed from country and western, 1970s pop ballads or reggae, Tiwi musicians are very successfully combining local stories and identity with non-Tiwi music. The band B2M (Bathurst to Melville), a group of six Tiwi men,[13] has had worldwide recognition and success, as well as being loved and constantly played on the islands. As Mr Simon put it, "We started the band in 2004 when our community had a really rough time, so we decided to use music as a tool to pass on really positive messages."[14]

---

13 B2M are Jeffrey Simon, Greg Orsto, Fabian Kantilla, Daniel Cunningham, Darren Narul and Shelton Murray. Greg Orsto passed away in 2021 aged 59.
14 Mr Simon quoted in James, F. (2015). "B2M Bathurst to Melville: Northern Territory band releases debut album after decade of touring", https://www.abc.net.au/news/2015-02-23/b2m-release-debut-album-home-after-decade-of-touring-and-playing/6227522.

Their songs are deeply planted in Tiwi spiritual and physical identity, with lyrics that use Old Tiwi words and phrases, new (spoken) forms of the language, and English lyrics in rhythm and blues and dance/pop musical styles. The use of "hard language" sung words in "calling out" style as well as in quasi-Yoi vocalisation, plus the use of phrases from extant Tiwi songs, gives their songs an integrity and familiarity for Tiwi listeners. Hip-hop/rap sung/spoken sections in English and in Tiwi highlight the similarity between extemporised spoken/sung composition that is the basis of classical Tiwi singing and those contemporary (non-Tiwi) music forms. Senior singers point out the similarities between B2M's hip-hop performance skills and those of singer/composers of Yoi, and hope that young people will take this connection to their interest in the classical song practice. Many of B2M's songs include elements of classical sung forms (performed the "old way") in pauses between the digitised beats, and Tiwi listeners tend to pause and react to those elements in a show of cultural pride. It is interesting to note how, in superimposing Tiwi language onto an American pop music pulse, the rhythms and emphases of the spoken form are altered, just as it is when sung onto Tiwi song metres. While some senior singers have been concerned that the popularity of B2M's songs (and the degree to which young Tiwi people sing and know them) might have the effect of undermining their capacity to sing classical Tiwi metre, most think the artistic use of Tiwi language in such well-loved music has only enhanced Tiwi people's openness to using their own language in their own songs, in whatever context that may be.

The regular, repeating pulse of the Yoi song-type is particularly well suited to transposition onto a four-beat pop structure, successfully combining Tiwi and non-Tiwi language and music. Particular songs have become very popular among young Tiwi listeners especially, and they identify strongly with those songs that refer to their own kinship groups through recognised song texts and the empowering messages in the new lyrics. In much the same way (although in different musical styles and in different cultural contexts) the Strong Women's Group are also meshing non-Tiwi and Tiwi linguistic elements into songs composed in new musical forms, reshaping them in order to make them meaningful in the Tiwi context.

I saw this in (very effective and interesting) action one evening in 2010 when the women were composing the healing song to be sung at the burial of Regina Kantilla's daughter. The ladies flicked through a dog-eared old bible choosing phrases they found meaningful, poetic or relevant. They then translated these into (Modern) Tiwi and formed them into song phrases. One institutional effect of the women's time in the mission school has been their attitude towards the bible as a symbol of their education and literacy. As young girls they learned words from it by rote, both in oral and in written English instruction. The bible has therefore become a resource for stock phrases that the older women turn to in order to express particular sentiments to do with healing, goodness and faith. As they composed the song for Regina's daughter, they called up Tiwi song words and phrases to express the woman's identity within her family, kinship and Country, but turned to the bible for phrases about heaven and the afterlife. The mining of two resources was therefore in play: the orally transmitted set of Tiwi words and phrases; and the written English of the bible. As they chose words and phrases from each resource to weave into the healing song, they were continuing the traditional process of ritual-specific composition in the context of current influences.

Extemporisation and improvisation within the context of epithetic Old and Modern Tiwi language elements such as this may well be the future if song composition cannot work using New Tiwi. The old recordings, with the associated transcriptions and translations, will become a resource of Old language words and phrases, much like the bible already is for the Women's Group, for use when composing their Kuruwala hymns for the Catholic mass part of funerals.

It might seem obvious, but it is important to reiterate how essential the songs – the words – are to enabling people to dance Yoi. While knowledge of one's Yoi dance is ubiquitous in the Tiwi community, the ability to sing the associated Yoi song is far from it. Whereas in archive recordings we hear a chorus of 20 or more voices joining in Yoi songs, these days it is two or three voices, while the assembled group waits to be beckoned to perform their specific dance. Young people are consciously taught their Dreaming Yoi (dance) but very often it is to clapping only, not song. It has become normalised for older people to sing (creating a class of singers) while others silently dance. Since about 2015, senior singers are trying to incorporate the texts of the Dreaming Yoi into classroom and extracurricular activities so that the words of young people's Yoi begin to be as familiar as their dances are. In Chapter 7 I will explain how the Strong Women's Group have taken steps (over close to 50 years) to embed epithets of the Yoi and other ancestral songs into their Modern language songs, with the aim of encouraging children to associate with the words as well as the dances.

Song language

Having introduced language as an important factor in any study of song, we now come to the language in the context of song composition, the complexities of the traditional song composition skills, and the procedures taken by Tiwi composers in creating song texts. Looking at the techniques used by composers, one can see how the language of songs, while being fundamentally the same as the (Old) spoken language, is altered to a degree that makes it unrecognisable by many Tiwi people today. By looking at the way some of these techniques are being used by composers today, in both traditional and non-traditional song forms, we find that two underlying elements of Tiwi song texts are fundamental to describing Tiwi song. These are: the arrangement of all Tiwi song texts into metrical units of five syllables; and the placing of the performance (through the text) in the present. Both of these rely on the Old language. Considering the fact of language shift, it is not surprising that there is a modification of song practice and a growing use of extant song texts and text elements, even within modern music contexts. Continuing my narrative of the role of the recordings' return in the current study of Tiwi song practice, I will use old recordings as examples of some of the compositional techniques found in the traditional practice as well as some reactions to them by current singers.

For a detailed description of the linguistic devices employed in Tiwi song text composition I direct the reader to Osborne's work (Osborne 1989). An overview here will give an idea of the difficulties Tiwi people have today in approaching the tasks of trying to transcribe and translate these old texts, as well as in teaching the process of composition to young adults who have no knowledge of the Old language on which the rules are based. It also explains to some extent why written texts are not always an exact representation of what is actually being sung. When transcribing song texts from recordings, Tiwi listeners often gave me the words that they *expected* to hear rather than what was actually on the recording. Often what I was hearing was quite different to what they told me was being sung. I asked Calista Kantilla about this and she told me that "not all the words are real".

There is a degree of alteration between the spoken, metrical and sung levels of a Tiwi song text (as there is in many other song cultures), and the process by which words are first set in prose, then modified to be set to metre, then modified further when sung, that are quite strict and methodical.[15] Thus, while allowing for an individual's artistic expression, they give today's student identifiable "rules" to follow in order to compose a classical Tiwi song. When approaching any written Tiwi song text, it is important to remember that performances of a line of text will be different with each performer, with the constancy of the metrical form compared with the relative variability of its

---

15   See Jakobson (1960), Turpin (2007), and Turpin and Stebbins (2010) for more on Australian spoken and sung levels. Among the literature this process is described using differing terminology. For example, what I am calling "metrical form", Jakobson (1960) calls the "verse instance" and my "performance stage" is Jakobson's "delivery instance".

treatment in the performance form creating potentially numerous "versions" of what might be considered an old or inherited song text. As I have said earlier, there are very few fixed song texts – and indeed no two performances of even those songs – that are considered fixed, being passed down through generations, that are identical, because there are always variations created by the singer at the point of performance.

Put most simply, the Tiwi composer goes through three stages:

1. Creating a line of prose.
2. Altering the spoken form to a metrically correct poetic form.
3. Altering the poetic form to a musically correct melodic form.

This process might be described as versification (into poetic form) and then cantillation (intoning that poetic form in a recognised musical pattern such as chanted prayers). This description holds up in the ritual context and we can certainly regard the epithetic texts presented at mortuary ceremonies and in the ritual stages of Kulama to serve a purpose not unlike chanted prayer. It is less useful however when we consider that Tiwi composers also apply this process to non-ritual performance contexts and song forms and melodies and that it has passed into the composition of the new song-types with non-Tiwi musical forms.

Osborne, with the help of his Tiwi consultants, transcribed the "verse" text (Osborne's term, 1974) of songs recorded by Spencer in 1912, Hart in 1928–29, Simpson in 1948, Mountford in 1954, and those that he himself made in 1972–75. I make the distinction between song text and verse text because Osborne presents the text as lines of verse, which adhere to strict metrical rules that apply to the first process of Tiwi song composition: that in which the spoken form is altered as it is set to a metrical verse form (that I will call the "metrical form"). While it is useful to study Osborne's metrical versions of song texts, I suggest that relying on the metrical version of a song for any study only gives part of the picture. Listening to recordings in the archive, even educated Tiwi listeners often find it difficult to marry what they are hearing with what Osborne has recorded in writing as the metrical form. The issue here is that the metrical form doesn't ever really exist. It is a construct of the composer and of the researcher, but it is never uttered – either spoken or sung. While essential to the process, it is a fleeting moment, often as the song is being performed, when the composer instinctively organises the words into syllabically regular metrical units, and then sings them in a musical form that suits the occasion (that is, the context shapes the song-type which therefore shapes the sung presentation of the words). It is a complex process which only those most fluent in the language and the process can achieve with any degree of ease, and indeed across the recordings and today singers often take pause to sort out a song as they present it. Osborne describes the process thus:

> The singer goes through the following steps; grammar, metre, music, performance. The hearer must go backwards through these steps to fully appreciate the artistic and poetic skill. (Osborne 1974, 204)

Eustace Tipiloura describes this in his words at the beginning of this chapter.

> You think about it and whisper it when you walking out bush or along the street, you think about it and the words come straight into your mind. Then you sing at ceremony. The words have to fit. The sounds of them. That's what is important.

As a live performance art form, the song may also include variations resulting from the individual's performance style. This means that when listening to a song recording one hears only the sung form of the words (which might be quite different from how they would be spoken). A detailed knowledge of the language is required in order to extrapolate the metrical and then spoken forms. Being two generations (at least) removed from fluent speakers of the language of these recordings, current singers are faced with a very difficult task when auditioning the repatriated recordings. At the time they were performed, the songs were heard by people who had a thorough command of the language in which they were composed and so could apply this knowledge to an understanding of the song. The performers of the (early recorded) songs would have had knowledge of the versification principles in much the same way as a native speaker has intuitions about language. Today the listener is working backwards through the levels of cantillation to attempt to prise out from among the additions, deletions and alterations first a metrical setting and finally the original phrase in prose.

The difference between spoken language and sung language

Hart reported that there was a form of the language used in song (C.W.M. Hart 1930, 178) that was different from the spoken form. Osborne is in qualified agreement with this, saying:

> It differs from spoken Tiwi very considerably in lexis, as many old words and incorporated forms which have died out in speech have been retained in song. However, it is unlikely that it differs from ordinary spoken Tiwi in syntax and morphology. (Osborne 1974, 3)

Jane Goodale writes of "special or 'literary' words not used in daily conversation" (Goodale 1974, 290) being used for Tiwi songs and that "My informants often said to me that they could not translate certain of the songs because they did not know the meaning of some of the words" (Goodale 1974, 291). To some degree this would have been due to linguistic change, but it also points to the likelihood that the language of song has always been in some way different from the spoken language.

The primary motivation behind Tiwi composition is innovation and creativity and it seems to have also been a feature of the Old language used in song. Indeed, Osborne comments that "[t]he complex morphological structures of the verb forms are not a mere static inheritance from the past, but are always being refined, improved and further developed" (Osborne 1989, 256). Osborne notes that when his Tiwi consultants in 1975 heard the Baldwin Spencer recordings they were not so much impressed by the similarities between song texts performed in 1912 and their own as by the developments that had been made since then.

As it creates an artistic, poetic level above that of everyday speech or prose, song language tends to be more florid, or more expansive than necessary to present the meaning in the most economical way. This is partly the result of insertions in order to make words fit the metre but is also a literary or artistic decision of the composer, who wishes to create songs whose language is rich and layered, showing the level of virtuosity to which their many years of training have brought them. In Yoi songs the length of a song's line is not simply a series of metrical units that fit a set length but rather stems from the original statement in prose – the first level of grammatical text. The song's meaning must remain intact through the process of versification then cantillation. In some songs the stages are the same, so when transcribing a recorded song item I have found that the singer has exactly articulated the metrical form of the text in the sung performance. In other cases, the performance transcription includes variations from the metrical form (that is, further deletions and/or additions). These are (in the opinion of senior singers) either small errors or idiosyncratic creative flair on the part of the performer. Certainly in the case of altered vowel and consonant sounds, crushed syllables and inserted syllables, they are seen as skilful, clever and indeed sometimes showy displays of performers revelling in the creativity and freedom the art form provides.

The sound of the words

When speaking of song texts, Tiwi composers often speak of the meaning *and* the sound of the words as mutually dependent and important. They want to create words that sound as musically fluent as possible. The lyricism of the melody is enhanced by vowel and consonant choices (such as the repeating *a* vowel sound and the soft *ng* and *m* consonants in the song shown at Song text 17) that in turn lead to word choices. This "sound" of particular words is part of the deep-level intuitive knowledge of the language of the songs that only the eldest singers have. Pirlingimpi Elder Anne Marie Puruntatameri explained to me her method of composition as wanting to create a continuous stream of syllables and avoiding giving two beats to one syllable so that the song flowed "like waves". She said that "filling up" the melody with even, aurally homogenous syllables in this way was much harder than stretching out a word across beats but it is worth it because "the words have to be the same as the melody". By this Anne Marie means that all metrical positions within a line should be filled. While melisma does occur in the unique introduction or cadenza sections of some song-types, that is entirely a result of the individual's performance style. The general rule is that each "note" or "beat" of a melody contains only one syllable. This makes extemporised composing more difficult because there is nowhere to hide (and why numerous recordings tell us that it was completely acceptable for singers to try out a line a few times, to abort a line and start afresh or to "pause" a song by singing "kurukangawakawayi" (akin to humming, which I mention in the next chapter)).

Similarly, the Amparruwu songs composed by Eunice Orsto in 2011 were, Eunice said, made up of "lovely words, lovely sounds, meaning, meaning". Eunice stated that she sang in such a way as to create, with the sounds of the words and the melody, an aural image of the snake (and by association, the couple) coiling in gentle lazy circles. Song text 17 shows how Eunice sings an *a* vowel for the line-final of Line 1 and drops the *i* from the end of Line 2 to give a repeating (she called it "rolling") aural pattern. In Line 1 she has repeated the word ngilimpangimikimi to emphasise the atmosphere of when she sang (the evening), but also to lengthen the line for poetic effect, in this case (she told me) to sound lengthened, like a sigh. (In the second iteration Eunice changes the consonant in muwi to murri, also (she told me) for the sake of this aural effect of "smoothing it out" and for interest.) In Line 2 the alteration of the *a* at the end of Jinarringa to *u* creates a repeating rhyme between *u* and *a* (shown in bold font). Listen also to Audio 16.

Song text 17: Eunice Orsto. Jinarringa (Black-headed python), 2011.

> L1. Spoken: Murtinayinga awungani muwi ngilimpangimikimi
> *[Ancestral name] like that we ourselves [sleeping]*
>
> Sung: Murtinayinga wunganimuwingilimpangimikima nimurrilimpangima
>
> L2. Spoken: Muwa Jinarringa awungani
> *We ourselves Black-headed python like that*
>
> Sung: M**u**wajinarring**u**wawung**a**n
> *We'll be like a snake*
>
> Understood meaning of song as a whole:
> *As husband and wife roll each other and I am your wife*

Patterns of five

The composition of lines of poetry (the first step of song composition) necessitates a degree of artifice that places Tiwi song text as a higher register than everyday speech. Tiwi poetry is "highly artificial, both in syntax and in diction ... in the sense that it is literary, the product of art, and so set apart from the common run of everyday discourse" (Osborne 1989, 255). The poetic devices employed by singers relied on full command of the language as well as thorough knowledge of the rules of poetic composition.

The principal rule of the vast majority[16] of Tiwi songs' structure is that text lines must be made up of metrical units of five syllables each (that I will call "unit A"), with the final unit made up of four syllables (that I will call "unit B").[17] There can be any number of A units in a line of song, but there are most often between two and six, and then the line must end with a B unit. The stresses fall consistently on the first and fourth syllables in unit A and on the first and third in unit B. This is not always the case now. Audio 3, 28 and 77 are performances of Arikuruwala songs by singers, who consistently place the stress on the first and third syllables of the A unit. They have not been able to tell me why this is, but it might be the result of non-Tiwi musical influences.

None of the senior singers I asked was consciously aware of the fact that all the song texts follow a pattern of units of five and none was able to speak the

---

16 While lullabies and love songs depart from it, they constitute a small percentage of the recorded songs and of the total number of songs composed. Osborne found that of the 1,309 lines of song text he studied, only 13 showed metrical irregularity (Osborne 1989, 131). The women's Modern Kuruwala song-type shows a modified and yet related version of this.
17 To facilitate the reader's cross-referencing I use Osborne's terminology: units A and B.

text in verse (they invariably sang whenever I asked for words or text). Those who compose did however adhere to the pattern and found it difficult to say the words in speech, as they were "song words" (words modified into verse structure).

Clementine Puruntatameri sang in what her peers referred to as "the old way" even within non-Tiwi musical treatments of song texts. I discuss her song Murrntawarrapijimi in greater detail in Chapter 7, but pertinent here is her treatment of the ancestral place name Rangini. While listening through the archive recordings one day in 2010, we came across the text of a song recorded by Simpson in 1948[18] and transcribed by Osborne in 1975. The unidentified composer has inserted *yija-* in order to make the place name Rangini the required five syllables, thus: Yijarangini. Clementine, who had not heard the 1948 recording when she sang her song, used a very similar alteration – Nijarangini – in her performance of Murrntawarripijimi in 2008.[19] Clementine told me that is the way one sings Rangini. She didn't make a distinction between the two words as being one for speaking and one for singing, but instead repeatedly said it was the same word – just spoken and sung. In this way we can see that Nijarangini (and the older version, Yijarangini) can be considered "song language". Some disyllabic forms, like *nija-, nita-, wangi-, wanga-* and *tani* have no linguistic function other than to turn a three-syllable word into a five-syllable word, thus creating a five-syllable metrical unit. Meaningful disyllabic conjunctions used in similar ways include *ngini* (as), *pili* (because), *nginta* (so), *karri* (when), *kuta* (indeed), *marri* (well), *niyi* (that there), *maka* (where?), *waya* (now), *naki* (here), *kwiyi* (there), *apu* (and) and *yati* (one).

In speech the penultimate syllable of each word is stressed (Lee 1993; Osborne 1974). The first syllable of the word has the first secondary stress and the other secondary stresses occur on the penultimate syllable of each incorporated stem in all but a very few words in Old Tiwi, and those few are mostly loan words from Iwaidja. The following line of a Tatuwali (Shark) song at Song text 18 (Osborne 1989) recorded by Simpson in 1948[20] shows how the stresses have moved in the process of versification. In the spoken form the stresses mostly fall on the first and penultimate syllables of each incorporated form,[21] whereas in the metrical form the stresses occur consistently on the first and fourth syllable of each unit of five. So, while there are stress rules, these apply to the metrical

---

18 Audio 2.
19 Audio 3. The Modern Kuruwala version of this song retains this linguistic device.
20 Audio 71.
21 The exception to this is wampáy (fin), which is not incorporated.

units, not to the words. The difference, then, is that the words are grouped by syllables, irrespective of word boundaries.

Song text 18: Unidentified singer. Tatuwali (Shark), 1948.

> Gloss:
>
> Ngénta tártuwáli mpiwúgha wampáy ám -p- entye -rre-ké- rrayawárri
> *So   shark   nz   fin   he -f- dur -lk-eve- thresh*
> *Free translation: The shark threshes the water with his dorsal fin.*
>
> Spoken: Ngénta tártuwálimpiwúgha wampáy ámpentyerrekérrayawárri
>
> Metrical: Ngéntatartúwa límpiwugháwam páyampentyrréke rráyawárri
>
> Unit: A   A   A   B
>
> Syllable count: 5   5   5   4
>
> dur = durative
> eve = evening word form
> f = feminine
> lk = linking syllable
> nz = nominaliser

In addition to the alterations made by the composer at the versification stage, the text is then further altered in order to fit the structure of the melody and rhythm appropriate to the song style being performed. Phonologically, the stress and intonation patterns are different, and the word boundaries have been obscured and then performed with the accents on the first and fourth syllable of each unit of five (and first and third of each unit of four). Phonetically there is also a difference, with vowel harmony employed by many singers, and in the women's Kulama response (see description of the Ampirikuruwala song form in Chapter 6) when an open throat *a* is used.

Strategies for fitting words into metre

There are certain specific procedures that take place in the construction of a line of Tiwi song text that result in the reduction or increase of word length. For example, strategies for reduction include deletion, vowel fusion and consonant lenition. Increase is achieved through syllable insertion and/or repetition. Once the correct metrical pattern is achieved the text is "ready" to be sung. If, while composing on the spot, in performance, the singer finds that the words do not fit the metrical pattern, various techniques can be employed. Bearing in mind that these alterations are only ever made while someone is singing, this does mean that the metrical form (which would not be written down) should not be taken as a complete song text. I have presented songs in metrical form here to show examples of the process, but it is important to remember that Tiwi listeners would have been hearing/recognising the complete words in their minds, with this metrical form a recognised version of the language in its own right. Remembering too that in many recordings we hear different approaches to fitting the same words into the metre within one song and we start to get an idea of how "of the moment" classical Tiwi songs are.

A song composed by Jurruputimirri (Tony Charlie) circa 1970 has the cargo ship *Marella* as its subject.[22] Because *Marella* is a word with only three syllables, the composer added *pi* and *wa* in order to create the song word pimiraluwa, which, having five syllables, completes an A unit. This addition of *w* between vowels is one method of adding a syllable. The final vowel sound *a* in *Marella* is altered phonetically to sound *u*, as is necessary when preceding *wa*.

If a desired word is too long to fit the required unit, the singer can reduce it through deletion of a syllable or the elision of two adjacent equivalent vowels. The word ampentyerrekerrayawarri (threshing in the water), for example, in the Tatuwali (Shark) song at Song text 18, has been shortened by deleting the *e* in the morpheme *entye* so that it can produce a five-syllable unit A (payampentyerreke). Such elisions happen quite frequently in association with the consonant *rr*. In this case the sung performance is identical to the metrical level. Many other instances of deletion and elision occur at the performance stage when vowels are "crushed" in order to fit syllables into the metre. This is similar to a contraction in English (*cannot* becomes *can't*, for instance) and so it does not affect the meaning of the word. This happens a lot in Tiwi songs, partly because there are numerous morphemes in the (spoken) language – many of which remain in today's New Tiwi – that begin and/or end with a vowel. In other songs we see syllable fusion. There are numerous instances in the recordings of the fusion of a word-final syllable into the following word-initial syllable. To give you an idea of the process a Tiwi singer/composer goes through I will describe how a simple line of spoken text might be transferred into song.[23]

A composer might want to sing: Ngiya akirlimighi naki awungani nginingilawa arawunikiri "I sneak up with my spear."

---

22   Recorded by Osborne. C04-003854-137.
23   This is not taken from a Tiwi composer's song. I have invented it by way of an example.

The first two words will join as the two *a* vowels are fused – Ngiyakirlimighi – but it would then have to be added to because Ngiyakirlimighi comprises six syllables. So, adding the next syllables to form Ngiyakirlimi ghinaki – then there is the choice between deleting the first syllable of awungani to create ghinakiwungani (again, six syllables) or to add a consonant between the two and form ghinakiwawungani or ghinakiyawungani (seven syllables). In both instances the unit is too long, so again they are split. Taking the third option ghinakiyawungani becomes ghinakiyawu nganinginila. Then the final syllable *wa* joins the front of the next word -wa arawunikiri and again it needs deletion (here elision) warawunikiri or addition wawarawunikiri to make it fit, but this still needs work to complete the line correctly! The options are (among many): warawunikirimi (finishing the line with a unit of seven syllables which is unusual but not impossible) or wawarawuni kirimuwa, adding two syllables to the end purely to complete the line with a unit of four syllables as is the standard pattern. So in order to sing one line of song, the composer has (in their head, often while singing) gone through all of these processes of readjustment to create a highly artificial and artistically pleasing line of song worthy of ceremonial performance.

Ngiya akirlimighi naki awungani nginingilawa arawunikiri

has become:

Ngiyakirlimi ginakiyawu nganinginila wawarawuni kirimuwa

Bearing in mind the fact that this example doesn't involve any re-ordering of words, any time-of-day or ritual context words or any attempt to shape the sounds, this is still a very complex process, and I hope it gives some indication of the level of intellectual skill involved in Tiwi song composition.

Dorrie Tipakelipa (Jipulimatuwu) was the widow singing for her husband when she performed the following Amparruwu song in 1975.[24] With their characteristic two-part melody, Amparruwu songs are performed at a slow tempo, with the drawn-out vocalisation and extremes of tessitura (an octave or more apart within one performance) requiring breaths to be inserted more often than in fast tempo songs.

Dorrie extended one line of metrically complete text across two parts of the melody and we can hear how she moved and reiterated syllables to fit her words into this pattern. She sang in the voice of her deceased husband as he watches his wife and classificatory wives (Dorrie's sisters) performing ceremony. This interpretation was offered by Eunice Orsto: "I am thinking about my darling wives."

First she forms the line in prose (in her head):

---

24 Dorrie Tipakelipa, 1975: AIATSIS: C04-003855B.

Ngiya	ngu	purnayuwi	ngiya	waya	pu - tuwunjingu	munguwamungu	rralangumani
I		*my wives*	*I*	*now*	*they - keep on*	*the mind*	*filling up*

Then, shaping that into metrical form, she sings, repeating the first four words across two "melodic parts", with a duplication of the end of the second unit [i] to make it fit into five beats (she didn't need a breath) and then clipping off the last syllable to take one at the end of the line (`).

Ngiyangupur   ngunayuwi[i]   ngiyangupur   ngunayuw(i)`
    5   5   5   4

She then sings the next three words, breaking them where they would not normally be broken in speech. Again the words span the two parts of the melody, but this time running the first unit of four straight on, by adding [wu] and deleting the last syllable so she can take a breath (but retaining the rhythm of the unit).

Ngiyawayapu   tuwunjingu[wu]   munguwamungu   rralanguman(i)`
    5   5   5   4

Variations to this pattern at the performance stage

Calista Kantilla, Jacinta Tipungwuti and Leonie Tipiloura sang what they called the Kulama (implying "proper" and "old" version) of a line of song (Song text 19) that was part of a larger song project that we worked on together in 2010. Having composed the lyrics and written them out in what they called "song language" (the metrical form) the women then changed the words in the sung performance. Singing in unison (following Calista), Jacinta and Leonie were able to pick up the changes as they sang. They fused the final of wutawa and the initial of walima to produce the correct metre. So nginiwutawa walima becomes nginiwutawalima. This fusion occurs not only when the segments are identical, but also when they differ, such as in the text of the love song at Song text 21, which includes fusion of *lu* and *wa* to create *la*.

Song text 19 (which corresponds with Audio 5) presents one line of the song text showing cantillation; having first created the correct metrical form of the text, the women added and subtracted syllables to make the words fit the melody at the cantillation stage. Having given me the metrical form, which included the meaningless *api* to create correct metre, the singers then omitted it in the sung form because of further changes that they made as they actually sang. I have shown the start of the line in bold to indicate how the women moved the final unit of the line to the beginning of the line. Being originally a line-final unit B (so comprising four syllables) they had to add *wu* in order to complete a unit A (five syllables). They also then altered the preceding syllable (the last syllable of the word ngimpurimi) to *ma* to create the "better sounding" *mawu* (underlined). Having created the correct metre at the versification stage, the women then (for Melodic Line (ML) 1) extended the first unit with an anacrusis *a* (1 syllable) to the phonetically altered *waya* (from *wayi*) to create a unit A comprising seven syllables (with an anacrusis) as well as a line-final unit of seven syllables (by adding *na*). The text is reiterated (ML2) to complete the form of the Ampirikuruwala song-type they were singing.

Song text 19: Calista Kantilla, Jacinta Tipungwuti and Leonie Tipiloura. Wutawa kuwayi (They call out), 2010.

Free translation: They, the ancestors are calling us.

Spoken:	Ngini wutawa walima ngawa kuwayi ngimpurumi			
Metrical:	Nginiwutawa	walima api	ngawakuwayi	**ngimpurimi**
	5	5	5	4
Sung form	A**waya**ng**impurumawu**	nginiwutawa	limangawaku	wayingimpurimi[na]
ML1:	1+2+5	5	5	7
Sung form	Nginiwutawalima	ngawakuwayi	ngimpurimi[n]	
ML2:	7	5	4	

In some performances of Arikuruwala songs the groupings of five-syllable metrical units are obscured by the overlay of seven-syllable melodic groupings. This reframing of the metrical structure cannot (in the opinion of senior singers) be called a rule as such (or indeed an exception to the rule) but is rather a case of "mixing it up" to make the compositions more interesting. Among the recordings are numerous examples of the metre being altered in this way at the performance stage. The song in Music Transcription 1 (Audio 38) by Christopher Foxy Tipungwuti, shows this. The metrical form is in correct metre (5+5+4). The singer uses a rise in pitch and strong accent at *ma* to delineate a new grouping, overriding the 5+5+4 metrical pattern to create two groups of seven syllables (shown with square brackets). I have also added the stresses on the spoken and metrical forms to give another example of how these are altered through the versification and cantillation process. The sung form suppresses all of the metrical stresses, apart from the rising in pitch on *tya* (although there is no accent).[25]

---

25 The word "night" in this song does not mean "at night" but indicates the time of the performance. I explain this further in the next section on indicators of time.

Music Transcription 1: Example of altering the metre in sung form.
Christopher Foxy Tipungwuti (Audio 38).

Spoken form: Wí- kuntyíngi   mátyatyumángili   púngurráya
               They- at night   hold on to/collect honey   have plenty

Metrical form: Wíkuntyingíma   tyátyumangíli   púngurráya
               5   5   4

Sung form:

The example in Music Transcription 2 is another Arikuruwala song in which the spoken and metrical forms are marked in differing ways in performance. It also shows a number of features found in the recordings. The melody of the song, by Barney Tipuamantimeri (Audio 11), is shown with indications of pitch fluctuation and percussive accompaniment in relation to the text. Characteristic of this song-type, the irregular percussive beats fall sometimes on and sometimes between notes and are not in the same place across different performances of the one line. Nor are they consistent, neither with other songs of this type nor within this performance. While the second stick beat falls on *na,* the first beat falls between *pi* and *me*.

In Figure 13 I have broken down the song into its elements to show how the words are treated (I also give a detailed translation in order to show the word breaks in spoken form). The insertion of a meaningless vocable *wa* at the start means that in the first unit the stresses (marked in bold) do not fall on the strong syllables that occur in the spoken form (also in bold). We can hear that the first two five-syllable units are marked with a higher pitch on the initial syllables, but a seven-syllable unit is also implied with a strong accent on the second syllable of the second unit. This partly defines the text at the spoken level because the first two words (six syllables, not counting the initial meaningless *wa*) are separate, whereas the remainder of the line comprises one 17-syllable compound verb warupingilimpangipimengangipimenangirrinti (he stood up). All syllables of this word are sung evenly and there is no vocal emphasis, apart from a slight accent on the initial of the final unit. The metrical structure is marked, however, with the quasi vibrato beginning in line with the start of the third unit and with a percussive clap on the start of the fourth and fifth units. We can see then that the third metrical unit, ngilimpangipi, is the only one which is not marked either by pitch, vocal stress or percussive beat. This unit coincides with a word boundary in the spoken form and so perhaps the singer felt it would be recognised as such without the need for any musical marker. In this case the singer has added an unpitched vocalisation *a* at the end of the line. This idiosyncratic feature is not part of either the spoken or the metrical forms of the text (hence enclosed in brackets) and is an example of the freedom that the individual singer has to make changes at the cantillation level.

Music Transcription 2: Melody in relation to text. Barney Tipuamantimeri.

Figure 13: Text breakdown of Arikuruwala song by Barney Tipuamantimeri.

Translation of spoken text (Osborne 1989, 617):

kwiyi   turrunguni wa- rupi-   ngilimpangi- pimengangi rrinti
there   clearing   ic- them-   sleeping-   get up-   stand

Free translation:

There on the cleared ground he stood up to defend them.

ic = incompletive
note: ngilimpangi does not literally mean sleeping but is a time-of-day and ritual stage marker

Song breakdown:

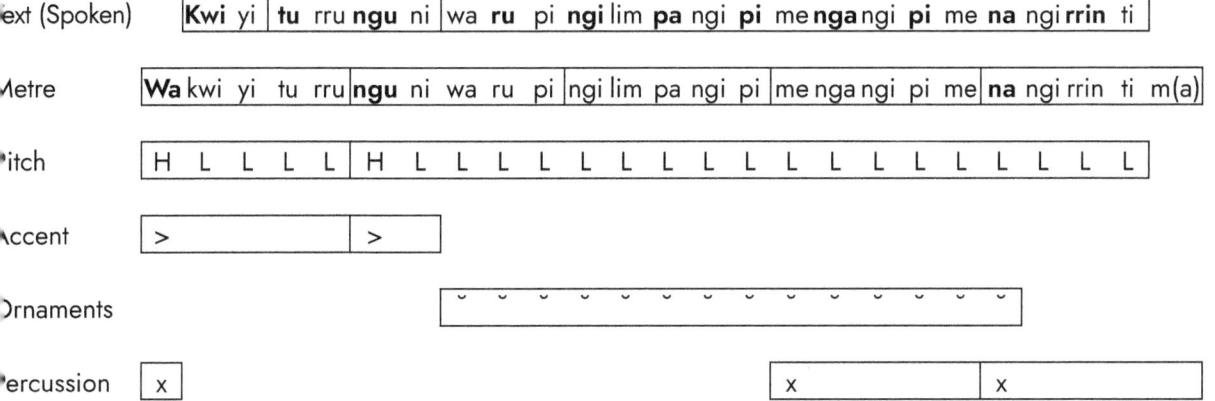

Calista Kantilla, who on New Year's Day 2023 turned 86, is one of the last two older women (the other is Leonie Tipiloura) to whom people turn on matters of language and song, and she explained to me how she creates a Kulama song. As a simple example, Calista chose to sing as though she was telling the news of her visit (with me) to Darwin. Song text 20 (also Audio 4) shows the song text in two forms: first as Calista would speak the line; secondly at the metrical level. Having suggested the subject matter, Calista sang the text as a Kulama song (within a minute or two of having spoken the sentence). She moved the position of the words, adjusted them to accommodate the metre, and made alterations as she sang "because it sounds good that way". When she arranged the words into the metrical form Calista could predict that the final unit would be two syllables short, so she inserted nginta ("so" or "indeed") into the penultimate unit to rectify the problem. It was pointed out to me by the other women present that this was a skilled way of doing it, rather than partial reduplication, to create a five-syllable metrical unit A from a three-syllable word and showed Calista's high level of compositional skill; pre-empting the pattern, knowing in her mind how the length of the various words would best align in order to complete the line and repositioning the words in an order that achieved a good flow of syllables and consonants. It should also be noted that this was achieved with no iteration of the text between Calista saying the sentence (stage 1) and then singing it (stage 3, which in this case did not change from the metrical stage 2). We can see that in this short song phrase she has moved words around, added a word (superfluous to the meaning), altered the emphasis and word breaks, and deleted syllables, and yet Tiwi listeners know exactly what she means.

Song text 20: Calista Kantilla. Awungarra Jiliyarti (Here in Darwin), 2011.

> 1. Spoken form.
>
> **Kiringarra wumunga ngintirrimu awungarra Jiliyarti**
> *Six days we were here Darwin*
>
> 2. Metrical form (as it was sung).
> Kiringarrawu mungajiliya rtingintangarra ngintirrimu

Versification using other metrical patterns

The love songs do not follow the rule of metrical units comprising five syllables, but they have the most regular melodic structure and so the singer does still employ a number of alterations in order to fit the text into the love song melody. The song I discuss here is a good example of the singer using specific cantillation techniques while also showing individual creativity. Song text 21 shows the three

5 The Tiwi Language(s)

steps taken by the composer: composition of the text in prose; its arrangement into metre; and then cantillation into the sung form. This corresponds with Audio 23, a recording made by Mountford in 1954 of an unidentified Tiwi woman performing an example of the Apajirupwaya (love song) type (see Chapter 6).

As I show in Music Transcription 3, the melody is in four phrases (numbered) and each cycle of the melody is broken up into two iterations of each line of text.

Music Transcription 3: Love song melody showing relationship between text and melody. Unidentified female singer 1954 (Audio 23).

As shown in Song text 21, each line is sung twice before moving on to the next. The first and second lines are treated differently each time, while the third line stays the same. In Line 1 the line-final *-uwu* is added to the second and fourth units to create a five-syllable then a four-syllable metrical pattern. In the second iteration of Line 1 the syllables ngantya are inserted (shown in bold). The syllable count is therefore increased from seven syllables (in the spoken form) to eight syllables in the sung form, so fitting the melody. In each iteration of Line 1 the singer deletes the first syllable of nyempatu to create an eight-syllable line.

Song text 21: Spoken, metrical and sung forms of love song, 1954.

Free translation:
L1. *I'm sad that you are leaving this morning*
L2. *I send all my thoughts to you*
L3. *He gave me a torch to light my way*

Spoken form:

L1. Ngatyi ngintya nguwuri ngatyi nyem -p- atu -   witya
     Like   you   alas   like   you   -np- morn - go

L2. Nga- ngi- lawa pukatawunga ngi -tu- wate- meny- tyingi ning- ity- amighi
     f-   my   own   thoughts   I   -p-   morn- you   dur-   send   go   caus

L3. Yita ngeni layit yi- nu- wate- meni- te- rrankining- iluwa
     em   as   light he- to- morn- me-   dur- light-   give

Metrical form:

L1. Ngatyingintyangu wuriyuwu ngatyinyempatu wityawuwu
L2. Ngangilawapu katawu[nga]ngentu [wa]tementyingini ngityamighi
L3. Yitangenila yitinuwate menityerraki ningiluwa

Sung form:[26]

ML1. [Ngatyi] ngintyang<u>u wuriyuwu</u> ngatyi[nye]mpatu witya<u>wuwu</u>
     Ngatyang[in]tyang<u>u wuriyuwu</u> ngatyi[nye]mpatu [wi]ty[a]<u>wuwu</u>
ML2. Ngangilampu kata[wunga]ngentu [wa]tementyingi[ni] ngityamighi
     Ngangilampu kata[wunga]ngentu [wa]tementyingi[ni] ngityami[ghi]
ML3. Yitange[ni]la yiti[nu]wate menity[e]rraki ningil<u>uwa</u>
     Yitange[ni]la yiti[nu]wate menity[e]rraki ningil[uw]a

In the first iteration of Line 2 the last syllable is deleted from pukatawunga, as is the first syllable of *wate* (all deletions are shown in square brackets). When the text is then sung, a number of syllables are deleted as the text is modified by the melody and the singer deletes *wa* and adds the consonant *m* to alter *-lawa-* to *-lampu*. On the first iteration the line is sung in full, but in the second the final syllable *-ghi*

---

26 The sung form is presented in this figure in comparative perspective showing omissions and insertions in relation to the metrical form. In Music Transcription 3, only the resultant syllable strings are shown.

is deleted. This creates a repeating pattern whereby each time we hear Melodic Line (ML) 2, the last syllable is shortened in relation to ML1, which has a double "quaver" length due to the fusion of *wuwu* (underlined). Line 3 has four deletions and the cantillation (text, pitch and rhythm) is the same in each iteration, except that the final of the first iteration is a fusion of the two syllables *lu* and *wa* to give a lengthened *la* (occupying the space of two syllables), whereas in the second iteration the *uw* is not sung at all, so the line is one syllable shorter, ending only with *la*.

Vocalisations

As Turpin and Stebbins note, "Song cannot simply be defined as a musical setting of words, as many songs contain vocables, such as 'tra-la-la', which are not words and yet are part of the song text" (Turpin and Stebbins 2010, 3). The function of vocables and phatic elements of song texts has been discussed in the literature, including notable examples from outside of Australia that are relevant to this study (Frisbie 1980; Browner 2009). There are many instances in Tiwi songs of individuals adding meaningless vocables at line beginnings, line endings or between lines. Open-throated vowel sounds, nasal closed-mouth sounds, throat coughs and other similar sounds serve to ornament and individualise performances. Other vocables are song-specific, such as the lip flutter that is added to Tatuwali (Shark) Dreaming songs, the growl sound of the Nyingawi people in Nyingawi songs and the short *wu* that is always added when singing Yirrikapayi (Crocodile), whether in the classical or modern forms.[27] The vocalisations used in the Sugarbag and Mosquito calls are called by all those present, regardless of identity affiliation.

Kawakawani and kawakawayi are defined in the Tiwi Online Dictionary as verbs "to sing in the traditional way": kawakawani means "to sing traditional style, sad singing" and kawakawayi means "to sing traditional style, happy singing". The vocalisation kawakayayi in Eunice's Amparruwu song occurs in most Amparruwu songs and is often sung between each line of text. Although kayayi is untranslatable it universally indicates sadness, wailing or crying. Elders say it might be a development of the word kayi "Listen!" and in the context of an Amparruwu song, means "Listen to me, hear my grief" (directed to the deceased).

There are many variations on the treatment of this vocalisation and it can be altered to fit any song-type. In the archive recordings are instances when the singer seems to stumble on a word, either at the beginning of or midway through a phrase, and they sing elements of kurukangawakawayi such as:

---

27   Examples of these can be heard in Audio Examples 71 (Shark) and 7, 65 and 68 (Crocodile).

kuruwu, kurukawanga, kurukawangaka, kurukangawakawayayi (and many other variations) before returning to the song proper. This allows the melodic line to continue uninterrupted, creating a filler that, as Eustace explained, is "more clever than just la, la, la", and the degree to which it is inserted seamlessly to avoid stumbling indicates a highly skilled singer. Singers tell me its purpose is to enable the song to continue uninterrupted while the singer prepares the next line or as an interlude between lines of the song if there is an interruption to the attention of their audience. In performances in both Arikuruwala and Mamanunkuni song types, recorded in 1975 (Audio 25, 26 and 27), Long Stephen Tipuamantimeri makes a mistake (Line 7, marked in Music Transcription 4) and immediately follows with a line of Kuruwakawakawayi[28] before attempting the line again. We hear him "humming while he's thinking what to sing next" (as Calista Kantilla put it).

Variations of Kurukangawakawayi are also added to almost every Modern Kuruwala-style song that is performed by the Women's Group, and often in traditional-style songs performed by men as well. It can be used to extend the length of a song or within a song if the following verse is temporarily forgotten. This happens relatively regularly when we perform together, either because the women are unsure who is leading (and so who is cueing the verse order), if we have to extend the length of a song to coincide with a staging requirement or if the women are dancing. It is also used to extend the length of an introductory section to allow the group (whether singers or dancers) to be ready. Music Transcription 4 gives just six of the many examples in order to show how the words can be altered to fit different rhythms and melodies. The song-type of each example is indicated. Stresses are marked with /.

Music Transcription 4: Six musical treatments of Kurukangawakawayi (Audio Examples 16, 27, 38, 46, 48, 51).

Example 1: Long Stephen Tipuamantimeri 1975. Mamanunkuni (Audio 27)

Example 2: Christopher Foxy Tipungwuti 1975. Mamanunkuni (Audio 38)

---

28 In the old recordings the *r* is a rolled *rr* sound. Some older singers use this, but the word is usually written today with one *r*.

Example 3: Eustace Tipiloura Brolga 2012. Ariwayakulaliyi (Audio 48)

Example 4: Women's Group. Wurrumiyanga Wellbeing Centre song 2009. Kuruwala (Audio 51)

Example 5: Women's Group. Kupunyi 2008. Kuruwala (Audio 46)

Example 6: Eunice Orsto 2010. Amparruwu (Audio 16)

In all these examples we see that the core of the words is comparable, with the beginning *kuru-* and the ending *-wakawayi* fairly consistent, but with the order of kawanga and the stresses being different depending on each singer and each melody.

Indicators of time

A feature of the language spoken by people older than 60 is the use of different grammatical verb forms to designate three general times of the day.[29] As I have mentioned, this temporal aspect is embedded in the polysynthetic verb structures of Old Tiwi. With some modification, it has been retained in the speech of older Tiwi people and their songs (suggesting it is a feature of Modern Tiwi but not New Tiwi). It creates a complex and mutlilayered understanding of song texts, their composition, delivery and reception.

The prefixes *wati-*[30] (morning) and *ki-* (evening) are used to identify when a song is being sung, not when the action described takes place. For example, Ngiya nguwatuwujamurrakupupuni means "I am going into the bush in the morning",

---

29   There is no affix specifically meaning midday, but the absence of one implies the general middle of the day (neither morning nor evening).
30   *wati* becomes *watu* when followed by a *w*.

and if spoken, it would tell us that the speaker intends to go into the bush in the morning. When sung, however, it does not necessarily imply the journey to the bush happened in the morning; rather, it tells us that the singer was singing in the morning. These time-of-day prefixes appear among the old song recordings and also in the songs composed by the eldest songmen and women who follow the Kulama way of composing, incorporating the stage markers (see Figure 14).

First person, present tense

In the vast majority of Tiwi songs, the singer sings Ngiya … "I am …", making that song performance a first-person, present narrative or personification. This bringing of the ancestor, the animal of the Dreaming or the deceased person into the present reflects the "self-manifesting and eternally active nature of the Dreaming" (Barwick and Marett 2003, 145). As the singer performs, they become the embodiment of the subject of their song and (re)tell the story or describe the imagery as though it is happening *now*. With each performance, therefore, a folding over of time is occurring, with the deep past and the present co-existing. Whether a Kulama song telling of current news ("I am talking into the gramophone"),[31] a bereavement song sung in the voice of the deceased's Dreaming ("I am the Crocodile") or a ritual stage-marking song ("I am the goose-feather ball") Tiwi songs are occasion-specific, with the singer activating or becoming a manifestation of the subject of the song. The degree to which the moment of performance was of primary importance is also evidenced by the text within many old songs that place the *performance* at a particular time. Song texts are tailored to the audience, the place and the time of day in which they are being created and (simultaneously) performed. At Song text 22 are four examples of this.

Song text 22: Unidentified man. Ngiya mampini (I am a canoe), 1912; Timarralatingimirri Daisy. Ngiya kulumurrunga (I am the crocodile), 1966; Warlakurrayuwuwa Paddy Sawmill. Ngiya jipilonti (I am the goose), 1975; Kitiminawulimguwi Declan Apuatjimi. Ngiya purrungi (I am the feather ball), 1975.

> **Unidentified man, 1912**
> Ngini myapinila muwingi nimuninginjirrikiliwingantirramawini
> *I am a boat carried in on the tide*

---

31   Audio 72 and Song text 4. While they wanted to give their own transcription of the Tiwi text (and use modern spelling), senior singers advised me to keep Osborne's translation. A further four lines of the song, while transcribed by Osborne, were not audible enough for the singers to be prepared to present it for this publication.

> **Timarralatingimirri Daisy 1966**
> Arranawu Ngyia wanga kulumurrunga
> *Be careful I am the female crocodile*
>
> **Warlakurrayuwuwa Paddy Sawmill, 1975**
> Ngiya jipilontimajiyawatiwuwa
> *I am the goose clearing the ground*
>
> **Kitiminawulimguwi Declan Apuatjimi, 1975**
> Ngiya purrungilimpangiliwaningimirri
> *I am the feather ball that they are holding*

When listening to old recordings, Elders often comment on the time of day the song was sung; for example, "He's singing for the evening, evening words, sounds like evening." The third song in Song text 22 for example includes -*wati*- not to place the story in the morning, but because the singer was singing in the morning. This is very often heard in the songs performed at the mortuary Yoi events and preparation of the dance-ground (to which this song refers) that are usually held in the morning. In the fourth song, Declan Apuatjimi includes -*ngilimpangi*- which places his performance in the evening. The song is not necessarily about the evening and indeed there was no word for evening in the text but the Tiwi listener could "hear" evening time in the sounds of the words. They were hearing the verbal affixes that mark temporality[32] – encoding the time of the day and/or stage of the ceremony at which it is performed – in this case either in the first evening of Kulama when bereavement songs are shared or during a mortuary ceremony. Across the song recordings is the regular addition by singers of -*ngilimpangi*-, the marker for the first day of Kulama, in the evening, the lying down or sleeping time. While adding no translatable meaning other than contextualising the performance itself, these temporal markers do create an aural mood for educated listeners. The feeling of the atmosphere surrounding the song performance is elicited in the listener through the threading of these words through the songs. Eustace Tipiloura explains the difference between hearing morning words and evening words:

---

32 There is no single word, analogous to "tense" or "aspect", that is commonly used to refer to the grammatical function of affixes of this type. R.M.W. Dixon (2010, 205) uses the phrase "temporal specification". Bernard Comrie, more discursively, calls such affixes "bound morphemes, attachable to the verb, which indicate the time of day at which a situation holds" and notes that they are rare across the languages of the world (Comrie 1985, 17–18). In Australia they occur in Yandruwandha as well as Tiwi, but elsewhere the only example Comrie gives is from the West African language Kom. In Tiwi, they have been described in grammars by Osborne (1974, 37, 46) and Lee (1987, 151, 186).

> He's singing for the morning, morning words, sounds like morning … the birds, the low sun … At midday the words are sharper, strong, like the bright sun … afternoon words, evening words … you know … they're more round, softer, sort of lazy maybe.

Close examination of song texts shows that there are two types of time markers: those found in the (almost obsolete) spoken language; and those found in song language.

Kulama stage markers

As song texts are always in the present, in Yoi songs performed at Pukumani-associated rituals the following will exist within the moment of the song's performance: the ancestor, a Dreaming image, a story from long ago, a ceremonial action, a Country place or a kinship marker. Kulama songs take this a step further with elements of song text specific to certain stages of the three-day ritual. Part of a student's initiation into Kulama and song composition entailed learning these grammatical structures and how to use them for performance at a specific time of day, and the part of the ritual performed then.

The words marking each part of Kulama are shown in Figure 14 (Osborne 1989, 281). Osborne refers to these as "Stage Markers" (Osborne 1989, 279). In the minds of my Tiwi colleagues some of these words and affixes (for example, *-ingilimpangi-* in the evening and *wati-* in the morning)[33] are now used more generally as an indication of the time of the day that a song is being performed, whereas other expressions (for example, *-kunji*) would be used only in a particular stage of the Kulama ritual. Senior singers can tell, from the use of a particular word in a recording, that the song must have been performed at that particular stage of Kulama, and, by extension, at what time of day. The placement of a song in a particular part of the day creates a strong existential inference on the part of the listener, placing the singer, the recording and the subject matter of the song in a very specific temporal environment. In dealing with the 1954 recordings, confusion was caused when songs were presented out of the correct Kulama sequence. For Elders, the time of day of the actual performance (even an elicited performance) should determine words to be used and so questions arise as to whether the singer was singing the wrong words for the time they made the recording or the correct words for the original performance context, but which are then incorrect for the part of ritual they refer to.

---

33   Here I use current spelling, but in song texts the initial vowel of *-ingilimpangi-* is spelled "u" following the advice of senior singers and/or where it elides with a preceding "u", such as in Declan's song in Song text 22. Similarly, the final vowel can be spelled "i" or "e". The same vowel change occurs in *wati-* which appears in some song transcriptions as *watu-*.

Figure 14: Ritual stage and time-of-day markers used in song texts.

Evening of First Day	-ngilimpangi-*, -ingilima[34] or ngi
Lying down time	*lying down/sleeping*
Afternoon of Second Day	-inji-rri-k-iningi-
Preparing ritual ground	*dur- cv- eve- hold*
Evening of Second Day	-jingi-ki or -ki-mirri-ki
Washing	*dur-eve*
Morning of Third Day	-wati-winginji-, or -wati-*
Fire burning down	*morning - dur*
Morning of Third Day	-kunji-
Cooking the yams	*cooking*
Afternoon of Third Day	-inkiri-piya
Painting face	*face-zero*
Evening of Third Day	inji-rri-ki-pi-*
Ayipa	

Expressions that have also been recorded or heard in recent non-Kulama songs

Wati- and *-ki-* (the time-of-day grammatical elements) are incorporated into the evening- and morning-stage words. Even though they can be glossed, none of these has any translatable meaning in the context of a song, apart from placing the performance in time. The listener (who, it is presumed, has prior knowledge about these markers and some years of attending Kulama) then engages with the song at a deeper level, feeling the sense of the time in the day when the performance occurs. Elders who listened to archive recordings (out of context of the ceremony structure) are able to establish the time of day (and, therefore, at which stage of the ceremony) a song was performed. They are hearing those elements found in spoken grammar, but they are also hearing what they call "the sound" of the time of day. Older listeners who are educated in these temporal markers tell me that the proliferation, throughout a song text, of these time-specific grammatical elements give a song an aural atmosphere, a "sound" or feeling that is created by the sounds of the words.

In the Cotton Tree song recorded in 1928, for example, every line includes the word *-ingilimpangi-* (sleeping) (see Song text 23 and Audio 70, Osborne 1989, 633). None of these implies that either the tree or the singer is sleeping

---

34 In current spoken usage *-ingilima* means "to kneel".

or has anything to do with sleeping. I must also point out that "sleep" is not a metaphor for death. Tiwi people don't see a dead person as having stopped engaging with the world. The word is there in order to place the song in the present at the time of the performance (the evening of the first day of Kulama). Tampungekerrayuwu is the name of the singer's daughter. He mentions three daughters in this way throughout the song. He is placing them as Cotton Tree people within the context of the deceased ancestor's clan. Ngampiripatumi is a place on Bathurst Island, and is the singer's Country.

Song text 23: Jimalipuwa. Use of -ingilimpange- as temporal marker in Tamunga (Cotton Tree), 1928.

L1.
Ngiya purr- wingilimpange- pili- muni- Tampungekerrayuwu
I they- sleeping- tree- fall- Tampungekerrayuwu
I am the falling Cotton Tree Tampungekerrayuwu [an Ancestral name associated with Jikilaruwu Country and Cotton Tree]

L2.
Ngiya purr- wingilimpange- Pilirrumawu
I they- -sleeping- Pilirrumawu
I am Pilirrumawu

L3.
Ngiya purr- -wingilimpange- Pilimunatuwu
I they- -sleeping- Pilimunatuwu
I am Pilimunatuwu

L4.
Ngini Timerrawila mwanjimi- ngilimpange- pili- muninga- piyanginiya
The Timerrawila ab- dur-me- sleeping- tree falling clear ground
The Timarrawila [Woollybutt clan] clear the ground for my fall

L5.
Ngampiripatumi tamunga nge-rr-wa-ri- ngilimpange- pili- yinti
Ngampiripatumi Cotton Tree I- p- ic- lk- sleeping- tree- stand
I am the Cotton Tree that stood at Ngampiripatumi

This song is exemplary of the rich implied meaning with few words of the Old Tiwi songs. When people hear this song they hear not only what the song is about but also, through the temporal markers, its context in time and where it fitted into the ceremony. The time of day a song belongs to is an important part of the overall meaning and significance of the text and of the associated feeling people have when listening to it. As well, there is a degree to which the lexicon places a song temporally (for example, words that literally mean "sunrise" or "dusk") but also that there is, according to senior songmen and songwomen, an overall aural imagery, resulting from the particular sound of the syllables of each time-marking word and the atmosphere invoked. Exactly what is meant by Eustace and others when they describe midday words as "sharp" and "strong", and evening words as "soft" and "round", proves difficult to specify, but Tiwi singers concur that the inclusion of these words and syllables creates an associated mood, so a song that has repeating iterations of -*ingilimpange*- throughout the text is often described as quiet, calm or sombre. This inference resonates with younger Tiwi listeners for whom the word is also now associated with bereavement/remembrance songs, in part because the lying down or sleeping time of Kulama is when those songs are traditionally sung. Without knowing why, they hear the song's ritual context and function – memorial – while they are actually hearing its performance context – evening. Both result in the same understanding of the intent of the song.

How these markers are used in song today

The temporal stage markers are used only by those very few men and women (now in their 70s and just passing 80) who still know how to compose for Kulama. Those aged between about 50 and 60 tell me they can hear the difference between the "old" way of singing (with the temporal stage markers) and the "new" way of singing (without) but cannot pinpoint the words from a given text. In what can be seen as a combining of two systems, the Women's Group does not use the Kulama stage markers in their compositions (because they are not singing at Kulama) but, perhaps because they follow the lead of the most senior women in the group for matters of song words, they do use the (Old Tiwi spoken language) time-of-day grammar that is appropriate for *when* they will sing the song. Teresita Puruntatameri said:

> Like say if a man is singing it's in the morning so when he sings he has to sing the words that he sings in that song's got to be morning words. Grammar kuwa [yes] and if he sings at night he's got to make the words into night. We do that now when, say, if we make a song for the funeral

and the funeral will be in the morning then we got to, you know, use the words in the morning.

Figure 15 shows one line of a song composed by Clementine Puruntatameri (the full text of which is at Song text 12). The text includes the chirping of the birds, as well as the grammatical morning marker *wati-* (shown in bold, noting that in sung form the vowel sound *i* is changed to *u*) to set the time of day at which she knew the song would be sung.

> It is "daylight, singing in the morning, let us know that it's morning", I was told by the women. "We hold the Mass in the morning so we sing those words."
>
> Calista Kantilla

Figure 15: Morning time marker in a healing song by Clementine Puruntatameri, 2011.

Mantirijipi rijipi aghayi*, yatipili **watu**wunkirijimi aghayi
[bird sounds] hey quickly the sun is coming up

*Aghayi is an interjection similar to "hey!" and here it is spoken in the voice of the bird saying, "Hey! It's morning!"

Eustace Tipiloura's song Going to Canberra (which I describe at the conclusion of this book) is another contemporary example of time stamping in performance. He sang it for me to record twice, once in the mid-morning and once in the evening. The texts differed only in the use of the relevant markers indicating the time of day of the recording. At Figure 16 is the same line of his song, with the same translation, but sung at different times of the day. When translating both of these texts, Eustace said it means "This is what I am doing". The evening time marker, *-limpanganayi*, is shown inserted throughout in my transcription (at Music Transcription 33) of his rendition sung in the late afternoon, in numerous variations as he sang to compose complete metric units. It serves as an interjection within the narrative, placing the singer in the present (of the late afternoon/evening performance) as if to remind the listener "that I am here telling you my story". When we consider that it occurs in almost all lines of text throughout the sung form, we can imagine how the song would sound quite differently with the corresponding number of insertions of (variations of) *watiwinginji*. Apart from the necessary alterations to surrounding text to make the metre correct, the words are phonetically quite different. These words are not heard in the narrative of the story. They *sound like when* he sings.

This setting of the performance in the present is another reason why the potential for learning, by rote, of old songs from recordings is a problematic thought for Elders. Although they do not mean anything to young singers, the time-of-day and ritual stage markers so strongly set the song in a particular time of day that older people feel the song is evoking a particular time and place. They told me they would not sing those words exactly at other times of the day because it wouldn't make sense.

Figure 16: Two iterations of the same song, at different times of the day (Eustace Tipiloura, 2012).

Sung in the mid-morning.
Ngirri watiwinginii ngirringuwi wayarri
This is what I am doing. I asked them. I want to take it back

Sung in the late afternoon.
Ngirri limpanganayi ngirringuwi wayarri
This is what I am doing. I asked them. I want to take it back

Interpretation of song subjects

In an attempt to document song texts, translation is only part of the picture. A strict translation will provide most of the words, and they are useful as a reference for future study and/or as a teaching tool for Tiwi song teachers, but it leaves out the associated and contextual meanings (Barwick and Marett 2003; Corn and Gumbula 2007; Magowan 2007; Turpin 2007). Due to the varying experiences, knowledge and affiliations of listeners there will always be more than one understanding of a song. Although, unlike in other Australian traditions, there is no attempt to create obfuscation due to secret, sacred or gender-restricted songs, Tiwi singers do aim at poetry with multiple meanings, ambiguity and evocation rather than literal meanings. Osborne states, "The technique of expression developed by Tiwi poets, especially in ritual contexts, is allusive, oblique and highly symbolic" (Osborne 1989, 392).

A group of people affiliated with a specific Country will share a unity of identity because of their recognition of those places when named in song. Similarly, among close members of a clan there would be understanding at a deep level of certain poetic metaphors and allusions within a song text. Osborne points out that:

> [T]he Tiwi vocabulary includes a wealth of synonyms, and it is the exploitation of these resources which permits the development of a

distinctive poetic diction … In any set of synonyms, one word … by virtue of its common usage in the everyday language, becomes the ordinary prose member of the set, while others … because they are less frequently used, acquire a literary or poetic character. (Osborne 1989, 310)

Eustace Tipiloura, Stephen-Paul Kantilla, Robert Biscuit Tipungwuti and Roger Tipungwuti, four of the last men who were qualified to sing for ceremony, all told me that it is too hard to compose using New Tiwi because it does not fit. On one level this is because the simpler, shorter forms of words (without the poly-agglutinative verb forms) are difficult to arrange into units of five syllables. Further, New Tiwi lacks the time-of-day word elements which always feature in the improvisation of text into metrical units, and perhaps the most significant factor (the one that has the potential to cause emotional and spiritual upset) is the fact that the modern language lacks the capacity for obliqueness and ritual-specific symbolism that creates a level of sung language deemed appropriate for ceremony. In much the same way as orthodox Catholics, Jews, Buddhists or Muslims might feel if their holy writings, hymns or chants were reworded using slang or mundane, everyday speech, singing Tiwi ceremonial song using New Tiwi lessens the import, reverence and respect for the religious observance. There is growing concern especially among Elders that "new" words are less respectful and cause harm as well as offence. Think about the symbolism (previously explained) for fathers' and mothers' kinship songs; for example, poetic allusion to breast, penis and groin present at a level above everyday speech, whereas blunt physical terms lower the tone.

With the Old language no longer spoken, even these old men have taken to studying the old recordings in order to re-learn these and other words as source material. Due to the obfuscation of many of the word boundaries and the stresses of the spoken language, the texts of the old, recorded songs are now only partially translatable by Tiwi people. Although the commonly used additions are recognised by older listeners, there are many words that have, through deletion, been altered beyond recognition today. This is (I surmise) why the few songs that have been passed down through the generations contain words that are not understood, not exactly translatable and are called "song only" words. The singers now compose using words or phrases that they cannot translate precisely but that have a meaning by association with a particular singer and their kinship group or because the song has been passed on in modified form. The train song (Figure 17) gives us an example of this. The word yontye, which in this song refers to the engine or carriage, is used in another song recorded in 1912 to describe a "saw". Yontye actually means "shellfish" or "something hard" and is used in other old song texts to describe any hard metal object. The 1912 text is taken from Osborne's translation (Osborne 1989, 850). The spelling used in Modern Tiwi and New Tiwi texts is the current orthography, a "j" having replaced "ty" in Osborne's transcription (Figure 17, Example 1) done in 1975. The changes in the first two vowels of the first word are, similarly, spelling changes that reflect the slight modification of phonetics.

Figure 17: Train song showing text change between 1912 and 2011.

Example 1: 1912 Train song (Old Tiwi)

Spoken form:

L1. Pe-   tu-   wuntying ala   yontye- rranungun- atyirr -ami
     They f-   dur   ?   engine   jolting   recip   mv

Free translation: *Wagons jolting forward one by one*

L2. Wong-   atyirr am-p-etye-   matyingikerirra- yala- pungilup- itya
     Alone- recip   she-f-dur-   linked together   ?   further   go

Free translation: *Each by itself moves a little further*

Sung form:

L1. Petuntyingala yontyerranungun atyirrami
L2. Wongatyirrampe tyematyingike rirrayalapu ngilupitya

Example 2: Current train song, consistent since the 1970s (Modern Tiwi).

Sung form:

L1. **Putajingala** yamarritipi **ajirrami**
L2. Tututingampi **kimajingiki rrayangilampu kuluputa**

Sung at Kulama by Tungutalum after a visit to Darwin when he saw a train, and recorded by Spencer in 1912, it must have been very well received at the time because it has become a well-loved and often-performed song, one of only a few songs that have been passed down for that reason. A train is an unlikely song subject for a composer living on an island north of Darwin in 1912. There has never been a train on the island, but there was a goods train in Darwin. Oral history tells us that Tungutalum (the singer) had travelled to Darwin in 1911 and had seen the goods train there, and on his return sang this song in the Ayipa stage of Kulama ceremony, a time for putting on public record the important or interesting news of the day.

A feature of Old Tiwi syntax, that makes it so different from the language spoken in the community today is noun incorporation, or the way the noun is embedded within the structure of the verb rather than being a separate word. This can be seen in Example 1, Figure 17, where yontye (onji in current spelling), the noun referring to "engine", is surrounded by the verb and its prefixes and suffixes.

A word containing 15 syllables works well for Tiwi song composition because it can provide either three units of five syllables for a non-line-final position, or two units of five syllables and one final unit of four syllables for a line-final position (by removing one syllable). In the sung form of the 1912 song *wu* is elided to create the correct metre (a five-syllable unit), Petuntyingala. It is interesting that Osborne could not find a meaning for ala in Line 1 or yala in Line 2. Presuming the *y* in Line 2 is an intervowel consonant, the two are synonyms. As an incorporated form -*ala*- is listed in the current dictionary as "the spirit of a dead person", and that has been added to the general associated meaning for people singing it today.

Since sometime in the 1970s (no-one is sure, but they guessed at this date because the old men they heard singing in the 1970s sang it this way) the text of the train song has been sung with words shown in Example 2 in Figure 17.[35] A recording made in the mid-1970s (*Songs of the Tiwi*, publication date unknown) includes a performance of Train with a variation of the words shown at Example 2. The extent to which these changes are the result of change in pronunciation and/or the change from one singer to another is not known. The loss of the *n* sound from the second syllable of unit one is another recent change. The second unit of the 1970s song has a couple of possible explanations, but neither can be confirmed. *Ya* is either an addition to complete the metric unit or a transitive verb root suffix to the first word meaning "look at". *Marri-* is a connective marker meaning "with". Marriji is a term for the Rainbow Serpent and might be a symbolic reference to the winding movement of the train. The Train song is still sung using the words from the 1970s version today, although they are no longer understood by singer or audience, as Barry Puruntatameri explained:

> I do that [song]. I learned as a young boy. It's not spoken language. This is thing that my great-great-uncle he sat by himself in the bush there. He made up those words about the train and it became a real Tiwi song today. People sing that song. He chose those words himself. The young boys, they wouldn't know the word meaning of it but they know the sound. You can't turn it into English. It's just the words.

---

35 The 1970s and 2011 text were given by my consultants. The spelling used in Modern Tiwi and New Tiwi texts is the current orthography, a "j" having replaced "ty" in Osborne's transcription done in 1975.

The onomatopoeic effect of the now meaningless words has become most important. We have no evidence of whether or not the text might have been onomatopoeic when it was first composed, but, since Osborne's consultants were able to gloss it, we know that it did not consist entirely of vocables, even though today people cannot translate any of the text. Those younger than about 50 years of age with whom I spoke had the opinion that the words are merely the sound of the train. Others agreed that the words mean nothing, showing the extent to which knowledge of Old Tiwi has disappeared. They said that much of the context of an old Yoi song such as this comes from the accompanying dance and that people imbue the song with associated meaning rather than from the text. Regina Kantilla said:

> It's only a word. You know it's a train by looking at the family and we recognise that Tungutalum – it's their song. Tipuamantimila. His father composed the song. It must be the dancing. That word [tututingampi] is I think the train sound but the first one is only a word.

My consultants, including Justin Puruntatameri (who, when he died in 2012 aged 87, was the oldest and most knowledgeable songman on the islands) said that tututingampi kimajingiki (the first and second units of Line 2) are onomatopoeic words describing the train's whistle and the way it clatters down the tracks. Whereas in 1912 this song was composed using the language spoken (and understood) by everyone, the distance of time and loss of Old Tiwi have rendered the literal meaning of this song (and many others on the archival recordings) incomprehensible.

An example of associations and speculation in relation to song: Allie Miller's Death of a Father song

Alluding to past occurrences, social norms or previously told stories is another way the composer can choose to imbue their song with contextual information. In many instances in addition to any common symbolic references, there will also be reference to a fact that only those who are part of the group connected to the singer will be aware of. Listening to songs or looking at the texts many years later has meant that even for Tiwi people many of the old songs are only partially meaningful because they were sung for a contemporary audience who were privy to recent news and the latest happenings in the community. Allie Miller's Kulama song, for example, composed in 1954 for his deceased classificatory father Waniyamperi, includes several poetic and linguistic devices that made it richly layered with different connotations and meaning for different people. Song text 24 is the full song text (this corresponds with Audio 1).[36]

Song text 24: Warabutiwayi. Allie Miller, Sorrow for his father, 1954.

> L1. Ngiya rringani perrantyuwali latemani ni-ngilimpange- marri- pumwari
> My father Prince of Wales letter-man loc-sleeping with leave
>
> *My father the Prince of Wales has left me*
>
> L2. Pantirri- wini ngurarri-n a-meni- me- ngilimpa- ngilani- kunte- rringilani yaketapumi
> Flag-m many-m he-me- wet- sleeping- flag- ? flag hold out
>
> *Many flags are held out for me*
>
> L3. Terayini tayikuwa- nga ngen-ti -wingilani- kitiraghi
> Train many- f l - f -flag- depart
>
> *In many trains I departed*[37]

Mountford (in a spoken introduction, Audio 1) gives the following free translation:

> This is Allie's song of the Pukumani. My father was King and I am Prince of Wales. As King George is King, so is the old man on the hill my father. I shall have war ships, money and a flag of red and white.

While this may have been the explanation given to Mountford by the singer, it is not a translation. The song text is not a close match. The allusion to the Prince of Wales is not literal. It is a term that was commonly used by Tiwi singers in the 1950s as symbolic of someone having power, being highly respected or being someone whose opinions should be heeded. Prince of Wales was a senior Larrakiya Elder and prominent dancer in Bagot (Darwin) in the 1950s. He had inherited the role of cultural leader from his father, whose English name was George King, similarly symbolic of his status in the community. It is likely that Tiwi men were aware of him. In this context it would have been used to mark the high status of the deceased. Similarly, a "letter man" alludes to people in positions of power: office workers or people from whom letters come (the written word in those days being something that "clever" or "powerful" people were capable of). The phonetic singing of English words appears in numerous songs throughout the archive. Perrantyuwali (Prince of Wales) and

---

36   Osborne's gloss and translation, including his question marks, presumably indicating text elements he was not able to elicit a gloss for (Osborne 1989, 644).
37   This is the translation for Line 3 given by Osborne. It makes no mention of flags.

latemani (letter man) in this song, and Kuwiyini Mirri Yilitpiti (Queen Mary Elizabeth) in Audio 59, rijiya (radio) in Song text 4 and Mindilipiji (Mindil Beach) in Audio 78 are just a few.

Bereavement songs often include imagery related to departing or being left behind. The reference in Line 3 to the deceased leaving in a train most likely came about because Allie had seen a train in Brisbane in March 1954 and so, singing at Kulama only a month later, the train would have been a newsworthy inclusion in his song.

In the following analysis of this song I will present the several different references that those I played it to have made, showing that one's relation to a song, and to its recording when heard out of context, is a very personal one, as well as being affected by the associations and experiences each listener brings to the occasion of listening. With word boundaries obscured in song form, it is difficult for modern listeners to determine what the word elements are, which can also lead to varying translations. Referring to Song text 24, I will comment on some of the words in turn.

- Elders recognised *-ngilimpange-* (Line 1) as a time marker indicating that the song belongs to the evening of the first day of Kulama, the lying-down time, when bereavement songs are sung. Those younger than about 50 years of age told me the word means "he has died" or "sadness for his death" because they recognise the word is always sung in these types of songs.
- In Line 2: *-me-* (now spelled *-mi-*) means "wet season" or "rain". Perhaps indicating that it was wet season (or raining) either when the song was performed or when Waniyampeni Sugarbag's death, Burial or Yiloti (Final) Ceremony took place.
- Osborne translates rringilani (Line 2) and wingilani (Line 3) as flag. Putting a flag outside the house of a recently deceased person was a common occurrence. The origin of this practice has not been confirmed but it might be from contact with Macassan fishermen. The connection has been made between this and communities in north-eastern Arnhem Land and it seems plausible that the same contact might have happened. The other possibility is that the custom came with the Iwaidja people. I have not been able to find *-ngilani* in either Osborne's or Lee's dictionary, however, and none of my consultants heard the words as flag. Among other songs in the recorded archive is the word pungila (flag),[38] and Elders recount a flag being indicative, in song, of a (European) settlement, perhaps from Fort Dundas (at Punata) in the 1820s and the army camps during the Second World War. Mourning songs note a flag to convey

---

38 The current Tiwi spoken word meaning flag is pantirra.

news of a death in hospital in town or in Darwin. A flag here might therefore suggest the location of the train in Darwin.

- In Line 1, rringani is translated as "father". The syllable *rri-* is a past-tense prefix and also a verb-stance prefix meaning "away from camp, at a distance" and some listeners understood this to mean the deceased father or ancestor was back in his Country.
- Osborne gives no translation for the word kunte in Line 2. Opinion is that it might be kunji, an Iwaidja loan word (from Hindi, via Macassan) meaning door, referring to the flags being held outside the door of the house of the deceased. Alternatively, kunji as an incorporated form relates to cooking – the time marker for the morning of the third day of Kulama. Some also heard kuntirri meaning "to be covered", symbolising the body or the coffin being covered at the funeral.
- *Wingilani* (Line 3) was heard differently and so resulted in different translations. It is likely a sung form of *-ngilani*, the *wi-* either a variation of *rri* from Line 2, the meaningless addition to create correct metre, or indeed a mis-hearing of *rri*. Some people heard wingi meaning "food". This fits with the singer's possible use of words marking the "cooking" stage of the Kulama ceremony. The word wingili means both "ochre" and "initiation song" and some listeners therefore heard in the text the symbolism of the Kulama ceremony's role as an initiation ritual or of the deceased's role as a songman. Instead of ti-wingilani some heard tiwingi, *tiwi* meaning people and the suffix *-ngi* meaning out bush or in Country. Not recognising *-lani*, they treated those syllables as metrical fillers. In the current dictionary *-riyi* is listed, meaning to depart – indicating there has been a vowel change from *-raghyi* to *-riyi*. The syllables *ki* and *ti* can be separated from kitiraghi – *ki* an evening time affix and *ti* a past-tense prefix – so ngilanikitiraghi suggests the deceased has gone to his Country.

This song and the train song are examples of the complexities faced by Tiwi listeners when approaching the old songs, but they also show how new ways of approaching the old texts are potentially just as meaningful in terms of their continued place in the Tiwi repertory. They are (as are all the examples in this book and in the sung repertory) also indicative of the multiple associations, inferences and responses that come from such richly allusive texts. An accumulation of meaning becomes attached to words and imagery as the songs are heard by listeners who bring their own understandings of ancestral stories, places and identities.

5 The Tiwi Language(s)

Continuing versification and cantillation techniques in modern song forms

In songs composed by the Strong Women's Group since the 1980s, a number of linguistic techniques found in the traditional song practice have been maintained, in the context of the newer Modern Tiwi language. While they are not creating the traditional songs' metrical structures, the women do employ some of the traditional techniques such as syllabic fusion, deletion and addition, as well as the obfuscation of word boundaries in their new songs. Modern Tiwi has lexical similarities with Old Tiwi, but with a simplified grammar. It is regarded as being appropriate for composition of some song genres, including those with the traditional five-syllable metre. With the lead composers in the group being the eldest, and so having the stronger connection with Modern Tiwi (now itself rarely spoken), as well as knowing some culturally significant words from Old Tiwi, these songs are now recognised as an important resource for the continuation of Tiwi song culture. Francis Orsto's version of Murli la (a derivation of the women's classical love songs) provides an interesting example of each of these techniques in the current repertoire and give some context as to how the renegotiation of language is a central part of both a song's composition and its reception. Francis Orsto (a Tiwi man in his mid-thirties) has been learning song skills from the senior men for some years and is emerging as a songman in traditional song practice. Having spent much of his childhood in the care of his grandmothers, and continuing his close relationship with the Elder songwomen, he has also become one of the core composers and performers of the Strong Women's Group, in the Modern Kuruwala song-type. He therefore has a relatively strong knowledge of the older forms of the language (Modern and Old Tiwi) in the context of song composition. His 2011 version of Murli la includes elements of both the Modern Tiwi and New Tiwi languages, treated in sung form in the "old" way, while in a non-Tiwi musical style.

Translating even this modern song we find it creates the same sorts of fluidity of understanding as some of the older texts do. With the (older) Tiwi listener expecting the singer to be altering words in certain ways, they can hear a number of meanings depending on their own inference. The Murli la song(s) are, in much the same way as the classical Crocodile song(s), one theme and one communally held story which is added to and retold as it is passed along the line of singers. Murli la is considered to be one song, despite these additions and alterations. At Figure 18 I've noted four understandings of one line of the version of Murli la attributed to Mr Orsto and recorded in 2011.[39] First is his understanding of the line of text, written out (by him) the way he sings it. Next is how the older women explained each word's meaning to me, and (at Example 4) the way they and Francis wanted it written down in English. Comparing these with the dictionary breakdown (Example 3) we can see how much room there is for interpretation when a song already holds an accumulation of meaning, as well as the impact of different generations of speakers hearing the language differently in song form.

Figure 18: Four possible interpretations of one line of Murli la, 2011.

Example 1: What Francis composed (in sung form), and his own translation.

Ngiyanuka nginta ngimpangintamurri
I will never forget you

Example 2: Women's glossing of text, and two opinions of the meaning of the line.

Ngiya arnuka nginta nimpangi nginta murri
I not indeed goodbye you us together

- I won't/can't forget what we mean to each other.
- I don't want to let you go.

Example 3: Dictionary glossing of what Francis composed.

Ngiya arnuka nginta ngimpa nginta murri
I not indeed I will indeed us

Example 4: Agreed transliteration.

Goodbye, I will never forget you and what there was between us.

The old women hear (and sing) nimpangi nginta, which is a song phrase they use in other songs, meaning "goodbye (to you)". They are expecting the syllable fusion of the final *-ngi* of nimpangi with the initial *ngi-* of *nginta* and so they hear both words, even though the syllable *ngi* is missing. In their translation the women have added the sense of being together (*murri*) and so we arrived at two "translations" from contemporaneous current sources, both with the same essential meaning, but using different words. It is an indication too of the associations of the whole song and of its connection to its Apajirupwaya (love song) predecessors which have longing as a central theme, that the word "forget" was offered by everyone I asked, although it is not there in the Tiwi text.

---

39 Audio 53.

5 The Tiwi Language(s)

The text of Example 1 shows Francis' understanding of the device of word alteration in traditional song composition. Although his song does not adhere to the classical songs' metrical structure and does not use a Tiwi melody, Francis still employs this device in order that the words fit the desired melodic phrase. To create the correct syllabic pattern for the melody, the words Ngiya arnuka ("I do not", "I will not" or "I am not") are fused into ngiyarnuka. Singers avoid adjacent vowels, so ngiya arnuka would be sung either as ngiyarnuka (deleting the final syllable of Ngiya) or as Ngiyamarnuka (inserting a consonant *m*). Francis uses the first option as he joins the words Ngiya and arnuka to sing the four-syllable Ngiya nuka. He chooses to change arnuka and retain Ngiya, therefore placing the important meaning on the action of the singer – "I am". The fact that Francis wrote it out in this way (changing the word arnuka to nuka) indicates that it was the sung form of the words that he wanted to document, creating Ngiya nuka. This has the potential to change the language further in future, because people learning the song from the written text or the recording might accept it as the way the word should be. The (older) women on the other hand heard arnuka as the more important – "not, can't, won't" – with the negative impact being the most important sense of the line. Some women also articulated the fused words, hearing the alternate usage of the prefix *ngi-* as "we", because they sing as a group while recounting the lovers' sad story. While a pedantic point, it makes a subtle yet important difference to the way it is understood by listeners and indicates how collaborative and adaptable researchers' approaches to song documentation must be.

What happens when the Old language is lost

Elders talk of "song language" but it seems this is in part because the language in the songs is Old Tiwi, a language that is no longer spoken but is only used by senior singers and composers. Perhaps this also reflects their understanding of the processes of text modification from prose through poetry to song. We know that song poetry composition was a skill taught over many years' immersion and participation in Pukumani- and Kulama-associated ceremonies. The attainment of the skill of composing was highly regarded. Grau notes that "[singers] gain prestige in creating songs and the audience appreciate a clever use of metaphors, allegories, and poetic images" (Grau 1983a, 55). Although word alteration and obscured word boundaries are features of almost all Tiwi songs, there is no overt aim to make the text opaque to the listener. Rather it is designed to display the cleverness of the singer. Perhaps, though, there is a sense that those who had attained the skill of how to compose in this way are revered for holding a knowledge that not everybody is able to access. It is consistently stated by Tiwi people in discussions about song composition that the alteration of words from speech to singing creates text that flows well and sounds good within the parameters of Tiwi artistic and musical aesthetics.

However, listeners have often commented that the language is "hard" and different from the spoken language. This is certainly in large degree today the result of the language shift and the fact that there is nowhere near the immersion in song that occurred in the past. While listening to the 1954 recordings, Calista Kantilla commented: "These songs are in hard language. I know the hard language but kids today don't know it. When I was young I was there when the old men sang those songs." Considering the fact that it took many years to achieve the status of becoming a senior man or woman in Kulama, those with the cultural authority to be leading ceremony and put forward as representatives of song to be recorded by the anthropologists were composing and singing following training they had received from teachers a generation older than themselves. This gives us a conduit back to pre-20th-century practices with idioms and ancestral stories passed down in an unbroken chain of transmission through Kulama. Tungutalum (a senior man recorded in 1912) would himself have learned from his Elder who would have been an old man in the mid-nineteenth century. Even listening to the more recent recordings from the 1980s we are hearing songs composed by people who would have been born in the 1920s and whose first language (and the language of their song initiation) is Old Tiwi. The breaking of this continuing transmission with the dismantling of the Kulama system has meant that much of the underlying intellectual process of song composition is now lost. Leading singers today do not talk about songs and song composition in terms of a precursor stage of creating lines of verse or by consciously constructing sung poetry. For those who can compose it is (and, they say, always has been) an intuitive skill that takes many years to absorb through experimentation and apprenticeship. Now as the language of the classical songs becomes more removed from everyday speech, it has become all the more imbued with notions of cultural heritage, art and spirituality. Elders speak of the metaphysical process of composing – Dreaming or finding or hearing the words in the bush and picking up snippets of song that the ancestors are singing. Justin Puruntatameri put it this way:

> We don't have school for singing like the old way when young boys sat with the old man to learn. Now they have to find the words on their own ... Maybe those old men are still out there, who knows? They're still singing and I hear them sometimes, you know, when we call out ... If they can sit and listen those words will come in somehow, maybe out hunting, maybe when they're asleep.

5 The Tiwi Language(s)

This is a dynamic, changing and fluid culture of song, sung knowledge and embodied identity with interpersonal engagement and heuristic learning at the heart of its traditions of transmission. Classical song must adhere to the correct metrical patterns (for the traditional song styles) and use the correct required vocabulary (such as the time-of-day markers) and (in order for it to be appropriate for that higher level) can only be composed using the Old Tiwi language. Only absolute fluency in that language and mastery of its grammar would make composing possible. Add to this the fact that singers would normally improvise their songs at the point of performance, and we start to get an understanding of how difficult the process is today for people who have never spoken the language. The additions, deletions, fusions and stress alterations that occur at the metrical level and then at the point of cantillation result in song text that is so different from the spoken language (and with that language now fallen out of use) that most songs in the recorded material are now only partially translatable. With language change and a marked shift in the role of song in the community, the "old" or classical songs have been raised from the everyday, becoming seen more as a part of a precious cultural heritage rather than a means of communication. Old words (many archaic and with suggested or imagined meaning) are now family heirlooms being passed down, like the stones from heirloom jewellery, reworked and embedded into new settings.

In the next chapter I will present a musical analysis of the song-types that make up the Tiwi song repertory and explain how, while most are still sung in Palingarri way, others are being renegotiated within the context of new musical forms. In both instances, the basic linguistic procedures of composition are followed in song texts using the Old and the Modern forms of the Tiwi language.

Plate 1: The Tiwi Islands, looking north along the Arruwulupini Kirluwagamini (the Big Creek), Apsley Strait. Photo: Genevieve Campbell.

Plate 2: Marralyaangimpi waterhole, Bathurst Island. Photo: Genevieve Campbell.

Plate 3: Delegation to Canberra, November 2009. L-R: (standing) Regina Kantilla, Francis Orsto, Agnes Kerinaiua, Wally Kerinaiua, Stephen-Paul Kantilla, Eustace Tipiloura; (seated) Genevieve Campbell, Mary Elizabeth Moreen, Teresita Puruntatameri, Jacinta Tipungwuti, Leonie Tipiloura, Mel Sheba Fernando. Photo: Terrilee Amatto.

Plate 4: Performing Kupunyi (Canoe) at NFSA, November 2009. L-R: Wally Kerinaiua, Teresita Puruntatameri, Stephen-Paul Kantilla, Eustace Tipiloura, Mary Elizabeth Moreen. Photo: Genevieve Campbell.

Plate 5: Unidentified man dancing Yirrikapayi (Crocodile), Bathurst Island. Still taken from footage by Baldwin Spencer, 1912. Photo: AIATSIS.

Plate 6: Performing with the 1912 archive footage. L-R: Gemma Munkara, Regina Kantilla, Frances Therese Portaminni, Katrina Mungatopi. NFSA, May 2021. "Eyes and Ears" presented by Canberra International Music Festival. Photo: William Hall.

Plate 7: Francis Orsto performing at NFSA, Alex Boneham in background, November 2009. Photo: Genevieve Campbell.

Plate 8: Collecting pandanus, Tikilaru Country, June 2014. Photo: Genevieve Campbell.

Plate 9: Eustace Tipiloura and Roger Tipungwuti in Wrangku Country, June 2014. Photo: Genevieve Campbell.

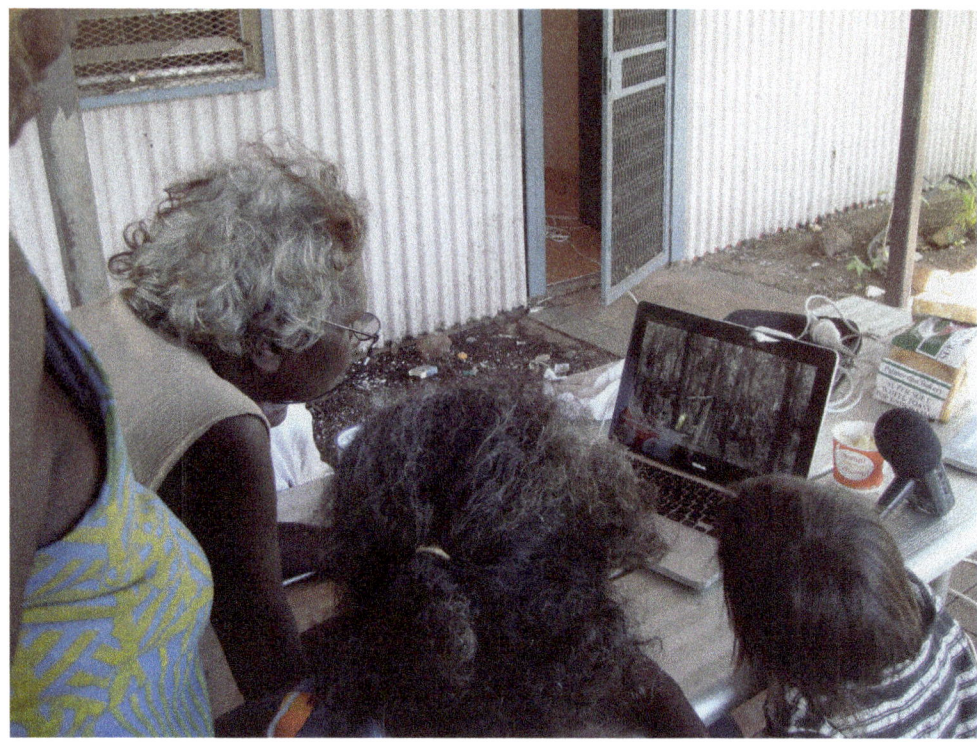

Plate 10: Marcella Fernando, Emerentiana Tipiloura and Tallulah viewing the 1912 footage. Wurrumiyanga, Bathurst Island, February 2010. Photo: Genevieve Campbell.

Plate 11: Jacinta Tipungwuti and Francis Orsto composing for an upcoming funeral. Wurrumiyanga, Bathurst Island, June 2012. Photo: Genevieve Campbell.

Plate 12: Performing at PULiiMA Indigenous Language and Technology Conference in Darwin, August 2019. L-R: Frances Therese Portaminni, Mary Elizabeth Moreen, Nola Tipungwuti, Regina Kantilla, Gregoriana Parker, Calista Kantilla, Concepta Orsto. Photo: Genevieve Campbell.

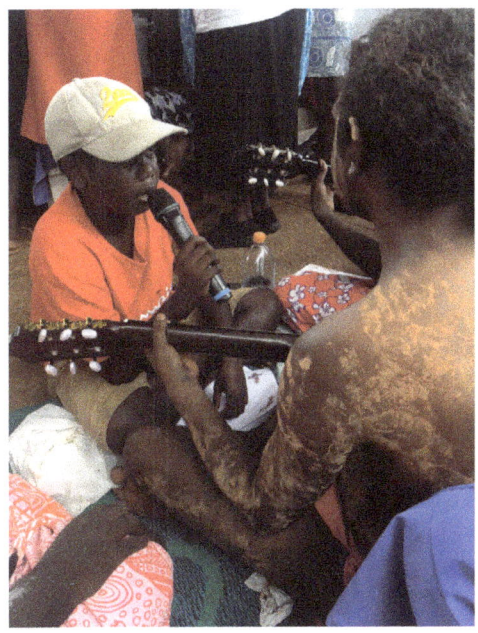

Plate 13: Jules Palipuaminni singing Kuruwala songs at a funeral for the first time, guided by Francis Orsto. At the funeral for Teresita Puruntatameri, January 2020. Photo: Genevieve Campbell.

Plate 14: John Louis Munkara performing his Jikilaru song. Darwin Entertainment Centre, March 2021. Photo: Libby Collins.

Plate 15: Performing Nyingawi at the Magic Mirrors Spiegeltent. L-R: Regina Kantilla, Mary Elizabeth Moreen, Jacinta Tipungwuti, Francis Orsto, Karen Tipiloura. Sydney Festival, January 2016. Photo: Prudence Upton.

Plate 16: Rehearsing the opening of Ngarukuruwala Yoi! Darwin Entertainment Centre, March 2021. Photo: Roger Press.

Plates

Plate 17: Mary Elizabeth Moreen and Eustace Tipiloura performing Yirrikapayi (Crocodile) at the Magic Mirrors Spiegeltent. Sydney Festival, January 2016. Photo: Prudence Upton.

Plate 18: Turtuni placed at the Milimika in preparation for Yiloti Ceremony. Wurrumiyanga, October 2012. Photo: Genevieve Campbell.

Plate 19: Calista Kantilla painting up for Yiloti. Wurrumiyanga, October 2012. Photo: Genevieve Campbell.

Plate 20: Transcription session. L-R: Marie-Carmel Kantilla, Regina Kantilla and Augusta Punguatji (behind). Wurrumiyanga, July 2017. Photo: Genevieve Campbell.

Plate 21: Ratifying the Tiwi display, part of the *Ambassadors* exhibition at Chau Chak Wing Museum, University of Sydney, 2021. L-R: Calista Kantilla (seated), John Louis Munkara, Regina Kantilla, Augusta Punguatji, Frances Therese Portaminni, Katrina Mungatopi. Photo: Genevieve Campbell.

Plates

Plate 22: Performing the Bombing of Darwin dance. L-R: Bobby Fernando, Ivan Fernando, Harold Munkara, Paul Tipungwuti. Bathurst Island, 1982. Photo: Patakijiyali Museum, Bathurst Island.

Plate 23: Justin Puruntatameri dancing at Kulama. Pirlingimpi, 1981. Photo: Andrée Grau.

Plate 24: Cornelia Tipuamantimeri dancing Winga (Sea) towards her husband, Long Stephen. Pirlingimpi, 1981. Photo: Andrée Grau.

Plate 25: Yilaniya (Smoking) ritual. Pirlingimpi, 1981. Photo: Andrée Grau.

Plate 26: Calista Kantilla leading singing at the funeral for Augusta Punguatji. Wurrumiyanga, September 2022. Photo: Genevieve Campbell.

Plate 27: Nina Black and Calista Kantilla, Bonnie Bush, Gabriel Wommatakimmi and Marcellus Mungatopi, Yanna Fourcroy, Doriana Bush, Nelson Mungatopi. Milikapiti, March 2010. Eunice Orsto, 2010. Casmira Munkara and Regina Kantilla, February 2008.
Photos: Genevieve Campbell.

Plate 28: Eustace Tipiloura, Calista Kantilla, Teresita and Barry Puruntatameri, Stephanie Tipuamantimeri. Wurrumiyanga, February 2010. Photos: Genevieve Campbell.

Plate 29: Juliette Puruntatameri and Clementine Puruntatameri. Wurrumiyanga, March 2010. Photo: Genevieve Campbell.

Plate 30: Calista, Clementine, Genevieve and Eustace. Women's Centre, Wurrumiyanga, 2010. Photo: Katherine Wood.

Plate 31: Justin Puruntatameri explaining language and Kulama to Francis Orsto, listening to the old recordings. Munupi Arts, Pirlingimpi, Melville Island, 2012. Photo: Genevieve Campbell.

Plate 32: Recording in the Old Church, Wurrumiyanga. L-R: Teresita Puruntatameri, Francis Orsto, Regina Kantilla, Genevieve Campbell, Karen Tipiloura. Photo: Simon Bartlett.

Plate 33: Shirley Puruntatameri and Regina Kantilla watching archive materials with Pularumpi Primary School children. Pirlingimpi, April 2016. Photo: Genevieve Campbell.

Plate 34: Singing "traditional way" songs at the Nguiu Social Club, 2010. L-R: Brian Ullungura, Eustace Tipiloura, Stephen Paul Kantilla, Walter Kerinaiua Sr, Leonard Tungutalum, Regina Kantilla, Calista Kantilla and Bede Tungutalum.

Chapter 6
The classical Tiwi music

> They sang really strong, you know? Hard words, proper way. I learned from them old men back then. I learned after them, bit by bit … [listening]. That line, that one, proper one for Kulama. Always the proper way for Kulama, then for Pukumani, for Yilaniya, or dancing … Pupuni, kuwa [good, yes] … So strong, those voices. I know Kulama way still. I'm the only one left.
>
> Justin Puruntatameri

As in many Indigenous Australian languages, there is no Tiwi word for music as a general concept. In current usage the word mujiki, borrowed from English, refers to pre-recorded music played on a sound system or radio. The closest Tiwi word is kuruwala (to sing). There is no Tiwi noun meaning "song" but instead people use a verb, saying they are singing: into Kulama, at Yoi, for their mother, etc. This points to the understanding that "song" does not exist as an object, but as an act. This is not unique to Tiwi culture. Indeed, many song cultures in Australia and around the world employ similar terminology (Ellis 1978; Stone 1998; Barwick and Marett 2007). Those who gave me words meaning "voice" explained that this is what a song is – the sound of one's voice – which is also the sound of one's body. Pupuni miraka, for example, means "good voice" and can also be said to a singer in praise of their performance. Other people suggested song-type names as the closest the language has for "song", although they understood the words to denote particular songs of that type rather than a song (of any type). Ngirramini was suggested as a word that describes what the song entails (a story, news, or a piece of instruction or law). It has, among practising Catholics, also taken on the meaning of "hymn" because it tells "the good news". Kawakawani is in the Tiwi dictionary meaning "to sing traditional style, sad singing" and kawakawayi[1] "to sing traditional style, happy singing". None of these however is a specific word for an individual song in the sense that we use the word in English.

As elsewhere in Australia, Tiwi music is predominantly vocal. Although in recent years the use of guitar has been incorporated into group singing at church and other community events, traditional and ceremonial Tiwi music does not involve pitched instruments. The didgeridoo,[2] common in other northern Indigenous communities on the mainland, has never been a part of Tiwi culture. Tiwi music consists of vocalisation, accompanied by percussion in the form of tawutawunga (clapping sticks), ngirini (mussel shells) hit together or hand clapping. When dressed in nagi (cloth tied around as short pants) for a formal performance occasion or a funeral the older men still use the method called pawupawu (slapping of hands on thighs or buttocks). Beating time with sticks or other found objects on soundboards such as pieces of corrugated iron sheeting is also common today and is first heard in recordings made in the 1960s. Although drums are not used for classical Tiwi musical styles, drum kits are played in rock band style music.

Traditionally the role of lead singer at a Kulama or Yoi event is performed by men, with women singing either in a supporting role[3] in Kulama or as part of the general group at the Yoi. While there are some song-types that tend to be sung either by men or by women, there are no song-types that must not be performed by a particular gender and, increasingly, men and women are sharing singing roles.

Before we can consider how Tiwi songs fit into the broader context of Aboriginal Australian music, it is important to have an understanding of the Tiwi musical culture and to give an overview of the song-types. The Tiwi song repertory comprises eleven musically definable song-types and one vocal call. Eleven different melodies have been identified among the ethnographic song recordings (although there may well have been more prior to the 20th century that were not recorded). These are performed in three performance contexts: the Pukumani (mortuary-related) ceremony; the Kulama (annual initiation-

---

1 Kawakawayi is a song text element that is widely used in Kulama and Yoi singing as well as in the more recent guitar-accompanied singing done by the women's group. I have discussed this text element in Chapter 5.
2 There is no Tiwi word for this instrument. The closest, arlijuta, meaning the "trunk of the bamboo plant", is also used as a synonym in the Tiwi online dictionary (Lee 2011), although I have heard Tiwi people use the words yidaki and didgeridoo, always in the context of the music of other people.
3 In the Ampirikuruwala song-type.

focused ceremony); and non-ritual occasions. Musically they are in one of two distinct styles – either in the Yoi (dance) style or Kuruwala (singing) style – and there are certain generalisations one can make based on this distinction. The Yoi-style song-types, being principally for group participation and dancing (and, functionally, to connect people through Dreaming or kinship groups) are more regular in tempo and structure and have a stronger marking of the pulse with percussive accompaniment. The Kuruwala-style song-types are primarily performed solo[4] and their purpose is to express an individual's thoughts (of grief, of love or of telling news). They exhibit a greater degree of variation in tempo, structure and embellishment of melody and are generally slower, with either sparing or no use of percussive accompaniment. Figure 19 lists the song-types with a general overview of their musical characteristics, function and performance context. I use both "mourning" and "grieving" to describe the function of Amparruwu and Mamanunkuni – "mourning" sometimes implying a state of being, not within a ceremony, and "grieving" referring to an act (of wailing or crying) within ceremony. Some of the women's songs, such as the Amparruwu, can also be considered keening, but, as it is a performed vocalisation, I distinguish it from the cries of grieving. Both song-types can be performed in both circumstances. Song-types 1 to 5 are performed as part of the Pukumani series of rituals, which is held in a number of stages over some days or weeks.

Figure 19: Overview of the Tiwi song-types.

Song-type	Traditionally sung at	Traditionally sung by	Function	Tempo and percussion	Currently
1. Jipuwakirimi Yoi (dance) style	Yoi [Pukumani] (mortuary ceremonies)	Lead singer/composer, then picked up by group	Dance support Kinship Dreaming Ritual	Fast Sticks and/or clapping	Sung at funerals, weddings, community events and public performances
2. Jalingini (Sugarbag) and Timilani (Mosquito) Call	Yoi [Pukumani] (final mortuary ceremony)	Group (traditionally men)	Calling of ancestral and Country names Opening Yoi event	Single long note. No beat	Sung at Yoi and at public and tourist events (Mosquito obsolete)

---

4   The recent forms of the individually created songs (song-type 11) and the Modern Kuruwala-style (song-type 12) do, however, often involve group singing (in a non-Tiwi, choral style).

Song-type	Traditionally sung at	Traditionally sung by	Function	Tempo and percussion	Currently
3. Arimarrikuwamuwu Yoi (dance) style	Preliminary mortuary activities Tree-climbing (obsolete) Yilaniya (part of the Yiloti (Final) Ceremony)	Solo, patrilineal male kin Group interjections	Bereavement status	Fast Sticks	Still sung at Yilaniya but not tree-climbing
4. Ampirimarrikimili Yoi (dance) style	At mortuary ritual, at battle events, for private entertainment	Women's Group, led by soloist	Non-specific	Fast Hand clapping	No longer performed
5. Amparruwu Kuruwala (singing) style	Throughout (and adjunct to) final mortuary ceremony	Solo. Spouse of deceased	Mourning/grieving Sorrow	Slow/moderate No sticks	Sung in the evening a few days before and throughout the day of the funeral and at Yiloti (Final Ceremony)
6. Mamanunkuni Kuruwala (singing) style	Adjunct to final mortuary ceremony Kulama ceremony	Solo. Male or female	Mourning/grieving Sorrow	Slow No sticks. Sometimes soft clapping of hand on knee	Sung at Yiloti (Final Ceremony), at funerals and associated gatherings and at any time
7. Arikuruwala Kuruwala (singing) style	Kulama ceremony	Solo male	Bereavement Bestowing names Airing grievance Imparting news	Slow/moderate Use of sticks varies between individuals	Public performances (male or female solo) Sung by male soloist at Kulama ceremony
8. Ampirikuruwala Kuruwala (singing) style	Kulama ceremony	Female individual or group	Response to male Arikuruwala	Slow/moderate No percussion	Sung at public performance and at Kulama ceremony
9. Ariwangilinjiya Kuruwala (singing) style	Anytime (non-ritual)	Solo, usually women	Lullaby	Slow No percussion	Sung by older women caring for infant grandchildren
10. Apajirupwaya Kuruwala (singing) style	Private social gatherings	Solo female	Entertainment	Moderate No percussion	No longer performed

6 The classical Tiwi music

Song-type	Traditionally sung at	Traditionally sung by	Function	Tempo and percussion	Currently
11. Ariwayakulaliyi Kuruwala (singing) style	Kulama ceremony Other (non-ritual) occasions	Male or female solo or group	Non-specific	Moderate Sticks and/or hand clapping	Melodies now used by Women's Group
12. Modern Kuruwala Kuruwala (singing) style	n/a	Women's group	Healing Entertainment Education	Moderate Guitar-accompanied Sticks and/or hand clapping	Healing, Yilaniya, funeral Community events, professional engagements

Performance context and variability

There is a general difference between the solo song-types and those that involve group singing. The Jipuwakirimi/Yoi, Arimarrikuwamuwu (tree-climbing ritual) and Ampirimarrikimili (women's) songs are, while composed and led by an individual, primarily for group participation, with the "lead" singer presenting their song and others joining in. The Arikuruwala (Kulama), Amparruwu (widow), Ariwangilinjiya (lullaby) and Apajirupwaya (love) songs are composed and performed by individuals as solos. The Mamanunkuni (sorrow) songs are composed and sung by individual men with one or more women singing in a quasi response.

Whether creating an entirely new song (for Kulama) or re-inventing a Dreaming or kinship song (for Pukumani), the Tiwi composer creates a new work while working within the parameters of the melodic contour, the subject context, and the phonetic and linguistic structures and rules of whichever song-type they are singing. While there are defining characteristics for each song-type, no two songs are the same. I will first address the group participation songs.

It is important here to note the fundamentally social and inclusive nature of the Yoi (dance) event and the songs performed therein.[5] Jipuwakirimi songs (commonly referred to as Yoi songs) were traditionally performed at the final stages of mortuary rituals and are now the central element of the funeral and Ceremony[6] in an event that is widely known as "the Yoi". Both the old recordings and the current practice confirm that the primary function of a Yoi song is as

---

5   This discussion refers principally to the Jipuwakirimi songs. There are very few recordings of Arimarrikuwamuwu or Ampirimarrikimili songs and they are no longer performed, so I cannot generalise to such an extent.
6   "Ceremony" is the term generally used today for the Final Pukumani (mortuary-associated) Ceremony. I therefore capitalise the word when it is used in this way.

dance accompaniment and group participation, regardless of the context (ritual or entertainment) in which it is sung. Yoi songs (and dances) are now also performed for non-ritual events such as the football grand final, a community occasion or for tourists.

The extent to which group participation is a feature of the Yoi-associated song-types has a clear impact on musical conventions and there is a demonstrable correlation between melodic variation, performance function and song-type. The consistency of tempo in Yoi songs (both within the song itself, throughout the often hours-long event and across years of the recorded archive) can be attributed at least in part to group participation and pervasion of regular events, similar to what has been analysed in the Djanba repertory sung at Wadeye, northern Australia (Bailes and Barwick 2011). For example, a Jipuwakirimi song is always performed first by the lead singer (usually the composer) and, after a few iterations of the text, the group joins in, singing the same words. Although there is much scope for extemporisation of this text (the song would be newly composed for the occasion), the tempo and pulse are regular so as to create a constant basis for the dancers. There is also the need for consistent repetition of text in order that the group can "catch" the words and join in. These are also the main reasons for the monotonic contour of Jipuwakirimi songs, as I discuss in the next section.

Just as group participation results in regularity of tempo, percussive pulse and melody in the Yoi-style song-types (1, 3 and 4), the solo performances given by individual singers of the Kuruwala-style song-types (5, 6, 7, 8, 9 and 10) are characterised by greater variability of tempo, pulse, melody and vocal style. Arikuruwala (song-type 7) along with song-type 8 (Ampirikuruwala, the woman's response sung in a supporting role) forms the basis of the Kulama ceremony. It is sung solo, traditionally by men (often with the female response creating a duet) and is a vehicle for innovation of subject matter, poetic technique and vocal artistry. Certain singers in the old recordings display vocal idiosyncrasies, which have, in many cases, helped my informants identify individuals. This is also the case with the Mamanunkuni (Sorrow) and Amparruwu (Widow) songs, which are solos, sung by men and by women, with none of the constraints associated with group singing. Melismatic introduction, falling or rising of pitch on different beats, vocal timbre variations and different line-final lengths render the melodies of the Kuruwala-style songs slightly different with each performer.

It is interesting to briefly consider how these relate to neighbouring Australian song genres. I'll begin with the elements in which we can see differences between the Yoi style and the Kuruwala-style groupings – melody, song structure, tempo and pitch – and will then discuss rhythm and text, the important features of which apply to all of the Tiwi song-types.

Melody

The general impression given in the literature of the song culture of the Tiwi Islands is that it is primarily monotonic (Moyle 1997; Osborne 1989; Simpson 1951; Stubington 1979) and even "entirely inexpressive" (Osborne 1989). This might be partly because the Jipuwakirimi song-type, which is broadly monotonic, is the song-type performed for all Yoi events – mortuary ceremonies and public dance events – and so was the subject of most observational study, and it also appears more often in the recorded archive. There are in fact 12 distinct melodic forms and (even across the "monotonic" songs) there are as many variations of poetry, musicality and vocalisation as there are singers and performances. This might be due simply to musical unfamiliarity or unavoidably selective observation, but it is certainly a misrepresentation of Tiwi song culture as a whole. I would suggest that this impression could also be the result of the fact that most of the songs recorded by researchers are Jipuwakirimi and Arikuruwala, the song-types that form the bulk of the Pukumani and Kulama ceremonies and which have melodic contours that are close to monotonic. The song-types that show a greater degree of melodic interest (sung by individuals and with more personal subject matter) are performed outside of the large ceremonial events (or, if during them, off to the side rather than as a focus of the proceedings). This perhaps goes some way to explaining Osborne's opinion that melodic interest is "a frivolity" and so only appropriate for secular songs "for entertainment" and that in ritual-related songs "plain monotoning ... is usually preferred so that the hearer's attention is not distracted from the meaning of the words" (Osborne 1989, 154). While it is true that it is the case for the (non-ritual) love songs (song-type 10), none of my Tiwi consultants agrees that the words are less or more important in any context, nor that melodic simplicity or complexity influences the listener's reception of them.

Most Tiwi songs employ melodies that undulate around a pitch range of close to a minor 3rd.[7] This small range sets the Tiwi genre apart from the octave-descent shape of some Central or Western Desert genres (Keogh 1990) or the series of pitch descents found in north-eastern Arnhem Land (Stubington 2007). Some Tiwi song-types are based around a cyclic melody, with each iteration corresponding with one line of text. Others use a melodic phrase that comprises two segments, across which one line of text is split, or a shorter line

---

7 The love songs (song-type 10) and the individually invented melodies (song-type 11) that have a range of up to an octave may be the result of the importation of non-Tiwi musical styles.

of text is repeated. The capacity for the extension of musical structures to allow for dancing, for ritual activity or to accommodate the desired text is a feature of most Tiwi song-types. The love songs are the only song-type that has a fixed line length. Similar variability occurs in many Australian song genres (Barwick 1990; Treloyn 2003, for example). Most Tiwi melodies follow a note-per-syllable pattern. In the introductory incipits of Arikuruwala songs, melismatic ornamentation is sung on vocables, but not on syllables of the song text.

In Tiwi songs, as with most other genres of Australian song, there are variations or nuances of pitch and vocal timbre that reflect individuals' performance styles but occur within the overall framework of the melodic contour, phrase structure and pattern of rhythmic cells that are indicative of that particular song genre.

Pitch

It seems that there is a certain degree of pitch memory among the Tiwi singers across separate Yoi events, and also by individuals in their own solo singing.[8] In the past, when Yoi sequences were preceded by the Sugarbag and Mosquito calls (that serve as an introductory "tonic"), the Mosquito call was always a full octave above the Sugarbag call, in a falsetto tessitura. Immediately after these calls the lead singer started the first song (on the same pitch as the (lower) Sugarbag call), which was then picked up by the group. The continuous nature of the song event meant, with each new song being presented soon after the completion of the preceding one, it was likely that the pitch stayed the same for each subsequent singer, often for some hours at a time. The likelihood of a collective pitch memory being established is greater when many such events were held with not a lot of time in between, and also in the era prior to non-Tiwi audio "interference" such as hymn-singing nuns, guitars, radio and television. Pitch memory is a widely studied topic across many musics, as is the notion of "perfect" as opposed to "remembered" or "learned" pitch. To a certain degree we (non-professional singers) all sing at a pitch we find physically natural and comfortable. Think about a group spontaneously singing "Happy Birthday". Each person begins on their comfortable note and so the group will often begin on varying notes, coming together to find a consensus with the loudest singer (or perhaps the person who started singing first, with varying success depending on the aural perception and vocal qualities of the singers!). It has been observed in children (including my own) who are exposed to regular repeats of audio

---

8   This capacity in other orally transmitted performance traditions has been the topic of discussion in the literature, for example Barwick (1989) and Will (1998). In the Tiwi context this is due to the collective nature of group singing occasions.

with a constant pitch centre – such as a favourite television show theme song or often played record – who will then sing that song at the same pitch as the recorded version even when not hearing it at the time. They have remembered the song at the original pitch and so for them the song always exists at that pitch. This (remembered pitch, rather than perfect pitch) is probably what's happening in the Tiwi context. Through the archives are instances of people singing at "their" pitch when singing alone and also of the current custodian of a songline singing at the same pitch as the previous holders/singers of that line. In my experience with Tiwi singers, Casmira Munkara, Clementine Puruntatameri, Ella Puruntatameri, Eustace Tipiloura, Calista Kantilla, Francis Orsto and Justin Puruntatameri have continued this trait.

Figure 20 shows the pitch of the Sugarbag call, the Mosquito call and the song series immediately following in some of the repatriated recordings.[9] While there would have been many other Yoi events that were not recorded that might have been sung at other pitches, this data does show that across many years there is a spread of only two tones (C4–E4) in the pitch of Yoi song events.

Figure 20: Pitch of Sugarbag and Mosquito calls.

Year of recording	Sugarbag	Mosquito	Songs
1955 (ABC)	D4	D5	D4
1965 (Wurm)	D4	D5	D4
1975 Songs of the Tiwi	E4	E5	E4
1975 (Osborne)	Db4	Db5	Db4
	E4	E5	E4
1976 (Moyle)		D5	
1981 (Grau)	E4		E4
1991 amateur video			Db4
2011 Campbell	C4		C4
2012 Campbell	C4		C4

---

9 The pitch of the 1912, 1928, 1948 and 1954 recordings is unreliable due to the quality of the recording equipment and the songs running too fast. While we have slowed them down to tempi my consultants are happy with, and found they are on D4 and E4, I do not include the data here because further work is needed to confirm the results are correct.

The pitch of the Kulama-associated song-types is not consistent. This could well be because Kulama singing is a solo performance, not involving group participation (apart from the women's response sections) and also not sung at the same occasion as the Sugarbag and/or Mosquito calls. While the recordings show some consistency of pitch among performances by an individual, each person sings at a different pitch from others.

Structure

There is no definitive structural pattern for each Tiwi song-type, although generalisations can be made about them. Just as the vocal ornamentation is greater in the solo song-types, there is also greater variation in the structure of the text. Across the different Tiwi song-types there are different structural organisations of text, some song-types showing similarity to the cyclic structural style of Central Australian and Western Desert songs (O'Keefe 2010; Turpin and Stebbins 2010) and others more like the strophic songs of Arnhem Land (Stubington 1979; Wild 1985).

The Yoi-style songs (and, to a lesser extent, the Arikuruwala songs that involve the female Ampirikuruwala response) involve group participation and so have a greater degree of regularity in text organisation. They tend to be lineal in structure, in that each line is repeated any number of times before moving on to the next line, which is repeated in its turn and so on. The lead singer, who is also often composing the song phrase as they sing, will often take more than one iteration of the line to "set" the words and will indicate by a subtle change of sound (projecting out to the assembled group to present the newly formed song) that the group is welcome to join. Singing of each line at least twice enables the group to pick up the words. In a large Yoi event, a song phrase might be repeated a dozen times or more to accommodate all those who want to take their turn to dance. The linear, repeating structure of Jipuwakirimi songs is one of its defining features.

Among the Kuruwala-style songs, on the other hand, the structural shape of Mamanunkuni varies the most, with variations in the length, symmetry and repetition of lines. By comparing the recorded performances of different singers, we can get a sense of how each person has their own style, and we hear that one singer will repeat (say) lines 1 and 2 a few times, then move on, to bring 1 and 2 back again, creating a pattern, whereas others will repeat 1, 2, 3 and re-order those in repetitions to create a section of variations of those lines, before moving on and singing 4, 5, 6, 4, 5, 6 and so on. The singer, free from having to work with a group, sings just as they desire with the random ordering of lines of text creating a stream-of-consciousness effect as they compose while they sing.

As well as in the structural arrangement of the lines, the length of lines and how they vary follows the degree of individual freedom each song-type allows.

The general rule across all the song-types is that the length of a line is varied by adding metric units (each comprising five syllables and, correspondingly, five rhythmic notes) at a particular point in the melody that is mostly consistent within each song-type. Broadly speaking, one can say that any extension occurs on the pitch that is arrived at on the second unit of text, then there is a motif that delineates the end of the line, so melodic interest occurs at the beginning and end of a line of text, with the majority of the text voiced on the plateau section of the melody. There are variations to these norms but we can note the characteristics of each song-type.

For example, in the Arikuruwala song-type, which has the potential for the longest lines, comprising up to about 11 units, we hear the extension usually occurring at the beginning of the second unit (the point at which the pitch arrives at the "tonic"). The melodic motif at the end of the line is then sung across the tenth or eleventh unit. The Mamanunkuni songs are extended by repeating alternating pitches in the middle section of the melody (not at the first or the last units, which have relatively regular motifs). The Amparruwu songs, rather than extending the melody to accommodate longer lines of text, comprise relatively short lines of text (of two or three units) which are then split across the two segments of the melody, with the singer altering the second text unit as it restarts on the following line before moving on, creating a dove-tailing or overlapping effect as each line moves on incrementally, taking part of the line before with it.

Amparruwu songs are personal narrative-style expressions of grief, often in the form of the singer talking to their deceased spouse or of the voice of the deceased talking to the singer. They therefore tend to be linear, with numerous interjections of the kayayi (crying) vocalisation and some repetition of lines, but with no set pattern. There are many versions of kayayi, mostly in the vocalisation of the initial *k* (with more or less aspiration and attack depending on the individual) and extensions of the vowel sounds to create drawn-out sighs and/or abrupt cut-offs and pitch falls to approximate sobs.

The incidence of the (untranslatable) kurukangawakawayi line is also noticeably higher in the Amparruwu, Mamanunkuni and Arikuruwala songs. This is not so much a word as a syllabic string, although Tiwi singers do call them "songwords" and make a point to differentiate them from the

English language equivalents of "la la la". Kurukangawakawayi, altered to fit whichever metrical, melodic and rhythmic positioning required, serves to give the composer time to formulate the next line of poetic text.[10] Kurukangawakawayi words are described by Tiwi singers as "a bit like humming" and also as "happy singing" (as opposed to the "kawakawani" (sad singing) words kayayi kayayi). They are often used in both current classical singing and in the choral Women's Group songs, either as a way of extending a song at the completion of the song (forming a coda) or within the song (between verses, for example). The Ariwangilinjiya (lullaby) song-type tends to comprise only one or two lines, which repeat at random, interspersed with "ayayaya" elongated to any length, as the singer's main purpose is to calm or to lull a baby to sleep. The only recordings we have are quite short, not having been recorded in the action of actually lulling a baby, but in an elicited recording session. With a baby in their arms a singer will continue on and off for as long as it takes.

Figure 21 gives a representative indication of the structure of each of the song-types. While of course this should not be taken as the definitive structural rule for each song-type, it does show the relative degree of variability found in each.

I use numbers for each line of text. "K" indicates the text string (kurukangawakawayi or kayayi variations) and A indicates "ayaya" in the lullaby texts. An aborted line is indicated with (ab). I have not indicated aborted lines in song-types 1 or 3, because many lines end part-way through as the singer cuts off to correspond with the end of each dancer's contribution.

Inaudible sections are indicated by "…" Song-type 2 is not listed. The Sugarbag and Mosquito calls don't include text and so don't have definable text line structure, although they are sung and so are included in the classification of song-types.

---

10 See a fuller description of this text element in Chapter 5.

Figure 21: Structural analysis of song-types.

Jipuwakirimi (Song-type 1)

Barry Puruntatameri. Yiloti. 2012 (Recorded by Campbell)[11]
1,1,1,1,1,1,1,1,1,1,1,1,1,2,2,2,2,2,2,2,2,2,2,3,3,3,3,3,3,3,3,3,3,3,3,4,4,4,4,4,
4,4,4,4,4,4,4,5,5,5,5,5,5,5,5,5,5,5,5,5,5,5,5,5,6,6,6,6,6,7,7,7,7,7,7,7,7,
7,7,7,8,8,8,8,8,8,8,9,9,9,9,9,9,9,9,9,9,9,9,10,10,10,10,10,10,10,10

Arimarrikuwamuwu (Song-type 3)

Black Joe. Goose. 1955 (Audio 17)
1,1... 2, 3, ... 3, 3... 3, 3, 4, 4, 3... 2, 3, 3, 3...

Stanley Munkara. Rich Man. 1975 (Osborne 1989, 1057)
K, 1, 1, 1, 2, 2, 2, K, 3, 3, K, 1, 1, 3, K

Ampirimarrikimili (Song-type 4)

Unidentified women. 1948 (Audio 21)
1 x 14, 2 x 3 (before recording fades out)

Unidentified woman. 1981 (Audio 20)
Song 1: 1, 1, 2, 2, 2,
Song 2: 1, 1, 1, 1, 2, 2, 2
Song 3: 1, 1, 1, 2, 2, 3, 3, 3, 2, 2, 2

Amparruwu (Song-type 5)

Christopher Foxy Tipungwuti. Rainbow. 1975 (Audio 39)
(Osborne C04-003855 song 207).

K, K, 1, 2, 2, 2, 3, 4, 1, 1, 4, 5, 5, 5, 4, 5, 3, 3, 2, 2, 4, 5, 2 (ab), K, K, K,
2, 2, 3, 3, 1, 1, 4, 5

Eunice Orsto. Snake. 2010 (Audio 16)[12]
1, 2, 3, K, 4, 5, 6, 7, K, 8, 9, 10, 11, 11, K, 12, 13 (12), 12(K), 14, 14, 14,
15, 16, 15, 16, K

Mamanunkuni (Song-type 6)

Long Stephen. Waking Up. 1975 (Audio 27)
K, K, 1, 2, 3, 3, K, K, 4, 4, 5, 6, 1, 2, 3, K, K, K

---

11 Audio not included at request of family.
12 In this performance, Eunice sings half a line at 13, with the remainder of line 12 and then half of line 12 with the remainder of the kayayi line.

Long Stephen. Silent Land. 1975 (Audio 69)
1, 1, 2, K, K, K, 1, K, 2, K, 3, 3, K, K, 4, K, 5, K, 2, K, 4, 5, 5, 5, 5, K

Arikuruwala (Song-type 7)

I have not included Ampirikuruwala (song-type 8) here because the woman's response is an immediate repeating of the man's words and so follows the same structure as his performance.

Unidentified man. 1912 (Spencer C01-00701-7)
...1, 1, 1, 1, 2, 2 ... 2, 3, 3, 3, ... 4, 4, 4

Tungutalum. 1928 (Audio 72)
1, 1, 1, 2, 2, 2, 3, 4, 5, 2, 1, 4, 5, 1, 1, 2, 6, 6, 6, 6

Tractor Joe. Grievance over a promised woman. 1975 (Osborne C04-003853-89)
This example shows a full performance in the Kulama ceremonial context. Only those recordings made in ceremonial context are of this length. Recordings made in sessions are much shorter.

(low octave) 1, 1, 1, 1, 2, 2, 2, 3, 3, 4, 4, 4, 4, 4, 4, 5, 5
(low octave) 1, 1, 1, 1, 2, 2, 2, 3, 3, 4, 4, 4, 4, 5, 5, 5, 5, 6, 6,
(upper octave) 1, 1, 2, 2, 3, 3, 4, 4, 4, 5, 5, 5, 6, 6,
(upper octave) 1, 1, 1, 2, 2, 3, 3, 4, 4, 4, 5, 5, 6, 6, 7, 7, 7, 7,
(upper octave) 7, 7, 7, 7, 2, 2, 3, 4, 4, 4, 5, 5, 6, 6, 7, 7,
(upper octave) 1, 1, 1, 2, 2, 4, 4, 5, 5, 5, 6, 6, 7, 7, 7,
(upper octave) 1, 1, 1, 2, 2, 3, 3, 4, 4, 4, 4, 6, 6, 7, 7, 7

Ariwangilinjiya (Song-type 9)

Unidentified man. 1954 (Audio 22)
A, A, 1, 1, 2, 2, 2, 1, A, A, A, A, 1, 1, 2

Unidentified woman. 1954 (Audio 23)
1, 1, 2, A, A, 1, 2, 1, A, A, 1, 2

Apajirupwaya (Song-type 10)

Unidentified woman. 1954 (Audio 23)
1, 2, 1, 2, 3, 3, 3, 3, 4, 4, 4, 4

Maria Woodie. 1975 (Osborne, 1989, 1109)
1, 2, 1, 1, 2, 1, 3, 4, K, 1, 1, 1, 3, 4, K, 1, 3, K

Ariwayakulaliyi (Song-type 11)

In these examples I group each three lines of text as they are sung to each melody, which itself comprises three melodic lines ML1, ML2, ML1 — ML1, ML2, ML1, etc.

Group of schoolboys. 1962 (Audio 43)
1, 1, 2 — 2, 2, 1 — 3, 3, 2 — 2, 2, 3 — 4, 4, 2 — 2, 2, 3 — 3, 3, 2 — 2, 2, 3

Christopher Foxy Tipungwuti. 1975 (Audio 42)
K, 1, 1, 2 — 3, 1, 1 — 2, 3, 3 — 2, 1, 2 — 3

Women's group. 2008 (Audio 52)
1, 1, 1 — 2, 2, 1 — 3, 3, 1 — 4, 4, 1

Tempo

When considering tempo, again we can see the performance style manifesting in song-type characteristics. In Yoi singing, a regular tempo and strongly accented pulse facilitate group dancing. Although they all have different actions, all Yoi dances are performed to a consistent tempo and pulse. The men's Yoi dance style involves foot stamping on each beat whereas the women shift their feet on each alternate beat, giving the effect of dancing at half speed to the same song, but this doesn't alter the tempo of the song's delivery. The regularity of tempo in Yoi singing also enables a large group to participate for an extended period of time and with numerous songs (and singers) added consecutively without disruption. The regular Yoi tempo is established and reinforced by sticks, clapping and danced foot stamping. Not only does this result in a largely regular tempo throughout an entire Yoi event, but it also means that people tend to dance Yoi at about the same tempo whenever it arises, whether in a group event or celebrating at the club or dancing impromptu just for fun. Exposure to the Dreaming dances from a very young age and the mortuary-related Yoi being so regular that people "just feel the way to dance it", as Ella Puruntatameri put it.

Kuruwala singing is far more contemplative and individualistic and so there is no need for a regular tempo, or to mark the pulse strongly. In the main Kulama style (Arikuruwala), when the (usually male) singer does use sticks he more often than not ceases beating while singing the text (the beating occurring during the introductory, melismatic section and between song phrases). The beats are often irregular, slower than and/or not related to the syllabic pulse as if the singer is absent-mindedly tapping the sticks while he composes the next text phrase. The range of tempi of Arikuruwala singing across the recordings is so varied that it is not useful to list them in any more detail than to give an approximation of the range in each recorded collection. Computing the tempo is made more difficult by the lack of stick beating and because the accents are often placed on the first and third syllables of each metrical unit and are thus determined by metre rather than by any underlying pulse.

Although the tempi might seem to overlap between the two song-types, the syllabic pulse of Yoi songs is much faster than Kulama. The percussive beat of Yoi marks groups of five or more syllables, whereas the tempo for Kulama singing is arrived at by creating a moderate "quaver" pulse with "beats" on each two syllables. The Kulama song-types are therefore slower overall than the Yoi song-types. Figure 22 gives tempi used for Kulama and Yoi singing among each recorded collection. The Kulama column shows the range of tempi found in that collection, while the Yoi column shows the average taken of the tempi recorded.[13]

Figure 22: An indication of the tempi (beats per minute) of recorded Kulama and Yoi song-types.

Recording	Kulama (Arikuruwala)	Yoi (Jipuwakirimi)
1954 Mountford	44–55	77
1962 Moyle	n/a	75
1965 Wurm	32	76
1966 Holmes	n/a	80
1967 Doolan	32–46	n/a
1972 Sims	37–59	77
1974/5 Osborne	45–64	84
1980 Grau	31	78
2009 Campbell	n/a	75
2011 Campbell	n/a	77
2012 Campbell	36–50	78
OVERALL RANGE	30–64	75–84

---

13 I have not included recordings made before 1954 because the speed cannot be trusted due to speed fluctuations in the original recordings.

Rhythm

The two main Tiwi song-types – Jipuwakirimi sung at Yoi and Pukumani (mortuary-associated ceremonies) and Arikuruwala sung at Kulama – tend to be isorhythmic (having a repeating rhythmic pattern), similar in this way to song genres of the Kimberley and Central Australia. While we can make generalisations about stick beating across the Tiwi song-types, no one type has entirely consistent rules of beating or clapping. Some singers mark the metrical sense of the text, while others mark the contours of the melody, their intake of breath or the periods between lines of text. There are no separate, overlaid percussion patterns in Tiwi song styles. This is quite different from either the northern genres or the Central Australian and Western Desert genres, which have an independent repertory of stick patterns and rhythmic modes (Marett 2005; Stubington 1979). The Yoi (dance style) song-type is similar to Central Australian genres in its relatively simple, pulse-based percussion. The Kuruwala-style song-types (which do not involve dance) either have percussive accompaniment that is not regular, or no accompaniment at all. The clapping or stick rhythms tend to be more a matter of the performer's own choice and depend upon how they perceive the underlying structure of the song, segmenting each phrase into multiple periodises accordingly. While there is an overarching pattern to which all performances of a song-type conform, no two performances have exactly the same rhythmic pattern. Small nuances in rubato, inflection and "crushed" notes that are not technically part of the generic song melody make each rhythmic rendition of a song-type different from others of that same type.

Text

The importance of improvised text in traditional Tiwi performance cannot be over-emphasised and it is a feature of all Tiwi song-types. Osborne wrote:

> [T]he great majority of the songs sung at every Tiwi ritual are new songs, composed specially for the occasion, and, as there are something like a dozen big mortuary rituals every year, as well as numerous yilanigha,[14] and at least half a dozen separate kulama rituals, the Tiwi are obliged to compose some hundreds of new songs each year. It is true that a few inherited songs are performed at mortuary rituals, but these are only a tiny minority of the total number of songs performed. (Osborne 1989, 115)

---

14 Yilanigha is a smoking ritual held in the lead-up to the Final Pukumani (mortuary-associated) Ceremony.

The song-types Arikuruwala, Amparruwu, Mamanunkuni, Apajirupwaya and Ariwangilinjiya are unique compositions. Manikay is similar in this regard (R.M. Berndt 1966), with innovation occurring within formulas and epithetic text portions that are combined in new ways by each singer. This is not unlike the way many Yoi songs relating to Dreaming, Country and kinship are extemporised using extant text elements. Tiwi songs are composed by the singer, not overtly attributed to having been passed down through dreams from ancestors, as is often the case in other genres such as Wangga, Junba and Nurlu. There are very few song texts that are fixed in any way and this distinguishes Tiwi song from most other Australian song genres. It is important however to say that older songmen and songwomen describe hearing words in the bush, in the voices of ancestors and in the natural sounds of the bush, and of formulating songs through subconscious thoughts and dreams.

The repertory of Tiwi songs is therefore enormous, but Tiwi people speak of songs that relate to a particular subject (a Dreaming, for example) as many manifestations of the same song, similar to the way Manikay songs are grouped (Corn 2005). Any Dreaming Yoi song about Crocodile, for example, is considered to be *the* Crocodile song because it brings into the present the Country places and ancestors connected with Crocodile Dreaming. The first five free translations given at Figure 23 are from a sequence of Yoi songs performed at a Final Ceremony in 1977 for a man with Crocodile Dreaming.[15] The next five are translations of texts that are sung today. Songs pertaining to the Crocodile, symbolically linking it with the family of the deceased (text 4 for example)[16] or to places it is found (text 7) are sung by a number of singers across a whole day of ceremony. These are all referred to collectively as Crocodile.

---

15 Quoted from the film *Good-bye Old Man, Or the Film of Tukuliyangenila (A Film About Mangatopi): A Tiwi Island Bereavement Ceremony* (MacDougall 1977).
16 This is also an example of bereavement imagery as I will discuss in the next chapter.

6 The classical Tiwi music

Figure 23: Transliteration of Crocodile song texts sung at a Yiloti (Final Ceremony) in 1977.

1. The Crocodile's tail leaves a mark in the sand.
2. The Crocodile is floating out to sea.
3. The Crocodile floats in the clear water, his legs and tail hang motionless.
4. Someone pulled the spear from Mungatopi's shoulder.
5. The Crocodile floats swimming slowly.
6. I am the Crocodile man.
7. I am in the mangroves breaking up everything with my strong tail.
8. I am the Crocodile man lying low down in the mud.
9. Crocodile goes out with the sea.
10. Wiyapurali [the Country place] he saw them – he was running very fast.

The use of embedded meaning and symbolism with the aim of obfuscation has been documented in the songs of other Indigenous Australian communities (Clunies Ross and Wild 1984; Magowan 2007; Marett 2005; Turpin 2007). For example, Wangga public songs have clearly defined word finals, delineated by the rhythm, whereas in secret songs opacity of text is the aim, with the rhythm obscuring word boundaries and placing accents on syllables that are not normally stressed in speech (and vice versa) (Marett 2005). This is not what occurs in Tiwi song composition. While there is a sense that senior Tiwi singers are the holders of important knowledge, with their songs holding embedded deep meaning that perhaps only they fully understand, there are no secret songs, no restricted knowledges and no obfuscations of meaning for the sake of excluding (or protecting) the listener. Justin Puruntatameri and Calista Kantilla spoke about this at length one day in 2012, confirming that there is neither spirit language nor intentional obfuscation of text for the purposes of secrecy – as is seen in some mainland genres (List 1963; O'Keefe 2010; Stubington 2007; Turpin 2007). The language used for Tiwi song texts is glossable, being based on spoken language.[17] However, modifications made by the singer at the metrical and sung level, with word boundaries obscured and speech stresses not followed in the sung form, mean that the sung text is often rendered difficult to understand for non-educated listeners. Word boundaries in Tiwi songs may be unclear. While in the Yoi songs the boundaries of text and melodic lines match up (similar to Junba songs of the Kimberley (Treloyn 2006)), in the Kuruwala song-types there is more evidence of text lines being split across melodic lines. This, and the technique of beginning a sung phrase part-way through a word,

---

17 The exception to this is the use of the language of the Nyingawi people in Nyingawi songs.

is similar to what has been reported in Central Australian genres in which the singing can begin and end at places other than the text boundaries. Tiwi singers always sing the entire line of text before taking a breath.

Performance context

Tiwi songs can be separated into three general performance context classifications: those connected to the Yoi events held at the mortuary-associated ceremonies; those connected to the Kulama[18] ceremony; and those songs that are secular (there is no overarching Tiwi term for secular songs). Tiwi songs are also categorised into two performance styles: Yoi (dance) style; and Kuruwala (singing) style. Modern Kuruwala songs (song-type 12) performed by the Women's Group do have actions, but in the traditional song-types, the Kuruwala song-type does not involve dance. In my discussions with Tiwi listeners, I have found that many of the song-types documented by Osborne and outlined in this chapter are referred to simply as Kulama songs rather than by the specific name such as Arikuruwala or Ariwayakulaliyi. While most of the song-types are recognised by senior singers, not many of the names are still used. People tend more often to speak simply of Yoi songs, Kulama songs and Kuruwala songs. Grau found similar: "They always use the verb kuruwala plus whatever the intention of the singer was: 'he sings to say goodbye', or 'he sings to give a name'". (Grau 1983a, 55)

Dynamic currency of performance practice

There are 12 musical song-types (including one vocal call) either in current use or at least recognised as what should be performed. Ten of these song-types were documented in the early 20th century and their interrelationship according to performance context is shown in Figure 24 (Figure 28 shows how these contexts have changed today with the addition of two new song-types). As I explain in my description of each song-type, there are occasions when some song-types are performed outside of the context I have specified. It must be understood that while they are traditionally performed in the context indicated in Figure 24 and Music Transcription 5, they are not confined to these. It must be said that with changes in ceremonial contexts since the most recent literature on the subject (Goodale 1988; Grau 1983b; Osborne 1989) as well as a difference of opinion depending on individuals' relative adherence to cultural orthodoxy, these designations must not be taken as the definitive state of affairs. I have found quite a lot of variation between my data and the data in previous literature. An inevitable feature of a knowledge system that is held by each subsequent

---

18   As explained in Chapter 4 Kulama is the name of the annual initiation-related ceremony. Kulama is also however often used to refer to all the songs sung at Kulama, as well as, more generally, "old" or "traditional" song styles (and this does tend to cause some confusion).

generation of Elders is that words, stories and understandings develop and change as they are re-owned and retold. There are for instance a number of quite different understandings among Tiwi of elements of information (about Skin groups and Country areas for instance) from what is in previous literature. Having spent some time reading Osborne's descriptions of the song-types and functional categorisations to the Elders with whom I have been working, they are of the opinion that his information is important for historical reference but is not what most people know now. The distinction between the classification of songs by functional and musical means is one such instance. Osborne identifies 14 song function-types (Osborne 1989, 119–25). As the function-types relate to the song subjects and/or when and by whom they are sung, rather than their musical form, I do not elaborate on those here. Some of the names given by Osborne to the musical forms are descriptive words in Old Tiwi, and most are no longer recognised.[19] I have found that there is not a consistent use of either song function or musical form name; while a few older people tend to refer to a song using the musical form name, most people (young and old) refer to songs by their function. I have attempted to give those musical form names that are still used a meaning, by glossing their definition.

By way of example, the word ampiriwayatyuwityighi (ampiriwayajuwijiyi in current spelling) is the musical form listed by Osborne for Mamanunkuni (sorrow) song function.

The word ampiriwayajuwijiyi was not recognised by any current Tiwi singers. A breakdown of the structure of the word gives us the rough translation "says (or sings) it at the end". We do find in the current language the noun-feminine prefix *ampiri-* with which most of these form names begin, but none of the words stemming from *ampiri* given by Osborne's consultants is in the current dictionary. Waya is an incorporated form meaning "words", "talk", "bite" and/or "mouth".

ampiri = noun feminine
waya = says
juwa = finished
jiyi verb subject PAST = he or she did something

Songs of this type are now called Mamanunkuni, along with all laments with this melodic form, and are sung at the funeral, during the Final Ceremony or in the bereavement songs stage of Kulama in the context at which Osborne's classification of ampiriwayajuwijiyi would be expected. When hearing a man sing what functionally was known as "singing at the end", Elders told me he

---

19 For a full listing of the song forms and functions see Osborne (1989).

was singing Mamanunkuni (i.e. a sorrow song, for the end of someone's life, and/or the end of the ceremony). The Yoi function song-type Jipuwakirimi is another example. Osborne calls it Ariwakirimi (Osborne 1989, 172), but again this term was not recognised by my consultants. This might be simply a matter of lexical change (*jipu-* and *ari-* being found at the start of many Tiwi words), and indeed older speakers decided that these two words actually mean the same thing. *-wakirimi* means to make up/compose words for a song or a story; to make law.

Elders surmise that, like this, the other names given to the forms are descriptive of why or when they were sung. With many of the specific stages of ritual now either not performed or performed in modified form (and at different times) today, this deeper level of classification and the accompanying descriptive names are not used, but songs are now known by their function type.

1. Numerous musical forms

In the course of his detailed analysis of song texts Osborne (1989) lists 40 musical forms, including two musical forms of Ampirikuruwala, six of Ampirijukwaya and ten of Ampiriwayajuwjiyi. It is the opinion of the Elders that these should not be regarded as separate musical forms (of each type) but, rather, the one form with variations due to the artistic individuality and spontaneity of each performer. For example, the ten forms of Ampiriwayajuwjiyi listed by Osborne are sung by ten different people, and the second to the sixth forms were each recorded only once in his data. It is likely that this is the result of the way those particular individuals sang that song-type. Christopher (Foxy) Tipungwuti and Stanley Munkara each sang two Arimajingipapujiya songs consecutively in a recording session and these are each classified by Osborne as a separate musical form. It is my contention that these recordings should not be taken as the definitive versions of two separate forms. Speaking of the way Foxy raises the pitch on the third syllable of the second metrical unit in each three-unit line, Osborne comments, "This feature is not found in any of the other recorded performances of laments of any type" (Osborne 1989, 187). It is feasible that Foxy used this embellishment in both songs because he sang them in succession for the recording. At another time he may well have created a slightly different pitch embellishment.

2. A change in a song-type name

Apuputyingapirni is the term Osborne gives to the "women's response" within the Arikuruwala style and he uses the term Ampirikuruwala to refer to the two elements together: the solo man's singing, with response from the women's group. Elders today say that Ampirikuruwala refers just to the women's response singing, both in Kulama and Ceremony. It seems there has been a change of definition between 1975 and 2023.

The obsolete song-type Ampirimarrikimili is another interesting example. This has fallen out of use as a song-type, and indeed the word has connotations today that make it an inappropriate term to call a song-type. *Ampiri-* is a feminine prefix. In the Tiwi dictionary *marri-* is a connective marker meaning "with" and *-kimili* means to have sexual intercourse. The derivation of this song-type might therefore relate to women's singing with reference to them being wives (with the connection then being drawn with sexual intercourse).

3. Sorrow songs

I must also include a note on the use of the word "sorrow" relating to song-types. In current usage "sorrow songs" refers to Mamanunkuni (which is the traditional sorrow song-type) but also refers to Amparruwu (widow) songs as well as Arikuruwala songs sung at Kulama. When I recorded Stephen-Paul Kantilla (Audio 31) and Eustace Tipiloura (Audio 28) in March 2012 (for example) singing their songs from the recently held Kulama ceremony, they both introduced their performances as "sorrow" and then sang the Arikuruwala melody. A recording made by Grau in 1981 suggests that this has long been the case.[20] Recording a Yiloti (Final Ceremony), Grau introduces the section as "sorrow songs". What follows are three Arikuruwala songs (two of which include a female Ampirikuruwala response) and then a Mamanunkuni by the same man (Audio 19) followed by the woman singing Amparruwu. It seems likely that Grau's consultants regarded all these as "sorrow songs" because they all referred to the deceased and were sung for grieving.

As it is not a Tiwi song-type, I will not discuss the Catholic hymns here, except to say that I include them (and the church as a performance context) in Figure 24 to indicate their long-standing presence in the Bathurst Island community, which has inevitably had an impact on subsequent song practice.

---

20 The beginning of A01-009278.

Figure 24: Performance context of Tiwi songs, early 20th century.

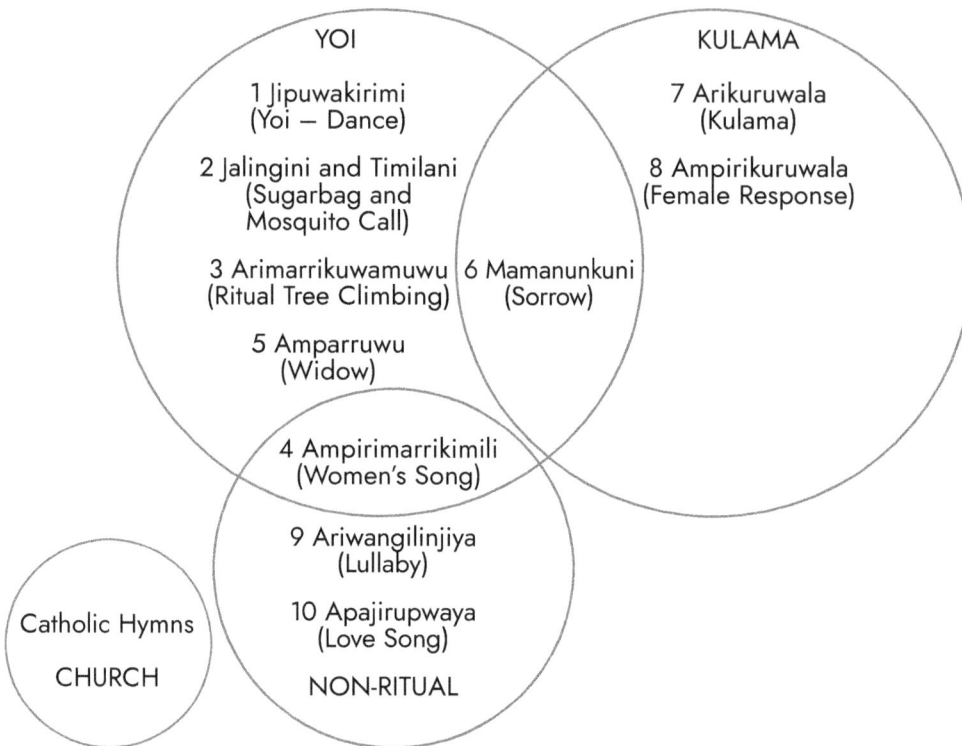

So, to summarise this introduction, the 11 song-types (and one vocal call) can be separated into three general performance contexts: Pukumani (mortuary-related rituals); Kulama (the annual Kulama ceremony); and non-ritual occasions, and into two broad performance styles: Yoi (dance); and Kuruwala (singing). I have introduced the notion of degrees of variability being determined by both performance context and song function and shown that, while there are defining characteristics for each song-type, no two songs are exactly the same. Whether creating entirely new text or extemporising on epithetic material, the Tiwi singer creates a unique composition, working within the parameters of the melodic contour and the musical characteristics of whichever song-type they are singing. This brings me back to the observation that the repertory of Tiwi songs is very large and must be considered as a dynamic, creative process of transmission of cultural knowledge.

It is only with at least some understanding of the linguistic and poetic complexities of Tiwi song composition that it is possible to appreciate how the melodies, rhythms and performance styles of the songs are intrinsically connected with the reasons they are composed. I will describe the song-types 1 to 10 in the order in which they appear in Music Transcription 5 (which gives their basic melodic structure). As it will transpire in the next section, Song type 11 (individuals' songs) can be seen as a pivot point in the evolving creativity of the story of Tiwi songs, with crossovers occurring between the classical song-types and non-Indigenous Tiwi music forms, resulting in the emergence of song-type 12 – the women's "modern" songs. Even these, as I will explain, are considered "old", while the classical songs continue to be composed and so continue to be "new".

Music Transcription 5: Outline of melodic contour for each of the Tiwi song-types.

Yoi

1. Jipuwakirimi Yoi (dance)

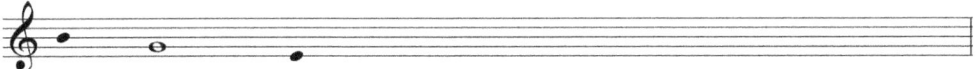

2. Jalingini (Sugarbag), Timilani (Mosquito) Call – and a 2023 variation.

3. Arimarrikuwamuwu (ritual tree climbing)

4. Ampirimarrikimili (women's song)

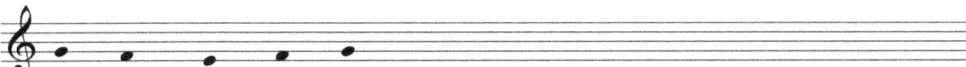

5. Amparruwu (widow)

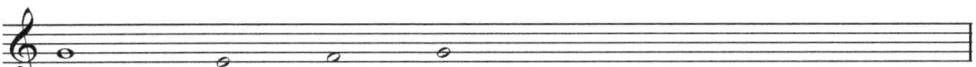

6. Mamanunkuni (sorrow)

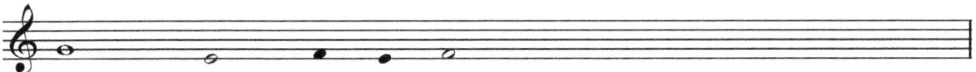

Kulama

7. Arikuruwala (Kulama)

8. Ampirikuruwala (female response)

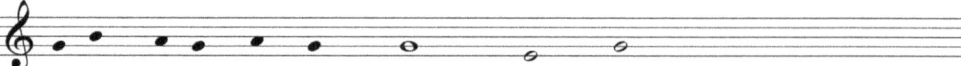

Non-ritual

9. Ariwangilinjiya (lullaby)

10. Apajirupwaya (love song)

11. Ariwayakulaliyi (individuals' songs)

12. Modern Kuruwala (Women's Group).

This song-type uses variations of melodies used in song-type 11 and non-Tiwi melodies, and therefore has no specific melodic contour.

I begin with the song-types performed at Yoi events (either within or around mortuary-related Pukumani or funeral ceremonies), then discuss those songs that are sung at Kulama and then songs that are not associated with ritual. Song-type 12 is the Strong Women's Group's Modern Kuruwala song-type. It uses a number of melodies (including those that are not Tiwi) and so I do not include a melodic contour in Music Transcription 5. Comparing the basic melodic structures, we can see some similarities between particular song-types. Jipuwakirimi (1) and Arikuruwala (7) songs employ the least pitch variation, with the majority of each line of text on one pitch, preceded by a fall from a higher note and followed by a fall of approximately a minor 3rd. Ampirimarrikimili (4) and Amparruwu (5) (both women's song-types) have a fall of a minor third and return, by tonal step, to the original note. Apart from the Apajirupwaya (10) (love songs) and the Ariwayakulaliyi (11) (individually invented songs), all of the Tiwi songs comprise an introductory higher pitch (sometimes with ornamentation) to an extended monotone and then a variable ending (either a pitch fall or a return to the main note).

1. Jipuwakirimi. Yoi style. Ritual (and now secular).

As I mentioned earlier, confusingly (for non-Tiwi readers!) Yoi refers to dance, song, Dreaming and the part of (any) ceremony or event in which Yoi is performed. In the opinion of the most senior Tiwi song custodians this song-type is most correctly called Jipuwakirimi,[21] although everyone calls it Yoi. Yoi songs are seen as accompaniment to dance and are rarely sung separately from a dance performance, or without someone instinctively dancing along. Without being of less consequence (indeed the dance would rarely be performed without the song), it is nonetheless primarily a support for a dance, and dancing always happens when a Yoi is sung. Some are new songs composed especially for an event, either prior to or at the time of performance, and most today are largely based on existing (Dreaming) Yoi song phrases.

Yoi songs are defined by their monotonic and isorhythmic structure. The syllables are presented with no break between words or metrical units and the text is structured in the standard five-syllable metrical pattern. However, the rhythmic enunciation of syllables within the constant pulse creates a rhythmic interest that varies with each singer. As is indicated by the examples in Music Transcription 6, the five syllables in each unit A can be altered at cantillation to produce rhythmic interest within a constant beat. At the fast tempo at which this song-type is performed, the standard pattern of stresses on the first and fourth syllables of a metrical unit is often not distinguishable. For each example, I present first the text in metrical form, and then show how it is altered in the sung form (the deleted syllables in parentheses). As Example 1 in Music Transcription 6 shows, the metrical units (shown with square under-bracketing) do not always match up with the rhythmic units because, at the performance stage, some syllables are not sung.

In her notes accompanying her 1962 recording, Alice Moyle describes the Yoi thus: "Despite variations in pitch the general effect is closer to monotone chanting than to singing" (Moyle 1997, 33). This is an appropriate description. Considering the (rapid) speed at which the words are sung (with one syllable per "quaver" and no melisma or long-held notes of more than a crotchet's duration), Yoi performance is closer to a rhythmic calling of the text. The Yoi song contour does, though, include raising and lowering of pitch approximately a third above and below the principal tone (on the initial and/or final of the song line).

---

21   The part of the word *-kirimi* means "to make something" and so the song name implies "making up a song".

This is the fastest song-type, with the stick/clap beats starting at about 75 beats per minute (bpm) and, at a particular point, doubling (cued by the dancer). A Yoi song consists of one line of text, repeated numerous times (as many as 30, according to Osborne 1989, 173), as determined at the time of performance. The lead singer also repeats one phrase at a time so that the group can join in, picking up more words with each iteration. Senior song and culture man Barry Puruntatameri told me that the lead singer might have to repeat the phrase a few more times "if the others can't keep up or if the dancing men need more time to get into the right spot". The composer will try their best to have the words sorted out before they sing, but if words are too difficult to remember or deemed to not fit well enough with the metrical pattern (units of 5+5+4 syllables, for example) then a new word or phrase will be used. The song must continue to enable the dancing of kinship and Dreaming dances. As well as group dancing, individuals take their turn to dance and so this will require more iterations of the song.

Looking at Example 1 in Music Transcription 6, the *wu* is an interjection specific to Crocodile Yoi, given as a cue by the dancer at the end of their dance and *a eya* is the immediate response, from both the lead singer and the group. Other Yoi have other vocal interjections specific to the Dreaming (if a Dreaming song). In a general subject, the interjection is *poop* or similar. All responses are *a eya*. This interjection can come at any point in the text, or at the completion of the line, with the singer then beginning that line again or moving on to a new line as the next dancer takes their turn. Sometimes people will finish their dance (by singing *wu*) in unison, but more often they choose their place to stop individually. If five people are dancing concurrently the singing will be interrupted at up to five separate points that do not correspond with a line final. The codependence and connection between singer and dancer in this song-type are extraordinary. The singer (who, we must remember, is likely extemporising on a theme around the kinship, Dreaming, Country and backstory of the people who are dancing and the person for whom they are dancing) watches each dancer intently so that they can break the sung line at whichever point the dancer gestures their final dance movement. The Yoi dances have short series of actions so there is no way the singer can pre-empt the conclusion of the dance, but watches, sings and responds to the exact beat that the dancer finishes. Each individual dancer might choose to dance for only four or five steps/beats and finish midway through a line of song, while another might (and often does) dance a full circle around the dance-ground, taking four or five full repetitions of the song text. The role of the lead singer is therefore one of support, both musical and physical. The dancer (who in this case is also a mourner and so will likely be in a state of distress or ritual self-focus) doesn't have to worry about what they are doing. It is the job of the singer to provide musical, chanted support for their paying of respect. This becomes even more complicated when a large group of spiritually and/or physically related kin (such as a group of sisters or of sons) takes their turn. First all the sisters will dance together, with the song repeating as they progress through their dance. Then one at a time each sister will decide in their own time and in no order or pattern when they will break across the repeating phrase to end by making the finishing gesture of their particular dance. The lead singer (and those around them who are watching closely) seem to anticipate this final dance move because they invariably call the *a eya* interjection in time with the dancer. It is a powerful example of social support and mutual trust enacted through music.

This is the only song-type that has the capacity for interruption of the text in this way. Audio 74 is the beginning of a Yoi event at a Yiloti recorded by Grau in 1981. I include it as a clear example of the group dynamic. The lead singer begins and is joined after two iterations of the text by others around him. At four points throughout the song (each about 30 seconds apart) we hear the *a eya* interjection as each dancer completes their turn dancing. At a point halfway through (01:38 in this example) the group sings Sugarbag (but not Mosquito) and then the song continues until approximately 03:05 when the end of that song text is marked by *a eya*. The percussive beat[22] continues and a new song begins. In the complete recording[23] the Jipuwakirimi singing continues for another 25 minutes (with no break in percussive beat) on the same pitch.

In the Jipuwakirimi/Yoi introduction to the Crocodile song (Audio 67), recorded in 2008, we can also hear that while the group is singing in unison, as each individual completes their section of dancing they interject with *wu* and the group responds *a eya*, regardless of the point of text they are up to. In his Parakajiyali song (Example 2 in Music Transcription 6 and Audio 55), Eustace Tipiloura has added similar calls to *a we* even though he sings solo, because, he told me, it is part of the form of this song-type and there would normally always be other people involved.

---

22 Percussive alignment with the vocal part is indicated in Music Transcription 6 and throughout with an "x".
23 A01-002970.

Music Transcription 6: Two examples of rhythmic interest within the constant pulse of the Jipuwakirimi/Yoi song-type (Audio 7, 55).

Example 1: Aloysious Puruntatameri. From Yirrikapayi song. 1976. (Audio 7).
Metrical form:
Wiyapurali yuwunjingima piyirumuji ngipijimi
In Wiyapurali [Country place] he saw them
Sung form:
C=E

Example 2: Eustace Tipiloura. From Parakajiyali song. 2011. (Audio 55).
Metrical form:
Ngawamukala pilajuwunji rrikimajirri miyajirra
He has given them flour, sugar, blanket, niki [nicotine]
Sung form:
C=B♭

The tempo and metre of Yoi songs are fairly consistent across the repertoire, and usually the beat will continue while one song moves seamlessly into the next, the only means of differentiation being the text change and perhaps a change of singer. A Yoi event, within the context of a Yilaniya (Smoking), Yiloti (Final) Ceremony or the Yoi dance stage of a funeral is, in effect, a continuous succession of songs with accompanying dances, linked by periods in which the stick beating (which can also be beating of a stick on a corrugated-iron sheet and/or hand clapping) continues while people organise the next person/s for dancing. Often the beats continue for a minute or so before people are ready for the next song/dance.

Across the recordings one can hear singers make small variations to the duration of the syllables. Similar to the process of "swinging" quavers in western music, Tiwi singers, to varying degrees, push and pull the quaver beats within the framework of a consistent tempo and pulse (marked by percussive beats)[24] determined by the metrical structure. The arrangement of words and syllables into complex rhythmic patterns that fit into the constant pulse is highly regarded and appreciated by Tiwi listeners. Music Transcription 7 shows how the rhythmic treatment and stick accompaniment of the same text (within one song) changes, although the pulse remains constant. This performance (Audio 6, recorded in 1912) is regarded highly by Elders as a complex example of a Jipuwakirimi/Yoi song. The singer begins in a rhythmically even pattern, presenting the words clearly and with no accents. As the song continues and the group joins in, accents are introduced and the rhythms shift until the patterns are very different, to the point where in section two we can say that the placement of the syllables has moved from a duple subdivision of the pulse to a triple subdivision of the same tempo pulse, further organised into compound 6/8 metre. The maintaining of a regular beat and tempo while varying the rhythmic organisation to this degree is highly complex and senior singers have discussed this widely. A similar example of this complex relationship between the two sections of a Yoi can be heard in a song recorded by Simpson in 1948 (Audio 2).

Music Transcription 7: 1912 Yoi performance showing alteration of rhythmic pattern between first and second sections. Yirrikapayi, Tungutalum (Audio 6).

First section.

Second section.

Yoi songs do not include this first section today. Within a constant pulse, the beating doubles part-way through a performance, and the relationship between the rhythms in the single-beat and double-beat sections is closer. The rhythm tends, however, to be somewhat looser in the single-beat section and more regular in the double-beat section due to two factors: accents on the first syllable of each metrical unit give more space to the singer to stretch syllables; whereas having a stick (or clap) beat twice as often confines the syllables into an even duple pulse. Music Transcription 8 shows a more recent performance of a Jipuwakirimi/Yoi song (the same performance as is in Example 1, Music Transcription 6) showing the single and double beat sections. I have used dotted

---

24   Audio 7 and 55 are clear examples of this.

bar lines for ease of comparison. The relationship between the lead singer and the group can be heard in this performance, which may well have involved some of the same performers as Goodale described in 1970:

> The composer begins by chanting one verse alone. The rest of the men [or women], who stand in a semi-circle around the dance ground, pick up the beat of the song and accompany the singer by slapping their thighs or buttocks with their open hands. Gradually they also pick up the words of the song and begin to chant with the composer. When enough of the men have learned the words, the singer stops singing and begins to dance to the accompaniment of the chorus of men who continue to chant and beat in time. (Goodale 1970, 292)

Music Transcription 8: 1976 Yoi performance showing alteration of rhythmic pattern between single-beat and double-beat percussive accompaniment (Audio 7).

Single beat.

Double beat.

2. Jalingini (Sugarbag) and Timilani (Mosquito) call. Ritual (and now secular).

Jalingini (also called Honey) is said to have originated with the ancestral people of the Honey/Sugarbag clan, who first performed Pukumani ceremonies. I use the term Sugarbag here because that is how it is most commonly referred to today.

The Sugarbag and Mosquito Call is listed along with the song-types because it is a performance item that has been recorded numerous times over the last century. Although they are named separately, Sugarbag and Mosquito can be considered one item made up of two parts, one of which (Mosquito) has now fallen out of use. Senior men on Melville Island have developed a new version of Mosquito, singing four or five short calls "Yo eya!" at the lower (Sugarbag) tessitura, followed by the upper octave (Mosquito) "Yiyi eya!" as part of calling out to ancestors at the opening of Yoi. See Music Transcription 5, Example 2. Examples of both Sugarbag and Mosquito are found among the live recordings made by Hart (1928), Simpson (1948), Mountford (1954), ABC Radio (1955), Groger-Wurm (1965), Holmes (1966), Sims (1972), Osborne (1975), Moyle (1976) and Grau (1980), so we can say that Mosquito was still in practice until then. People cannot recall exactly when or why the Mosquito part of the call stopped being performed but speculate that it is not performed anymore because it is very difficult vocally. Elders agree they would like to see it reinstated in the future, and let's hope a Tiwi singer comes along who decides to stretch their abilities and have a go! Some people refer to the call sung today (which is at the lower pitch) as Mosquito, no longer making a distinction between the two. The calls were always performed together – Sugarbag being the lower (mid-range in a man's vocal tessitura) sung first, with the Mosquito sung a complete octave higher (up to F5). These vocalisations are unique to the Tiwi Islands and, due to the very high pitch, two calls among Spencer's 1912 recordings have caused some confusion among researchers as to whether they were vocalisations or produced by an instrument of some sort (Moyle 1959, 13; Osborne 1989). Alice Moyle incorrectly thought the calls in Boat and Train (recorded in 1912 by Spencer) were produced with a high-pitched didgeridoo. The audition notes accompanying the material from AIATSIS list "conch" in these song items. Without direct information from the singers we of course will never know but, although these calls are vocally similar to Mosquito, according to Elders listening today they are descriptive of the boat's siren and the train's whistle. Both come during the song (not before the text as the introductory call). Sung by a group of men at ceremony, or more recently at tourist performances, the classical Sugarbag and Mosquito calls served as the opening to the Yoi event, and also as markers for new sections of ceremony.

The Sugarbag call was sung on an open vowel (*yo*) lasting about ten seconds. The lead singer then switched to the high Mosquito call, one octave higher than the preceding Sugarbag call, and in the (male) singers' falsetto tessitura. The group followed, staggering their breathing so as to give an unbroken sound that continued for about 20 seconds. The Mosquito call was not a single note, but each singer enunciated *yiyiyi* … giving the overall effect of a high-pitched vibrating sound (imitating a mosquito). Today at group events such as Yoi dance sessions held either as part of mortuary rituals or public performances for visitors, the proceedings open with Sugarbag and the calling of Country placenames.[25] I have included an example at Audio 18, recorded by Simpson in 1948. Simpson describes how it was impossible to accurately capture the

---

25 The Strong Women's Group also begin their performances with Ngarukuruwala in this way.

intensity and timbre of the falsetto and very high pitch with the recording equipment available at the time and how he had to ask the men to perform the call repeatedly in an attempt to alter the recording levels to avoid distortion.[26]

3. Arimarrikuwamuwu (tree-climbing). Yoi style. Ritual.

This is a type of bereavement song that was sung at the tree-climbing stage of the Yilaniya (Smoking) ceremony, a preliminary stage of the Final Ceremony rituals (Goodale 1974). Possibly as a result of the demise of the initiation function of Kulama, today tree-climbing is not done and Yilaniya is often held at a time separate to the Final Ceremony, so songs of this type are rarely sung. They were performed (solo) by men in the same patriline as the deceased and saw young men in the process of moving through Kulama forced/encouraged to climb a tree while the Yilaniya fire smoked them from below. Although it is a bereavement ritual song-type, the subject matter is light-hearted and often humorous and the tempo is faster than the Mamanunkuni or Amparruwu. Recorded examples range from 144 to 168 bpm. Osborne comments on the consistency of tempo in his three recordings of Stanley Munkara (which I was not able to obtain), saying that he sang at exactly 152 bpm each time, a number of days apart (Osborne 1989, 188).

This song-type comprises lines of varying length and varying amounts of lines. A pattern is created by the singer using a higher pitch for each non-final line and a lower one for the final line, creating a pattern of AB, AB and so on. There is one example of Arimarrikuwamuwu among the Hart recordings from 1928 but the sound quality is not good enough for more than recognising the melodic contour. The 1976 recording was made at an outdoor tourist performance and so includes atmospheric noise. The clearest recording is one made in 1955 for an ABC radio program. The tempo is approximately 172 bpm, although this might be slightly too fast and indeed current singers' opinion was that all of the performances on this recording are faster than they should be. Music Transcription 9 is taken from the 1955 recording. The text was given to me by Clementine Puruntatameri. It is incorrectly introduced on the 1955 recording as a "battle song". The singer, Wampayawityimirri Black Joe, Bartholomew Kerinaiua begins with an incipit while the group is singing Sugarbag. The melody proper is in two parts. The first melodic line (ML1) features a drop of a major third on the final of each alternate metrical unit of five syllables. The second part (ML2) is a tone down and alternates between semi-tones. The text segment, tyonta, is the call of the Goose and is regarded (by my consultants) as an interjection by the animal. In

---

26 Simpson also describes how, being in a recording session rather than in a proper Yoi event, the Tiwi singers listened back to their performance and comparisons were made as to the quality on each attempt (Simpson 1951).

6 The classical Tiwi music

the recording (Audio 17) we hear that the singer begins his song while the group is singing the Sugarbag call. Unlike all other Yoi event performances I have come across (in which the soloist takes the pitch of the group call), the singer begins his song on a lower pitch, as indicated in Music Transcription 9 (the singer in 1976 does the same). Also unusual is the fact that the group holds their unison note for some beats after the soloist has begun, whereas in Jipuwakirimi singing the Sugarbag and/or Mosquito call finishes before the soloist begins. A feature of this song-type is the interjections shouted out by the group throughout the song in order to show support of the singer and approval of the song he is creating.

Music Transcription 9: Arimarrikuwamuwu tree-climbing song.
Wampayawityimirri Bartholomew Kerinaiua, 1955 (Audio 17).

The free translation is:

I rose up on my behind
Tyonta, tyonta
I counted the crowd of Tyuwantipila

4. Ampirimarrikimili women's songs. Yoi style. Ritual and secular.

Ampirimarrikimili songs were recorded by Hart in 1928, by Simpson in 1948, by Osborne in 1975 and Grau in 1981.[27] They were sung by women, either solo or by a group with a leader. Although Osborne recorded two examples, he reported they were no longer sung or composed at the time of his fieldwork (Osborne 1989, 192). This song-type is not performed today, although the older women recognise it as a woman's tune. Back in 2012 Leonie Tipiloura and other older women remembered this style and have since been listening to the recordings with the aim of perhaps singing it again. The songs had a variety of functions and were sung both at Pukumani-associated ceremonies and at informal gatherings.

The melodic contour of the Ampirimarrikimili is consistent across the recordings. It is similar in contour to the women's Amparruwu songs in that it covers a minor third by steps, beginning and returning to the tonic.[28] The function, context, performance style and tempo of this song-type vary across the recordings as the two examples I present here show. Example 1 in Music Transcription 10 is from the recording of a group of women made in 1948 by Simpson. The performance style is typical of Tiwi group singing, with a regular beat (marked with hand claps) and a high dynamic level. The eight-syllable text of ML1 is fitted over three percussive beats while the 14-syllable ML2 is fitted over four percussive beats. In order to show this change in the musical metre clearly, I have used time signatures. This does not imply, however, that the singer was consciously using these time signatures. Note that, unlike the second line, the first line does not conform to the standard metrical structure (5+5+4). The first line of text is repeated almost identically fourteen times. The second line of text (and ML2) is sung three times before the recording is faded out so I cannot say how many

---

27 Two items by Hart in 1928 (one of which is at Audio 40); two items by Simpson in 1948; three items by Osborne in 1975; and six items by Grau in 1981. I was unable to access Osborne's recordings.

28 I use the term "tonic" to refer to the note that serves as the principal pitch reference of the melody, either because it is the pitch with the largest time allocation, or it is the melody final (with a melodic contour that leads towards it).

more repeats there might have been or whether there was a return of ML1. This recording was edited together with others for the radio piece *Island of Yoi*[29] and so the singing is faded out under the return of the narrator.

Example 2 is a solo performance by an unidentified Tiwi woman recorded in 1981 by Grau. The singer did not use any percussive accompaniment and the pulse and space between phrases (indicated with breath marks) are less defined. The melodic contour is used for this and four subsequent songs on Audio 20. I have marked three melodic lines (numbered and with brackets above the stave). Although ML1 and ML3 are very similar, the singer makes a distinction between the pitch initials of ML1 and ML3, and ML1 is a two-part repeat of the motif. I have presented the rhythm (of the first song) as closely as possible to show how, within the relatively regular contour of each melodic line, the rhythm varies each time, with the musical stresses reflecting the patterns of the words as they would be spoken. This is an important point of difference (also found in the love songs) compared to the other song-types, which do not reflect speech patterns.

Music Transcription 10: Two Ampirimarrikimili melodies.

Example 1: Unidentified women. 1948 (Audio 21)
Free translation: *You [Crocodile] are running fast on the beach*
C=G

Example 2: Unidentified woman. 1981 (Audio 20)
Free translation:[30] *Well, really, we are going away from here*
C=F

---

29 The radio documentary piece *Island of Yoi* was an episode of the radio series "Walkabout" produced by the Australian Broadcasting Commission. See catalogue listing in List of other recorded material in the AIATSIS archive.
30 Text transcription and translation by author with Calista Kantilla.

5. Amparruwu (widow songs). Kuruwala style. Ritual and secular.

Amparruwu[31] songs are sung by the spouse of the deceased – or if the spouse is not alive, the role is taken by the spouse's sibling, of the same gender, so that, for example, a sister of the widow would sing Amparruwu for her (deceased) brother-in-law – and are still sung by older people. It is now unusual for young widows to sing Amparruwu, but instead older women (or men) with appropriate kinship to the widow tend to sing in their place. Amparruwu songs often have a sexual connotation because they typically describe the relationship between the singer and their spouse. They are sung at any time during the final stages of the Final Ceremony, either off to one side while the rest of the group are continuing on with the main event or after the day's activities are over, in the silence of the night. They do not require an audience. In some circumstances (depending on individuals' cultural/religious motivations) the Amparruwu singer takes on the role of keening on behalf of the assembled group and senior women have described to me their act of taking on the burden of mourning.

The melody follows a definable contour: a rise of a tone on alternating line initials followed by a monotonic middle section, and then a drop of a third before stepping up by tones to the original note on each alternate line ending (see Music Transcription 11). This return to the original note makes the Amparruwu melody similar to the Ampirimarrikimili melody (song-type 4) and establishes both as a woman's tune.

Music Transcription 11, Example 1 is a transcription of a performance by Dorothy Tipungwuti, recorded by Osborne in 1975. I show lines 5, 6, 7 and 8 of her performance, showing that lines 5 and 6 are the repetition of one line of text across the two-part melody. Lines 5, 6 and 8 each comprise two metrical units and line 7 comprises three units (each unit marked with square brackets). In Example 2 (a recording I made of Eunice Orsto in 2010) I have shown how the singer does not define the five-syllable structure but extends the second unit to 12 syllables by creating a string of evenly produced notes.

---

31 Ampiripijukwaya is the name listed by Osborne as the musical form. In all my discussions with Elders I have not heard this term. As I mentioned earlier, it seems that many of the sub-category terms collected by Osborne are no longer in use. I include it here for the purposes of record.

Music Transcription 11: Two examples of the Amparruwu melody.

Example 1: Dorothy Tipungwuti 1975 (Audio 14)
Free translation (from Osborne 1989, 953): *Now we must stop what we used to do, and be chaste, wife*
G=A

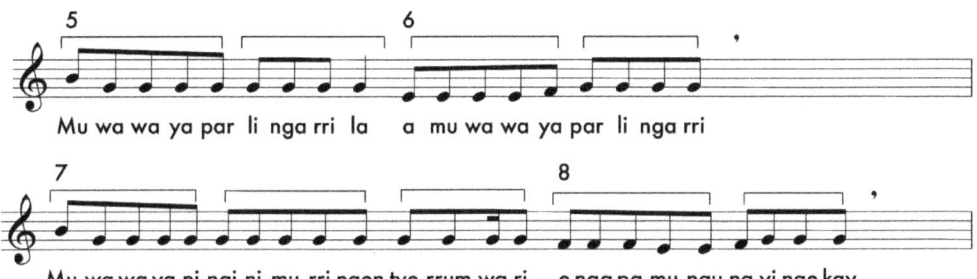

Example 2: Eunice Orsto 2010 (Audio 16)
Free translation (from Eunice Orsto): *We lie together coiled like a snake*
C=E
Handclaps marked with x

6. Mamanunkuni (sorrow songs). Kuruwala style. Ritual and secular.

Mamanunkuni (sorrow) songs can be sung at any time in the lead-up to or during a funeral, Yiloti (Final Ceremony) or at Kulama. They are quite slow and there is often a melismatic introductory section, sung in a wide variety of ways, and the pattern of line repetition is not consistent. The standard melodic contour is similar to Amparruwu, the difference being that Mamanunkuni songs do not return to the tonic. There is no stick or clap beating in this song-type. Music Transcription 12 shows a full performance by Long Stephen, recorded by Osborne in 1975 (Audio 26). The melody is broadly similar across all recordings of Mamanunkuni, with two melodic lines. Line 4 shows how text line extension is achieved by singing three rather than two five-syllable A units (shown with square brackets). The third unit A of Line 4 is accentuated by the singer with a raise of pitch (on *tyi*). In this performance Melodic Line 2 always comprises one unit A and one unit B. I have included the complete performance transcription here in order to show the variation to the melodic contour that occurs, as well as the irregular order in which the text is presented.

Music Transcription 12 shows the lines of text (numbered 1–9) indicated with square brackets above each corresponding melodic phrase. "K" indicates a line of meaningless vocalisation. The order in which the lines of text are sung and the pattern of their repetition are unique to this performance. I include this example also as an indication of the variability of line order.

Music Transcription 13 is of Line 1 of a performance by an unidentified woman, recorded by Mountford in 1954.[32] The singer sings an extended unit of kayayi – a vocalisation indicating sadness (I have used stemmed notes in this example to show the rhythm) and then two iterations of the text line, once on Melodic Line 2 (because it follows Melodic Line 1) and once on Melodic Line 1. Each line consists of one five-syllable unit and one four-syllable unit (marked with square brackets).[33]

The function of Mamanunkuni is, like that of Amparruwu, the expression of the singer's personal grief at the loss of a loved one. While Amparruwu singing is directed specifically to the singer's (deceased) spouse and is performed around the time of the related rituals for that person, Mamanunkuni songs are sung during Kulama in remembrance of (sometimes long-since departed) loved ones, and at any time of private grieving. Audio 62 (Mariano singing in 1928) and 63 (Foxy Tipungwuti singing in 1975) show how, across the span of 50 years, the contour and purpose of Mamanunkuni haven't changed.

---

32   Mountford states on the recording that it is an Amparruwu song. Although the woman may have been Amparruwu status to the deceased, the musical song-type is actually Mamanunkuni.
33   As it is not metrical, I have not bracketed the kayayi phrase. It is the same length temporally as each of the two-unit phrases of text.

6 The classical Tiwi music

Music Transcription 12: Full performance transcription of Mamanunkuni song. Long Stephen, 1975 (Audio 26).

Music Transcription 13: Mamanunkuni melodic contour. Unidentified woman, 1954 (Audio 15).

Unidentified woman, 1954 (Audio 15)
Free translation: *Why did you leave me?*
C=C#

The recording context has a marked impact on the way Amparruwu and Mamanunkuni are sung. The tempo also varies greatly between the recorded examples – the slowest being around 60 bpm and the fastest up around 80 bpm. In recording sessions, the performance style is calm and the melody more clearly defined than in recordings made at ceremonies when, understandably, the emotional state of the singer is heightened and the surrounding noise of the group (from the others continuing to sing and from general talk, children crying, dogs barking, etc.) give the recording a degree of vocal fluctuation and wailing that makes transcription and analysis all but impossible. It is also inappropriate to include either in transcription or audio the grieving of a person in distress when it is unclear if they knew they were being recorded. What I will say is that, while wailing and sobbing form a large part of the recorded Amparruwu, these do not alter the melodic structure beyond recognition.

It is in the Amparruwu and Mamanunkuni songs that we find the most variation and individual expression of performance (Audio 31–36 give an idea of this). Through lengthy and sometimes meandering songs the singer is able to express personal emotions, from intense grief to quiet sorrow, within the melodic formalities of the song-type. Free from the constraints of having to sing a regular, repeating song that others can join in with and dance to, singers in this context add their own melodic motifs, the length of phrases varies, the repetition of phrases varies, percussive accent shifts are far less regular and singers add extra vocalisations that are not part of the song phrase. These song-types share some of the variability of the introductory section of the next song-type (Arikuruwala) in which we hear similar freedoms of the solo singer.

7. Arikuruwala (Kulama songs). Kuruwala style. Ritual.

Kulama is the name of the annual ceremony that was traditionally held at the start of the dry season. Arikuruwala singing is the backbone of Kulama, its melodic form being heard across the three days and nights of the ceremony. It is perhaps due to its ubiquitous role that the name Arikuruwala means simply "singing" (with either the masculine *ari-* or feminine *ampiri-* prefix) and that people call it "Kulama style".

The Arikuruwala melody was also used for bereavement-related songs during the Pukumani ceremony (when they were held over the course of some days). Today the melody is similarly used for bereavement songs performed within or outside of the Kulama ceremony and, in fact, with the almost complete demise of the ceremony, Kulama songs are these days most often sung out of context, either spontaneously by an older person as part of telling a story or as an introduction to a "modern" style song performed by the Women's Group. In the past Arikuruwala/Kulama songs were performed by a male soloist but today women perform them just as often, although when a Kulama ceremony is held, the traditional gender roles are adhered to. Like Jipuwakirimi, each line of Arikuruwala text is sung on evenly spaced regular syllables with no breaks between units, and word boundaries going across the metre. The tempo ranges from around 65 up to 110 bpm across various singers, although the "quaver" pulse is slower than the Yoi song-types. The general rule is that the (self-accompanying) beating at the start, before the singing begins, is slower than the subsequent song proper. The downward-stepping melodic contour is consistent across recordings and contemporary performances, with the individual adding their own variation to the introductory melisma, using the vocables *ma*, *mm* or *aa*.[34] Once the song proper begins, the text is sung with even timbre and smooth-flowing syllables, avoiding accents and with softened consonants, almost like a chant. In Music Transcription 14 I give five examples of individuals' incipits in the Arikuruwala song-type.[35] The motifs used in these introductory sections return throughout the song, creating small interludes between lines of text. It is this idiosyncratic ornamentation that sets one performance apart from others of the same song-type. In the archival recordings Christopher (Foxy) Tipungwuti, for example, was easily identified by Elders because of a cough he gives on the beginning of each line (see Example 3). Similarly, when listening to recordings made of Barney Tipuamantimeri, the then very elderly Justin Puruntatameri and his wife Alberta recognised the vocalisation of *mawu* that is distinctive to Barney (and his father). A particularly impressive example of melismatic incipit can also be heard among the recordings made by Hart in 1928 (Audio 62).

---

34   Audio 24.
35   For ease of comparison, I have transposed the tonic to C in each. In the performance each incipit is followed by the song proper (indicated with the word "text" above).

Music Transcription 14: Five examples of Arikuruwala incipits showing individuals' variation.

Example 1: Unidentified man 1928 (Audio 9)
C=E

Example 2: Justin Puruntatameri 1975 (Audio 10)
C=E^b

Example 3: Foxy Tipungwuti 1975 (Audio 37)
C=E^b

Example 4: Barney Tipuamantimeri 1975 (Audio 11)
C=F

Example 5: Stephen-Paul Kantilla 2012 (Audio 12)
C=A^b

The line length in this style is variable, with anywhere from three (the minimum) to eight metrical units recorded in the data. The point at which the pitch steps down is not exactly fixed. In Example 1 in Music Transcription 15, for example, the singer uses the pitch fall to mark the fourth syllable of the first metrical unit, whereas in Example 2 the pitch changes occur at the line initial, the second syllable of the second metrical unit, the start of the third metrical unit and (at the second iteration) on the line final.

When the line is extended in length the added metrical units are sung on the note that is arrived at on the second metrical unit (the third pitch of the melody, used for the monotonic section of the song), with the phrase-beginning and the phrase-end remaining consistent in pitch and duration (a unit A and a unit B respectively). Vibrato is often added to the second and subsequent units. Example 2 at Music Transcription 15 comprises an incipit with stick beats and then the first line of text, which is five units long (four A units and one B unit). The complete song comprises nine different lines of text, each repeated a varying number of times to result in a performance that is 85 lines in length (and three and a half minutes long). Each iteration of one line of text (in this case comprising four A units then one B unit) is separated with a breath, and the metre is marked with accents on the first and fourth syllables of each unit.

Music Transcription 15: Two examples of the Arikuruwala melody. Foxy Tipungwuti (Audio 37) and Tractor Joe (Audio 29).

Example 1: Foxy Tipungwuti 1975 (Audio 37)
C=B

Example 2: Tractor Joe 1975 (Audio 29)

A varying number of repetitions of the line is performed, first with the soloist seated, and singing at a relatively low pitch; then, with the soloist standing, a number of iterations are given at a higher pitch (close to or actually an octave higher).[36] The entire sequence lasts for about ten minutes. Each singer begins with stick beating that is irregular and much slower than the tempo of the song. The sticks can continue under a melismatic vocable, but they do not always accompany the song text. In between each line of song there might be a few stick beats, not of a specific number. The overall impression we must get from Arikuruwala is that it is a musical form that no two singers perform in exactly the same way. As well as two examples in Music Transcription 15, at Song text 31 I give a full performance transcription of another Arikuruwala song.[37] Comparison of these three versions (and of those at Audio 9, 25, 28, 33 and 61) exemplifies the range of vocal ornamentation that makes each performance unique.

8. Ampirikuruwala (Kulama songs). Female response. Kuruwala style. Ritual.

The Ampirikuruwala is the response sung by one or more women as part of the man's Arikuruwala song. It is never performed without the Arikuruwala solo (whether that is sung by a man or by a woman). It has a melodic contour not unlike the Arikuruwala except that it includes improvised ornamentation on the first unit. Traditionally these are sung at Kulama ceremonies, but today they are also performed by the women's group in Ngarukuruwala performances.[38] The important feature of this song-type is the polyphonic effect created by the way in which the supporting individual (or group) follows the soloist in a response form. The response begins in time with the start of the last metrical unit of the soloist's first line. The line final is then repeated before the singer starts from

---

36   See also Figure 21.
37   Audio 78.
38   When a group sings the response the entries are staggered as individuals begin in turn, adding to the polyphonic effect.

the beginning of the line. This creates a seven-syllable unit with shifted accents so that the first, third and sixth syllables are stressed. This means the response is sung two syllables behind the soloist, with the accents falling on different syllables for each singer. Two or three iterations of the line will be sung, with no pause between the lines (unlike the soloist's rendition).

In performance the (usually male) soloist repeats the line a number of times alone. When the Ampirikuruwala singer feels confident that she has picked up the words, she begins. The traditional function of this song-type, creating a duet between husband and wife, was an important symbolic gesture of spousal support, respect and sharing the knowledge within the song. In a recording made in 1975 by Osborne,[39] Tractor Joe continues to sing the text while first one woman (who unfortunately is not identified) and then a group sing the response. It is impossible to transcribe the two vocal lines with any exactness because of the rhythmic looseness of the singing. Music Transcription 16, however, shows the melodic contour of each, to represent the polyphonic effect and to show how the staggered entry places the text two syllables apart. The text is taken from Osborne's transcription (1989, 459).[40] This is from the same performance as Music Transcription 15, Example 2. I have removed pitch fluctuation markings and have bracketed the start of each line of text.

Music Transcription 16: Arikuruwala with Ampirikuruwala response. Tractor Joe and unidentified women. 1975 (Audio 29).

---

39   Audio 29.
40   To make this example clearer, I have not included the microtonal variation.

In Music Transcription 17 I give an example of the singer continuing to vocalise, while not singing the text, when the female response is sung. This is a common variation of this song-type.[41]

Music Transcription 17: Showing relationship between Arikuruwala and Ampirikuruwala vocal lines. Foxy and Dorothy Tipungwuti, 1975 (Audio 37).

In the old recordings I have studied, the response follows the same format as is used today. The response singer replaces any iteration of ngiya (I) with nginta (you), creating a dialogue between her and the soloist (or the animal or ancestor he is the embodiment of). In performances recorded by Mountford and Osborne, the woman's response is also altered by transposing all vowels to an open *a* sound. The effect of the man's continuing to sing (either the same text or vocables) while the woman sings is to create an undulating melody with the two lines revolving around each other in heterophony. Listening to the recordings one can hear the man responding to the pitch fluctuations of the woman's line. The result is, aurally, highly complex. These singers show considerable musical skill in their ability to sing a line of text starting part way through a word, altering the accent pattern and giving all syllables equal weight and value while hearing those same words sung concurrently but a step behind. The fact that in most cases the song text would be new to the "response" singers

---

41   This corresponds with 00:30 in Audio 37.

adds to this. In the Strong Women's Group's performance context, the words are usually known by the group because the Kuruwala song texts are relatively set. The words are not exactly the same, however, as the soloist will usually change the text slightly each time and so the response group is in effect repeating what they have just heard. It is therefore always a feature of Ampirikuruwala that the response is just that – a direct response to the words being sung by the lead singer, which establishes their authority as custodians of the song and also enacts the connection and mutual support between all participants. Tiwi singers agree that this type of singing needs both people to be listening carefully to each other. Whether the soloist continues singing after the response begins is not consistent and whether this is due to the circumstances of the recording session or the singer's personal style, we do not know. In the recording at Audio 31[42] the lead male singer, Stephen-Paul Kantilla, vocalises on an open vowel (similar to the 1975 example) while two women, Leonie Tipiloura and Calista Kantilla, sing the response. Audio 60 and 61 give two other performance styles within the characteristics of Ampirikuruwala.

9. Ariwangilinjiya (lullaby). Kuruwala style. Secular.

This song-type is slow and monotonous and the structure of the song includes a repeating meaningless vocalisation (*ayayaya* …), the aim being to induce sleep. There is no percussive accompaniment in this style because the singer is usually holding a small child and waving the fingers of one hand in small gentle circles above the child's face. In the recording made by Mountford in 1954 (Audio 22) a man sings first, followed by a woman who performs the same song. Two important and interesting features of Tiwi song practice are evident in these songs: the differences between individuals' renditions of the same song; and the style of the Ampirikuruwala response in which the woman sings her version.

The woman sings almost entirely monotonically. The syllables are slurred together into quasi-melismatic phrases, giving a hypnotic soothing effect, more as one would imagine a lullaby being sung. While the singer uses metrically correct units, she fuses the last two syllables (*puwi*) of Text Line 1 (shown underlined in Example 1, Music Transcription 18) and truncates the final unit of that line in all but two of the seven lines of the full performance, creating a breath while not affecting the pulse (marked with //). Transcribing this song proved very difficult because my consultants were unable to recognise most of the text. Patipatingini (a small lizard), the first word of the song when sung by the man, is known but the words wankelarrampuwi, to close one's eyes,

---

42   Recorded by the author on Bathurst Island in 2012.

and kuwunawina, flea, given by Osborne (1989, 1142) bear no resemblance to equivalent words in today's language. The text and translation given by Osborne for the 1954 recording and for his recording of Kituwulumi singing the same lullaby in 1975 use identical text apart from the replacement of the word lizard by ant (walawalinga).

The most obvious difference between the two renditions of this lullaby in the 1954 recording is that the man uses more variation of pitch and articulates the syllables and rhythm more strongly. The man sings a melody moving across a minor third and the rhythmic and syllabic delineation is more accentuated than in the woman's performance. He makes similar alterations to the end of Line 1, sometimes deleting the final syllable *wi*. Current Elders' opinion is that the man was singing "to show off the words" whereas the woman sang "to really put a baby to sleep" – and that she might have been holding a baby, although we can't be sure from the audio. The melody used by the man is not recorded elsewhere, nor is it known to current singers. I have included the text of these examples (with translation at Song text 25 (Osborne 1989, 1142)) to show how the woman has started part way through the line, following the Ampirikuruwala method of "response" singing.

Song text 25: Unknown singer. Ariwangilinjiya (lullaby), 1954.

Patupating-am	pu-	nginyu-	wankelarrampuwi
Lizard-she	*np-*	*you-*	*close eyes*

Lizard will close your eyes

Kuwunawin-	a-	minyi-	ngu-	wankelarrampuwi
Flea-	*he-*	*you-*	*hw-*	*close eyes*

Flea will close your eyes

Music Transcription 18: Ariwangilinjiya (lullaby), 1954 (Audio 22).

Woman's performance:

6 The classical Tiwi music

Man's performance:

10. Apajirupwaya (love songs). Kuruwala style. Secular.

Love songs were performed solo and unaccompanied. Goodale mentions love songs being sung by young women and that each belonged specifically to the woman who composed it, and should only be sung by that woman (Goodale 1974, 40, 131). From the mid-1970s this might have begun to change because Osborne notes that a song can become well known and sung by women around the community. Among his 1975 recordings are songs that were performed (for the recording) by a woman who was not the composer. The love songs are a product of the time when physical liaisons outside of the marriage-promise system (under which girls were promised, often before birth, to adult men in order to fulfil mutually beneficial obligations and kinship groups) were common and, if not publicly condoned, it seems that as long as they were in secret and no public shame came to the family, extramarital liaisons were tolerated as an inevitable result of the large age gap between husband and wife that the system produced.[43] These songs therefore refer to secret meetings, mostly at night, with allusions to sexual encounters veiled under references to longing, waiting and meeting by torchlight.

The Apajirupwaya songs serve a similar social function to Iwaidja Jurtbirrk (Barwick, Birch and Evans 2007). While Jurtbirrk are composed and performed by men, Tiwi love songs are exclusively a women's genre. There are similarities, however, in that the text of a Tiwi love song relates to real events and real people (rather than spiritual or sacred subjects) and that they are implicit rather than explicit. They are considered far more suggestive and evocative than the Amparruwu songs (described earlier) that overtly mention sexual acts and body parts. The texts are not specifically about or descriptive of actual physical contact, but they paint a picture of the atmosphere, the night-time, the secrecy, the waiting to meet and then thinking about it during the day with longing or secret thrill. It is precisely the lack of detail that makes them all the more sensual. As Eunice Orsto said to me, the listener "can fill in the blanks with whatever they imagine". These were songs to be sung for the entertainment of women and were sung at informal gatherings. They were not secret, however, nor regarded as inappropriate, and recordings of them have been played openly (sometimes in the presence of men) in listening and transcription sessions together. The old ladies recall the songs from the days they were young girls in the Bathurst Island mission and the women from across the Aspley Strait at Paru would sing that melody. They didn't sing love songs themselves because they grew up at the mission and so were not exposed to them or their social function. This manifests in Mountford's recordings in 1954 and Osborne's recordings in 1975 that are all from Melville Island. The melody of the love songs

---

[43] For further explanation of the pre-mission marriage system see Goodale (1974), Hart and Pilling (1988), Mountford (1958) and Venbrux (1995).

(Audio 75) is the most florid of the traditional song-types, with a rising and falling scalic passage on the second, third and fourth units. While these songs are no longer sung as love songs, the Women's Group version (Murli la) has become very popular and is performed at public events and professional performances.

The recordings of only one singer's Apajirupwaya were available to me (recorded by Mountford in 1954). It is therefore difficult to say what degree of variation might have been employed by other singers, including those whom Osborne recorded. Osborne says that the love songs he recorded in 1975 are, while "broadly similar" in musical form to the 1954 recordings, different in melody (Osborne 1989, 198). This is the only song-type whose lines of verse are of regular length, presumably because the melody has a fixed length. This makes the love song structure different from all the other song-types, in that it is regular and always comprises eight metrical units in total.

The women I spoke with about these songs tell me the melody is from Mantiyupi Country. This concurs with their memories of it being sung primarily by the women at Paru, which is in Mantiyupi Country. I was not able to obtain the recordings of the love songs that Osborne made in 1975 but, comparing his description of the melodic contour (Osborne 1989, 199) with the melody sung by an unidentified woman in 1954 (recorded by Mountford), we can presume it is basically the same. Music Transcription 19 shows this melody with the four melodic parts numbered. The metrical pattern of five- and four-syllable units is not always followed in this song-type. It shows how she has used the basic melody with the same cycle of four melodic parts repeating once, but with less ornamentation and so conforming to the metrical pattern. Three further text phrases, sung by the same woman, are presented at Music Transcription 3.

Music Transcription 19: Apajirupwaya (love song) melody. Unidentified woman, 1954 (Audio 75).

Waiting All Night.
Free translation:
I thought of him last night where he was sleeping.
C=C#

11. Ariwayakulaliyi (individuals' songs). Kuruwala style. Secular (and Church).

There are other songs in the data that do not fit any of the song-types listed above. Osborne gives these a collective term, Ariwayakulaliyi, although none of my consultants knew of this word being used as a song-type. The word itself is understood to mean "changing the words around" or "singing one's own words in one's own way". Each of these extra-classificatory songs has a different melody, and none is particularly similar to any of the traditional song-types. Whether they are of various functions that are no longer known or they were always "one-offs" is a matter of conjecture. Osborne suggests these might not be Tiwi melodies, wondering whether they might be of Macassar origin (Osborne 1989, 194), and Moyle says of the second song of this type (in the liner notes to the recordings published as *Songs of the Northern Territory*) that it is "more ample in scope than others connected with traditional ceremonial styles of this Australian island region". We have not been able to establish a non-Tiwi source for these melodies, and Tiwi singers consider them to be Tiwi.

The following three Ariwayakulaliyi song melodies are credited to particular composers.[44]

Melody 1: Music Transcription 20: Long Stephen.

A song performed by Long Stephen in 1975 is credited as having been composed by Tungutalum, who died in 1935 (Osborne 1989, 1076). There is no record of whether Tungutalum created the melody or only the text, but Long Stephen does not use this melody in any of his other recorded performances. It is different to the other songs in that it spans a fourth and uses major scale.

---

44   My consultants advised that Examples 1, 2 and 3 should be included in this section, despite Osborne not classifying them as Ariwayakulaliyi songs.

Music Transcription 20: Ariwayakulaliyi melody, Long Stephen 1975 (Audio 47).

Free translation (given by Long Stephen):
L1: I am the shooting star, Wurangampityimirri
L2: Showing off, anyhow, I walk right through the middle of everyone

Melody 2: Music Transcription 21: Eustace Tipiloura.

Eustace Tipiloura composed this melody and it has been used by the Women's Group in their Kuruwala-style healing songs in recent years. Here he explains how he owns the song, but that others have learned it from him and it is now sung at funerals for members of his kinship group:

> They use it for when my family die, my father's side, blood side. That's the one they sing in the church. That's mine it's only me. They just catch it. Somebody took it from me at Garden Point and I said "all right".

Music Transcription 21: Ariwayakulaliyi melody, Eustace Tipiloura (Audio 48).

Free translation (given by Eustace Tipiloura):
I am Brolga. I am watching in [my homeland] Wurangku

Melody 3: Music Transcription 22: Enrail Munkara.

Enrail Munkara's melody is unique to Nyingawi songs. It is similar to the Arikuruwala melody in which additional metrical units in a line are accommodated by additional repetition of the tonic pitch. The tonic pitch in these songs is defined not by final position but by internal repetition; in other words, it is the most frequently repeated note. The final unit is marked by a rise of a tone (at a non-specific place) and fall of a third occurs on the penultimate note. In this performance the singer has retained the metrical form of the text, although the rhythmic treatment of each four-syllable unit B differs each time. In the first iteration of the line, each unit B is extended to five "quaver" beats and in the second iteration it becomes seven "quavers". The melodic treatment of the text also differs on the second iteration. The pulse is even and consistent, a feature of Nyingawi songs in the old recordings. This has been modified in performances of Nyingawi by Casmira Munkara (Audio 57). She places stresses on the first and fourth syllables, creating a rhythm similar to the Paujimi melody that has developed into some of the women's Modern Kuruwala songs.

Music Transcription 22: Ariwayakulaliyi/Nyingawi melody. Enrail Munkara, 1954 (Audio 56).

Free translation (given by Stanley Munkara): *First two units of each line are untranslatable Nyingawi language*
Third and fourth units of each line: *The branches make a cracking noise*
C=F

12. Modern Kuruwala (Strong Women's Group songs). Kuruwala style. Secular (and Church).

The most recent song-type is called Modern Kuruwala (modern singing) by the Strong Women's Group. It is characterised by the influence of non-Tiwi music and the years the women spent as children in the mission, learning to sing Catholic hymns in a guitar-accompanied choral style. It uses modifications of the melodies of the Ariwayakulaliyi song-type that have become associated with Country groups, although they can be sung (in the context of the Modern Kuruwala song-type) by people from any Country group. This song-type also includes songs whose melodies have been "borrowed" by the women, having heard pop and folk-music songs on the radio and being taught by the nuns at school and at church (in the 1960s and 1970s).

At Music Transcription 23 I give three examples of original Tiwi melodies that are now used for numerous songs. To show the similarity of melodic shape and structure I present them on one system (they would not, however, be performed simultaneously). They are generally at a moderate tempo and often feature group singing in two-part harmony. They are (melodically) most like the love songs in that they have scalic passages and larger intervallic leaps than the ritual-associated song-types. While they have demonstrably different melodies, they are all based on a ternary structure in which the first line starts on the tonic, the second line starts on a pitch higher and the third line returns to the tonic (sometimes with slight variation to the return of A, as in the case of Example 3). Traditionally performed solo and with hand-clapping or sticks accompaniment, this song-type has been transplanted onto the guitar-accompanied musical style of the Women's Group songs with minimal melodic change and retains the capacity for line expansion following the rules of classical song composition. As I will expand upon in the next section on emerging musical genres, these three melodies have become known as Country tunes: melodies affiliated with the traditional Murrakupuni groups that are drawn on in new songs composed by women from those particular groups and so they continue to be referred to as Country melodies (albeit with non-Tiwi musical treatment).

Music Transcription 23: Three Ariwayakulaliyi melodic contours, composers unknown.

Example 1: Murli la. Free translation: *Hey, let's go, together*
Example 2: Yirrikapayi (Crocodile). Free translation: *The crocodile man is sitting down making a spear*
He was at his Country, Wiyapurali, on the beach

Example 3: Wunijaka (Spirit of the wind). Free translation:
Jipayamurriningimirri *[ancestral name]*
He is high up above us

Having documented ten traditional/old/classical song-types, one traditional vocal call and one recently created song-type, I will now describe those song-types that are considered "modern". These have definable characteristics, while showing capacity for variability. As we find with the classical song-types, this capacity correlates with the performance context of the song-type, with group participation resulting in more regularity while the more soloistic song-types show a greater degree of melodic, rhythmic and tempo variation.

Chapter 7
Emerging musical genres

Pupuni miraka, you have a good voice, your throat, miraka, is where your voice comes through from your body, from your mind. We say in old way, your voice is arlikirraka, which is also the frog – maybe because his whole body makes the sound. He is his own voice, not separated like in our throat. We don't need anything in the way when we sing, tell those stories of our ancestors before us. Those words come straight through to your ears, nothing in the way.

Clementine Puruntatameri

With its demonstrable variability, wide use of extemporisation and performance-focused currency, Tiwi musical culture predominantly values novelty and innovation – a contemporary music scene if ever there was one. When an Elder songman or songwoman "puts up" a song, they are creating something new. Their song is unique to them, and to their performance. They have perhaps been singing quietly to themselves for days beforehand, mulling over ideas for words that will fit with the melody they will use. At the actual time of performing, though, they extemporise around the structure of melodic, metrical and rhythmic rules that they know well. The process the Tiwi singer goes through in the moment of performance is a complex one, made to seem easy. Just as a jazz instrumentalist or singer creates rhythmic and melodic variations as they perform, so too does a Tiwi singer extemporise on a standard melodic and metrical form and respond in the moment of performance. The melody, the text and the musical feel of a jazz standard remain similar enough to the original for it to be recognisable and yet each performer (singer or instrumentalist) has the creative freedom to modify, ornament and improvise around the elements that define it. The Tiwi Yoi songs can be regarded in the same way. The Dreaming Yoi (Shark, Crocodile or Moonfish, for example) can be regarded as "standards" and yet each time they are sung they are varied according to the creative improvisation of the performer. In rap and/or hip-hop we can also find comparisons, perhaps closer, with singers of that genre creating sung poetry, drawing from extant phrases, idioms, linguistic devices and street vernacular in quasi-melodic spoken/sung form that strings syllables together in patterns that neither match those of speech nor of a melodic form. Some young Tiwi people who sing along with the rapping sections of B2M have commented that it sounds a little like what the old men are doing in ceremony, and indeed within B2M songs one can hear a connection between the rapped English language elements and the syllabic strings of Tiwi language sung phrases.

This stylistic assonance comes as a result of familiarity on the part of the singers in B2M with the aural and physical processes of performance that they've been surrounded by in the course of cultural practice. It is a similarly embodied and often spontaneous transplanting of Tiwi words, rhythms or dance actions onto non-Tiwi melodies and musical structures that the women exhibit in their Modern Kuruwala songs. One striking example that is relevant here occurred in 2008.

In a break in rehearsals in 2008 the (non-Tiwi) band started noodling around the song Murli la (which we had been working on in that session) and the women began to riff on words, inserting Yoi song texts into the Murli la melody. In this instance the women were singing Dreaming Yoi to a new melody (and not Jipuwakirimi, that is usually used for Yoi). They were also singing (and dancing) Yoi to a non-Tiwi musical form. The jazz ostinato played by the band set up a continuing pulse and repeating rhythmic pattern, not unlike in a Yoi event, allowing for repetition of each song to accommodate numerous dancers and the change from one song to the next without the beat stopping. The women told me too that it was the text that enabled them to dance their Yoi even though the music was quite different (and not traditional).

So, even though they were dancing to non-Tiwi music and singing a non-Yoi melody (although Tiwi), they were able to dance Dreaming Yoi because they were singing the words. It is the words that enable the connection between Dreaming Yoi and embodied, danced Yoi.

In this Chapter I will describe how many of the traditions and motivations of Tiwi classical song practice have been superimposed onto non-Tiwi musical styles and performance contexts. While in some cases the musical outcome is quite distinctly altered from the classical Tiwi form, it's clear that the underlying meaning, function and approach to composition and/or performance remain.

7 Emerging musical genres

Daniel Paujimi's melody

This melody (in the Ariwayakulaliyi song-type) is now most often performed in the Modern Kuruwala song-type. Different song texts are composed using the melody, in the same way that other Tiwi melodies are used for numerous song texts and for different functions. My information confirms that it was composed by Daniel Paujimi, presumably sometime in the 1940s or 1950s. It was used in church for parts of Mass sung in Tiwi by Daniel (who was a church assistant). By association it has come to be owned by the Tikilaru Country group (Daniel's Country). When Daniel Paujimi's son died, this melody (used also for Kupunyi, Yinjula and a couple of Catholic hymns) was closed for a period of time but it has continued to be a widely used melody. In a recording made by Father Michael Sims in April 1972, Daniel Paujimi sings eight songs in Tiwi but with Catholic subject matter, all of which use this melody (see Example 1, Music Transcription 24).[1] Daniel's tune is fluid and lilting and repeats a small circling melody around a tonic, not dissimilar to European liturgical chant. Comparison with the motivations behind the composition of church Lirrga in Wadeye (Barwick 2003) can be drawn. Metrical and rhythmic patterns of the traditional song practice were set by the composer to texts relating to Christian liturgical stories, in a sense creating a Tiwi version of the liturgical singing he heard in church (performed by the priest, and that he learned as an acolyte). Local opinion is that Daniel started to sing this melody in the church and it has since been taken up by others, taught to children at school for secular and religious texts, and also sung by the Women's Group.

Although it is not the oldest recording of this melody, I present Daniel Paujimi's performance (recorded in 1972) first in Music Transcription 24 because it is regarded as the original version (he being the composer). Seven items using this melody were recorded by Osborne in 1975. The six of these that were sung by Daniel Paujimi are unfortunately not available for audition.[2] Osborne also recorded Christopher (Foxy) Tipungwuti singing an Apajirupwaya (love song) composed by Marjorie Wonaemirri.[3] The melody that Mr Tipungwuti uses (Example 2 in Music Transcription 24) is the same as the first phrase of Daniel

---

1   The recording Sims lodged at AIATSIS is a re-dubbing of the original recordings that he made, and we hear him speak and then press play on a second machine (on which the original performances were recorded). That machine has a regularly undulating pitch that should not be regarded as part of Paujimi's melody or singing style. Unfortunately, this has also meant that the audio is unclear and so we have not been able to elicit a complete text transcription.
2   Osborne lodged all but one of his field tapes from 1974–75 at AIATSIS, and these songs are on that tape.
3   Song number 204 on C04-003855B. I list this as an Ariwayakulaliyi song-type because although the text is from an Apajirupwaya (love song) it uses the Ariwayakulaliyi melody.

Paujimi's melody (not the love song melody). The melody used by a group of Bathurst Island schoolboys, recorded by Moyle at the Darwin Eisteddfod in 1962 (see Example 3, Music Transcription 24) also has this melodic phrase, as well as what we can presume would have been sung as the alternating phrase by Daniel in 1975 when recorded by Osborne.

It was also used by school children at Milikapiti in 1964, recorded by Groger-Wurm, for their Dugong, Yinjula and Whirlwind songs (Example 4, Music Transcription 24). The women I have played this recording to are confused as to why Milikapiti children would have known that melody, as it is firmly associated with Bathurst Island people (the Tikilaru group) and the mission school. They guess that someone from Bathurst Island had taught it to them.

The 1962 recording is interesting because it is the earliest recorded example of what the Strong Women call the Modern Kuruwala style. In this performance (Audio 43) we can hear the beginning of a shift from a straight duple beat to the swung compound beat that is the rhythmic feature of the women's Kupunyi (Canoe) song (Audio 46), which also uses the same melody. It is evident from the recordings that over the years the "quaver" beats have been modified as a duple time signature imposed on to the traditional form. What are almost exactly evenly spaced syllables grouped into units of five in Paujimi's and Tipungwuti's solo performances (Examples 1 and 2, Music Transcription 24) become a triplet, duplet in the 1962 and 1964 recordings (Examples 3 and 4, Music Transcription 24), in which the clap beats (in Example 3 only) delineate the units of five syllables following the standard pattern, which places a stress on the first and fourth syllables. In the two recordings I have of the Women's Group singing this melody (Examples 5 and 6, Music Transcription 24) the addition of guitar sets up a four-beat pulse over which the first three of the five syllables of the metre are set into a "swung" quaver rhythm.

7 Emerging musical genres

Music Transcription 24: Six variations of Daniel Paujimi's Ariwayakulaliyi melody (Audio 41, 42, 43, 44, 45, 46).

Example 1: Daniel Paujimi. 1972 (Audio 41).
C=F

Example 2: Pearling boat. Foxy Tipungwuti. 1975 (Audio 42).
C=F

Example 3: Tiwi schoolboys. 1962 (Audio 43).
C=F

Example 4: Yinjula. Milikapiti schoolchildren. 1965 (Audio 44).
C=D

Example 5: Yintoola. Leonie Tipiloura. 2011 (Audio 45.)

Example 6: Kupunyi. Ngarukuruwala Women's Group. 2008. (Audio 46).

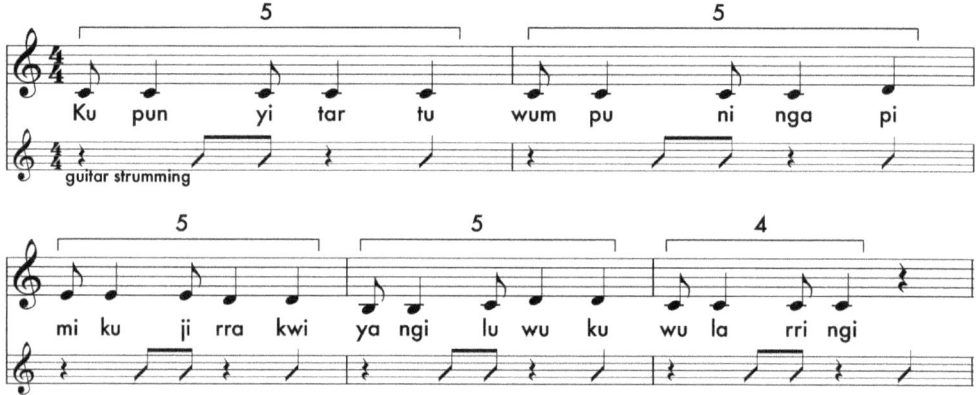

Sometime in the late 1980s the women rearranged the song into a western-style guitar-accompanied song Kupunyi, keeping elements of the old melodic structure intact. The rhythmic pattern of the Kupunyi text/melody follows the metre of the old songs. Although the language is Modern Tiwi, the words have been arranged into a five-syllable metre with stresses aligning to the metre rather than to reflect natural or everyday speech. Every line is metrically correct, comprising four five-syllable A units and one four-syllable B unit. The rhythmic pattern is "swung" to a greater or lesser extent depending on the style of guitar, but the groupings of five remain clear. In Music Transcription 25 I have marked the metrical units with square brackets to show how the women have modified the rhythmic pulse from the traditional song form to fit into a 4/4 time signature but kept the sense of groups of five syllables.

Music Transcription 25: Three treatments of the word rrakwiyangili (dugong) in the Modern Kuruwala Kupunyi song. 2008. (Audio 46).

In this song the Old Tiwi word for dugong, rrakwiyangili, is used (the New Tiwi word is marntuwunyini or jimayi). Comparing Line 1 (Example 6, Music Transcription 24) with Lines 3 and 4 (Music Transcription 25)[4] one can see how in each line the women have altered the sound of this word and the stresses within it in order to fit the metre, in much the same way as was done in the past. The two renditions of Line 3 differ in that part of the word is deleted in each, and in all three lines the stresses fall on different syllables, none of which corresponds to the spoken form of the word. Another feature of the old song technique is that the women change the vowel sound at the end of rrakwiyangili to a *u* in order to smoothly join it to wumurupiya (Line 3) and to wumiringarra (Line 4). Similar vowel harmony happens in Line 1, with tarti becoming tartu to join it to the next word wumpuni. In performance the women further elide vowels and/or add syllables to fit the words into this five-syllable pattern. Song text 26 shows that Lines 1, 2 and 3 are the same, but 4 and 5 change. Song text 27 shows Romuel Puruntatameri's performance of this song in 1975 (Audio 8), as comparison of the use of old song words and metrical arrangement.

---

4 The first iteration of Line 3 was an error, and the women corrected the metre as they sang.

Romuel's song was composed to fulfil his role as son for the mortuary Yoi held for Wampayawityimirri (Black Joe). The last line marks the patriline and the Dreaming of the deceased (dugong) and references the mirawani (son) status of the singer through the spear symbol. The fact that the classificatory son "kills" the dugong (his father) follows the etiquette of mortuary songs, in which the son symbolically kills his father, thus taking on the responsibility and obligations he has inherited, having replaced his father in the patriline. Rrangini, a place in north-western Melville Island, has significance for Romuel's Yiminga clan. In the text of the women's song is Mirntati. This is a rock off the coast of Melville Island. Another meaning given by younger women (aged in their 60s) for this line is "He looks like a big stone – his back is smooth", suggesting the rock is associated through this song with marntuwunyini, the New Tiwi word for dugong.

The first line = the text as requested for documentation, second line = what is sung.

Song text 26: Strong Women's Group. Kupunyi (Canoe), 2008.

> L1: Kupunyi tarti wumpuningapi mikuji rrakiyangilu kuwularringi
> *Three men were paddling in a long canoe looking around*
> sung:
> ML1, ML2 Kupunyitarti wumpuningapi mikujirraki yangiluwuku wularringi (x2)
>
> L2: Pilamingarra purukunji rrakiyangilu munukumuni
> *The tail of the dugong is very big*
> sung:
> ML1 Pílamingárra pú[ru]kunjirráki yángiluwúmu núkumuní
>
> L3: Putupwarra ayikunji rrakiyangilu wumurupiyangirramiya
> *The tail of the dugong is flipping around on the water*
> sung:
> ML1 Pútupwarrá(tu pwárra)[a]yikúnji níkunjirráki [yangilu] wúmurupíya ngírramiyá
> ML2 Pútupwarrá(tu pwárra)[a]yikúnji [níkunji]rráki yangilu wúmurupíya ngírramiyá
>
> L4: Nginingaji Mirntati waranga ampiniwingi rrakiyangilu wumiringarra
> *The dugong is swimming around the stone in the sea*
> sung:
> ML1, ML2 Ngíningajímirn tátiwarángaam píniwingírra kíyangilúwu míringarrá

7 Emerging musical genres

> L5: Piripati rrakiyangilawu, Piripati rrakiyangilawu.
> *Spearing the animal*
>
> sung:
> ML1 Pír[i]patirráki yángiláwu, Pír[i]patirráki yángiláwu.
> *They are happy because they have speared the dugong*
>
> L6: ML1,ML2 Kurukawangawakawayi
>   (humming)

Song text 27: Kilupwarlapiwiyi Romuel Puruntatameri. Rrakwiyangili (Dugong), 1975.

> **Spoken form:**
>
> Rangini-nga- la tyakupwayinga ngen- ti- ni-mi-nge- rrignart- ighi
> Rangini- f-   *of bark canoe*   I -   f- *to-him-hw-* *immerse* tr
>
> Pakinya ngen-ti- ni-mi-nge rrakwiyangili - pu- murarrinty- ighi
> *First*   I —   f- *to-him-hw-* *dugong-*   /   *coil*   -tr
>
> Mapetyan- yi-   nu-wa-ngi-nge-   rrakwiyangili pi- nge- rruninkuwa
> *Muddy water-he-* *to- ic- me-hw-* *dugong -*   /   /   *line up*
>
> Krrupukini ngen-ti-wi-nge- rrakwiyangili -matyerrangil ighi
> *Harpoon* I- f- cv- hw-   *dugong*   *spear*   tr
>
> **Metrical form:**
>
> Ranginingala tyakupwayinga ngentiniminge rrignartighi
> *I launched my Rangini bark canoe to go after him*
>
> Pakinyangenti nimingerrakwi yangilipumu rarrintyighi
> *First I coiled up the rope in readiness*
>
> Mapetyaninu wangingerrakwi yangilipinge rruninkuwa
> *When he made a trail in the muddy water*
>
> Krrupukiningen tiwingerrakwi yangilimatye rrangilighi
> *I speared the dugong with my harpoon*

Singing current events into a 21st-century oral tradition

The football song and the Wurrumiyanga Wellbeing Centre song, and one version of Murli la that I discuss later in this section all use variants of a broadly similar three-part melody, which I have defined as one of the Ariwayakulaliyi song-type (see Example 1, Music Transcription 23). It has a three-phrase structure similar to the melody composed by Daniel Paujimi (Music Transcription 24) and is also demonstrably similar to Eustace Tipiloura's melody (shown at Music Transcription 21). While it is similar to the melody used for Kupunyi and other individually composed songs, this melody creates a different relationship between text and rhythm. This melody is set to text in an additive rhythmic pattern. The rhythmic duration of a line is determined by the number of syllables in the text. A section of the melody can be extended from the second metrical unit through to the penultimate unit when the melody steps down through that and the final unit of the line (as I will show through examples here). In the opinion of older members of the Strong Women's Group, this melody (belonging to Mantiyupi Country people) is considered a derivation of the love songs from Paru (on the south-western shore of Melville Island, in Mantiyupi Country) recorded by Mountford in 1954. The tune is known these days as the "happy" tune that was sung by old women when they went out bush in order to keep in contact with each other and not get lost. (The women still do this, but they also sing other songs.) Senior knowledge holders tell me it is definitely a pre-guitar melody and would have been used for unique compositions and one-off performances.

This melody has become a standard, in a way similar to that in which the traditional melodies were used for new compositions. In the performance context the women maintain the traditional practice of "putting up" lines of song even while following a verse/chorus structure and chord progression and the number of beats may change from line to line. The structure comprises three melodic phrases, each of which has a variable length. In order to accommodate the varying lengths of each line of text, rather than thinking in terms of bars and phrases of a set length Tiwi singers count the number of syllables, and this determines the number of bars and therefore the length of the phrase. Even when a song text is fixed (having been written out and added to the song book *Murli la: Songs and Stories of the Tiwi Islands* that they have produced for the community) the order of the lines will most likely change each time it is sung as either the lead singer (if there is one) or women in turn "put up" a line that everyone knows and so can join in after the first word or so that acts as a cue. This creates an ensemble dynamic very similar to the traditional Yoi singing, where the lead singer/composer sings a line and repeats it until the group joins in (in the modern style, the phrase is repeated once only). In a clear example of the women continuing old performance practices within a new style of performing we can also draw a comparison between a song with several text lines performed in changeable order and a string of Yoi songs that makes up a Yoi event.

An important feature of the role of the women's songs is that they are embraced by the whole Tiwi community and continue to provide a vehicle for the community noticeboard in much the same way as the Ayipa songs of Kulama.

As well as being popular favourites for locals and tourists, the women are providing accumulating oral records of local history as they update their songs each year to suit the circumstances. Within a mostly fixed text that tells the story of a football game (in the case of Yiloga, the football song), they make small changes to reflect the teams that are playing and the Country place they affiliate with. This is a direct parallel with the women's funeral songs and traditional songs for ceremony which, while to some extent are fixed, are altered to include the individual's kinship, Dreaming and Country. The women's alteration of words to fit metre and melody also follows traditional practice in a way that overrides the guitar-strum rhythms and clapping along of an audience. In Music Transcription 26 we can see how the rhythm changes to accommodate the words and that certain words have syllables deleted (shown in parentheses) in order to fit the melody, again, in a method similar to that of classical song composition. The five-syllable-unit rule is not strictly followed in this song, although we can see groupings of five in the first unit of each line. Examples 2, 3 and 4 also show how the melodic line is extended from the second metrical unit (shown in square brackets) in order to accommodate the required text, just as ceremonial singers would. Example 3 names the Muluwurri and Wurangku teams, Example 4 names Imalu and Tapalinga. The four examples show a variety of rhythmic alterations made to the first two crotchet beats to incorporate the different texts, including appropriate team names. At Song text 28 is the full text as composed and performed by Wurrumiyanga Strong Women's Group for the game between Imalu and Tapalinga on 8 March 2010, sung to the Mantiyupi Country Melody (the traditional owners who are the "hosts" of the grand final at Wurrumiyanga (Audio 50). Also interesting to note are the different spellings for the Tiwi word for umpire in these two presentations of the text. In Example 1 in Music Transcription 26, "Umpirrimani" was given by older singers and in Line 2 of Song text 27 "Ampayamani" was given by younger singers. Both are considered correct as each reflects the way older and younger singers pronounce that word.

Music Transcription 26: Football song examples of line extension.

1. Um pi rri ma ni lo wa ji wun jing(im) pi ya man ta(wu) ni
2. Nga ji nga wu la Ti wi ma mu rru ta wi nga ri pi ngu ji(ngi) ma(ja) ku(lu) mu
3. Mu lu wu rri la Wrang ku wu la wu ta ka li wi(ngu) ti ngi ma rru wu(ngi) li pi
4. Im u lu wu la Ta pa li ngu wi wu ta ka li wi(ngu) ti ngi ma rru wu(ngi) li pi

Song text 28: Strong Women's Group. Yiloga (Football), 2010.

ML1, ML2 Najingawula Tiwi mamurruntawi ngaripinguji ngimajakulumu (x2)
All of us, Tiwi people and white people, are watching the game

ML1 Imuluwula Tapalinguwi wuta kali winguti ngi marruwungilupi
The Imulu and Tapalinga teams are running into the field with the ball

ML1, ML2 Ampayamani yilowaji wunjingimpiya mantuwuni (x2)
The umpire with the football bouncing the ball

ML1 Wijilipayamanangirri pulamuningayurugi
[Descriptive of the umpire's action bringing the knee up and arms down to indicate a goal]

ML1, ML2 Wúrrukurrunúwi wújingimarri píningijirri ngájirrami (x2)
Young people are pulling each other's football jumpers

ML1 Kuruwamuta wutawungaji wíngumjingímpi nawajirri
Punching, pushing, tackling one another

ML1, ML2 Jipakawularumagha ampijipiningintagayi (x2)
He gets a free kick and he kicks a goal

ML1 Najingawula yajilotuwi kukunari ngaripingujingimarrimi
Every one of us [Australians] are really happy to see the best team win

ML1 Nirrawaya awungarra yilowa ampijingi piningimpaya
That's the end of the football season 'til next year

7 Emerging musical genres

As I've explained earlier, Ayipa songs played an important role in the Kulama ceremony as a means of putting news and current events on record. In the Strong Women's Group's modern storytelling songs are examples of the continuation of the Ayipa song function, composed for any occasion they feel should be chronicled in the community's history. As well as the songs composed for the annual Tiwi football grand finals, new compositions were performed for the arrival of the Olympic Torch Relay in 2000, a Kidney Health Day, the 100th anniversary celebration of the mission in 2012, and the Bombing of Darwin song performed at the 75th anniversary commemoration in 2012 and in 1975, soon after Cyclone Tracy.

Songs of this type also serve as a public forum in which matters of socio-political community affairs are put on the public record. Songs in the archive also refer to landowner/custodianship and the responsibilities and rights of traditional owners to particular areas. The Wurrumiyanga Wellbeing Centre song was composed by the women in October 2009 to celebrate the opening of this centre, a facility for the provision of mental health services. At the time, there had been discussion around the renaming of Nguiu to Wurrumiyanga (a name particular to the Country in which Nguiu stood, and owned by one group of Tiwi traditional owners). The naming of the centre and, further, putting the change on record by embedding it in this song, were significant. The name change was (and still is) a matter of varying opinions, with the acknowledgement of traditional Country seen as an important gesture, but also with some concern that it disenfranchised the many Tiwi residents who are the traditional owners of other land areas, and who live in the town purely because of the congregation of services and housing that brought people in from the lands after the mission was established on the site. The song mentions the name Wurrumiyanga four times, and the narrative makes clear that the project was achieved by the traditional owners (understood by Tiwi listeners to mean the owners specific to that area of the island). Just as singing something into Kulama was a way of putting it beyond reproof, putting it on record and giving it validity, with a view to settling the matter, this song can be seen as having this same function. As with any name change, perhaps, some people continue to use the old name for the town, and there is a general understanding and agreement that people feel differently about the matter. Music Transcription 27 includes a free translation (provided by the composers) of the first line of the story.

Music Transcription 27: Line 1, Wurrumiyanga Wellbeing Centre song. 2009 (Audio 51).

Ngam pi Wu rru mi ya ngim pi la pi   ka rri ngi ni yi pu rru wun ji ni   ni ya ngi rri

Free translation:

The people from this Country, the traditional owners, wrote a letter to the government

Imparting cultural knowledge in new musical ways

I have mentioned that the Strong Women's Group have made a conscious effort to use their Modern Kuruwala songs as a medium for engaging Tiwi children with their culture. Although I have also discussed them in reference to other features, Nyingawi, Kupunyi, Murrntawarripijimi and Tikilaru songs were all composed to pass on long-held ancestral knowledge. The song Ngariwanajirri ("We all work together and help each other") is the result of a language-based project that saw senior songwomen work Old, Modern and New Tiwi into song phrases composed (in the main in English) by children who then learned the song in language, and which has been transferred on to different Country-based melodies and in a "dance mix" created by the children (at Audio 58 and 76).[5] Among their repertoire is a number of songs created by the women fundamentally in order to embed cultural knowledge in a musical medium and language that are, in their opinion, more approachable for young people than the traditional songs and language. The guitar-accompanied nursery-rhyme-style Mopaditi song, for example, which is taught to children of pre-school age, tells of the Mopaditi (the spirits of the deceased) and warns to be wary around ceremony grounds so as not to be taken by them. It is a mock-frightening song (the text includes (translated) "run away quickly or they might eat you!") that children love (in the same way as they do Nyingawi), but it also imparts deeply held ritual belief. The Tiwi Yoi song is another example, having a simple lyric about being Tiwi people, and then listing each of the Dreaming Yoi in turn, and embedding the traditional Yoi song text of each Dreaming (Shark, Buffalo, Crocodile, Junglefowl, Rainbow, etc.) so that children learn to dance and sing their Yoi. Another song, which the women have composed recently for inclusion in a new project to record children's

---

5   The Strong Kids Song Project was funded by Red Cross N.T. Communities for Children Program in 2011.

songs for use in the schools, is the Pupuni Yingiti (Good Food) song, which lists the bush foods endemic to the islands and surrounding waters.[6] These songs have been composed over the past 40 years as the women have brought up their children and grandchildren and have continued their traditional role of imparting such knowledge and information, but within a new musical (and linguistic) context.

As well as composing songs with overtly educational purpose and content, the women continue to compose songs that function within mourning rituals where Yilaniya and Mamanunkuni songs would traditionally be sung. These new choral songs don't replace the classical song-forms but are found alongside them at funerals and related rituals. The following song, Wrangku Murrakupuni, is an example of preserving old song language as well as passing on an ancestral story. It is ostensibly a collection of phrases that could be presented as single song items presented in turn at a Yilaniya (Smoking) or at a funeral, and the language alteration and inclusion of allusion to kinship and to Country are very similar to what we hear in classical mourning songs. The Wrangku Murrakupuni song (at Song text 29) was composed by the Strong Women's Group, and sung for a funeral that I attended in 2010. They sang to the Malawu Country Melody (Audio 49). Melodies are named for where they first emerged but are not restricted to singers of those areas and, in this case, kinship lines would have connected mourners to both Wurangku and Malawu Countries. I have since heard this song performed a number of times, in remembrance of a departed loved one from Wurangku Country at informal occasions; each time the text had overall similarity with some variations. At the pre-funeral Yilaniya in 2022 for a woman of Wurankgu Country and Crocodile Dreaming, the group sang it with some alterations to line order, and they sang "sister" rather than "daughter". The Old Tiwi phrase Pikilijipiyanginila (at Lines 12 and 16) was repeated throughout as mourners danced Crocodile, altering their tempo to suit the guitar style, rather than the classical Jipuwakirimi. This phrase would be sung and danced in the Jipuwakirimi form at the funeral the following day and it has become a "standard" for Crocodile as Elders have heard it in the archive of classical songs and repeated it for Crocodile people.

---

6   This song has become particularly important to the women not only because it lists the Tiwi names of many flora and fauna, but it also impresses upon children the high nutritional quality of traditional food and will, they hope, inspire at least a partial return to a healthier diet.

Song text 29: Strong Women's Group. Wurangku Murrakupuni (Wurangku Country), 2022.

> L1. Ngampiwutawu rankuwula pirratuwuji ngumuwani
> *Their land, Wurangku people*
>
> L2. Ngapiwutawa tangarima payawurrura tingatawi
> *Their home at the Payawurra beaches*
>
> L3. Pilingurupa yuwunyirraji watujingima rruwari
> *The ancestors were calling out*
>
> L4. Kapinyirrarra ampiyawungaji jiwatiwungu jiliyarra
> *You have gone there our daughter for a long time we will talk to you*
>
> L5. Jiwatiyingu jingiminta wanganuwangi miraninga
> *Our daughter has really gone, our granddaughter*
>
> L6. Karripilimatuwu nyirra wangatagaji watu wujingima
> *Mangrove fruit [for healing] is hers and the ancestors'*
>
> L7. Wutawaya awungarri Yiminga jiwiningujirralilimigi
> *Since long ago we are all her people*
>
> L8. Wutangimiraninga pituwa tuwu jilanikitimighi
> *They the father's sons [ancestors] are now embracing her*
>
> L9. Pilikitima manukuni pirratuwujingiwaya mukurigi
> *All of us [Crocodile people] are crying together*
>
> L10. Kulumutunguwi yirrikipayi yiwatuwujingikiringirri
> *She was only a young [Crocodile] woman*
>
> L11. Marruwamirrila nyirra jiwatuwujingiwangiwura
> *Remembering her even though she is gone away to the ancestors*
>
> L12. Pikilijipiyanginila winga winga ampakulumurri
> *Big mangrove roots, the sea goes out*
>
> L13. Payawurrurawula pirratuwujingiwaya kinajirri
> *Payawurrurawula people are talking to us from a long way away*
>
> L14. Pikilijipawama ayinguji liyampi ngimayawalari
> *Pikilijipawama [ancestor's name] since a long time his spirit is here*
>
> L15. Kurukawangakawayi akurukawangakawayi
> *[singing words]*
>
> L16. Pikilijipiyanginila winga winga ampakulumurri
> *Big mangrove roots, the sea goes out*

7 Emerging musical genres

I have described the Ampirikuruwala response sung by women in the Kulama ritual. Ampirikuruwala appears largely unchanged within Modern Kuruwala. A feature of this type is the fact that the woman sings in direct response to a song she is hearing for the first time, and so the resulting duet is loose. Perhaps as a result of rehearsing together with the desire to make their songs sound more polished, the Women's Group now sings the response quite differently. In a recording made of the Women's Group in 2008 (Audio 54) the soloist does not sing while the response happens. They have modified the exclamatory first unit into a melodic motif, kept the stress pattern of first and third syllables of each unit of five (that the soloist sang) intact, and do not change the vowel sounds as women of the past did (to the same degree that the older women do). The response begins on the last syllable of the last metrical unit of the line. The line final is then reduplicated, which has the effect of creating a seven-syllable metrical unit with accents on the second and fifth syllables. A recent development to further enhance the polyphonic effect is that sometimes the response group splits into smaller groups, each with their own entry point (and the quavers do not align as rigidly as the notation suggests). Following the rule of the classical Ampirikuruwala response singing, each group begins in sync with the first syllable of the last metrical unit of the sung line that they are following. In Ngarukuruwala performances the women have split the response group further, setting up a three-part canon to create three or four concurrent lines depending upon whether the soloist also sings or not. This came about after the women had heard a Women's Group response among the archived recordings in which some singers did not align their entries while others did. Rather than have randomly staggered entries the women decided to set up a three-part canonical effect, predetermining who will sing in each part and whether the lead singer will continue or not. They have performed this way with great success, enjoying the enhanced "echo" effect that it produces. Since this (rehearsed) method of performing their version of Ampirikuruwala there has also been a loosening of the set-up and individual women (especially when singing something with deep ancestral significance) will begin at their own entry point which (while always following the alignment with the final metrical unit and the shift of syllabic accent) does not adhere to the group parts. This is a return to the traditional way of singing the individual response within a newly created way of performance. Music Transcription 28 is taken from a video recording of the women in rehearsal in 2010.

Music Transcription 28: Example of rehearsed Ampirikuruwala singing. Strong Women, 2010.

7 Emerging musical genres

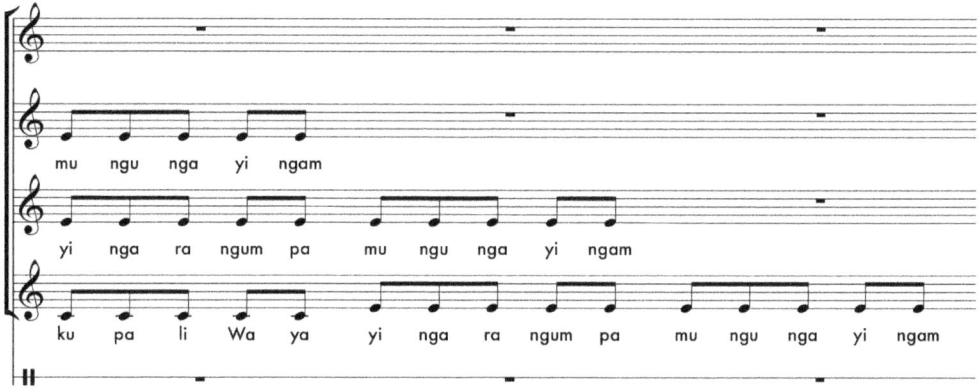

Continuing traditions despite (and because of) cultural change

One of the very interesting things about the Strong Women's Group is the way they have adapted introduced musical styles – and indeed particular songs – into their song practice. This goes further than singing "covers" or picking up musical ideas. It shows how individuals' context-driven composition and performance are the overriding factors which allow for invention, change and adaptation while remaining inherently Tiwi. The Modern Kuruwala song-type is demonstrably a continuation of the traditions of Tiwi song practice and of the role of women in Tiwi song practice.

Traditionally there are three main roles for women in singing:

1. Solo singing of widow songs (song-type 5), the lullabies (song-type 9) and the love songs (song-type 10).
2. The wife of the composer (or a group of women led by her) singing in response to the male lead (song-type 7).
3. Singing Yoi as part of a group (of women and men) joining in a song being led by the male composer (song-type 1).

Added to the traditional roles (above) is the recent growing call on older women to lead ceremonial singing because of the dwindling number of qualified men available. Songwomen were traditionally central to healing, and they have taken the lead in navigating the conflicts and confluences between Tiwi and Catholic imagery and rites in order to maintain the essence of Tiwi ceremony. The practice of mourning ceremony and associated rituals remains central to 21st-century life on the Tiwi Islands, with inherited knowledge of ritual melodies and language, and new occasion-specific songs composed for every funeral and ceremony. As well as reconfirming kinship identity and obligations, these songs enable metaphysical connections between individuals and their ancestral totems and sacred places in Country. In Tiwi cosmology the unborn, the living and the dead co-exist in their Country, but in different states of perception, with song being the conduit between them through the embodied voice of the (living) singer. The Yilaniya (Smoking) ritual comprises songs that create direct conversation between the living and the dead, acknowledging the deceased's new place among the ancestors and encouraging their spirit to leave, thus allowing the living to move on and heal.

As the impact of colonial rule over the last century has resulted in changes to the logistics of holding ceremony, Yilaniya – traditionally male-led and relatively small; now widely also called Healing – is increasingly sung by senior women and has expanded to include new song forms. The composition and performance of old and new forms of Yilaniya songs have resulted in a blurring of traditionally gendered roles in song composition and custodianship, as well as broadening the motivations and understandings of Smoking and Healing beyond their ritual context – both in their own right remaining pivotal to the spiritual and, equally important, the social health and wellbeing of the Tiwi community. As I will explain in this section, the songs being composed and performed by the Women's Group can be divided into three categories: re-workings of traditional songs; substitutions of traditional song-types (continuing the former's function); and entirely new songs. In Figure 25 I have listed the categories of women's Modern Kuruwala songs along with the classical song-types with the same function.

7 Emerging musical genres

Figure 25: Functional correlation of traditional song-types and Modern Kuruwala songs.

Function	Traditional song	Women's Modern Kuruwala songs
Sorrow, bereavement. Sung at Kulama, Funeral, Yilaniya (Smoking) and Pukumani.	Mamanunkuni (mourning). Amparruwu (widow).	Healing songs.
Telling news, putting events on record.	Ayipa songs sung on third day of Kulama.	Storytelling songs – building openings, current events, historical events.
Entertainment.	Love songs.	Murli la songs.
Imparting cultural knowledge.	Kulama songs in initiation ritual stages.	Songs about bush foods, hunting, Skin groups, ancestral stories and ceremony procedures.
Dreaming and Country.	Yoi (Dreaming totem).	Dreaming songs, Country songs.

Within the Catholic missions[7] at Nguiu, Bathurst Island (1911–69), and Garden Point (Pirlingimpi), Melville Island, at least three generations of Tiwi children grew up being educated in English and converted to Catholicism. The removal of Tiwi children from family to reside in the mission school and the missionaries' discouragement, disruption and banning of local ritual practice are well documented, both in oral history and in the literature (Goodale 1974; Hart in Hart and Pilling 1988; Morris 2003). There is a good deal of evidence in the sung and written literature that, during the years when the mission had most influence on the islands, the observance of traditional ceremonial practice was actively discouraged by the missionaries (Goodale 1970, 1974; Morris 2003; Mountford 1958; Venbrux 1995). The current interactive AuSIL Tiwi–English Dictionary entry for Yoi gives the following as an example of the word's

---

7   From 1941, children from the Alice Springs and Darwin "half-caste" compounds were moved to Garden Point Mission, as well as the healthy children of patients at the Channel Island and East Arm leprosariums, and Tiwi children with Japanese parentage were moved there from the Bathurst Island Mission. The Garden Point Mission closed in 1968.

definition and use in a sentence. The fact that this example is used is indicative of the openness with which people speak of this issue:

> *Yoi: Free-form verb.* to dance. Awarra Pata Mankara yimani ngini, "Ngajiti yoyi ngimp-a-ri-mi, ngajiti ngimp-a-ri-mirnikuwa pili awarra yita mapurtiti awarra." "Father McGrath used to say, 'Don't dance, don't dress up for the dance, because that is sinful.'"

Although resistance to Tiwi ceremonies eased over the last few years of the mission, many traditional practices had already declined or disappeared.[8] The women's Modern Kuruwala songs include Tiwi translations of Catholic hymns and other songs that are received by Tiwi audiences as symbolic of Tiwi and Catholic spirituality together.[9]

The 1970s marked a resurgence of culture. The closure of the mission on Bathurst Island in 1969, the legislated (re-)establishment of Indigenous land ownership through the *Aboriginal Land Rights Act 1976* (Cwlth) and the formation of the Tiwi Land Council in 1978 are regarded by locals today as pivotal, with many Tiwi people (especially on Bathurst Island, most affected by the mission) able for the first time to embrace their culture and their language. Teresita Puruntatameri said:

> In 1974 Aboriginal people all over moved away from the mission to develop self-determination and that's when we voted for leaders from each Skin group to become members of the Council or in Local Government. This later became the Tiwi Islands Shire Council.

At the same time, however, Brother John Pye wrote "[a]nd so in 1976 we find that the cross has replaced the totem pole, not only on the graves but in their way of life" (Pye 1998, 61). Although it is true that the big Pukumani (mortuary-associated) ceremonies such as those recorded on Melville in the 1970s had disappeared from Bathurst Island, people were embarking on somewhat of a cultural revolution.[10] What is pertinent to this story is the cultural resurgence

---

8   Opinion expressed in the documentary film *Mourning for Mangatopi* (1975). Director Curtis Levy. Mountford (1958), Gsell (1955) and Venbrux (1995) make correlating statements to the effect that the practice of Tiwi ceremonies was banned by the church in the early years.
9   While this may well be a case of acculturation and interruption of ceremonial practice (which is regarded with sadness and anger by many locals), there was also a combining of Catholicism with Tiwi spirituality (Grau 2001b) that has endured. While Catholic hymns are sung in the community, they are not the focus of this book, which instead centres on the Tiwi song-types.
10 Although the presence of the church has continued to be strong, and the blending of Tiwi and Catholic rituals is evident (Frawley 1995; Gardiner and Puruntatameri 1993; Grau 2001b), attitudes towards the mission era and to the associated loss of Tiwi culture vary between individuals, and these are not the subject of this study.

the community has seen in post-mission days, led, in large part, by the Strong Women's Group.

In the 1970s, when the women were in their late teens and early twenties, the Strong Women's Group made a conscious effort to reconnect with their parents, learn their language and attend ceremony. As they became mothers and teachers,[11] they grew increasingly proactive in maintaining elements of Tiwi culture (such as traditional knowledge, ceremony and language). They translated hymns into Tiwi language and sang guitar-accompanied choral-style music (in Tiwi and English) in church and at local events, not unlike other Indigenous women's groups with a similar mission background, such as those in Galiwin'ku or Maningrida, and the Torres Strait and Pacific islands (Choo 2001; Diettrich 2011; Lawrence 2004; Mackinlay 2010; Magowan 2007).[12] Some men of this generation (now in their 60s, 70s and 80s), whose schooling was in the mission, join in singing those songs that are regarded as hymn translations, especially in the context of Catholic Mass (and there is no restriction against doing so) but it is widely regarded as a women's group form of singing.[13]

Since the 1980s the Women's Group has continued its activities in the preservation of their culture, moving on from simply singing hymns in Tiwi to using song as a vehicle for preserving language and passing on stories of Tiwi ancestors and Country – absorbing introduced musical styles with the aim of engaging young Tiwi people with their culture.

As I've explained earlier, there is a degree of variation in many of the melodic forms across individuals, with unique songs created for the performance occasion (ceremonial or mortuary-related) with newly composed text relating to the people singing, those listening, and to the time and place the songs are sung. This means that (across both the traditional and the modern musical forms) there is a very large repertoire of unique songs, with transmission found in song words, epithets and stories rather than the entire songs themselves. The performance of the Modern Kuruwala form is no different, with variable text across performances and individuals, referencing the performance event, participants and/or the kinship and Country heritage of the singer/s.

---

11   Teresita Puruntatameri (1954–2019), one of the Strong Women's Group, was appointed as the first Tiwi principal of Murrupurtiyanuwu Catholic School, Nguiu, in 1997. Leah Kerinaiua was the second, in 2003. Ms Kerinaiua was tragically killed in a car accident in 2012.
12   It should be noted, however, that the experience of the Tiwi Strong Women's Group differs from that of many other Australian Indigenous communities as the mission was established much earlier (1912), with the resulting removal from Tiwi culture and language beginning a generation earlier.
13   There is increasingly a sharing of singing roles between Elder men and women as their numbers dwindle, while the need for singers with the capacity to provide ceremonial song continues.

A large repertoire of original songs was composed for the Tiwi Mothers Club Eisteddfods held during the 1980s and 1990s.[14] There are 50 songs documented among audio-visual and written records from the period, and the women continue to compose songs for every community occasion: funerals, weddings, community building openings, football finals, school graduations, etc., most of which have not been documented since the end of the eisteddfod era. Work in 2020 to translate and document these has confirmed that their language and subject matter were of their time, just as the classical songs were, and so many are not fully translatable. While the eisteddfods were run as competitions (with about a dozen small groups competing) they are remembered more as festivals of song, dance, language and culture, and for the empowering effect they had on the women in particular. They reflect a continuation of traditional song practice as a vehicle for knowledge transmission and for documentation of social history. Just as classical Tiwi Kulama songs record ancestral stories, ceremonial processes, and kinship affiliations to land and current events, the eisteddfod songs were composed for the occasion, with some used to describe culture and others as event-specific sung "moments in time".[15]

At Figure 26 is a selection of song subjects in songs preserved in the recorded archive and Modern Kuruwala songs created by women's groups since the 1970s, which have similar subjects and motivations.[16]

Figure 26: Comparing song subjects in the archive with Modern Kuruwala song subjects.

Classical Tiwi songs in the recorded archive	Women's Modern Kuruwala songs
• Crocodile (1912)	• The story of the man who became a Crocodile
• Priest building mission houses (1912)	• Karitiriki — the song about felling timber for houses
• Nyingawi (1928)	• Nyingawi
• Bombing of Darwin (1948)	• Bombing of Darwin

14   Tiwi performers appeared in the Northern Australia Eisteddfods in Darwin in the early 1960s and the women recall taking part as schoolchildren (see Campbell et al. 2022).

15   In studying the texts of the eisteddfod-era songs, we have come across many that are no longer sung simply because they refer to the occasion at which they were sung and so they are no longer relevant.

16   Songs recorded in the archive are dated by the year of each specific recorded example (see List of audio examples; List of other recorded materials in the AIATSIS archive). Those not dated are found across the entire catalogue of recordings. The women's group songs are anecdotally attributed to the 1970s through to today. For audio recordings and/or written texts of the Women's Kuruwala songs, see Ngarukuruwala Women's Group and Campbell 2023.

7 Emerging musical genres

Classical Tiwi songs in the recorded archive	Women's Modern Kuruwala songs
• A storm (1954)	• Bush food is good for us
• The moon landing (1970)	• Cyclone Tracy (soon after 1975)
• Cyclone Tracy (1975)	• Olympic Torch song (2000)
• Going to Canberra (2012)	• Wellbeing Centre opening (2009)
• Country affiliation songs	• Country affiliation songs
• Yoi Dreaming identity songs	• (Listing all of the) Tiwi Yoi song
• Ancestor songs	• Ancestor songs
• Marking ritual stages	• Song about Pukumani ceremony

Murrakupuni melodies in a new musical genre: the aural landscape changes

We know that in the pre-colonial Tiwi community there were at least 11 distinct melodies and (within the parameters of function-specific recognisable melodic forms) much embellishment and variation invented by individual singers. It is often said among Tiwi singers that those old melodies come from the ancestors, having been passed down through Kulama teaching and practice-led learning. Where did the melodies themselves come from? Opinion among senior song and culture men and women is that they came from the bush – the aural environment (in the pre-radio, pre-television era) would have been far more enveloping and visceral – knowing too that Tiwi ancestors are still there, in their Country and part of the natural world so are still heard in the bush.

Concepta and Francis Orsto explained it this way:

> Natural, normal, it came from them. They made their own melodies, you know, how they perform dancing in Kulama, they make up their own tune. Maybe from bush. Wherever they are sitting alone, listening, maybe hearing the breeze, the sound of the winds, birds and they reflect themselves where they are singing. Maybe the birds singing or the wind blowing they get their melodies from the wind, the birds, animals. Like they hear the ocean they hear the animals, nature and the wind blows and the oceans wave and the seas.

The natural sonic environment creates a strong tangible connection to Country, to ancestors and to ceremony for Elders who continue the "old" song practice.

The way in which the choral groups in the eisteddfods picked up introduced melodies can be seen as a continuation of this absorbing of aural environments. The composers of the choral songs absorbed a tune from the radio, for example, and reworked it, with the phrasing of the Tiwi text overriding it structurally, rhythmically and melodically.

When a strongly aural-focused song tradition that has continued unbroken through generations over many thousands of years is exposed to the aural additions of the 20th century it is not surprising that the songs heard on the radio seep in – sometimes subconsciously no doubt, but often quite consciously. The deeply ingrained practice of the oral transmission of culture and knowledge has resulted in cultural leaders embracing the melodies around them with the same cultural integrity and intent as their predecessors embraced the natural soundscape. Just as the traditional song melodies have specific functions in ceremonial and social contexts, the Kuruwala songs with introduced melodic inspiration have certain functions, largely following the functions of the old songs. Francis Orsto continued:

> When we listen to music, we pick up the tune from that song, and so today we've got traditional songs, traditional music that amawu [old lady] introduced to us all. They used to listen to music [on the radio] and make up a song, them old ladies. They choose the music that goes with the song[text].

Likely due to the popular music landscape when the women were in their young adulthood, the melodies they have incorporated into their repertoire come from the 1960s, 1970s and 1980s mainstream music media. The introduced melodies of some Kuruwala songs have been absorbed into the song culture to the point where they are now referred to as Country[17] melodies (with equally strong associations as the Ariwayakulaliyi melodies with Murrakupuni (Country)), identified with the choral groups who sang them in the eisteddfods and to family groups related to the composer/s who created the song in that form. At some time in the past (40 or 50 years ago), a (non-Tiwi) song would have been heard on the radio and become popular. In the tradition of improvisation and compositional creativity, people made it their own by reworking the words and the rhythms while learning the chord progressions to play on the guitar (which tend to follow western musical traditions as the guitar doesn't exist in

---

17 The association of the Ariwayakulaliyi melodies with Murrakupuni (Country) groups and their songs – called "Country" tunes – alongside the importation of country and western tunes (for songs also associated with Murrakupuni groups) leads to some confusion for a non-Tiwi researcher! Speaking with the women about a particular melody that they were singing, I asked, "Is that a Country tune or a country tune?" They answered, "Kuwa [yes]".

the classical Tiwi musical context). I am aware of seven songs (out of about 50) that comprise melodies borrowed from the radio. Some of the songs use tunes the women learned from the nuns while they were at the mission school.[18] They often have direct connection to an existing songline, such as the Nyingawi songs which exist in Kulama form recorded in 1928 and 1954, as well as in a popular Modern Kuruwala form to the tune of "Sing a Song of Freedom" and the Murrntawarrapijimi song (an ancestral story telling of an inter-clan fight and ensuing community peace), which uses the melody from "Ten Guitars", as well as being sung in Kulama form.[19] In all these cases the words are not translations of the original song, but are entirely new compositions, meaningful and specific to Tiwi people. The issue of copyright becomes an interesting one in this instance.[20] It was only while registering the women as composers with the Australasian Performing Right Association (APRA) that these "borrowed" melodies were consciously recognised as not being Tiwi-owned. They are original poetic compositions created for specific occasions, just as song texts are created using the "traditional" song forms.

In this section I will discuss some examples of Modern Kuruwala songs that serve the traditional functions of Kulama Murrakupuni (songs with Country affiliation) and Yoi (songs with Dreaming identity) – regarded equally as "traditional" Tiwi songs whether sung to a Tiwi melody or to an introduced melody.

Among the classical song tradition are melodies associated with and "owned" by particular Murrakupuni (Country) groups and, especially in the Kulama ritual stages that involve individuals' presentation of song, these melodies are passed down accordingly. The eisteddfod choral groups were originally based on class groups the women had been in as schoolchildren and, over the years, groups joined from the three towns across the islands and were informally organised into Skin group and/or Country groupings.[21] All written records of songs from

---

18 One such song is "Ngarikuruwala nginingawula Murrakupuni (We are singing about our Country)", which uses the melody of "The Bush Girl" by The Seekers. The Tiwi women remember being taught by the nuns to sing the song "Tribal Girl" (itself a reworking of The Seekers' original lyrics) in English as children. They see now that this was rather patronising and are pleased to have overwritten the English words to create a song about Tiwi traditional lands.
19 Both songs are always preceded in performance by a rendition of the Kulama version, sung by the singer holding custodial authority of the song.
20 They are not covers of the original songs, and our advice from APRA is that they have been altered sufficiently to avoid any suggestion of plagiarism.
21 The Tiwi Islands AFL league is another example of teams being organised along traditional Country identities.

the eisteddfods credit the performing group name (as "composer"), and that is often enough to indicate the melody to be used.[22]

Considering the central importance of the Country groups and of the recognised meaning of melody associated with the ritual stages and with emotional and ritual response, the way in which "new" and non-Tiwi melodies have been incorporated into the Tiwi song culture shows how embedded the entire aural atmosphere is to the Tiwi culture, and also how fundamentally it is the words that remain the most important part of what makes a song "Tiwi". I will now describe this by looking at Murrntawarrapijimi – a song that continues the transmission of Yoi (Dreaming) identity and incorporates the (pre-colonial) Old Tiwi; this is an example of an old ancestor story Kulama song that has been passed down a generation by being embedded into a new song with an introduced melody. I will then look at two versions of a Country song called Tikilaru, both considered Tiwi Murrakupuni songs, both considered old, and both adhering to and continuing traditional Tiwi song composition and performance practices, even when they are based on (non-Tiwi) musical styles.

The song about Murrntawarrapijimi

This song was composed and first sung by Pilayapijimi (senior songwoman Clementine Puruntatameri's husband's father) at Kulama in 1949, shortly after the death of Murrntawarrapijimi (Emmanuel Puruntatameri). Murrntawarrapijimi was Pilayapijimi's eldest son, so was Clementine's husband's older brother. Clementine told me that this is a song that her mother sang, although Clementine formally learned to sing it from her brother. In the time of my association with the song, Clementine was the only person who could perform the Kulama rendition of the song. Her daughter Ella Puruntatameri has emerged as a leader in song composition and since her mother's death is taking on increasingly senior roles in musical practice. She told me, "Kulama words are very strict and really special. It is important to stay with those words because that is what holds all the connections with our ancestors and where we come from."

The text tells the story of how Murrntawarrapijimi's death was central to the dissolution of a dispute between the Jilarruwi and Takaringuwi (Brolga and Mullet people) who were involved in a tribal war that involved throwing spears. These spear-throwing "mock fights" were not intended to end in death (Osborne 1989) but were an important part of community politics. When Emmanuel was struck in the temple and killed, everyone was so shocked that they stopped these mock fights. His death is regarded as emblematic of the change in the

---

22 Unless otherwise indicated, the Malawu group would sing their text to the Malawu tune, for example.

Tiwi community regarding "the old ways", and since then there have been no tribal fights of this kind.

The song "Ten Guitars", from which the Modern Kuruwala song borrows its melody, was written in 1966 by Gordon Mills (and sung by Engelbert Humperdinck).[23] "Ten Guitars" became popular in the Tiwi community in the 1970s in the form of Tom Jones's 1968 cover. It is still played often on the Social Club CD player.

Clementine composed an expansion of her family song Murrntawarrapijimi to this melody for her daughter Ella to perform at a local eisteddfod in 2002. By composing a song for this modern forum, Clementine was officially passing it to her daughter (and continuing its patrilineal transmission) with the same cultural integrity and import as presenting the Kulama form in ceremony would have. By performing it publicly, Ella was reaffirming ties with her ancestors and at the same time taking custodianship of the story in the next generation. In Ngarukuruwala performances the women performed the Kulama introduction, with Clementine leading, in the Arikuruwala/Ampirikuruwala song-type which created a polyphonic canon.

At the end of the modern song a coda is always performed (with accompanying actions): kurawu (junglefowl) and kurrupu (referring to a native night bird) which signify Emmanuel's great-great uncle, then "aaiii" (the noise one makes when nervous or afraid) and then the word nginja (peace to you, the end) on the final beat. Even with its non-Tiwi melody and up-beat musical feel, this was always a serious song for the women because of its subject matter. Since Clementine's death the recording we made of her performance in 2008 has also taken on extra significance. I have on a few occasions witnessed older women calling young people to stop and listen carefully when it is played, both out of respect for the story of the fight and for Clementine as a revered songwoman. It is a striking example of the interposition of "traditional" and "modern". Clementine Puruntatameri first sang it to me sitting out under a tree at Nguiu with dogs scuffling around in the dirt, other people chatting about other things and small children tugging at her, wanting her attention. Even with these interruptions she wept as she sang. The story, she said, "is terrible and sad and it is my father's story". In August 2007 she sang the old version in front of 600 people at the Darwin Festival and then led the group singing our new arrangement. The new version included solo improvised jazz flute, walking bass and swing drums and sounded (in the opinion of one audience member) like "Tiwi Lounge". Very

---

23   It became something of an anthem among Māori people in New Zealand. See http://folksong.org.nz/tenguitars/index.html.

cool, laid back – hardly resonant of a story about the violent death of a man. Still – it made Clementine weep. When I checked with her that it was appropriate to re-work this song in such a way, she told me, "There's no point keeping a sad story sad. You might as well make it happy and get on with things." To her, and the other women, the meaning and importance of the song – including reverence for the deceased – was still strong. Whereas audience members with little or no knowledge of the cultural significance of Murrntawarrapijimi were tapping their feet, responding purely to the musical elements of the piece, the inherent meaning was still very much present to those of us who knew the story.

In much the same way as in the previously mentioned women's Modern Kuruwala-type Nyingawi and Yirrikapayi songs, Murrntawarrapijimi includes Old Tiwi Yoi song words embedded in a Modern Tiwi text to create a narrative that tells the larger story (to which the Yoi song alludes). While the story remains the same, at each performance of the Kulama section of the song the lyrics or the order of lines will change. As each line of text was a separate entity, the order did not affect the narrative of the song. Clementine said that it is more important that the story of the song is told, than to sing the same words every time. This meant that, as I have mentioned in the context of other Women's Group songs, when the song was performed,[24] the group followed Clementine and picked up the words as she sang.

At Music Transcription 29 I show the old Arikuruwala text that Clementine sings in the introduction.[25] At Music Transcription 30 we can see how the text is directly transferred into the Modern Kuruwala song (with the "Ten Guitars" melody).[26] The repetition of pirrukutuwiya (which would normally happen when Clementine sang this in Kulama style, as can be heard in Audio 77) is deleted. The imposition of the introduced melody has altered the stresses of the words and created the need to lengthen some syllables. I have included time signatures in these examples to indicate the difference between the Kulama introduction, which is in a strongly accented five-beat pattern defining the underlying metre of (in this case) four units of five syllables and one of four syllables, and the Kuruwala song, which is in common time. Clementine always put stresses on the first and third beats of the unit whenever she sang this

---

24 I use past tense referring to performances of this song as, since Clementine died in August 2011, the song has not been performed by Ngarukuruwala. She also owned the modern version, which she had composed. On her death the song was closed for the Pukumani period, although, in a break with the Pukumani protocols, the Ngarukuruwala recording of the song was played at Clementine's funeral. It was first sung again by the Women's Group (although without the Kulama song) at the funeral of Clementine's son in late 2012.
25 Also Audio 3.
26 Audio 54, 06:36.

song-type, as can also be heard in her performance of Purrukapali (Audio 77). Although, across the recordings, most singers place the stresses on the first and fourth beats, it is no longer consistently one pattern or the other.

Music Transcription 29: Kulama introduction to Murrntawarrapijimi. Clementine Puruntatameri, 2008 (Audio 54).

Text: Ngintarangini nginiwatu wunturruwiyapirrukutuwiyapirramanimpa
People are looking at him flying

Music Transcription 30: The chorus of the Modern Kuruwala version of Murrntawarrapijimi 2008 (Audio 54).

Text: Ngintarangini nginiwatu wunturruwiyapirramanimpa
People are looking at him flying

The Tikilaru Country song

In order to show how the Tiwi traditions continue to accommodate new music alongside the continuation of old songs, I will now describe two songs that are "the same song" and provide an example of the recasting of traditions in new music and of the continuation of oral knowledge documentation and transmission practice.

The Tikilaru song belongs to the descendants of Munkara and the Tampurampi group. At a Kulama or Pukumani ceremony in the past, singers from Tikilaru Country would incorporate Country placenames into their compositions to acknowledge their affiliation with that land. Maria Munkara wrote a Modern Kuruwala style song sometime in the 1980s or 90s using the tune of "Happy to be on an Island in the Sun" by Demis Roussos. Just as a Murrakupuni song presented at a Kulama or Pukumani ceremony would, this song enables singers of Tikilaru

Country order to mark their affiliation with that land. It is now sung by older women to teach their grandchildren the placenames within Tikilaru Country and give them a sense of identity with that Country group.[27] The full text is given below at Song text 30, and I show part of the song in Music Transcription 31 by way of comparison. Example 1 is the Demis Roussos song. The rhythms, while syncopated in places, serve to outline the stresses of the words as they would be spoken. In Example 2 we see that while the melody of the Tiwi song is almost exactly the same, and the women have followed a feature of traditional Tiwi song, altering the words in order to fit the melody obscures the word boundaries and the spoken stresses.

Music Transcription 31: Text/Melody relationship comparison between "Happy to be on an Island in the Sun" and "Tikilaru Song" (Audio 73).

Example 1: "Happy to be on an Island in the Sun". Demis Roussos.

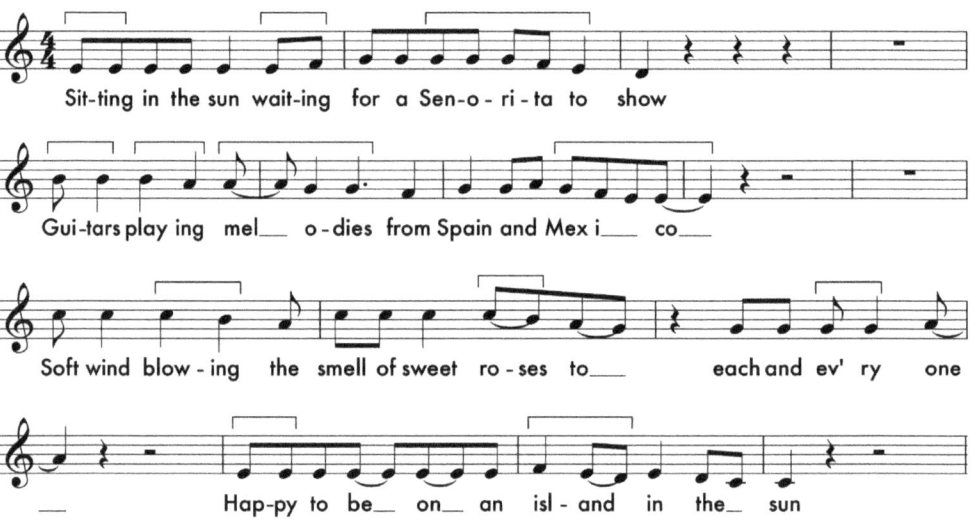

Example 2: "Tikilaru Song". Women's group.

---

27   The acknowledgement of Country and calling of ancestral names (whether in song or adjunct to performances) is a trait found in other Aboriginal song genres. "Naming evokes a multiplicity of social and ancestral themes which determine the identity of the performer and their connections to others through the ancestors" (Magowan 2007, 125).

7 Emerging musical genres

Nga wa tu a wu nga wu nga wa ngi ni nga wu la Mu rra ku pu ni Ti ki la ru

Nga wa ku ku na ri ngim pi ri mi ngi ni nga(wu)la ti ma ni

The Tikilaru Country song has been rendered into another composition, this one by John Louis Munkara, who wrote the words and music in 1993. I will describe his performance of his song at the Darwin Entertainment Centre in March 2021. John Louis plays guitar and bass guitar in the pub-band, rock-music style heard regularly in the social clubs on the Tiwi Islands and in pubs in Darwin. The song structure is fairly standard of the rock song genre to which it (musically, at least) belongs – verse, chorus, verse, bridge/guitar solo, chorus. The relationship between music and text, especially when comparing John's treatment of the English text and the Tiwi text, is best appreciated aurally, so I refer the reader to Audio 66.

Song text 30: Strong Women's Group. Tikilaru Murrakupuni (Tikilaru Country), c. 1995, and John Louis Munkara, 1993.

Strong Women's Group, circa 1995

Ngawa nginingawula Murrakupuni Tikilaru
Our country Tikilaru

Wuta ngawa-ampi, awungarruwu tangarima yimamini
Our grandparents, long ago they used to live there

Ngawatu awunganuwanga ngawa nginingawula
It is also ours

Murrakupuni Tikilaru, ngawa kukunari ngimpirimi Nginingawula timani
Country Tikilaru, we are all happy in our country

Mawuntuwu, Kilimaraka, Yilinapi, Turtuyanguwu,
Yawalinga, Japarrinapi, Tangiyawu, Ampwanikiyiti,
Kukuni, Atawunampi, Wulipingirraga, Pawunapi
Jipirriyapa, Pirnimata, Malikuruwu, Jawularimi
[Country places within Tikilaru]

Ngumpupji jupunyini amintiya Kilimipiti
Looking from the cliff and at Kilimipiti

> **John Louis Munkara, 1993**
>
> *Where the sun sinks down to the west, slowly across the sky*
> *I'm sitting under the old pandanus tree, thinking about this land*
> *Along the golden sand I walk, looking at the sun slowly going down*
>
> Mawuntuwu, Kilimaraka, Yilinapi, Tangiyawu, Pwanikiti, Pumpuruwu
> [Country places]
> Ngawa ngawa nginilawula Murrakupuni
> Our Country
> Tangarima, tangarima Tikilaru
> Our home Tikilaru
>
> *Sitting with my family by the campfire light, singing and dancing away*
> *As moonlight shines through the night and the fire keeps burning all night through*
> *Well I'm sad that I'm leaving my country, but I'll be back this way again.*

Looking at the text of the women's song and of John Louis' Jikilaru,[28] we can see that both serve the same purpose (an acknowledgement of Country), but John Louis's is different in that it includes English lyrics, and it was the only song to do so at the performance that evening.[29] The chorus text names (in Tiwi) places in Tikilaru Country and expresses the phrase "our home, our Country", just as the women's Tikilaru Country song does. On stage at the Entertainment Centre, both in the rehearsal and in the performance, it was those women who are custodians of Tikilaru Country who danced to support John Louis's singing. The others sat back – appreciative and moving with the music, but not actively participating in the performance as it was not their Country, so not their role to do so. Again, we found that between rehearsal and performance there were changes to the way John Louis placed his words in the structure of the melody, and so the phrase lengths varied. He repeated some words and added strummed beats on his guitar in between sung lines. As a singer coming from classical Tiwi song traditions, he rendered this non-Tiwi song and music style very much Tiwi, but he also ticked all the boxes of the rock 'n' roll singer, employing amplified guitar, keyboards and drums in well-known musical clichés of that genre, with the extensions of

---

28   John Louis' song is spelled this way, using the more recent spelling that was current when he composed the song. The women always refer to the older spelling for their song.
29   The women's song here shows translation into English for the reader's benefit and only the text in Tiwi language is sung. In John Louis's song, the chorus is only (and entirely) in Tiwi and the verses are in English.

metre giving it an irregular phrase structure and so bringing it back closer to Tiwi singing. In both its "new" versions, the Tikilaru song sits firmly in the space between Tiwi and non-Tiwi music and culture. Whether singing Tiwi or non-Tiwi melodies, the Tiwi singers follow a central characteristic of classical Tiwi song, altering the words in order to fit the melody, so creating and obscuring the word boundaries and the spoken stresses, lengthening phrases, creating irregular bars and shifted chord changes – all interesting challenges for the band, who were expecting a regular common time beat and symmetrical pattern of chord progressions.

Darwin Entertainment Centre 2021

The Tikilaru songs were performed within a concert presentation in 2021 at the Darwin Entertainment Centre (DEC).[30] The concert theme and promotion title was "Yoi", a consciously general word encompassing dance, song, dance event and identity, which allowed for the organic, collaboratively arranged event we knew it would be as well as accommodating whichever performers were able to be involved; Sydney-based band members confirmed only a few weeks beforehand due to changing travel restrictions and the list of Tiwi performers changed right up until the day of the performance. This meant that, much like a "traditional" Yoi event held in and for the Tiwi community, the songs reflected and were created by the participants present. Until we were in the (only) rehearsal – ostensibly an on-stage sound check – the day prior to the concert, the majority of discussion and planning was around who should be involved in each item, according to cultural authority, knowledge of songs, kinship representation and pro-active encouragement of young singers earmarked as emerging cultural leaders.

In all our Ngarukuruwala performances we are aware that our audience when on the mainland will be largely non-Tiwi and so there is potentially an element of touristification and, through a post-colonial lens, questions raised of hybridity, cultural authenticity and "otherness" (Hollinshead 1998; Bhabha 2012; Husa 2020). The Strong Women are particularly aware of their work in showcasing Tiwi song culture with an accompanying view to encouraging its maintenance, so we are always conscious of following the wishes of the most senior singer in

---

30 *Ngarukuruwala Yoi!* 19 March 2021. Presented by Darwin Entertainment Centre and supported by Tiwi Islands Education and Training Board and Tiwi Regional Council. This concert was a re-scheduling from March 2020, cancelled due to the emerging COVID-19 pandemic. We were very fortunate to have a small window in early 2021 in which to present the concert while borders were open for a short time.

the group, who decides which songs are to be included and why, and how they will be treated musically.

As I have outlined earlier, the songs being composed and performed by the Women's Group today can be divided into three categories: re-workings of classical/traditional songs; substitutions of classical song-types (continuing their function); and entirely new songs. Across the large repertoire of unique songs following both the classical and the modern musical forms, generational transmission is through songwords, epithets and stories rather than in finite song texts. Just as classical Tiwi Kulama songs record ancestral stories, ceremonial processes, kinship affiliations to land, and current events, the songs that evening were performed for the occasion, to record the participation of individuals and to denote Country and others as event-specific sung "moments in time". It was evident at that performance that the connection of Tiwi people through song, to Country, kinship and cultural protocols, remains an over-arching factor. Even in a non-Tiwi physical, cultural and musical space, and with many of our goals for the concert shaped by European notions of performance, venue, audience and exhibition, the core motivations for the musical decisions were Tiwi. Modern Kuruwala songs served the traditional functions of Kulama Murrakupuni (Country affiliation) and Yoi (Dreaming identity) equally alongside their classical forms. In Figure 27 I have listed the songs performed that evening, along with the categories of women's Modern Kuruwala songs and classical song-types with the same function. The Tiwi melodies performed using the classical form are indicated by C, Modern Kuruwala songs with Tiwi melodies MK (the numbers referring to the four Modern Kuruwala melodic variations shown at Music Transcription 32,[31] and those using introduced, non-Tiwi melodies marked by (*).

At Music Transcription 32 are four structure outlines of melodies that belong to the aforementioned classical, pre-colonial Tiwi song-type Ariwayakulaliyi, each using a Country-affiliated melody.[32] When used for various song texts, passing notes are added and rhythms altered to accommodate text. The ternary form (marked ABA) is consistent across this song-type, both in classical practice and in the Modern Kuruwala style. It is worth remembering here that, just like the classical melodies, the Modern Kuruwala melodies can be used across song subjects. The fact that numerous songs in the Modern Kuruwala genre share a melodic contour is a direct continuation of ritual song traditions. As I have

---

31   See also Music Transcription 23 which shows three of these with rhythmic and textual delineation. Ngawatu is marked 3b as, while it is closest to that contour, it is sung in binary (A, B) form.

32   Transcriptions are nominally in concert pitch for ease of comparison.

noted, in ritual and ceremony, each song function has a defined melody which gives the listener an immediate indication of the intent and inference of the song. The melody denotes the song's function, and the text is what changes for the occasion. Certain songs and melodies in the "modern" genre have also become affiliated with particular Country and kinship groups and so in this performance, with a number of the senior women belonging to a particular group, the canoe song, the Bombing of Darwin song and the Purrukapali song shared a melody.[33] In this guitar-accompanied musical style this then leads to a consistency of key and tempo, which has been another interesting factor of our work together. A leading singer who sings in their comfortable tessitura as they would in classical Yoi, now plays guitar as they sing and so, consecutive songs led by them tend to be in that same key. A regular tempo conducive to (the women's pace) dancing will also tend to be consistent across songs of the same style. While most of the women's songs involve danced actions and gestures that express the narrative, the Yoi dances are also included, usually in "chorus" or "coda" sections. This recurring pitch/key centre and pulse/tempo again stem directly from Tiwi traditions in which, for some hours at a time, a song series continues, on a regular pitch and with a regular pulse to enable group participation and as a support for the ritual dances.

Music Transcription 32: Four classical Ariwayakulaliyi melodic contours used across multiple songs.

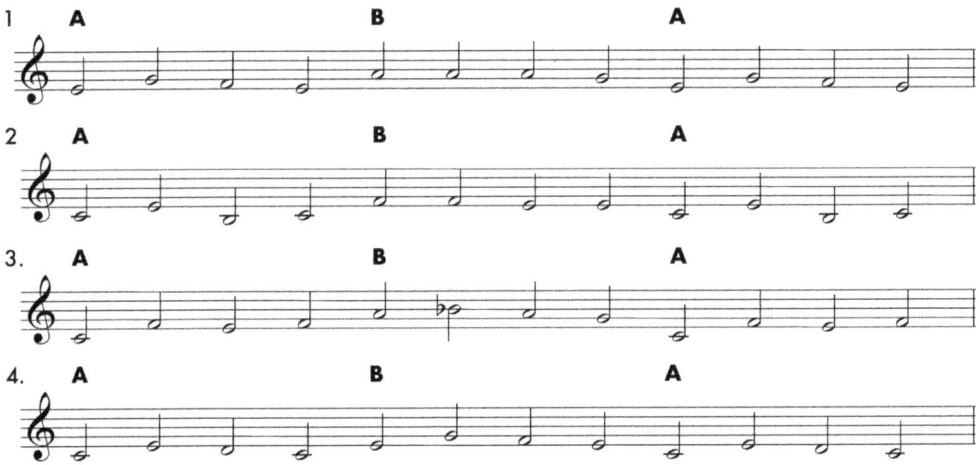

---

[33] The football song uses the same melody as the Crocodile story song, often performed by women with Crocodile Yoi. It was removed from the program due to its closure after the death of a leading man who sang that song.

In the context of our collaboration, these melodies are something we treat carefully and with a greater degree of social, family and kinship considerations than an audience would ever realise. To the non-Tiwi musicians involved, they have been the subject of discussion too – why are so many songs (with different words, different subject matter, and different intent and mood) performed to the same melody? For our instrumentalist colleagues it was a concern both to convey each song's intent and to avoid repetitive musical items. With three songs in a row with the same melody, the same basic underlying rhythms and in the same key, the urge to create variety was strong. Considering the fact that most of the audience would not understand the Tiwi lyrics, we worked to create a different feel for each song – along the lines of mood (a stronger back beat and drums for the football song or a gentler, more hymn-like feel for a healing song, for example) while being careful not to alter phrasing or tempo to the point where the singers couldn't present their words or dance actions comfortably.

The consistency of key has been another interesting factor of our work together. Far from being simplistic, a recurring key centre again stems directly from Tiwi traditions. In the group dance events of mourning rituals, a leading singer will create an almost unbroken series of songs, each with text specific to each mourner's relationship to the deceased. The fact that numerous songs in the modern Tiwi genre use the same melody is a direct continuation of these ritual song traditions. Fighting the urge to want to create more variety the band had to remember that it is not so far from Bach's ostinati or 1990s dance music and that in the Tiwi case the regularity serves an important cultural purpose. Fundamentally it was the text of each song that took precedence over the music. The primacy of the words, the metre of the poetry and the intent of the words shaped our musical phrasing, chord changes and rhythmic treatments. It is also another strong indication of the identity of the Tiwi women as cultural custodians, at all times, whether on stage or at ceremony they are holders of sung and embodied knowledge and culture first, and performers second. Alongside this there has always been an overt acknowledgement that the common goal is to care for and respect the Tiwi songs and their provenance above all else.

7 Emerging musical genres

Figure 27: Functional correlation of traditional song-types and Modern Kuruwala songs and how they were incorporated into a public performance in 2021.

Performed at DEC	Strong Women's Modern Kuruwala	Traditional song form	Function
Junglefowl (C) and (3) Ngawatu (3b)	Healing songs	Mamanunkuni (mourning) and/or Amparruwu (widow)	Sorrow, bereavement. Sung at Kulama and mortuary-related rituals
Bombing of Darwin (C) and (2) Football (4)	Story-telling songs – building openings, current events, historical events	Ayipa songs sung on third day of Kulama	Telling news, putting events on record
Murli la (1) and (*)	Murli la songs	Love songs	Entertainment
Calls to Country (C) Mumtankankala (C) Purrukupali (C) and (2) Nyingawi (*)	Songs holding cultural knowledge and ancestral stories	Kulama songs in initiation ritual stages	Imparting cultural knowledge
Yoi dances and songs(C) Tikilaru (*) Canoe (2)	Dreaming songs, Country songs	Yoi (Dreaming totem)	Dreaming and Country
Remix Disco medley by young group (1, 2, 3 and 4)	n/a	Yoi and Kulama songs	Identity

Onstage cultural negotiations

The order of the songs (which was planned in group conversations prior) created a general "journey" from palingarri (long ago) to ningani (today) and, as the older women put it, the future generation. This performance held particular significance as, although children and young adults have been involved in song-based community activities led by the Strong Women's Group, this was the first time that young people had joined a professional Ngarukuruwala performance. There had been a great deal of talk to encourage them to join in and it brought an extra degree of anticipation and importance to the occasion. The older women took the lead as instructors in the classical songs, the older kuruwala songs and dance movements and what unfolded on stage was, in one sense, real-time cultural transmission. When we look at the program as it came together through the course of a couple of days leading up to this performance, the centrality of song as cultural vehicle (as well as, and/or in spite of, entertainment for a non-Tiwi audience) becomes clear. With Calista Kantilla and Leonie Tipiloura, the two 81-year-old Elder women, present, it was an unspoken certainty that they would be celebrated on stage. They played clapping sticks throughout the evening and were turned to a number of times in the two rehearsals for opinion and advice on songwords and the positioning of performers on stage.

Each choice of song had a particular social or kinship significance. The calls out to Country, led by Calista Kantilla as the group moved on to the stage, three carrying ceremonial spears, was an acknowledgement both of the Tiwi ancestors and a sign of diplomacy and acknowledgement of the ancestors and current custodians of the Larrakia land they were in that night. The Murntankala story of the creator woman in Kulama form was composed and performed (solo) by Calista while the full story (in Tiwi and English language as I have presented in the Prologue) was shown on the backdrop of the stage. The Purrukapali story was presented in both Kulama and Modern Kuruwala sung versions, again led by Calista, as respect for the first and all ancestors and the inclusion of this song (even knowing that the audience would not understand any of the words) was particularly important to the older singers. Tikilaru is the traditional Country of the main group of women present that night and so that song was performed immediately following the creation stories to acknowledge the Country of this leading group. "Nyingawi", the song telling of the first (pre-human) people who lived in the bush and who taught the Tiwi people how to hold ceremony and how to sing, was the story the group wished to present next to a non-Tiwi audience – explaining how they all learned to perform ceremony, again, regardless of the fact that the text, all in Tiwi language, was beyond most in the audience. The Bombing of Darwin song was an important inclusion, taking the opportunity of being in Darwin to share this story which to Tiwi people is a part of their history, symbolic of their ties to the mainland and also emblematic of their distance and difference from the mainland (as it reminds us how the mainland ignored warnings from the islands of the incoming aeroplanes). Each person in turn then performed their individual Yoi (Dreaming) totem dance; Junglefowl, Horse, Crocodile, Shark, Dingo, Warship and Rainbow were represented. Francis Orsto as an emerging songman led the singing and presented the appropriate text for each Yoi, and (as would happen in traditional ritual) the group joined him singing as they picked up the words on the second or third iteration. The ancestral song belonging to Junglefowl people was performed by Ella Puruntatameri in honour of her mother Clementine Puruntatameri (who is still considered a cultural leader although she died in 2012). After performing the classical Kulama rendition, Ella led the song with a classical Tiwi melody in the chorale style used for healing songs both within the Catholic Mass and (with different texts) within Tiwi mourning-related rituals. Although it was "her" song as current custodian, she deferred to Francis Orsto for help because, though younger than Ella, Francis has the stronger knowledge of the old songwords. To mark the Tiwi AFL Grand Final that was to be played two days later, the group performed the football song and the words were updated to name the 2021 Grand Finalists. The three eldest Rainbow Dreaming women (Calista Kantilla, Leonie Tipiloura and Jacinta Tipungwuti) were then given centre-stage to speak about, sing and dance their Yoi (Dreaming), Ampiji (Rainbow Serpent). This was a significant moment for the Ngarukuruwala group and for those in the audience who knew them and the Tiwi community. The sad reality is that as Indigenous Australians, they are considered extremely elderly at their age and it was highly likely this would be their last appearance with the group.

The old women now often take a supporting vocal role to Francis Orsto and in their newest rendition of Murli la, they sang an echo response similar to the women's Ampirikuruwala classical song form. Francis's use of Old Tiwi words, metrical grouping and spacing between lines of text (with resulting asymmetric and irregular phrase lengths) made this the most complex of the songs for the band to pick up. It was important for the group too that John Louis Munkara was included in this performance as a male Elder of the Country of the main group of performers. As described earlier in this chapter, he sang and played guitar for his Jikilaru Country song, with young Tiwi man Dion Wilson Apuatjimi also on guitar – Dion's first time joining the women in performance. Then, in a first for the Ngarukuruwala group, came Remix – a medley of traditional songs that the young singers had reworked with disco backing track. The language is in the old form (sung by the women) and so the young singers had to work hard to learn it, and to fit the long and complex words into an otherwise musically regular pop-song metre. The Tiwi singers and band on stage were particularly impressed and applauded the young people's achievement, creating an audience within the performing group. The canoe song about hunting dugong and turtle is a story-telling cultural song that the women perform often. As its melody belongs to a Country group to which many of the participants belong, this melody also featured in the Purrukapali and the Bombing of Darwin songs. A healing song, Ngawatu, was inserted into the program that day in memory of two of the Women's Group who had passed away in December 2020. The group decided to also include the audience in the healing song and so announced on the night that they were singing healing for the world as it suffers through COVID-19 and for all those who had lost loved ones. Old Murli la was chosen as the finale for its light-hearted, fun content. The melody is also readily repeatable, so it accommodated the women dancing their individual Yoi Dreaming dances again as they took their bows. This Murli la is now known in the community as the Strong Women's "famous" song, having been featured in the 2019 film *Top End Wedding*, and this was also why they chose it to finish the evening.

With 27 Tiwi singers on stage as well as two Tiwi guitarists joining a band of five non-Tiwi musicians,[34] archive recordings playing in the auditorium alongside live performance and photographic imagery of significant Tiwi places, the intra- and inter-cultural diplomacy and staging, lighting and sound logistics became complex. Much of the rehearsal time was spent on these considerations, all based upon hierarchies within kinship groups, Country groups, gender, age and knowledge. All were negotiated within the context of each song at the time it was about to be sung – at the rehearsal, again at the sound check and then again within the performance itself. This was not due to disorganisation or lapses of memory. Far from it, the group was following procedures of respect, intergenerational interaction and participation in the true Tiwi way of sharing sung culture and identity, primarily for the benefit of the Tiwi participants themselves. Correct knowledge-holding protocols were followed to honour the Elders present and to impart instruction and encouragement to the younger participants. On top of that was the desire to present a good show. It was interesting (and amusing and endearing for the band and younger Tiwi singers in the group) to see the eldest women take the microphone and give detailed instructions about harmonies, introductions, chorus sections and vocal entrances, watching for guitar cues and the importance of moving nearer to microphones when taking lead singing parts. Again, Tiwi traditions of instruction and knowledge sharing came across in this otherwise very un-Tiwi physical and cultural environment. Several essentially Tiwi characteristics were at play in this concert: the onstage placement of singers according to kinship grouping; the physical and musical group dynamics of ensemble performance; the respect afforded vocal soloists following social and cultural hierarchy; alteration of text, variation and idiosyncrasy in individuals' renditions of otherwise standard song forms; and the giving of space and time to individuals to perform within an over-arching sense of group participation and communal input. Notable too was the absence of any difference between rehearsal and performance in demeanour, voice projection or stage-presence. The Tiwi group performed consistently in the rehearsal and in the concert.

---

34   Violin, horn, acoustic guitar/blues harp, keyboards/bass, drums.

7 Emerging musical genres

While there was excitement and, among the younger performers who were on stage for the first time, some nerves, the constant breaking of the "fourth wall" was and always has been a feature of our concerts. Our "performances" usually feature older women speaking directly to the group on stage about what is to be sung next, directing dance movements or placings mid-song and saying hello to someone recognised in the audience. Comparing a non-Tiwi musician's experience in music making and performance with working with Tiwi singers, perhaps mostly what I hear in their voices is a complete lack of ego. They sing not as performers but as the current custodians of the songs they present to listeners, regardless of the context. While individual talents, composition skills and vocal quality are highly regarded, the essential purpose of song is to facilitate diplomacy, mourning, ritual, kinship, dance, healing, celebration and the imparting of knowledge.

Considering that Tiwi song practice is firmly grounded in invention and the reflection of the aural, physical and relational space contemporaneous with its composition, I suggest that re-presenting old song texts in new ways in Ngarukuruwala performances is a continuation of what the Strong Women have been doing for at least 50 years and which songmen and songwomen have been doing for centuries. Melodies, words and sung motifs change, texts evolve and alter to accommodate generational transmission, mourning protocols and social and kinship politics are followed and, just as composers heard (and still hear) melodies on the wind, in the trees and in the creeks, they hear tunes on the radio and incorporate them into their sung affirmation of identity and accumulation of cultural record. The lines between Tiwi and non-Tiwi music, while blurred, are understood, acknowledged and embraced.

There are plenty of instances in which a non-Tiwi audience misses the Tiwi deeper cultural meaning of a song and why it is presented in a certain way. In preparation for each public performance much discussion is had about the amount of translation (into English) that is deemed necessary and how much of an audience's appreciation relies on understanding the words. Considering the fact that many of the songs sung by the older Tiwi women include language that is beyond the understanding of most Tiwi people, the need for complete understanding of text in order to appreciate the essence of a song is not paramount in their minds. The intrinsic Tiwi meaning and integrity of purpose are what is important, to all of us, regardless of our respective understandings, and the music becomes a product of our mutual experience as we perform it. Jacinta puts it this way:

> We sing old words that we heard in the past. Young people listen and they know. Sometimes they don't know the hard words but they know what we sing about because it's there. For them [a non-Tiwi audience] we

might put some words in English so they know what we're singing about, but I think they'll know. The dance can tell them, and the sounds, the words. Maybe they can feel how they want to feel when they listen.

We as musicians with different musical backgrounds, objectives and aspirations are finding ourselves meeting in a middle that is neither entirely our own, nor that of the others. Our Ngarukuruwala performances reflect a continuation of traditional song practice as a vehicle for knowledge transmission and for documentation of social history.

The role of the Tiwi singer as the next conduit in the ongoing transmission of oral knowledge, the communal thread of stories, places and names that are bigger than any individual and that form a bond of identity along kinships, sung journeys across country and through generations sits in balance with the celebration of individualism, idiosyncrasy and invention in composers and performers. In our work together there will always be recognition of the fact that we are different people from different cultures and therefore with different goals, responsibilities, insights and responses. The resulting artistic and cultural mutual space creates an experience that is artistically and emotionally enriching for all of us as practitioners of our respective cultures.

Compared with Figure 24, the diagram in Figure 28 shows that the performance contexts of Tiwi songs have become more overlapping, with the diminishing of the Kulama context and the expansion of the Yoi context to include church and funeral occasions as well as non-ritual events. It also shows that many of the traditional song-types are now performed by the Strong Women's Group and emerging young Tiwi singers (shown in Figure 28 as Ngarukuruwala[35]), continuing the fundamental functions of song traditions in their new work. Looking again at the overlappings of song functions we can see these songs through the following considerations:

- The recasting of traditional musical features into modern forms.
- Functional substitution of traditional songs with a new song-type.
- The imparting of cultural knowledge.
- Absorbing non-traditional melodies into the Tiwi repertoire.

We can see that since becoming active in song composition in the 1980s, the Strong Women have continued to compose new songs with a number of motivations that can be seen as equivalent to the composers of the classical song-types: linguistic instruction; the transmission of stories and cultural knowledge; marking Dreaming, kinship and Country; and as social record. The

---

35 Ngarukuruwala has become the eponymous name for the Strong Women's Group when identified as singers.

7 Emerging musical genres

Modern Kuruwala song-type is emerging as one with the potential to take on (and potentially replace) the functional role of some of the traditional song-types. It has become one of the traditions in which Tiwi cultural knowledge and accumulating social history are recorded. Modern Kuruwala can be regarded as a crossover between the traditional and the contemporary song practice, with a number of reinterpretations of the former manifesting in the latter.

Figure 28: Tiwi song performance contexts today.

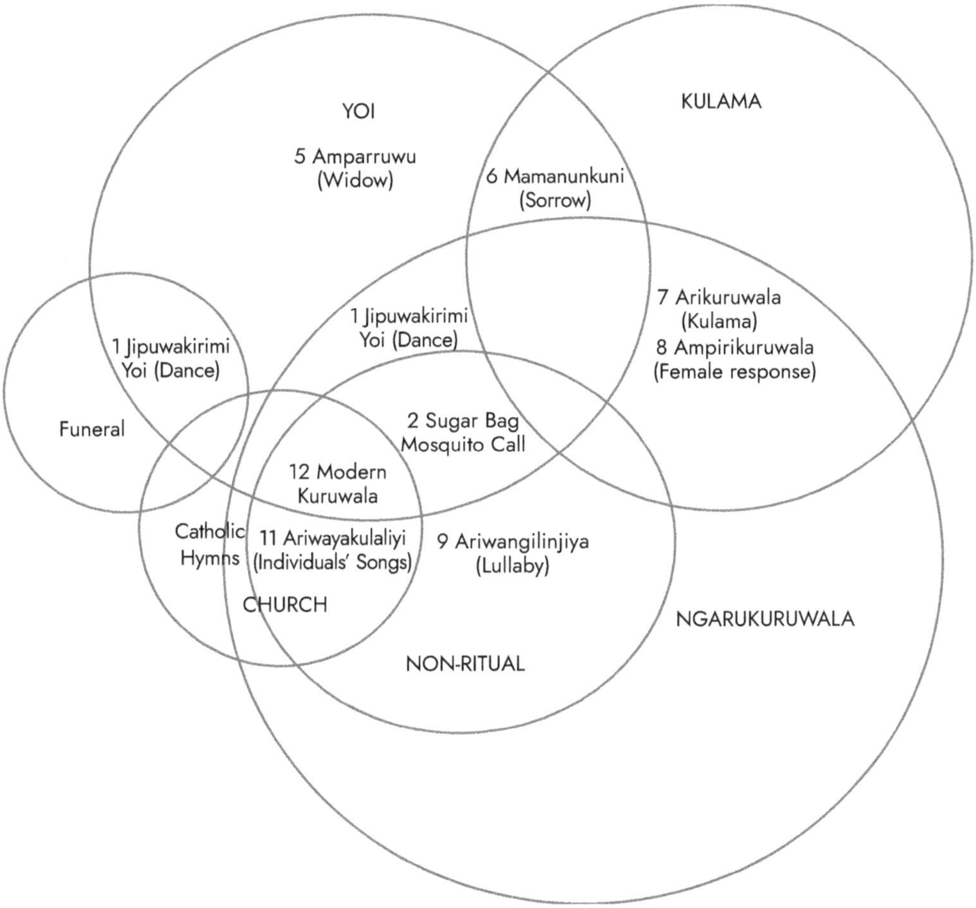

Returning to the archives: The old songs are new songs

Having given descriptions and examples from the Tiwi song repertoire it is now timely to refer back to the archive, the recordings that – although perhaps anathema to the continuation of lived, embodied, extemporised currency of practice – have nonetheless preserved the richness of poetry and music that the next generations of Tiwi singers will aspire to achieve. Notwithstanding the cultural, legal, personal and social complexities and conflicts involved in the taking of, returning of and reconnection with recorded voices of now deceased ancestors, the archive has become a cherished piece of Tiwi cultural and artistic heritage. It exists now as both a finite resource and as a tangible opportunity for conversation between Tiwi people and their ancestors. It also brings the voices of Tiwi singers and knowledge holders of the present into conversations with those of the (physical) past.

There are two ways of looking at the descriptions in this book. They are preserved, with respect and permission, in order to create a record of the melodies, metres and other musical elements that define their essence. It is important to remember though that, while this fixes those melodies in print, it does not set them in stone in terms of performance. Every time it is sung, each melody (while recognisable for its song-type) contains the idiosyncratic features of spontaneous creativity that come from live performance. Indeed, an interesting outcome of recording and transcribing is that while the recordings have "trapped" these unique performances, the process has also confirmed extemporisation as the dominant feature of Tiwi performance practice. Importantly, the process of audition and transcription has also reaffirmed individuality and invention as characteristics of the tradition that are, in the opinion of Elders, worth maintaining as well as being the catalyst for new discussion around the state of the song culture and its future. No-one will ever sing a Tiwi song the same way twice and today's Tiwi singers – Elders and young people – are continuing to extemporise using traditional elements to create unique, new songs.

Over the last century, the pre-colonial Tiwi society that enjoyed the luxury of an environment rich with the intellectual pursuits of poetry and song composition has largely gone. Social, linguistic and cultural pressures now necessitate the creation of a canon of songs in order that the rituals fundamental to Tiwi spirituality can continue. A fixed repertory of set-text pieces, in a song culture that was always based on the creation of contemporary songs, would constitute a big change. It would take a deal of rethinking and changing of perception for older people to accept the repetition of old songs in this way.

7 Emerging musical genres

The challenge for the current Elders is how to retain the spiritual, social and artistic functions of Tiwi song culture in a new language and new musical frameworks. My observation is that there are two responses emerging. Senior men and women are developing strategies for preserving the skills of singing in the old way and sustaining and potentially building upon the performance of Kulama. They are also (and these are not mutually exclusive) maintaining a strong connection between culture and song by embracing new music styles and making them work to the advantage of Tiwi song practice.

With the work the senior singers are doing to reinvent old songs, create new syncretic musical forms and engage children in song-based cultural activities, song will continue to hold an important, relevant and contemporary place in Tiwi culture. The role that the recordings are having now and will have into the future is multi-faceted. This corpus is not just an archival record but a social artefact of continuing relevance and reference today. It is a source of linguistic and musical material and a repository of ancestral, ritual and cultural knowledge. The individual recordings have also become highly valued items of cultural heritage. Unique, improvised songs have long been the main vehicle for individual and collective expression and affirmation of cultural identity. In a new, but arguably no less "traditional" way, the art of Tiwi song may well continue to provide these. One could say that Tiwi practice is in a state of flux, but then one could also say that it always has been.

There will inevitably be questions as to the motivation of both researcher and performer in anthropological research, especially in the context of perceived cultural loss. The written preservation of an oral art form is challenged by entangled questions, motivations and aspirations. Both for Tiwi song custodians and for me as a non-Tiwi musicologist, analysing and describing Tiwi songs while also continuing to create and perform them makes for a dynamic and, by necessity, changeable research methodology as the songs – supposedly the object of our research – add to and alter that research in real time. As the voices of ancestors sing out from the bush or from the archives, they are still teaching, maintaining the line of transmission of oral knowledge. What we need to do now is enable the current and next generations to understand what they are singing. On a personal and metaphysical level too, these recordings have joined the ongoing conversation and dialogue between generations of singers and knowledge holders.

Epilogue

So we come, full circle, to the song Going to Canberra.

As a senior cultural authority and highly respected custodian of song practice, Yikliya Eustace Tipiloura was among the group in Canberra in November 2009 and was central to the repatriation of the material and to subsequent musicological and linguistic documentation. In the Kulama of 2012 Eustace decided to present a song that would enter the delegation to Canberra into the public oral record, because, he said, "We all know what you and us have done and how we've been to Canberra and all that, but it wasn't official, you know?"

A few years after he sang it at Kulama he asked me to record it, to add to our collection and to the archive. Eustace's song was then reworked in 2015[1] with his instructions and input (Audio 78). Fragments of the archive recordings were added to bring the voices of the various protagonists (and their interactions) together. Interweaving the voices of the Tiwi singers, the researchers who recorded them and the archivists who catalogued the recordings, we've also captured their aural landscapes – the sounds of the Country, the rooms of the library and the reels of the archive. Eustace suggested that I should be involved, on horn, taking the role of the Kulama Ampirimarrikimili woman's response that echoes the line of the male singer. As I would if I was a Tiwi woman at Kulama who was backing up his song, I am now putting his song in writing. Eustace also chose certain old vocal recordings to add to his. At the time, this created for Eustace a powerful and tangible connection with his predecessors as he sang Kulama with those

---

1   Eustace's song is part of a 2016 album produced by Ngarukuruwala, *Ngiya Awungarra – I am here, now*, comprising vocal and instrumental responses to archive recordings of Tiwi songs and featuring the voices of deceased Tiwi singers.

past voices. The fact that he is now also deceased adds his voice to those of the ancestors. This song is the next in the line of songs recorded over the last century that tell of Tiwi people's relationship with recordings. It tells of his journey to Canberra to collect the material. The translations are his.

Song text 31: Yikliya Eustace Tipiloura. Kapi Canberra (Going to Canberra), 2012.

> L1. Ngintirri ngirranguwungimiji
> *I grab the canoe (paddling from there to Darwin)*
>
> L2. Ngirruwingi ngatirrapuji Mindilipiji jimani
> *I get there with the canoe to the beach*
>
> L3. Warjingala ngirrimamani kapuwutawa kunukuluwi tangarima awungaji
> *I was walking I went down to where the big shots are*
>
> L4. Ngirrilimpanganayi
> *This is what I am doing*
>
> L5. Ngirringuwi wayarri
> *I asked them. I want to take it back*
>
> L6. Apuwaya awarra yingiti ngirrimatakupawuli
> *I took back the stuff*
>
> L7. Wartjinga ngirrimamani
> *I started walking on the hillsides and walking back*
>
> L8. Mindilipiji tongulaka nginti wirramiji
> *I got back to Mindil beach [in Darwin] and got the canoe*
>
> L9. Kapungawula tangarima Tuwarrampila tangarima awungaji ngirramajirra purti
> *With the canoe I have come back home with all the stuff for my people*

Eustace gave me the text of this song immediately after he had sung this performance (which I recorded).[2] The additions, deletions and repetitions in the sung form render the words quite different from the song text that, although he'd sung it immediately prior, Eustace offered as the "correct" text. Eustace and I transcribed the recording phonetically in an exercise aimed at showing clearly what a Tiwi singer is doing when they sing. It is an indication of how instinctive the process is that Eustace agreed that even he could not exactly define the distinction between the (spoken form) words he knew he was singing and the

---

2 The full performance is transcribed at Music Transcription 33.

sounds that he actually sang. There is a large degree of word alteration with the addition of vowels (such as the addition of *i* in Mindil Piji (Mindil Beach) to become Mindili Piji to create correct metre).[3]

Eustace sang in the Old language, now used only in song and understood by very few. Following the poetic traditions of song composition, the trip to Canberra and the long bureaucratic process of the recordings' repatriation are presented in symbolism, to (in his words) "tell the story in the Tiwi way, with words that will always stay true". The canoe (Line 1) is symbolic of the journey away from the islands (he actually flew to Darwin). Similarly, the return journey was by aeroplane, not on foot, but telling of "walking across the hillsides" symbolises the great distance and difficulty of the journey. The "stuff" (the recorded material) is referred to in Tiwi as yingiti, meaning "food" or essential belongings or goods. This gives a sense of the high importance of the material. The word Ngirrilimpanganayi in the fourth line is an example of the Kulama words that place the song's time of performance (in this case the evening). We can refer to the audio and notated record of his performance in relation to the variability of percussive accompaniment (the degree to which the stick beats both align and misalign throughout), the order of lines of text in Kulama singing, and with reference to alterations made to words in the sung form, and use of time-of-day markers. As an example of the Arikuruwala song-type, we can compare the text and the performance transcription to see how words given by a consultant in prose can differ from what they sing.

The act of recording individual, contemporaneous, one-off songs risks changing what they fundamentally are: non-repeatable. This is a conflict that senior Tiwi singers and I discuss often as they find a balance between preserving near-lost song language and allowing for the ongoing innovation and currency that underpin Tiwi song practice. Tiwi custodians tell me that as they sing the old words, they are learning from, adding to and passing on their accumulating cultural story/history. A recorded archive makes that accumulated history tangible, perhaps, but it was always there regardless. What has become particularly fascinating for us working together, and what we hope will come through is that while we are studying the old recordings, transcribing the old songs and creating an archive of written knowledge, the current holders of that knowledge are all the while adding to it.

---

3   I use stemless noteheads for the regular "quaver" pulse of the phrase and indicate the other rhythms with standard note values. I have used spacing to indicate the breaks between phrases, and notated rests only when they are in "time". The placement of the stick beats is as close a representation of the performance as possible. This performance is indicative of the many recordings of Kulama singing in the way the sticks align with metrical units in some lines and are very loose in others.

The Old Songs are Always New

As well as being an example of Tiwi knowledge, history and identity held and passed on through song, Going to Canberra is included here as a beautiful example of a rich, complex linguistic and musical art form. In text, music transcription and recorded sound, we have "trapped" Eustace's voice and his story, but we have also added his voice, his intellect and his actions to the archive.

This song has come to symbolise the development of this book, with the returned archive song recordings at the heart of conversation, listening, learning and discussion as Elders have come together to help me relate the complexities and intricacies of Tiwi song practice. This book is not intended to be a definitive description of Tiwi songs but a resource for future Tiwi singers, knowledge holders and students that preserves just some of the richness and skills of past song custodians. It also aims to inspire admiration and respect among non-Tiwi readers and listeners for a musical genre that encompasses art, poetry, spirituality and social history, and is in an ongoing process of passing the words and thoughts of ancestors through the oral and embodied canon of cultural identity. Tiwi songs are very old and yet will always be new.

I give the last word to Yikliya, who said to me in April 2011:

> It's really brilliant because something that belongs to us has been released. It was locked for … many years. Many decades. So it was good. Something that I didn't even see when I was a kid, growing up. Now I realise how important it was for us to go down and have a look. For what they've done which they've left for us. I think it's going to help us for a strong culture and hopefully we'll carry on the hearts of our ancestors – what's left behind so we can carry on. Those young ones, they'll learn, gradually, they'll pick up the words. It's not really hard, especially if you're a Tiwi person you can pick it up. If they can't pick it up they can still always ask the old people what it means and how you pronounce it. That's the most important thing.

> It's really great. It's like they're all here. I hear all of these voices and I sing with them you know? Hearing the old men back then I have to learn their words too. Even though I'm old and I should teach them young fellas, I can still learn too so I'll sing with them instead.

Music Transcription 33: Going to Canberra, Yikliya Eustace Tipiloura. Full performance transcription.

The Old Songs are Always New

Epilogue

The Old Songs are Always New

References

Anderson, J. (2005). Access and control of Indigenous knowledge in libraries and archives: ownership and future use. American Library Association and The MacArthur Foundation, 5–7 May.

Bailes, F., and Barwick, L. (2011). Absolute tempo in multiple performances of Aboriginal songs: analyzing recordings of Djanba 12 and Djanba 14. *Music Perception: An Interdisciplinary Journal,* 28(5), 473–90.

Bhabha, H.K. (2012). *The Location of Culture*. Hoboken, N.J.: Taylor & Francis.

Barwick, L. (1989). Creative (ir)regularities: the intermeshing of text and melody in performance of Central Australian song. *Australian Aboriginal Studies* (1), 12–28.

Barwick, L. (1990). Central Australian women's ritual music: knowing through analysis versus knowing through performance. *Yearbook for Traditional Music*, 22, 60–79.

Barwick, L. (2003). Tempo bands, metre and rhythmic mode in Marri Ngarr "Church Lirrga" songs. *Australasian Music Research,* 7, 67–83.

Barwick, L., Birch, B., and Evans, N. (2007). Iwaidja *Jurtbirrk* songs: bringing language and music together. *Australian Aboriginal Studies*, 2, 6–34.

Barwick, L., and Marett, A. (2003). Endangered songs and endangered languages. In J. Blythe and R.M. Brown, eds. *Maintaining the Links: Language Identity and the Land; Seventh Conference of the Foundation for Endangered Languages*, 144–51. Bath, UK: Foundation for Endangered Languages.

Barwick, L., and Marett, A. (2007). *Studies in Aboriginal Song: A Special Issue of Australian Aboriginal Studies*. Canberra, ACT: Aboriginal Studies Press.

Barwick, L., and Thieberger, N. (2006). Cybraries in paradise: new technologies and ethnographic repositories. In C. Kapitzke and B.C. Bruce, eds. *Libr@ries: Changing Information Space and Practice*. Mahwah, NJ: Lawrence Erlbaum, 133–49.

Barwick, L., Vaarzon-Morel, P., Green, J., Zissermann, K. (2021). Conundrums and consequences: doing archival returns in Australia. In L. Barwick, J. Green and P. Vaarzon-Morel, eds. *Archival Returns: Central Australia and Beyond*. Sydney: Sydney University Press.

Basedow, H. (1913). Notes on the Natives of Bathurst Island, North Australia. *Journal of the Royal Anthropological Institute*, 43, 291–323.

Beaudry, N. (2008). The challenges of human relations in ethnographic enquiry. In G. Barz and T. Cooley, eds. *Shadows in the Field: New Perspectives for Fieldwork in Ethnomusicology*, 224–45. New York: Oxford University Press.

Bell, D. (2002). *Daughters of the Dreaming*. 3rd edn. Melbourne: Spinifex Press.

Bell, D. (2008). *Kungun Ngarrindjeri Miminar Yunnan (Listen to the Ngarrindjeri Women Speaking)*. Melbourne: Spinifex Press.

Bendrups, D. (2008). Pacific festivals as dynamic contact zones: the case of Tapati Rapa Nui. *Shima*, 1(2), 14–28.

Berndt, C.H. (1950). Expressions of grief among Aboriginal women. *Oceania Monograph*, 20(4), 286–332.

Berndt, R.M. (1966). The Wuradilagu Song Cycle of Northeastern Arnhem Land: content and style. *The Journal of American Folklore*, 79(311), 195–243.

Berndt, R.M. and Berndt, C.H. (1964). *The World of the First Australians*. Sydney: Ure Smith.

Bracknell, C. (2019). Connecting Indigenous song archives to kin, Country and language. *Journal of Colonialism and Colonial History* 20 (2). https://doi.org/10.1353/cch.2019.0016.

Brady, W. (2000). Indigenous insurgency against speaking for others. Paper presented at the 'Subaltern, Multicultural and Indigenous Histories', Transforming Cultures Winter School, University of Technology Sydney, 2000.

Brandl, M. (1970). Adaptation or disintegration? Changes in the Kulama initiation and increase ritual of Melville and Bathurst Islands, Northern Territory of Australia. *Anthropological Forum*, 2(4), 464–79.

Brandl, M. (1971). *Pukumani: The Social Context of Bereavement in a North Australian Aboriginal Tribe*. Perth: University of Western Australia.

Brown, M.F., Barnes, J.A., Cleveland, D.A., Coombe, R.J., Descola, P., Hiatt, L.R., et al. (1998). Can culture be copyrighted? (with Comments and Reply). *Current Anthropology*, 39(2), 193–222.

Brown, R., Manmurulu, D., Manmurulu, J. and O'Keefe, I. (2017) Maintaining song traditions and languages together at Warruwi (western Arnhem Land). In J. Wafer and M. Turpin (eds), *Recirculating Songs: Revitalising the Singing Practices of Indigenous Australia*. Hamilton, NSW: Hunter Press.

Browner, T. (2009), *Music of the First Nations: Tradition and Innovation in Native North America*. Illinois: University of Illinois Press.

Campbell, G. (2012). Ngarriwanajirri, the Tiwi "Strong Kids Song": using repatriated recordings in a contemporary music project. *Yearbook for Traditional Music*, 44, 1–23.

Campbell, G., Tipungwuti, J. Harris, A. and Poll, M. (2022). Animating cultural heritage knowledge through songs: museums, archives, consultation and Tiwi music. In Linda Barwick, Jakelyn Troy and Amanda Harris, eds. *Music, Dance and the Archive*. Sydney: Sydney University Press.

Capell, A. (1942). Languages of Arnhem Land, North Australia. *Oceania Monograph*, XII, 364–92.

Choo, C. (2001). *Mission Girls: Aboriginal Women on Catholic Missions in the Kimberley, Western Australia 1900–1930*. Perth: University of Western Australia Press.

Christen, K. (2006). Tracking properness: repackaging culture in a remote Australian town. *Cultural Anthropology*, 21(3), 416–46.

Clunies Ross, M., and Wild, S.A. (1984). Formal performance: the relations of music, text and dance in Arnhem Land Clan Songs. *Ethnomusicology*, 28(2), 209–35.

Comrie, B. (1985). *Tense (Cambridge Textbooks in Linguistics)*. Cambridge: Cambridge University Press.

Corn, A. (2002). Nurturing the sacred through Yolngu popular song. *Cultural Survival Quarterly*, 26(2), 40–42.

Corn, A. (2005). When the waters will be one: hereditary performance traditions and the Yolngu reinvention of post-*Barunga* intercultural discourses. *Journal of Australian Studies*, 28(84), 15–30.

Corn, A. (2007). To see their fathers' eyes: expressions of ancestry, fraternity and masculinity in the music of popular bands from Arnhem Land, Australia. In F. Jarman-Ivens, ed. *Oh Boy! Masculinities and Popular Music*, 77–99. Oxford: Routledge.

Corn, A., and Gumbula, N. (2007). Budutthun ratja wiyinymirri: formal flexibility in the Yolnu Manikay tradition and the challenge of recording a complete repertoire. *Australian Aboriginal Studies*, 2, 116–27.

Corn, A., Marett, A., and Garawirrtja, B. (2011). To proclaim they still exist: the contemporary Yolngu performance of historical Makassan contact. In A. Duschatzky and S. Holt, eds. *Trepang: China and the Story of Makassan–Aboriginal Trade*, 73–79. Melbourne: University of Melbourne.

Diettrich, B. (2011). Voices from "under-the-garland": singing, Christianity, and cultural transformations in Chuuk, Micronesia. *Yearbook for Traditional Music*, 43, 62–88.

Dixon, R.M.W. (2010). *Basic Linguistic Theory Volume 1: Methodology. Studies in Language*, 34(10).

Earl, G.E. (1853). *The Native Races of the Indian Archipelago: Papuans*. London: Hyppolyte Balliere.

Ellis, C. (1984). Time consciousness of Aboriginal performers. In J. Skinner and J. Kassler, eds. *Problems and Solutions: Occasional Essays in Musicology Presented to Alice M. Moyle*, 149–85. Sydney: Hale & Iremonger Pty Ltd.

Ellis, C. (1978). Classification of Sound in Pitjintjara-speaking areas. In L.R. Hiatt, ed. *Australian Aboriginal Concepts*, 68–80. Canberra, ACT: Australian Institute of Aboriginal Studies and Humanities Press.

Feld, S., and Fox, A.A. (1994). Music and language. *Annual Review of Anthropology*, 23, 25–53.

Frawley, J. (1995). Tiwi culture must be at the centre: an analysis and synthesis of Tiwi views on education. *The Aboriginal Child at School*, 23(4), 8–21.

Frisbie, C.J. (1980). Vocables in Navajo ceremonial music. *Ethnomusicology*, 24(3), 347–92.

Garde, M. (2006). The language of Kun-borrk in Western Arnhem Land. *Musicology Australia*, 28, 59–89.

Gardiner, A., and Puruntatameri, A. (1993). *Melding of Two Spirits: From the "Yiminga" of the Tiwi to the "Yiminga" of Christianity*. Darwin, NT: State Library of the Northern Territory.

Goodale, J.C. (1970). An example of ritual change among the Tiwi of Melville Island. In A. Pilling and R. Waterman, eds. *Diprotodon to Detribalization: Studies of Change Among Australian Aborigines*, 350–66. East Lansing: Michigan State University Press.

Goodale, J.C. (1971). *Tiwi Wives: A Study of the Women of Melville Island, North Australia*. Seattle; London: University of Washington Press.

Goodale, J.C. (1988). The Tiwi Revisited: 1954–1987. In C.W.M. Hart, A. Pilling and J.C. Goodale, eds. *The Tiwi of North Australia*. New York: Holt, Rinehart and Winston Inc.

Grau, A. (1983a). Dreaming, dancing, kinship: the study of "yoi", the dance of the Tiwi of Melville and Bathurst Islands, North Australia. Belfast: The Queen's University of Belfast. PhD thesis.

Grau, A. (1983b). Sing a dance – dance a song: the relationship between two types of formalised movements and music among the Tiwi of Melville and Bathurst Islands, North Australia. *Dance Research: The Journal of the Society for Dance Research*, 1(2), 32–44.

Grau, A. (1994). Dancers' bodies as the repository of conceptualisations of the body, with special reference to the Tiwi of Northern Australia. *Semiotics Around the World: Synthesis in Diversity – Proceedings of the Fifth Congress of the International Association for Semiotic Studies, Berkeley*, 929–32.

Grau, A. (2001a). Ritual dance and "modernisation": the Tiwi example. *Yearbook for Traditional Music*, 33, 73–81.

Grau, A. (2001b). Tiwi Catholicism: dance and religious syncretism among a Northern Aboriginal People. In S. Porter, M.A. Hayes and D. Tombs, eds. *Faith in the Millennium*, 468–80. Sheffield: Sheffield Academic Press.

Grau, A. (2005). When the landscape becomes flesh: an investigation into body boundaries with special reference to Tiwi dance and western classical ballet. *Body & Society*, 11(4), 141–63.

Grau, A. (2011). Intercultural encounters among the Tiwi of Northern Australia: dance, tourism and museification. Paper presented at the 41st World Conference of the International Council for Traditional Music.

Gsell, F.X. (1955). *The Bishop with 150 Wives: Fifty Years as a Missionary*. Sydney, Wellington: Angus & Robertson.

Hanssens, L. (2009). Submission to the Senate Community Affairs Committee Inquiry into Suicide in Australia. A Joint Submission from Lifeline Australia, Suicide Prevention Australia, The Inspire Foundation, OzHelp Foundation, The Salvation Army, The Mental Health Council of Australia, and the Brain and Mind Research Institute, University of Sydney.

Harris, A. (2014). Archival Objects and the circulation of culture. In A. Harris, ed. *Circulating Cultures: Exchanges of Australian Indigenous Music, Dance and Media*. Canberra, ACT: Australian National University Press.

Harris, A. (2020). *Representing Australian Aboriginal Music and Dance 1930–1970*. New York: Bloomsbury Academic.

Hart, C.W.M. (1930). *The Tiwi of Melville and Bathurst Islands*. Sydney: University of Sydney.

Hart, C.W.M, Pilling, A., and Goodale, J.C. (1988). *The Tiwi of North Australia*. 3rd edn. New York: Holt, Rinehart and Winston.

Hollinshead, K. (1998). Tourism, Hybridity, and Ambiguity: the Relevance of Bhabha's "Third Space" Cultures. *Journal of Leisure Research*, 30(1), 121–56.

Holmes, S. (1995). *The Goddess and the Moon Man: The Sacred Art of the Tiwi Aborigines*. Roseville East, NSW: Craftsman House.

Husa, L.C. (2020). The "souvenirization" and "touristification" of material culture in Thailand – mutual constructions of "otherness" in the tourism and souvenir industries. *Journal of Heritage Tourism*, 15(3): 279–93.

Jakobson, R. (1960). Linguistics and poetics: closing statement. In T. Seboek, ed. *Style in Language*. Cambridge, Mass: MIT Press.

Johnson, H. (2011). "The group from the West": music, modernity and endangered language on Guernsey. Paper presented at the 41st World Conference of the International Council for Traditional Music.

Kahunde, S. (2012). Repatriating archival sound recordings to revive traditions: the role of the Klaus Wachsmann recordings in the revival of the royal music of Bunyoro-Kitara, Uganda. *Ethnomusicology Forum. Special Issue: Ethnomusicology, Archives and Communities – Methodologies for an Equitable Discipline*, 212, 197–219.

Keogh, R. (1990). *Nurlu Songs of the West Kimberleys*. Sydney: University of Sydney.

Kirschenblatt-Gimblett, B. (2006). *Destination Culture: Tourism, Museums and Heritage*. Berkeley, CA: University of California Press.

Knopoff, S. (2003). What is music analysis? Problems and prospects for understanding Aboriginal songs and performance. *Australian Aboriginal Studies*, 1, 39–51.

Lancefield, R.C. (1998). Musical traces' retraceable paths: the repatriation of recorded sound. *Journal of Folklore Research*, 35(1).

Lawrence, H. (2004). The great traffic in tunes: agents of religious and musical change in Eastern Torres Strait. In R. Davis, ed. *Woven Histories, Dancing Lives: Torres Strait Islander Identity, Culture and History*, 46–72. Canberra, ACT: Aboriginal Studies Press.

Lee, J. (1987). Tiwi today: a study of change in a contact situation. Vol. 96. Canberra, ACT: Department of Linguistics. Research School of Pacific Studies. ANU.

Lee, J. (1988). *Tiwi: A Language Struggling to Survive – Australian Aborigines and Islanders Branch*. Darwin, NT: Summer Institute of Linguistics.

Lee, J. (1993). *Ngawurranungurumagi nginingawila ngapangiraga: Tiwi–English Dictionary*. Darwin, NT: Summer Institute of Linguistics.

Lee, J. (2011). Tiwi–English Interactive Dictionary. In M. Lecompte (ed.), *AuSIL Interactive Dictionary*. https://ausil.org.au/Dictionary/Tiwi/lexicon/main.htm

Levy, C. (1975). Mourning for Mungatopi. In C. Levy, J. Gaden and Australian Institute of Aboriginal Studies. Canberra, ACT: Aboriginal Studies Press.

List, G. (1963). The Boundaries of Speech and Song. *Ethnomusicology*, 7(1), 1–16.

MacDougall, D. (1977). *Good-bye Old Man, Or the Film of Tukuliyangenila (A Film About Mangatopi): A Tiwi Island Bereavement Ceremony*. Canberra, ACT: AIATSIS.

Mackinlay, E. (2010). Big women from Burrulula: an approach to advocacy and applied ethnomusicology with the Yanyuwa Aboriginal community in the Northern Territory, Australia. In K. Harrison, E. Mackinlay and S. Pettan, eds. *Applied Ethnomusicology: Historical Approaches and New Perspectives*, 96–115. Newcastle, UK: Cambridge Scholars Publishing.

Mackley-Crump, J. (2013). The festivalization of Pacific cultures in New Zealand: diasporic flow and identity through transcultural contact zones. *Musicology Australia*, 35(1), 20–39.

Magowan, F. (2007). *Melodies of Mourning: Music and Emotion in Northern Australia*. Oxford: James Currey.

Marett, A. (2000). Ghostly voices: some observations on song-creation, ceremony and being in NW Australia. *Oceania Monograph*, 71(1), 18–29.

Marett, A. (2005). *Songs, Dreamings and Ghosts: The Wangga of North Australia*. Middletown, CT: Wesleyan University Press.

Mashino, A. (2011). Classic or modern: the aesthetic and social evolution of Balinese *arja* from the 1990s to 2010. Paper presented at the 41st World Conference of the International Council for Traditional Music.

McIntosh, J. (2012). Preparation, presentation and power: children's performances in a Balinese dance studio. In H. Neveu Kringelbach and J. Skinner, eds. *Dancing Cultures: Globalisation, Tourism and Identity in the Anthropology of Dance*, 194–210. Oxford; New York: Berghahn Books.

McIntyre, K.G. (1977). *The Secret Discovery of Australia. Portuguese Ventures 200 Years Before Captain Cook*. Menindie, SA: Souvenir Press.

McMillan, A. (2007). *An Intruder's Guide to East Arnhem Land*. Nightcliff, NT: Niblock Publishing.

Morris, J. (2001). *The Tiwi: From Isolation to Cultural Change – A History of Encounters Between an Island People and Outside Forces*. Darwin, NT: Northern Territory University Press.

Morris, J. (2003). Continuing "assimilation"? A shifting identity for the Tiwi 1919 to the present. Ballarat: University of Ballarat. PhD thesis.

Mountford, C.P. (1958). *The Tiwi: Their Art, Myth and Ceremony*. London: Phoenix House.

Moyle, A. (1959). Sir Baldwin Spencer's recordings of Australian Aboriginal singing. *Memoirs of the National Museum of Victoria*, 24, 7–36.

Moyle, A. (1997). *Songs from the Northern Territory*. CD re-issue. Canberra, ACT: AIATSIS.

Moyle, R. (1993). Save the last dance – for me? *Musicology Australia*, 16(1), 48–57.

Muratorio, B. (1998). Indigenous women's identities and the politics of cultural reproduction in the Ecuadorian Amazon. *American Anthropologist*, 100(2), 409–20.

Nakata, N.M. (2003). Indigenous knowledge, new times and tomorrow's archives. The Inaugural Ben Haneman Memorial Lecture, State Library of New South Wales, Jumbunna Institute for Indigenous Education and Research, University of Technology, Sydney.

Ngarukuruwala Women's Group with Genevieve Campbell. (2023) *Murli la: Songs and Stories of the Tiwi Islands*. Melbourne: Hardie Grant Explore.

Niles, D. (2012). The National Repatriation of Papua New Guinea recordings: experiences straddling World War II. *Ethnomusicology Forum*, 21(2), 141–59.

O'Keefe, I. (2010). Kaddikkaddik ka-wokdjanganj "Kaddikkaddik Spoke": language and music of the Kun-barlang Kaddikkaddik songs from Western Arnhem Land. *Australian Journal of Linguistics*, 30(1), 35–51.

Onishi, H., and Costes-Onishi, P. (2012). An introduction to the Philippine Kulintang. Paper presented at the The Performer's Voice, 2nd Symposium. 25–28 October. Singapore.

Osborne, C.R. (1974). *The Tiwi Language: Grammar, Myths and Dictionary of the Tiwi Language Spoken on Melville and Bathurst Islands, Northern Australia* (Vol. 55). Canberra, ACT: Australian Institute of Aboriginal Studies.

Osborne, C.R. (1989). Tiwi chanted verse. Unpublished microfilm. University Microform International.

Pearson, N. (2009). *Radical Hope: Education and Equality in Australia.* Melbourne, Vic: Black Inc.

Pilling, A.R. (1970). Changes in Tiwi language. In A. Pilling and R. Waterman, eds. *Diprotodon to Detribalization: Studies of Change Among Australian Aborigines,* 256–74. East Lansing: Michigan State University Press.

Pye, J. (1998). *The Tiwi Islands.* Darwin, NT: Coleman's.

Ritchie, P.H. (1934). *North of the Never Never.* Sydney: Angus & Robertson.

Roach, P. (1982). On the distinction between "stress-timed" and "syllable-timed" languages. In D. Crystal, ed. *Linguistic Controversies* 3–79.

Robinson, G.W. (2003). What to make of Tiwi history? Book review essay of Morris, J. (2001). *The Tiwi: From Isolation to Cultural Change – A History of Encounters Between and Island People and Outside Forces. Australian Journal of Anthropology,* 14(2), 249–52.

Seeger, A. (1987). Do we need to remodel ethnomusicology? *Ethnomusicology,* 31(3), 491–95.

Simpson, C. (1951). *Adam in Ochre.* Sydney: Angus & Robertson.

Spencer, B. (1914). *The Native Tribes of the Northern Territory.* London: Macmillan & Co.

Spencer, B. (1928). *Wanderings in Wild Australia.* London: Macmillan & Co.

Stone, R. (1998). *Africa: The Garland Encyclopedia of World Music.* 1st edn. New York: Garland Publishing.

Stubington, J. (1979). North Australian Aboriginal music. In J. Isaacs, ed. *Australian Aboriginal Music.* Sydney: Australian Aboriginal Artists Agency.

Stubington, J. (1989). *Collecting Folk Music in Australia: Report of a Forum Held 4–6 December 1987.* Sydney: University of New South Wales.

Stubington, J. (2007). *Singing the Land: The Power of Performance in Aboriginal Life.* Sydney: Currency House.

Stubington, J. and Dunbar-Hall, P. (1994). Yothu Yindi's "Treaty": ganma in music. *Popular Music,* 13, 243–59.

Szego, C.K. (2003). Singing Hawaiian and the aesthetics of (in)comprehensibility. In M. Berger and M.T. Carroll, eds. *Global Pop, Local Language.* Jackson: University Press of Mississippi, 291–328.

Taylor, J.P. (2001). Authenticity and sincerity in tourism. *Annals of Tourism Research,* 28(1), 7–26.

Thieberger, N., and Musgrave, S. (2007). Documentary linguistics and ethical issues. *Documentary and Descriptive Linguistics*, 4, 26–37.

Thomas, M. (2007a). The rush to record: transmitting the sound of Aboriginal culture. In D. Bennett (ed.), Who Am I?, *Journal of Australian Studies*, 90, 105–21.

Thomas, M. (2007b). Taking them back: archival media in Arnhem Land today. *Cultural Studies Review*, 13(2), 20–37.

Tiparui, J. (1993). It is important to save this language because it is our culture. *Kularlaga*, 5, 16.

Tiwi Land Council (2020). https://tiwilandcouncil.com, retrieved 23 July 2020.

Tomlinson, G. (2007). *The Singing of the New World: Indigenous Voice in the Era of European Contact*. Cambridge; New York: Cambridge University Press.

Toner, P.G. (2000). Ideology, influence and innovation: the impact of Macassan contact on Yolngu music. *Perfect Beat*, 5(1), 22–41.

Toner, P.G. (2003). History, memory and music: the repatriation of digital audio to Yolngu communities, or, memory as metadata. Refereed conference paper. *Researchers, Communities, Institutions, Sound Recordings*. Sydney: University of Sydney.

Treloyn, S. (2003). Scotty Martin's Jadmi Junba: a song series from the Kimberley region of Northwest Australia. *Oceania Monograph*, 73(3), 208–20.

Treloyn, S. (2006). Songs that pull: Jadmi Junba from the Kimberley Region of Northwest Australia. Sydney: University of Sydney. PhD thesis.

Treloyn, S. (2012). Stopping the freeze: finding a place for musical analysis in a repatriation-focused song maintenance project. Paper presented at the Joint Annual Meeting of the American Musicological Society, the Society for Ethnomusicology and the Society for Music Theory. 1–4 November, New Orleans.

Treloyn, S. and Dowding, A. (2017). Thabi returns: the use of digital resources to recirculate and revitalise Thabi songs in the west Pilbara. In J. Wafer and M. Turpin, eds. *Recirculating Songs: Revitalising the Singing Practices of Indigenous Australia*. Hamilton, NSW: Hunter Press.

Turpin, M. (2005). Form and meaning of Akwelye: a Kaytetye women's song series from Central Australia. Sydney: University of Sydney. PhD thesis.

Turpin, M. (2007). The poetics of Central Australian Aboriginal song. *Australian Aboriginal Studies*, 2, 100–15.

Turpin, M., and Stebbins, T. (2010). The language of song: some recent approaches in description and analysis. *The Australian Linguistic Society*, 30(1), 1–17.

Venbrux, E. (1995). *A Death in the Tiwi Islands: Conflict, Ritual and Social Life in an Australian Aboriginal Community.* Cambridge: Cambridge University Press.

Venbrux, E. (2007). "Quite another world of Aboriginal Life": Indigenous people in an evolving museumscape. In N. Stanley (ed.), *The Future of Indigenous Museums.* Oxford; New York: Berghahn Books.

Wafer, J. and Turpin, M. (eds) (2017). *Recirculating Songs: Revitalising the Singing Practices of Indigenous Australia.* Hamilton, NSW: Hunter Press.

Walsh, M. (2007). Australian Aboriginal song language: so many questions, so little to work with. *Australian Aboriginal Studies*, 2, 128–44.

Ward, T.A. (1990). *Towards an Understanding of the Tiwi Language/Culture Context: A Handbook for Non-Tiwi Teachers.* Nguiu: Nguiu Nginingawula Literature Production Centre.

Whittaker, E. (1994). Public discourse on sacredness: the transfer of Ayers Rock to Aboriginal ownership. *American Ethnologist*, 21(2), 310–34.

Wild, S.A. (1985). Oceania. *The New Grove, Ethnomusicology*, 29(1), 175–76.

Wild, S.A. (1992). Song of experience: the Aborigine's long vocal tradition is now grafting popular Western styles to its own customs. *The Musical Times: Aspects of Australian Music*, 133, 336–38.

Will, U. (1998). And what if they say nothing … ? English version of *Et quand ils n'en disent rien … ? Cahiers de musiques traditionelles*, 12, 175–85.

Wilson, A. (2013). Tiwi revisited: a reanalysis of Traditional Tiwi verb morphology. Melbourne: University of Melbourne, Department of Linguistics and Applied Linguistics.

Index

Amparruwu (widow songs) 31, 129–130, 180, 181, 182, 199, 214–215
  melodic contour 200, 212
  performance context 200, 218
  purpose 214, 216
  revenge songs 77
  sound of words 124
  structure 188–190
  tempo 129, 210
  vocalisation 129, 137
Ampiji (Rainbow serpent) 62, 150, 275
Ampirikuruwala 180, 198, 222–225, 251, 275
  Arikuruwala with Ampirikuruwala response 223–224
  Ariwangilinjiya with Ampirikuruwala response 225–226
  melodic contour 202, 222
  performance context 200, 223
  polyphonic effect 222
  structure 186
  traditional function 223
Ampirimarrikimili (women's songs) 180, 181, 199, 212–213, 283
  melodic contour 201, 212–213
  performance context 200
  structure 189
ampiriwayajuwijiyi 197–198
Apajirupwaya (love songs) 180, 228–231, 237–238
  composition 194
  Daniel Paujimi's melody 237–238
  free translation 136
  melody 134–135, 182–183, 202
  metrical form 136
  performance context 200
  purpose 228
  spoken form 136
  structure 190
  sung form 136
Apiniapi (New Tiwi). *see* New Tiwi
Apuatjimi, Dion Wilson 275
Arawanikiri 33
archive recordings. *see* recordings
Arikuruwala 7–8, 50, 180, 181, 182, 183, 198, 219–222, 264
  Ampirikuruwala response 222–225
  composition 194
  melodic contour 201, 219–221
  performance context 200
  performance variations 131–134
  rhythm 193
  structure 186, 187, 190
  tempo 191
  vocalisation 138
Arimarrikuwamuwu (tree-climbing) 180, 181, 210–212
  melodic contour 201
  performance context 200
  pitch 210–211
  structure 189

Arimarrikuwamuwu (tree-climbing) *continued*
   tempo 210
Ariwangilinjiya (Lullaby) 180, 181, 225–227
   Ampirikuruwala response 225–226
   composition 194
   melodic contour 202
   pitch 226
   structure 188
Ariwayakulaliyi 181, 230–233
   Daniel Paujimi's melody 237–243
   melody 231–233, 245, 270–272
   Modern Kuruwala 234
   structure 191
Arnhem Land 6–7, 13, 15, 27, 51
artistic space 100–106
Arts NT xxxi
audience 44, 46, 269
   associations and experiences 153–154
   ceremony and performance, distinguished 46–47
   non-Tiwi 277–278
   performance, impact on 44–45
   song subjects, and 151–154
   songs tailored to 140
Australian Institute of Aboriginal and Torres Strait Islander Studies (AIATSIS) xxxii, 24, 34, 41
   ethnographic Tiwi song material 24
   Spencer recordings 48–52
   visit to 26–30
Ayipa (news-telling) 45, 51, 74, 98–99, 102, 149
   "favourites" 99–100
   song subjects and current affairs 100, 244
   Yiloga (football song) 244–246
   Yiloti, and 99

B2M 117–118, 236
Basedow, Herbert 28
Bathurst Island xxxi, 3, 4, 5, 48
   Catholic Mission 9, 31, 67, 69, 93–94, 112, 228, 233, 255–256
   Countries 59
Belyuen (Delissaville) 15
bereavement 74–77, 153
   Arikuruwala. *see* Arikuruwala
   Arimarrikuwamuwu.
      see Arimarrikuwamuwu (tree-climbing)

Ayipa song 102
family knowledge, transmission of 80
Black Joe. *see* Wampayawityimirri, Bartholomew Kerinaiua
Black, Nina xli, 117, *171*
Black, Paul xli
Bombing of Darwin
   dance 102, *169*
   song 99–100, 247, 258, 271, 273, 274, 275
Boneham, Alex *163*
Brown, Danny (Jipuwampi) xli
Brown, Kaye xli
Buffalo (Dreaming). *see* Jarrangini (Buffalo)
burial 70, 71, 75
Bush, Bonnie *171*
Bush, Doriana *171*
Bush, Paddy xli

Campbell, Genevieve *161*, *173*, *174*
Canberra 10, 23, 47–48, 146
   Canberra International Music Festival 31, *162*
   delegation *161*
   visits to 26–30, 31–32, 42, 283–290
cantillation 121, 122, 123, 130–131, 134–135, 155, 159
   Jipuwakirimi 203
   modern song forms 155–157
Catholic mission. *see* Bathurst Island, Catholic Mission
Chau Chak Wing Museum 32, 33
   Tiwi display 32–33, *168*
Christian music 237
clapping 193
   hand 178
   sticks. *see* tawutawunga (clapping sticks)
Cobourg Peninsula 8, 15, 51
composition 53–55, 100–106, 134, 278–279. *see also* performance
   extemporisation 9–10, 105–106, 119, 182, 194, 235, 280
   first person, use of 140–142
   improvisation xxxii, 12, 13, 20, 37–38, 119, 260
   language change, impact of 114–119
   metaphysical process 158
   novelty and innovation 16–17, 100–102, 117–118, 123, 182, 235

patterns of five 125–127
present tense, use of 120, 140–142
song language. *see* song language
sound of words 123–125
stages of 121
text, and 193–202
conches 50
consonant lenition 127
Cooper, Robert (Joe) 8, 51
Coorab in the Island of Ghosts 27
copyright 24, 29, 36, 261
Cotton Tree song 143–144
Country. *see* Murrakupuni (Country)
creativity 10, 102
Crocodile (Dreaming) *162*. *see also* Yirrikapayi (Crocodile)
cultural change
   continuing traditions 253–259
   language and 114
cultural heritage 105, 158–159
   cultural negotiations, on-stage 273–279
   cultural practice 11
   custodians 272
   film footage 31–32
   maintenance 105
   new musical ways, and 248–253
   reclaiming 25, 29–30, 32–33
   recordings. *see* recordings
   tangible and intangible 26
   transmission through language 116
cultural misunderstandings 31, 68–69, 86
Curry, Mary 78

Daly 15
dance. *see* Yoi (Dreaming)
Darwin
   bombing. *see* Bombing of Darwin
   removal of people to 8
Darwin Entertainment Centre *165*, *166*, 267, 269
Darwin Festival xxxi, xxxii
deceased people 19
didgeridoo 178
Doolan, Jack 24, 41, 99
   material 100
Dreaming xliii, 278. *see also* Yoi (Dreaming)
   family groups 61, 62–63
   New Dreaming 61

dugong (rrakwiyangili) 238, 241–242

education 92–96
   Catholic 119–120, 255–256
   Kulama and 92–96, 263
   "modern" songs, and 250–251, 278–279, 283
   senior singers, and 93, 104, 119, 155, 158, *174*, 281
extemporisation 9–10, 105–106, 119, 194, 235, 280
group participation 182

Fernando, Bobby *169*
Fernando, Ivan *169*
Fernando, Marcella *164*
Fernando, Mel Sheba 29, *161*
Final Ceremony. *see* Yiloti (Final Ceremony)
Football song. *see* Yiloga (Football song)
Fort Dundas 7, 99, 153
Fourcroy, Yanna *171*
funerals 40
   European influence 69–70, 86–87, 253
   Pukumani. *see* Pukumani

Gagudju people 8
Galiwin'ku 257
Garden Point. *see* Pirlingimpi (Garden Point)
gender 64–68, 178
Giles, Ray 45
glossary xliii–xlvi
Good-bye Old Man, Or the Film of Tukuliyangenila (A Film About Mangatopi): A Tiwi Island Bereavement Ceremony 101
Grau, Andrée 24, 42–43, 61, 69, 102
grave post. *see* Pukumani
grievance songs 95, 96–98
grieving. *see* mourning
Gsell, Father Francis Xavier 9, 93
guitar 178, 238, 248, 271

happy singing. *see* kawakawayi
"Happy to be on an Island in the Sun" 265–266
Hart, C.W.M. 33
   material 29–30, 32–33, 45, 46, 100
healing songs 87, 254, 275

heuristic learning 10, 39, 90, 115, 159
Holmes, Sandra 24, 29–31, 46–47, 69
Horse (Dreaming). *see* Pika (Horse)
Humperdinck, Engelbert 263–264
   "Ten Guitars" 263–264

identity 253, 278. *see also* kinship; Yoi (Dreaming)
   maternal. *see* Skin group; Yiminga
   metaphysical connections 56, 62, 69, 253
   person, family and Country 63–64
   singing 53–55
   song subject, and 147–148
   transmission through language 116, 159
improvisation xxxii, 12, 13, 20, 37–38, 119
   language change, impact of 115–116
   melodic inspiration 260–261
individualism 10, 11, 40, 98
   community, and 41
Indonesian sailors/fishermen 7
inherited knowledge 11
initiation 66, 89–91, 104–105
   education 92–96
innovation 16–17, 100–101, 117–118, 123, 182, 235
intuition 11
isorhythmic structure 193, 203
Iwaidja people 8, 15, 51, 153, 154
   Jurtbirrk 228

Jalingini (Sugarbag) 179, 188, 205, 208–210, 210–211
   melodic contour 201
   performance context 200
   pitch 184–186
   vocalisations 137
Japanese
   bombing of Darwin 99–100
   pearlers 8, 99
Jarrangini (Buffalo) 15, 49, 61, 101
Jilarruwi (Brolga) 262
Jimalipuwa 7–8
   Tamunga (Cotton Tree) 144
Jipapijingimirri 8
   Jipuwakirimi song 8
Jipuwakirimi 8, 49–50, 74, 102, 179, 183, 198, 203–208, 219, 236
   group participation 181–182

   interruption/interjection 205
   melodic contour 201
   metre 206
   performance context 200
   rhythm 193, 206–208
   singer and dancer, co-dependence 204–205
   structure 186, 189
   tempo 203–204, 206–207
Jones, Tom 263
Junba 194
Jurruputimirri (Tony Charlie) 128
Jurtbirrk 228

Kantilla, Calista xlii, 2, 31–32, 33, 120, 130–131, 134, 158, *165, 167, 168, 170, 171, 172, 173,* 195
   Awungarra Jiliyarti (Here in Darwin) 134
   composition technique 134
   Darwin Entertainment Centre 2021 274, 275
   pitch memory 184
   Wutawa kuwayi (They call out) 131
Kantilla, Marie-Carmel *168*
Kantilla, Regina xxxi, 62, 118, *161, 162, 165, 166, 168, 171, 174, 175*
Kantilla, Stephen-Paul 28, 97–98, 104, 148, *161,* 199
   Arikuruwala incipits 220
Kapi Canberra (Going to Canberra) 283–290
Karla Tractor Joe xli, 41
   Arikuruwala 222
   Arikuruwala with Ampirikuruwala response 223
   bark paintings 27
   Yipunjinga mayingi (Calling spirit) 57
kawakawani (sad singing) 137, 178
kawakawayi (happy singing) 178
kayayi (crying singing) 137, 187–188, 216
Kerinaiua, Agnes *161*
Kerinaiua, Kardo 27
Kerinaiua, Marguerita 97
Kerinaiua, Max 43
Kerinaiua, Wally 23, 28, 43, 104, 105, *161*
key, consistency of 272
Kimberley 13, 15
kinship 55–64, 253, 270, 278. *see also* identity; Yoi (Dreaming)
   Ayipa song 102

Index

bereavement symbols 76
maternal. *see* Skin group; Yiminga
status songs 74–77
Kirilima (Junglefowl) 61, 63, 85, 95, 102, 274–275
Kulama xliii, 5, 12, 38, 41, 43, 45, 77, 149, 178, 182, 196, 200–202, 265, 278
   ancestral story, and 95–96
   Arikuruwala. *see* Arikuruwala
   artistic space, maintaining 100–106
   Ayipa. *see* Ayipa
   chain of transmission 158
   changing role of 91
   decline, reasons for 67–68, 91–92, 93–94
   descriptions of 91–92
   education, and 92–96
   functional classification of songs 95
   gender, and 64–65, 178
   grievance songs 95, 96–98
   melodic forms 54
   Modern Kuruwala 263–265
   Murrakupuni 261
   performance context 278–279
   pitch, consistency of 186
   purpose 89
   ritual elements 90–91
   ritual stage markers 96, 142–147
   social history, and 98–100
   social politics, and 96–98
   song composition and performance 53–55, 100–106
   song subjects 54–55
   Tiwi language, and 89–90
   Yoi 261
Kulangana (South West Vernon) Island 3
Kupunyi (Canoe) *161*, 238, 244, 248, 271, 275
   Daniel Paujimi's melody 239–240
   Strong Women's Group 242–243
kurukangawakawayi 137–138, 187
   musical treatments 138–139
Kuruwala 16, 87, 155, 177, 196
   Catholic hymns, and 256–257
   melodic inspiration 260
   Modern. *see* Modern Kuruwala
   song-types 179–181, 214–216, 225–234, 255
   structure 186
   tempo 191–192

Langa. *see* New Tiwi
language. *see* song language; Tiwi language
listening, importance of 11
Lorrila/Marntimapila (Rock) 58–59
love songs. *see* Apajirupwaya (love songs)

Macassans 6–7
Macleay Museum 26, 32
Malawu Country 59
Mamanunkuni (sorrow songs) xliii, 81–83, 102, 179, 180, 181, 182, 199, 210, 215–218, 249
   Ampiriwayajuwijiyi 197–198
   composition 194
   melodic contour 201, 215–218
   performance context 200, 218
   purpose 216
   structure 189
   tempo 218
   vocalisations 138
Manikay songs 194
Maningrida 257
Mantiyupi Country 59, 229, 244
markings used xv–xvi
Marralyaangimpi waterhole *160*
marriage
   Catholic 67–68
   Skin groups, and 58–59
   Tiwi system 67–68, 93–94
Marrikawuyanga Country 59
Matingalia Island 3
melismatic introduction 182, 191, 215, 219
melismatic ornamentation 184, 222
melody 13, 43, 127, 183–184, 201–202, 257–258, 271
   alteration of words 245
   Amparruwu 201, 212, 214
   Ampirikuruwala 202, 222
   Ampirimarrikimili 201, 212–213
   Arikuruwala 219–221
   Ariwangilinjiya 202, 225–226
   Ariwayakulaliyi 230–232, 244, 270–271
   Daniel Paujimi 237–243
   love songs 134–135, 183–184
   Mamanunkuni 215–216

melody *continued*
   Modern Kuruwala 233–234, 257–258
   new musical genres 259–269
   origin of 259–260
   performance context, and 16, 54
   song-types 178–181
   sound of words, and 123–125
Melville Island 3, 4, 7–8, 15, 27, 48, 242, 255
   Countries 59
   Japanese pearlers 8, 99
   Portuguese slavers 7
metaphor 103, 147. *see also* symbolism
   metaphorical roles 74
   natural world, references to 85
metre 118, 120, 240–241
   Ampirimarrikimili 212–213
   Arikuruwala 221
   classical song, and 159
   fitting words to 123, 127–130, 245
   Jipuwakirimi 206
   metrical patterns 134-137, 195
   patterns of five 125–127
   performance variations 130–134
   syllable insertion/deletion 127–131, 155, 157
microtonal fluctuation 12
Mijuni 75
Milikapiti (Snake Bay) 4, 238
Milimika (dance ground) xliii, 72, 84, 96, *167*
Miller. *see* Mungatopi
Minjilang (on Croker Island) 15
Miyartuwi (Pandanus) 58–59
Modern Kuruwala 181, 196, 202, 232, 233–234, 238, 253–259, 270, 278–279
   classical and modern, combining 258–259, 270–273
   key, consistency of 272
Modern Tiwi 108, 110–111, 112, 240, 264. *see also* Tiwi language
   language shift 112–114
   Old Tiwi, relationship to 109–110, 155
   song tradition, impact on 118–119
monotonic structure 183, 203
Mopaditi (Spirits of the dead) xliii, 56–57, 77
   kinship, and 56–57
   new musical ways 248
   Yilaniya, and 71–72

Moreen, Mary Elizabeth Mungatopi 29–30, *161*, *165*, *166*, *167*
Mosquito. *see* Timilani (Mosquito)
Mountford, Charles 24, 27, 152
   material 29, 45, 100
mourning 46, 65, 86–87, 179, 253
   ceremony and performance, distinguished 46–47
   grieving, distinguished 179
   kinship status songs 74–77
   Kulama, and 95
   Pukumani. *see* Pukumani
   widow songs 31
Moyle, Alice 24, 43, 50–52
Muma (East Vernon) Island 3
Mungatopi, Eleanor 30
Mungatopi, Katrina *162*, *168*
Mungatopi, Marcellus *171*
Mungatopi, Nelson *171*
Mungatopi, Polly 29, 46–47
Mungatopi, Warabutiwayi Allie Miller xli, 29, 45, 46–47, 101, 108
   Death of a Father song 151–154
Munkara, Casmira 44, *171*, 232
   pitch memory 184
Munkara, Enrail 232–233
Munkara, Gemma *162*
Munkara, Harold *169*
Munkara, Jipwarlamparripa Stanley 77, 198, 210, 232
   A song for his father at Yilaniya (Smoking) 77
   Mangulumpwarni (Tide) 80
   Pajipajuwu (Turtle eggs) 84
Munkara, John Louis *165*, *168*, 267
   Jikilaru 268–269, 275
Munkara, Maria 265
Munupi Country 59, 84
Murli la 155–157, 229, 234, 236, 255, 275, 276
Murntankala 1–2, 274
Murrakupuni (Country) xliii, 4, 74, 270
   affiliations 4, 34, 59–60
   kinship, and 55–57, 64
   Skin groups, and 58
Murriny Patha people 15
Murrntawarrapijimi 126, 261, 262–264
Murrukuliki (Macassar Man) 5, 6
music, emerging genres 235–237, 259–269
musical forms 198

nagi (cloth tied around as short pants) 178
names 19–20
  deceased people 19
  family. *see* Tiwi family names
  personal 19
National Film and Sound Archive of Australia (NFSA) xxxii, 26, 31–32, 42, 43
National Museum of Australia (NMA) 26
  Tiwi artefacts 28
natural sonic environment 259
New Tiwi 18, 108, 111. *see also* Tiwi language
  language shift 112–114
  song tradition, impact on 117–119
Ngariwanajirri ("We all work together and help each other") 248
Ngarukuruwala performance group (We sing) xxxii, 23–24, 32, 222, 251, 263
  Darwin Entertainment Centre 2021 269–279
Ngawatu 275
ngirini (mussel shells) 178
ngirramini (story, song) xliii, 177
Nguiu. *see* Wurrumiyanga
Ngurlmak 51
nicknames xli–xlii
Nodlaw Island 3
non-Tiwi music, incorporation of 117–118, 233–234, 259–269, 277
Norm, Yirripungiwayamirri George 84
  Kujupurruwatuwu (Turtle) 84
novelty 16–17, 100–102, 235
Nurlu 194
Nyarringari (Goose) 63, 65
Nyingawi (Mangrove spirit people) song 43–44, 232, 248, 261, 264, 274
  performance *166*
  vocalisations 137

Old Tiwi 105, 108, 109–110, 112, 264. *see also* Tiwi language
  composition, and 105, 159
  language shift 112–114
  Modern Tiwi, relationship to 110–111, 155
  noun incorporation 149–150
  song tradition, and 117–119, 157–159
  time-of-day markers. *see* time-of-day markers

oral traditions 278–279
  recording 20–22, 38–39, 281–282, 285
ornament 12
Orsto, Concepta 3, *165*, 259
Orsto, Eunice 124, 129, 137, *171*, 228
  Amparruwu 124, 129, 137, 139, 215
  Jinarringa (Black-headed python) 125
Orsto, Francis 28, 155, *161*, *163*, *164*, *165*, *166*, *174*, 259, 260
  Darwin Entertainment Centre 2021 274–275
  Murli la 155–157, 275
  pitch memory 184
Osborne, Charles 5, 12–14, 24
  material 29
  song-types 196–199
  Spencer material, on 51
  The Tiwi Language 108
  transcriptions 120–122

palingarri (Old way) 66, 159, 273
Palipuaminni, Jules *165*
pandanus, collecting *163*
Parakajiyali song xxi, 205, 206
Parker, Gregoriana *165*
Paru 4, 8, 228, 229, 244
patipatingini (a small lizard) 225
Paujimi, Daniel 237–238
  Ariwayakulaliyi melody 237–243, 244
pawupawu (slapping of hands on thighs or buttocks) 178
Payijayi (payday) songs 79
performance. *see also* composition
  breaking the fourth wall 46, 277
  ceremony, distinguished 46
  context 181–183, 196–198, 200, 278–279
  cultural negotiations, on-stage 273–279
  extemporisation 9–10, 105–106, 119, 194, 235, 280
  first person, use of 140–142
  group and solo 181–183, 186, 204–205, 253
  improvisation xxxii, 12, 13, 20, 37–38, 119, 260
  novelty and innovation 16–17, 100–102, 117–118, 123, 182, 235
  present tense, use of 140–142
  recording, effect of 40, 44–48

performance *continued*
  rehearsal and 276
  song language, variations 130–134
  sound of words 123–125
  text, and 196–198
  time stamping. *see* time-of-day markers
  Tiwi characteristics 276
  variability 181–183
phonemic inconsistency 108
Pickertaramoor 4
Pika (Horse) 61, 63, 101, 274
Pilayapijimi 262
Pirlingimpi (Garden Point) 4, 8, 108, 255
Pirripitiriyi (Seagull) Island 3
Pitapituwi (Unborn) 55–56
  kinship, and 55–56
pitch 41, 44, 183–185, 198
  Arimarrikuwamuwu 210–211
  Ariwangilinjiya 226
  Ariwayakulaliyi 230–232
  fluctuation 132, 192
  Jipuwakirimi 203
  memory 184–185
  Modern Kuruwala 270–273
  primary 13
  rising 131, 182
Portaminni, Frances Therese *162, 165, 168*
Potinga (Vernon Islands) 3
Prince of Wales 152
Puantilura, Aloysious 43
Pukumani xliv, 19, 21, 32, 46, 49, 68–73, 86, 178, 200, 265
  ancestral story, and 80–83
  burial 70, 71
  cultural misinterpretation 68–69
  gender, and 64
  kinship status songs 74–77
  melodic forms 54
  protocols 56
  revenge songs 77–78
  ritual, allusion to 79–80
  ritual songs and stages 70–73
  song composition and performance 53–55
  song subjects 54–55
  Turtuni poles 28, 70, 72, 167
  Yilaniya. *see* Yilaniya (Smoking ceremony)
  Yiloti. *see* Yiloti (Final Ceremony)
  Yoi song 73–87

Pukwiyi. *see* Yiminga
PULiiMA Indigenous Languages Conference 165
Punguatji, Augusta *168, 170*
pupuni miraka (good voice) 177
Pupuni Yingiti ("Good Food") song 249–250
purakutukuntinga (talk about) songs 99
Purrapinarli (Karslake) Island 3
Purrukapali 113, 265, 271, 274
Purrumunupi (Harris) Island 3
Puruntatameri, Alberta 219
Puruntatameri, Aloysious 206
Puruntatameri, Anne Marie 124
Puruntatameri, Barry 150, *172*, 204
Puruntatameri, Clementine 26, 46–49, 80–82, 126, *173*, 210, 235, 275
  Mingatalini Mamanunkuni (Sorrow) 81–83
  Murrntawarrapijimi 126, 262–265
  pitch memory 184
  time markers, using 146
Puruntatameri, Ella 185, 191, 262, 263, 275
Puruntatameri, Emanuel. *see* Murrntawarrapijimi
Puruntatameri, Joe 39
Puruntatameri, Juliette *173*
Puruntatameri, Justin 94, 98, 99, 151, 158, *169, 174*, 177, 195, 219
  Arikuruwala incipits 220
  pitch memory 184
  song for Kulama 95
Puruntatameri, Kilupwarlapiwiyi Romuel 85, 241
  Rrakwiyangili (Dugong) 243
  Wantangini (Firewood) 85
Puruntatameri, Shirley *175*
Puruntatameri, Teresita xxxi, xxxii, 28, 63, 116, 145, *161, 172, 174*
Putaka (next-of-kin sisters) 75
Pye, Brother John 256

recordings 10, 20–21, 23–52, 281–282
  access to 23–25
  archive 37–40, 276, 280–282
  collections, engagement with 31–33
  cultural restriction appraisal 25

Index

emotional/personal responses 35–36
engagement 33
misinterpretations 48–50
ownership 21–22, 24, 29, 34, 35, 36–37, 47–48
Palingarri 29, 45
performance, effect on 40, 44–48
reclaiming 25, 29–30, 47–48
repatriation of 21, 33–43, 47–48, 285
respect for singers of the past 41–42, 263
song as artefact 27–31, 47–48
source of old/lost words 148–149
taking voices away 26–27
teaching resource, as 37–40, 117, 119, 280
vocalisations 50–52
Remix 275
revenge songs 77–78
rhythm 193, 245
    Ampirimarrikimili 213
    Jipuwakirimi 193, 206–208
    performance context 16
    Yiloga (Football song) 245
ritual stage markers
    Ayipa song 102
    Kulama 96, 142–147
    Pukumani 70–73
    used in song texts 143
    used today 145
Roussos, Demis 265–266
    "Happy to be on an Island in the Sun" 265–266
Rrangini 242
rubato 12

sad singing. *see* kawakawani; kayayi
Sawmill, Warlakurrayuwuwa Paddy xli, 5, 6, 65
    Mayimampi (Goose) 65–66
    Yirranikara Pajimuna (Burning leg) 80
senior singers xli, 10, 11, 16, 18, 20–21, 37, 40, 74, 105, 155, 158, 269
    cultural custodians 272
    education, and 93, 104, 119, *174*, 278, 280
    gender roles, and 64–68, 178
    holders of knowledge 195
    new styles, embracing 118, 281–282
    non-Tiwi music, on 118
    Old language, and 157

preserving traditions 281
respect for 41–42, 263
stage markers, and 142, 145
Shark (Dreaming). *see* Tatuwali (Shark)
Simpson, Colin 24, 27, 99
    material 100
Sims, Michael 24, 237
    material 29
singers
    recording process 44–46
    respect for past 41–42
singing
    identity. *see* Yiminga; Yoi (Dreaming)
sistagirls 66–67
Skin group. *see also* Yiminga
    associated clans 58
    identification of artefacts 28
    kinship 57–59
Smoking ceremony. *see* Yilaniya (Smoking ceremony)
Snake Bay. *see* Milikapiti (Snake Bay)
social history
    Kulama and 98–100
    transmission through language 116, 159
social politics
    Kulama and 96–98
song xxxi–xxxiii, 9–22
    act not object, as 177
    artefact, as 27–31
    ceremony and performance, distinguished 46–47
    continuum of tradition 43–52
    definition xliv
    generational transmission 270
    individuality/uniqueness 12, 285
    language change, impact of 114–119
    lineage and associations 24
    modern and classical, distinguished 15–17
    novelty and innovation 16–17, 100–102, 117–118, 123, 182, 235
    ownership 34, 47–48, 261
    owning and holding, distinguished 37
    preservation and acknowledgement 11
    privileging certain songs 40
    purpose 9–11
    sharing 14–15
    stages 14
    text, and 13–14, 43

song *continued*
  traditions, rediscovery of 42–43
  transcriptions 12–14, 17, 120–122
  translations 17, 147–154
  types 178–181, 196–199
  Yoi song. *see* Yoi (Dreaming)
song language 119–137
  metre, fitting words to 123, 127–130
  metrical patterns 134–137
  onomatopoeic words 151
  patterns of five 125–127
  performance variations 130–134
  phonetic singing of English words 152–153
  renegotiation of language 155, 159
  "song only" words 148–151, 157
  sound of words 123–125
  spoken language, distinguished 122–123
  transcriptions 12–14, 17, 120–122
  word boundaries, obscuring 126–127, 148, 153, 155, 157, 195
song subjects. *see also* text
  accumulation of meaning 154, 156
  associated and contextual meanings 147, 151
  audience specific references 151–154
  Classical and Modern Kuruwala 258–259
  dance, and 151
  identity, and 147–148
  interpretation of 147–154
  symbolism. *see* symbolism
sorrow songs. *see* Mamanunkuni (sorrow songs)
spears 33, 78, 274
  mock fights 262
spelling xxxv–xxxvi, 18–20, 108–109
Spencer, Baldwin 9, 24, 33
  material 46, 48–50
  misinterpretation of recordings 48–50
  vocalisations 50–52
Spirit children. *see* Pitapituwi (Unborn)
Spirits of the dead. *see* Mopaditi (Spirits of the dead)
sticks. *see* tawutawunga (clapping sticks)
Stolen Generations 8
Strong Women's Group xxxi–xxxii, 16, 87, 202, 225, 233–234
  Ampirikuruwala response 251
  continuing traditions and cultural change 253–259

cultural negotiations, on-stage 273–279
cultural resurgence 256–257
Kulama stage markers 145
Kupunyi. *see* Kupunyi
Modern Tiwi sustainable song tradition 116, 281
Murli la 155–157, 229, 234, 236, 275, 276
new musical forms 118, 181, 196, 219, 244, 270, 277
Strong Women, definition xliv
three-part melody form 244
Tikilaru Murrakupuni 267–268
traditional techniques, using 155
vocalisation, examples 139
women's roles 253–254
Wrangku Murrakupuni (Wrangku Country) 249–250
Yiloga (Football song) 245–246
structure 86, 125, 131, 179, 182, 186–191
  cyclic 186
  language 110–111, 115–116, 123, 139, 142
  linear 186, 187
  Pukumani ritual 69, 75
Sugarbag. *see* Jalingini (Sugarbag)
symbolism 74, 81, 83, 101, 147, 195, 285. *see also* metaphor
  contemporary subject matter, and 102
  conventions of imagery 85
  non-Tiwi objects 85–86
  ritual 102–103

Takaringuwi (Mullet) 58–59, 262
Tallulah *164*
Tambu 113
Tarikulani (Turtle) 40, 61, 63, 84
Tatuwali (Shark) 40, 61, 63, 126–127, 128, 274
  vocalisations 137
tawutawunga (clapping sticks) 178, 274
tempo 179, 191–193
  Amparruwu 129
  Arimarrikuwamuwu 210
  Jipuwakirimi 203–205, 206–207
  Mamanunkuni 218
  Modern Kuruwala 270
  performance context 16, 182
  song-types 179–181

"Ten Guitars" 261–262
Tepuwaturinga (Wallaby) 42–43, 49
tessitura 184, 209, 271
  Amparruwu songs 129
text 193–202
  importance of 43, 193–194
  obfuscation 195
  performance, and 196–198
  song subjects. *see* song subjects
Tikilaru Country 59, 238, 274
  song 237, 248, 265–269
Tikilaru Country group (Daniel's Country) 237
time
  importance of 11
time-of-day markers 110, 115, 139–140, 141–142
  aural mood, creating 141
  Kulama stage markers 142–147, 153
time-of-day words 110, 141–142
  New Tiwi, and 148
time stamping. *see* time-of-day markers
Timilani (Mosquito) 63, 137, 179, 188, 205, 208–210
  melodic contour 201
  performance context 200
  pitch 183–185
Tipakelipa, Dorrie (Jipulimatuwu) 129–130
Tipiloura, Emerentiana *164*
Tipiloura, Karen *166*, *174*
Tipiloura, Leonie xli, 53, 130–131, 134, *161*, 212
  Daniel Paujimi's melody 239
  Darwin Entertainment Centre 2021 275
  Wutawa kuwayi (They call out) 131
Tipiloura, Yikliya Eustace 28, 30, 45–46, 102, 104, 107, 115, 138, 148, *161*, *163*, *167*, *172*, *173*, 199, 286
  Ariwayakulaliyi 139, 231, 244
  Kapi Canberra (Going to Canberra) 283–290
  Parakajiyali song 205–206
  pitch memory 184
  time stamping 141, 145, 146–147
Tipuamantimeri, Barney 132–133, 219
  Arikuruwala incipits 220
Tipuamantimeri, Cornelia *169*
Tipuamantimeri, Long Stephen 39, 138, *169*
  Ariwayakulaliyi 230

Mamanunkuni 138, 217
Tipuamantimeri, Stephanie 43–44, *172*
Tipungwuti, Christopher Foxy 131–132, 198, 219
  Apajirupwaya 237–238
  Arikuruwala 220, 221
  Arikuruwala with Ampirikuruwala response 224
  Daniel Paujimi's melody 239
  Mamanunkuni 138
Tipungwuti, Dorothy 102, 214, 215
  Arikuruwala with Ampirikuruwala response 224
Tipungwuti, Jacinta xxxi, 2, 32, 89, 130–131, *161*, *164*, *166*, 277
  Wutawa kuwayi (They call out) 131
Tipungwuti, Nola *165*
Tipungwuti patriline 5
Tipungwuti, Paul *169*
Tipungwuti, Robert Biscuit 148
Tipungwuti, Roger 104, 105, 148, *163*
Tiwi xliv, 4
Tiwi consultants xxxvii–xli
  names used in Palingarri recordings xli
Tiwi culture 12
  cultural autonomy 16
Tiwi family names xli
Tiwi family systems 9
Tiwi Islands (Yirrara Ratuwati (Two Islands)) xxxi, 3–5, *160*
  creation story 1–2
  early visitors 5–9
  population 4
Tiwi Land Council 29, 40, 60, 256
Tiwi language
  changes 13
  Kulama, and 89
  language shift, reasons for 112–114
  Modern Tiwi 108, 110–111
  New Tiwi 18, 108, 111
  Old Tiwi 105, 108, 109–110
  orthography/spelling xxxv–xxxvi, 18–20, 108–109
  phonetic changes 108–109
  pronunciation xxxvi
  recordings, importance of 37–40, 148–149
  song language. *see* song language

Tiwi language *continued*
  spoken language 107–114
  structure 110–111, 115–116, 123, 139, 142, 181
  synonyms 147–148
  Tiwi–English Interactive Dictionary 114
Tiwi Mothers Club Eisteddfods 258
Tjadpa corroboree 52
Tractor Joe. *see* Karla Tractor Joe
traditional, definition xliv
traditional owners, definition xliv
train song 148–150, 154
transcriptions 12–14, 17, 120–122
transgender people 66–67
translations 17, 147–154
  fluidity of understanding, and 155–157
trepang 6–7
Tungutalum 33, 45, 52, 230
  Gramophone, 1928 45
  train song 149
  Yirrikapayi (Crocodile) 75, 207
Tungutalum, Bede 33, *175*
Tungutalum, Leo 43
Turiturina Island 3
Turtle (Dreaming). *see* Tarikulani (Turtle)
Turtuni poles 28, 70, 72, *167*. *see also* Pukumani
Tyukuliyanginila 51

Unborn. *see* Pitapituwi (Unborn)

versification 121–122, 123, 127
  metrical patterns, using 134–137
  modern song forms 155–157
vibrato 12, 132, 221
vocalisation 50–52, 137–139, 178, 187
  Amparruwu songs 129, 137
  Arikuruwala with Ampirikuruwala response 223
  Ariwangilinjiya 225
  growl sound 137
  lip flutter 137
  nasal closed-mouth sounds 137
  non-Tiwi music, and 118
  open-throated vowel sounds 137
  throat coughs 137
vocal talent 41
vocal technique 41

vocal timbre 12, 182
voice 177, 235, 280
  reclaiming 32
vowel fusion 127–130, 241

Wadeye (Port Keats) 15, 182, 237
Wampayawityimirri, Bartholomew Kerinaiua (Black Joe) xli, 210, 242
  Arimarrikuwamuwu tree-climbing song 211–212
  bark paintings 27
  Pitapituwi (Spirit children) 56
Wangga 194, 195
Waniyamperi 151
Warabatj (North West Vernon) Island 3
Warlapini, Mickey Geranium 43, 94–95
Warntarringuwi (Sun) 58–59
wax cylinders 48, 49
Whirlwind 238
widow songs. *see* Amparruwu (widow songs)
Winga (Sea) *169*
Wommatakimmi, Gabriel *171*
Wonaemirri, Marjorie 237
Wonaemura, Brian 104
Wrangku Murrakupuni (Wrangku Country) 249–250
Wulurangkuwu Country 59
Wunijaka (Spirit of the wind) 234
Wurangku 4
Wurangkuwu Country 59
Wurm, Helen 24
Wurrumiyanga (formerly Nguiu) xxxi, xliv, 4, 42, 104, 247
Wurrumiyanga Wellbeing Centre song 244, 247–248

Yangarti 65
Yeimpi 8
Yilaniya (Smoking ceremony) 69, 75, 79, 84–85, *170*, 249, 254
  Arimarrikuwamuwu 210
  Ayipa, and 98
  First Yilaniya 71
  healing songs 87, 253
  Main Yilaniya 71, 72
  revenge songs 77–78
Yiloga (football song) 245, 246, 272, 275

Yiloti (Final Ceremony) xliv, 19, 69, 71, 72–73, 84, 86
  Dreaming songs 78
  framework 79
  Mamanunkuni. *see* Mamanunkuni (Sorrow songs)
  Pukumani poles 28, 72
Yiminga (Skin group) xliv, 57–59, 63, 66
Yimpinari Country 59
Yinjula 102, 238, 239–240
Yipinuwurra (Clift) Island 3
Yirrara Ratuwati (Two Islands). *see* Tiwi Islands (Yirrara Ratuwati (Two Islands))
Yirrikapayi (Crocodile) 40, 49, 61, 75, 81–82, 85, 102, *162*, *167*, 204, 205, 249
  Modern Kuruwala 233, 264, 274
  song texts 194–195
  vocalisations 137
Yirripurlingayi (Buchanan) Island 3
Yoi (Dreaming) xlv, 5, 12, 19, 42, 60–61, 66, 196, 270, 278. *see also* Dreaming
  artistic innovation 100, 123
  Country, and 64
  group participation 181–182
  Jipuwakirimi. *see* Jipuwakirimi
  kinship status songs 74–77
  meaning 61–62, 74, 203
  monotonic and isorhythmic structure 203
  new musical ways 248
  non-Tiwi music, and 118
  performance context 278–279
  rhythm 193
  song 43, 49, 60, 62, 72, 73–87, 119, 123, 181–182, 236, 244
  song-types 179–181, 200–202
  tempo, role of 191–193
Yungunki (Old Tiwi). *see* Old Tiwi
Yuwunki (Modern Tiwi). *see* Modern Tiwi